PAYING THE PRICE

by

MADGE WALLS

*To Lori —
Persistence!
Aloha,
Madge*

"Dialogue"
PUBLISHING, INC.

ISBN 0-9764904-7-1
LCCN: 2005928852
Copyright © Madge Walls, 2005

First Edition, 2005

Dialogue Publishing
16990 Cherry Crossing Dr.
Colorado Springs, CO 80921
http://www.dialoguepublishing.com
info@dialoguepublishing.com

Editing and book layout by Dorrie O'Brien, Grand Prairie, Texas
Cover design by Gail Cross, Desert Isle Design, Mesa, Arizona

Printed in the United States of America

1 2 3 4 5 6 7 8 9 10

To my parents, Jeanne and Val Tennent,
who gave me the priceless gift of a happy childhood in Hawaii.

Acknowledgements

So many wonderful friends gave me help and encouragement along the way. My original critique group, Liz Engstrom, Marie Smith, Maggie Doran, Geri Kaeo and Brooke Brown met weekly in the dusty, termite-ridden Kihei Library when I was still knee-deep in children but determined to someday become a serious writer. Jill Engledow, formerly with the *Maui News*, said something to me at a New Year's Eve party at Nancy Nevius's home in Maui Meadows fifteen years ago. Those long-lost words got me up early on New Year's Day to begin my first novel. Jill later consulted regarding Hawaiian word usage.

Along the way, Cross Country Writers critique group members Liz George, Connie Vines, and Lori Di Anni worked over every word of this manuscript by mail over a period of five years. Liz and I had a mai tai-drenched rendezvous on Maui one day (she lives in Pennsylvania), and I hope someday to meet Connie and Lori to say thanks in person. Linda Boyden and I met regularly at Barnes & Noble in Kahului for critique and friendship. Gael Mustapha set me on the path of professional writing and gave an early draft an excruciating but necessary line edit. Ken Grimes, Donnell Bell, Lynn Sweet, and Nancy Mills critiqued later drafts, all returning valuable, detailed feedback. Sue Murray, my former broker at Prudential Locations on Maui, tackled the manuscript like a tiger, throwing back questions, suggestions, and observations that took it to a whole new level.

Shannon and Earl Tolley, I learned my profession with you in my car. Lauren Jardine was ever a keeper of the literary faith. Dorrie O'Brien performed a final professional edit and then called her publisher friend Sue Lutz of Dialogue Publishing and said, "You don't know it yet, but I'm holding your next book in my hands." Thank you, Dorrie, and thank you, Sue, for agreeing. Pam and Dave Keller encouraged me to turn my focus to writing while continuing to support my habit with employment at Keller Homes, Inc. Debbie Sinclair and Leeann Bee tossed around titles while doing water aerobics at the Briargate YMCA and gifted me with *Paying the Price*. And how can I thank Jerri Lilevjen, who handed me the last, maddeningly elusive resolution of Laura's inner dilemma with Annie while we were casually walking through a new model home ten days before the manuscript was due to the publisher?

Mahalo, most lovingly, to my sons, Christopher, Burke, and Alan, who have given me joy and happiness every day of their lives. They have encouraged me in all my endeavors but particularly in my writing, which keeps me off the streets and out of the stores.

Glossary of Hawaiian Words and Local Expressions Used in *Paying the Price*

Awapuhi	Wild ginger
Blalah	Slang for brother
Confunnit	Slang for confound it
Da kine	"The kind," a slang substitute for a word someone is too lazy to say or can't remember; a linguistic wild card
Great Mahele	In 1848, King Kamehameha III, under pressure from foreign interests, released his ownership rights to much of his land in the kingdom to the chiefs and commoners in fee simple. The process, which took about 50 years to complete, was called the Great Mahele. All land titles in Hawaii date back to that process.
Haole	Caucasian
Hanai	Adopted or foster child, often informally within the family or among friends
Hapa haole	Half Caucasian; a person of mixed blood
Hapai	Pregnant
Ihe pakelo	Wooden lance
Kamaaina	A local person; strictly speaking, a native-born Hawaiian, but nowadays someone who has lived in Hawaii for a long time
Kiawe	Algaroba, a common tree with thorny branches, popular for making charcoal
Kim chee	Korean pickled cabbage, pungent and peppery
Koa	Acacia koa, the largest of the native forest trees, yielding beautifully grained wood. Formerly used for canoes, surfboards and calabashes; now prized for furniture and ukeleles

Kukui	Candlenut tree, a large tree with light green, star-shaped leaves whose polished nuts are strung as leis
Lauae	Fragrant, low-growing fern used for landscaping
Lauhala	The leaves of the hala tree, used for weaving mats
Lolo	Stupid; crazy
Lomilomi salmon	Raw salmon that is hand "massaged" into small pieces, mixed with tomatoes and green onions and served at luaus
Lua	Toilet
Mahalo	Thank you
Naupaka	Native mountain and beach-growing shrub with white half-flowers
Nene	Hawaiian goose, rare and endangered
Ohia	The most abundant native tree in Hawaii. Its red, pompom-like flower, *lehua*, is the offical flower of the Big Island.
Okole	Buttocks
Okolehao	A liquor distilled from the ti root
Olena	Turmeric, a ginger whose root is used as a spice and dye
Ono	Delicious; tasty; savory
Opakapaka	Blue snapper, a mild, tender and very popular fish
Opihi	A limpet that lives on the rocks in tidal waters

Opu	Stomach, belly
Pau	Done; finished, ended
Pikake	Arabian jasmine, a small, fragrant white flower, popular for leis
Piko	Belly button
Pilau	Spoiled; rotten; foul; no good
Pilikia	Trouble; nuisance; problem; inconvenience
POG	Passion fruit, orange, and guava juice mix produced by Haleakala Dairy on Maui
Poi	Hawaiian staple food made from cooked and pounded taro roots, fermented and soured over several days
Poino	Ill luck; misfortune
Puka	Hole
Punee	A moveable couch, often a single bed, used for sitting
Ratoon Crop	The second and third sugar cane crops grown from roots left in the ground after the harvest; an unplanted crop
Shibai	A scam; a lie
Shishi	To urinate
Stink eye	A nasty glare
'S why hard	That's why (whatever you are talking about) is hard; life is hard; usually meant as a commiseration
Ti	A large-leaved ornamental shrub popular in landscaping and flower arrangements, also used to wrap food and make hula skirts

Tita	Slang for sister
Ulua	A large Pacific game fish, popular on restaurant menus
Wikiwiki	Fast; speedy

A word about the term Realtor: REALTOR® is a registered collective membership mark that identifies a real estate professional who is a member of the NATIONAL ASSOCIATION OF REALTORS® and subscribes to its strict code of Ethics and Standards of Practice. In the interests of simplicity, and following common usage in the press, I have taken the liberty of referring to Laura McDaniel and other licensees in this novel as Realtors.

Chapter 1

That day, I must admit, I was scraping the bottom of my energy barrel. Since Diana Coleman had announced to her husband Jerry that it was time to move again, we had looked at every listed property that could possibly work for them. Everything one liked, the other hated. Everything they both liked was above their means, didn't have enough of a view, or needed too much work. I was ready to take them both by the ears, whack their heads together, and boot them out of my life altogether.

Still, Diana and Jerry were jewels, my first real clients after earning my real estate license on Maui six years ago. They had become good friends, as well as a golden source of repeat business. As soon as Diana ran out of decorating ideas, they moved.

When she called that Friday afternoon in 1993 to see what I could show them over the weekend, I begged for time off. A rare weekend to myself, to read, lie on the beach, maybe cook a real dinner—even cleaning my apartment sounded appealing.

"No dice, darling," Diana said, laughter simmering beneath her charming British accent. "I saw a new For Sale sign in Makawao Highlands this morning. Not my favorite neighborhood, of course, but the house does look interesting. And the garden is a gem."

When Diana decided to buy a new home, she was relentless. She prowled the island, doing much of the legwork herself, presenting her finds as proudly as a Labrador retriever places a mangled duck at the feet of its master.

"But you were set on Kula," I exclaimed. A mixed district of cattle ranches, onion farms, and glamorous estates, Kula sits high on the slopes of Mt. Haleakala with sweeping views of the entire south shore of the island.

"Of course, Kula would be ideal," Diana replied. "But Makawao might not be bad. It's a bit lower on the mountain and closer to the highway, just a zip down the hill for Jerry in the morning. Perhaps he could grab a few extra winks."

Jerry was a stockbroker who needed to be at his desk by 4:00 AM in order to be live with the New York Stock Exchange six time zones away. His early-to-bed, early-to-rise lifestyle was a constant source of irritation to Diana, a confirmed night owl in every way.

"All right," I replied, trying not to let my Friday afternoon exhaustion creep into my voice. I sifted through the loose papers on my desk until I found a pen. "What's the address?"

She gave it to me, but it didn't sound familiar. "It must be a brand new listing. I'll check out the details and make an appointment for us. Nine o'clock tomorrow morning, okay? I'll pick you up." With an early start, there was hope for a free and relaxing afternoon—unless they decided to make an offer.

When I got home, I diligently combed through the Friday real estate section of the *Maui News*, sorry that I couldn't just leave work and forget about my job for the weekend like normal people do. Saturdays and Sundays, when clients are free to look at property, tend to be my busiest days. I found two more new listings for the Colemans that wouldn't make it into the Multiple Listing Service, the MLS, until Monday, and made appointments for us in the morning. In a tight seller's market, you have to stay on top of the inventory and check out every possibility before someone else snatches it.

While I was at it, I scanned my several listing ads: "Laura McDaniel, Realtor Associate, Blue Rock Realty." My photo was taken on a rare good hair day: straight, light brown, clipped to curve in just below the chin, wispy bangs touching my eyebrows. Smiling hazel eyes, a pleasant face, not too glamorous, easy to trust—at least, that's what I hoped it said.

Satisfied my ads were properly set out like baited hooks for prowling prospects, I finally allowed myself to relax. An evening of peace and quiet, with business in order and the ghosts of my past temporarily at rest. These were the rare moments I treasured.

Saturday, I stretched awake to the brisk morning scent of seaweed and saltwater two blocks away. All I had to do was dress, gather my files, and walk out the door. Once Diana and Jerry were in my car, we'd be laughing and joking, sharing the latest gossip, and having a grand time. Maybe we'd even stop for lunch on the way back. My treat, of course. I loved the social aspects of my job. The properties would be interesting, too, and who knew? Maybe this would be my lucky day. In truth, I needed another sale fast.

Quickly, I toasted a bagel and slathered it with cream cheese and guava jelly, intending to eat it in the car. As I picked up my briefcase, the phone rang. *If that's Diana calling to cancel, I'll kill her*, I thought. She'd done it several times in the recent past, always at the last minute for her own self-centered reasons. It meant an apologetic unraveling of our appointments with the listing agents, who then had to call their sellers and tell them they had tidied their homes for nothing. I hated doing that to people.

I smiled into the phone, forcing a cheerful note into my voice. "Hello?"

There was no response. I tightened the cord around my fingers and slipped into my sandals. An unintelligible, tinny babble buzzed against fading strains of music. At first I thought it was a bad connection. Something familiar in the melody caught my attention, though, and kept me from hanging up. Closing my eyes to focus on the sounds, I made out wisps of steel-guitar music in the background, barely discernible, but unmistakable. My ears straining, I spoke again, louder. I didn't try to hide my irritation. "Hel*lo*?"

Again a pause. I turned toward the door, poised to hang up.

"Mommy?"

I almost didn't catch it. It was no more than a whisper, childish and uncertain. It couldn't be my youngest son, David; he was always loud and exuberant when he called from college in Utah. When Damien, my eldest, called from El Salvador, the international operator came on first, asking if I would accept the collect call. That only left . . .

My heart began to pound so hard the blood whooshed in my ears. With superhuman effort, I reined in my voice to match hers. "Annie?" My heart shouted, *Where are you? Are you all right?*

The slightest hint of desperation or judgment from me would send her running again. The only other time she had called, about six months ago, I'd made every motherly mistake in the book. She'd hung up when I'd rushed in with one too many frantic questions. I vowed then that if God granted me a next time, I'd bite my tongue and let her lead the way.

"Ma." She sounded relieved.

"Sweetheart, I'm here." Again, the Herculean effort to calm my voice, to stifle my instinct to overwhelm her. The pause on the line continued. Every nerve in my body flared. I dared a prompt, "Honey?"

"Can you come get me?" Spoken as matter-of-factly as if she were across the island at a high school football game.

"Sweetheart, where *are* you?" For three years I'd been desperate to know. At age sixteen, my only daughter had dropped out of my life as cleanly as a chunk of loose coral thrown from the bow of a canoe into the dark depths of the sea. The sleepless nights, the gnawing anxiety, the fathomless anguish, not to mention the endless sums spent on a private detective, had all been to no avail.

"At the airport." Deadpanned, as if it should be obvious.

Lord, let me shake her. "*Which* airport?" *New York? Hong Kong? Siberia, for God's sake?* Then the steel-guitar music clicked in my mind. An amplified voice put her squarely on the map. "Hawaiian Airlines flight six-one-four departing for Honolulu in fifteen minutes. Passengers please line up for boarding at gate seventeen." She had to be calling from Kahului, right here on Maui. Her next words confirmed it.

"Ma, it's all changed. It sucks. What happened to the big tree?" The offended tone was Anna Kaleialoha McDaniel to the core, as if the airport's recent multimillion-dollar renovation, including the removal of the ancient, insect-infested banyan tree at its center, had been done specifically to aggravate her. This daughter I loved to distraction, who had challenged me at every turn since the day she was born, who had caused me endless tears and heartache well before she ran away, was still impossible to please.

I swallowed my exasperation, fearful that if I didn't hang up and get going that instant, she would disappear again by the time I could drive the twenty-five minutes to the airport.

"Where will I find you?" I asked, trying not to push her. Even giving her directions as to where I would pick her up could be interpreted as ordering her around, my capital crime of her high school years.

"Um, I just got off the plane. I'm upstairs somewhere."

I pictured her at the bank of pay phones in the passenger lounge. "Do you have any baggage with you?" I heard myself enunciate each word as if I were speaking to an idiot.

"No, Ma, at least . . . not at the baggage claim." She snorted, as if that were meant to be funny.

"Okay, take the escalator down and go through the exit at the bottom. Stand outside in the shade, and I'll pull up right there. I still have my green Honda, so you should be able to spot me easily."

"Like I wouldn't know my own mother."

I sucked in my breath at her sarcastic tone, but refused to rise to the bait. Softly, with as much enthusiasm as I thought she could bear, I replied, "I'm glad you're home, honey."

"Yeah, Ma." She hung up.

I stood frozen in my living room. Insanely, the only thing I could think of was how was I going to rearrange my office in the small alcove off the living room for Annie. I'd purchased the condominium four years after my divorce from her father, two years after Annie had disappeared. With island real estate prices so high, the one-bedroom unit was all I could afford at the time.

The ringing phone yanked me out of my paralysis. It was Diana, breathlessly cheerful in her lilting British way. "Darling, oh, good, you haven't left yet. Are you bringing your MLS book? There's another property we haven't seen, a friend was telling me about it. It sounds positively smashing. We can look up the details as we're driving."

"Oh God, Diana . . ." I raked my fingers through my hair, pulling until it hurt. How could ordinary life still be going on?

"Laura, what's wrong?"

"My daughter, she's waiting for me to pick her up at Kahului Airport."

"Your daughter? Annie? After all this time? You must be ecstatic." I could see Diana's face light up with her megawatt smile. She'd been a solid, empathetic friend when Annie ran away in 1990.

My voice surged with urgency. "Diana, I have to beg off on the showings we set up for this morning. Right now all I can concentrate on is getting to the airport. I'm sorry."

"Don't even think about it, darling. Is there anything I can do?"

I tried to unscramble my thoughts. "If I give you the phone numbers, could you call the listing agents and cancel our appointments? I can't waste a minute. I've got to get there before Annie does something rash . . . or slips away again."

"Of course, darling. Just leave it to me. Go take care of your daughter, with our blessing."

I rattled off the agents' names and phone numbers, grabbed my purse, and raced to the elevator, the bagel on the counter forgotten.

Pulling onto Piilani Highway, I narrowly missed a pickup truck that turned across my path without signaling. Shaking, I swore at him as he swerved past. What if I had an accident today, of all days? Annie would accuse me, once again, of messing up her life.

Crossing the flat, central Maui plain, my car sped past the tall, dark green *wiliwili* hedges on either side of the narrow, pot-holed road. Their leafy branches shot straight up thirty feet, thanks to the irrigation of the sugar cane fields that stretched for miles behind them. The *wiliwili* cast alternating stripes of light and dark across the road, a dizzying staccato of sunshine and shadow that flickered across my windshield like an old black-and-white movie. The hippies had called it the Psychedelic Road. The effect was usually hypnotic, but not today.

I rounded the curve at the old Puunene Sugar Mill, then turned right onto Dairy Road, heedless of the red light. What on earth would I tell Annie's father if she got all the way home to Maui, and I somehow missed connecting with her? Worse yet, what if I got her home only to offend her so deeply that she took off again? *Blessed Virgin, grant me the wisdom and patience to be the mother Annie needs this time.*

As I pulled into the airport passenger pickup lane, I scanned the area where I had asked Annie to wait. A Chinese family stood at the curb, watching the oncoming traffic for their ride. Beside them, a group of Hawaiian, Japanese, and Filipino boys carrying green-and-white Molokai High School sports bags joked and punched each other while puffing on cigarettes. To the rear, a stream of chattering tourists in wrinkled shorts and gaudy aloha shirts burst through the electronic doors and streamed toward the baggage claim. No one remotely resembled my daughter.

Frank's voice whispered in my ears: *All you had to do was pick her up.*

I switched off the car with a trembling hand and got out. Shading my eyes, I stepped past the Chinese family and the Molokai athletes, and scanned the concourse. An eerie silence lingered in the wake of the tourists who had trotted out of sight. A car door slammed behind me. I spun around to see the Molokai athletes drive off in a white van. Resuming my search, I resented every second it took my eyes to adjust to the shade. I almost missed the teenager who slouched in the shadows against a concrete wall maybe thirty feet away, his back to me.

Scruffy, short, he wore a long-sleeved black sweat suit with filthy, untied running shoes. His smudgy blond hair hung well below his shoulders. He must be sweltering in that bulky garb, I thought. No sane person wears a black sweat suit in Hawaii in August.

Dismissing him as a yet another hippie who came to Maui to live the laid-back banana-patch lifestyle without visible means of support, I turned to look in another direction. But something about him reclaimed my attention. That scraggly fair hair, that careless slouch . . . Shifting his stance, he turned to lean his back and shoulders against the wall. As if to ease a crick, he pushed his fist into the small of his back. In stark profile, I realized that kid was no boy. The black sweatshirt stretched across a very pregnant belly.

The youngster cocked her head to one side and flipped her bangs away from her eyes. And then I knew. That gesture was pure . . .

"Annie!"

CHAPTER 2

She turned toward me in that same instant of recognition, her face a study of cocky boredom. Or was it self-protection, unsure of her welcome? I stood riveted to the concrete floor, unable to move. She looked defeated and worldly-wise far beyond her nineteen years. She was my child, though, returned to me at last. A rush of love propelled me forward, banishing every vestige of anger and doubt.

"Oh, Annie." I pulled her close and buried my face in her hair. I had prayed for this moment day and night for three years, but never anticipated the thrill of holding her in my arms, breathing the sweaty, earthy scent of her. My child was home.

Her arms slipped around my waist, loose, tentative, but around me nevertheless. Her bulging stomach pressed taut against mine. God help us, on top of everything else, we were going to have to deal with that.

With one hand, I smoothed her flaxen hair down the back of her neck and nestled her head against my shoulder. I closed my eyes and rocked her back and forth, drinking in her familiar essence, allowing three years of worry and pain to melt away. She was still my little girl.

Too soon her arms dropped from my waist. She shrugged her shoulders in gentle but definite disengagement. Forcing myself to let go, I stepped back, then took her gamine face between my hands and kissed her on both cheeks. Her turned-up nose was as perky as ever, but her complexion was pasty, unhealthy. Deep purple shadows smudged her eyes; gone was their feisty blue sparkle of old.

Pigeon-toed and awkward, she suffered my fussing, her face a study in wary-eyed detachment, giving back very little. That was Annie, always holding herself in check except when angry. Anger was the one emotion she expressed without restraint.

"Oh, sweetheart. Just let me look at you. You'll have to get right to the beach and start working on a tan. You look like a regular mainland *haole*!" I said it lightly, playing on our lifelong amusement at being taken for newcomers. We might not look it, but we were as local as anyone who wasn't native Hawaiian. My mother's island roots dug back five generations to the days when Lahaina served as the whaling capital of the Pacific.

Annie shook her head. "Don't start ragging on me, Ma. Like, I don't know how I look?"

"No, no, of course not. I'm just thrilled that you're home. I can't get over it." I was rambling out of sheer nervousness. Seeking a diversion, I pointed to a ragged backpack with a split seam near her feet. "Is that yours?"

So quickly that she almost tripped, she bent down, snagged the straps, and slung the tattered bag over her shoulder with a grunt. I reached out to steady her, but she twisted away. "I've got it," she declared with an angry frown that set out a firm fence of boundaries.

Swallowing hard, feeling my own anger rising but determined to allow her whatever space she needed for now, I turned and started toward my car.

Annie followed, catching up with me in a few quick steps. She eyed me slyly. "Are you sure you have enough room for my pack in your trunk, Ma?"

Grinning, I put an arm around her shoulders and relaxed. It had been a standing family joke that whenever we picked someone up at the airport, we had to clear out the For Sale signs and other real estate paraphernalia from my trunk—even though I was only a fledgling part-time agent at the time. We both laughed at the memory of trying to fit luggage or groceries into that perpetually overloaded compartment.

As we drove away from the airport, I stole another look at her. The seat belt strained across her protruding stomach. Tears sprang to my eyes at the glimpse of her stick-like wrists poking from the ragged black sweatshirt cuffs, of one thin, bony hand resting on her belly mound. She looked like a refugee who hadn't eaten for weeks. I wanted so much to touch her, to hold and kiss that fragile hand.

"Are you hungry, sweetheart?" I asked. "Should we stop somewhere?"

"Nah. Let's just drive. Can we go the long way through Wailuku?"

That suited me, because it meant more time to talk. The kids always opened up to me in the car, away from the distractions of television and music players. Besides, I wasn't quite sure what I was going to do with her once we got home.

Annie seemed fascinated by the sights of downtown Kahului—the new shopping center on Dairy Road with K-Mart, Eagle Hardware, Office Max, Border's Books and Music, and a full menu of fast food places. I often wondered what visitors thought after they got in their rental cars and headed for their hotels. Except for the coconut trees and bougainvillea, the road from the airport must look much like home.

Annie couldn't have returned on a more spectacular day. The sun had climbed high over Mt. Haleakala and burned off the upper layers of mist. Across the central plain, the West Maui Mountains rose lush and green against the cloudless blue, the result of a recent Kona storm. I prayed this spectacular beauty would resonate with my wayward daughter, speak to her soul, reclaim her for her island home.

As we drove up the hill past her high school on the right, I searched for something to say. The low-rise Mediterranean-styled complex overlooking Kahului Harbor was the last place anyone had seen her before she disappeared. I glanced at her, hoping to find a clue to her thoughts. Her gaze was hard and far away, her fists clenched bloodless on her thighs. One lonely tear glittered on her cheek. She brushed it away quickly. I let the moment go. It was too soon to begin asking questions.

We drove under the bridge into old Wailuku Town, the Maui County seat. Her voice a little shaky, she said, "I dreamed about that bridge. Of all the things from home that stuck in my mind, that old lava rock bridge . . ." She trailed off into her own private thoughts.

My heart ached for my daughter. What dreadful experiences had tempered her during her three years away? When would it be safe to ask so I could begin to understand? Best simply to enjoy being with her, I decided, and hope she'd gain a sense of security from the familiar scenery. I couldn't begin to imagine what disturbing memories had triggered the clenched fists and the tear when we'd passed her school. Or how they related to the unknown path that had led her to run away.

Several miles beyond Wailuku, we passed through the old plantation town of Waikapu—a porch-fronted wooden grocery store, two old churches and a sign shop. We hit the open road again, accelerating under a scarlet canopy of royal Poinciana trees.

"Did the boys do everything they planned?" Annie asked, apparently recovered, making an effort to be sociable by asking about her brothers.

"Pretty much," I replied. "They'll be thrilled to know you're home. David transferred from UH to Brigham Young University in Utah last year. He'll graduate next June. He stayed up there this summer to work."

"BYU? Boy, what did Grandma say?" She grinned like the Annie of old. My heart lifted.

"She had a fit, as you can imagine. Her nice Catholic grandson going to a Mormon school with all those pagans?"

"I bet. I wish I'd been here for that!"

We both laughed. Margaret Wildethorne Henderson lived her faith in black and white. Either you were a member of the one true church or part of the devil's fold. The idea of her grandson attending a Mormon university had nearly done her in.

"He got a football scholarship," I continued. "We all held firm against her. For once, Grandma had to back down. But it wasn't pretty."

"Good for David." Annie always cheered for anyone who broke the rules. "What about Damien?"

"Finished University of Washington; joined the Peace Corps."

"No way!"

I chuckled at her genuine surprise. "He's in El Salvador, teaching English and business classes. Coaches basketball, too. It's primitive—electricity but no running water. In spite of the cool splash baths, he seems happy. The postman always laughs at me, spending twelve bucks to send him five dollars' worth of homemade chocolate-chip cookies."

"Wow, I can't picture Damien living like that. Such a neat-freak slug." She contemplated this remarkable change in her eldest brother, then asked cautiously, "How about Dad? Do you talk to him?"

"Occasionally." *Mostly when he calls to find out why I'm so far behind on my payments to the detective we hired to find you*, I refrained from adding. "He seems to be okay, living with Holly and Georgie in Maine."

"Maine?"

"Gee, I guess you wouldn't know. Shortly after you left, he lost his job in New York, big time."

Annie squirmed in her seat belt so she could face me. Concern showed on her face. "What happened?"

"I honestly don't know. The hotel chain was bought out by the Japanese. I expect it was a clash in management styles. You know Dad, he can be pretty outspoken. He never told me, though, and I never asked. Whatever happened, it seems to have ended his hotel management career."

"But Maine?"

"He and Holly bought a bed and breakfast in the country. Sounds kind of rustic. Cranberry House, they call it. I call it The Bog. They've kind of dropped out, partly because of Georgie, I guess. And get this—when Dad wasn't sloshing around The Bog, or helping care for Georgie, he wrote a book."

"Wow, Ma. Trippy." She twisted a strand of blonde hair and gazed out the window while she mulled that over. "What kind of book?"

"Hotel management." I smiled at her. "Surprised? He's an expert, you know, at taking small to mid-sized hotels in trouble and turning them around. When Cornell University Hotel School picked it up as a required text, there was an article about him in the *Maui News*. Island boy makes good and all that."

"Bad," she uttered, suitably impressed. Then she asked, "How's Georgie?"

"No better, no worse, as far as I can make out. Your dad doesn't say much."

Frank and Holly had a four-year-old autistic son. What little I knew about Georgie was mostly secondhand from the boys. Frank only mentioned him when I asked for money, denying me because they were barely making it with the B&B, and Georgie's needs came first.

"He'll be beside himself when he hears you're back. We'll call him as soon as we get home," I said.

Annie sucked on a knuckle and turned to look at the mountains out her side window. Suddenly she seemed lost again in her runaway memories. Was she worried about what her father would say? Frank had been very good with the kids, and especially close to Annie, despite the long hours and late nights required of a hotel general manager. I couldn't begin to predict how he'd react to her pregnancy, however.

Still on Honoapiilani Highway, we headed toward the Kihei-Lahaina junction. Sandalwood Golf Course spread out in manicured perfection at the base of the West Maui Mountains on our right. To the left, across the central plain toward Haleakala, red dust swirled over recently harvested pineapple fields. Ripped shreds of black plastic sheeting littered the acres of raw dirt. The plastic served as mulch between the rows of newly planted pineapple starts, leaving an unsightly mess after the fruit was harvested.

"Honey? I've got to tell him. He's been worried sick, just as I have."

She popped her wet knuckle from her mouth. "It's like . . . what's he going to do? Rush over? I don't want Dad to see me like this." Her voice trembled, as it had when she was a toddler and had done something to disappoint him. It was the first time she had alluded to her pregnancy.

Trying to sound casual, I pursued the opening. "Looks like you're, what, about seven months along?"

She hesitated for a long moment. So softly I could barely make it out, she finally said, "I'm not sure. Maybe early October."

If that was true, I'd be a grandmother in two months! If this were me, my scandalized mother would have shipped me off to Europe posthaste, where the baby would have been born behind convent walls and put up for adoption without my ever holding it. But times had changed; girls now thought nothing of keeping their babies and growing up with them.

Glancing at Annie, I ventured another gentle probe. "Ah, well, have you been under a doctor's care, then?"

"Yeah, well, not really." She fiddled with the frayed cuff of her sweatshirt.

"What do you mean, not really?"

She pulled on a loose string and broke it off. "When I figured I might be *hapai*, I went to a free clinic. They told me it was, like, too late."

"Too late? Too late for what?" I gripped the steering wheel, braced for the answer I knew was coming.

"Come on, Ma. Don't be dense. I figured I could, like, keep it, kill it, or give it away. I wised up too late to kill it. So here I am—stuck with keeping it or giving it away."

My mind reeled. How could she be so flip, so cold about her own child, *my grandchild*? Of course I knew abortion was rampant. In 1970 Hawaii had become the first state to make abortion legal, three years before *Roe v. Wade*. My mother had led the local opposition, picketing with her right-to-life cronies outside the state capitol week after week, not giving up until long after the ink dried on the paper.

Fueled by outrage, I waded in deeper. "May I ask if there's a father in the picture?" Someone who would do his blessed duty and make everything right? Not, please, a disreputable sort who might this very moment be hovering just out of sight, waiting to jump in and stir up our lives even more.

Annie's eyes flashed with anger. "Yeah, right, Ma. That's the first thing Dad's gonna ask, too. You guys are so out of it." She crossed her arms over her belly, an awkward gesture at best, clearly warning me away from that line of questioning. I backed off. Annie was home. That's all that mattered for the moment. Besides, there were other things to consider.

Until moments ago, it hadn't hit me that I would have to deal with

Frank on this. He would swoop in from The Bog and blame it all on me, again, for not having kept a proper lid on Annie when she was younger. Was he right? Frank could be ultra-charming when it suited him, but I couldn't bear the thought of him pushing onto the scene and taking over with his usual bluff and bluster. Nor was I anxious to deal with Frank's and my unresolved past—at least, it was unresolved to me. He'd moved on, but I still had questions, questions he'd never answered satisfactorily. My wounds may have scabbed over, but they continued to fester underneath.

My silence apparently softened her. "No, Ma, there's no father. At least, no one I'd recognize if I ever saw him again."

I gasped. Obviously we were not speaking of conception by the Holy Ghost, but still . . . All things considered, I was thankful for one less complication. God knew what kind of a person the father was or where she'd picked him up. We'd have to deal with his genes, which was bothersome enough. What we really needed to do was to concentrate on getting Annie safely through the last two months of her pregnancy and the birthing. Life as a runaway could not have been conducive to good prenatal health.

"Did you continue to go to the clinic for prenatal care?" I asked.

"No. But I managed." She flashed me a defiant look, as if that were something to be proud of.

I bit my lip and silently vowed to get her to a doctor as soon as possible.

Ahead of us, the road sloped gently toward Maalaea Bay. Out to sea, three low, gray clouds hung between the uninhabited island of Kahoolawe and the jutting cinder cone Puu o Lai. Rain squalls drifted down, casting shadowy veils across the whitecaps like ghostly jellyfish trailing their tendrils in the drifting tide. To the right, cresting the West Maui Mountains, the sky was as blue as Annie's eyes. No matter what happens with Island weather, blue sky always smiles somewhere. I would have to keep that in mind as the ramifications of Annie's return settled in.

CHAPTER 3

I opened the door to my apartment and stood back, poised to place a calming hand on Annie's shoulder. When she'd left, we were still in the grand house near Frank's Wailea hotel. Marble floors, bougainvillea-draped terraces, gourmet kitchen, swimming pool overlooking the ocean—we'd lived a life of pampered luxury until Frank lost his New York job and could no longer support us in the manner to which we'd become accustomed.

I waited silently while she took it in. My daughter did not do well with change. When she was in first grade I bought her a Cinderella bedroom set, white wood with gold accents and a pink satin bedspread. I set it up while she was at school. That afternoon she walked through the door, took one look at her unfamiliar furniture and shrieked to the heavens. Nothing consoled her. She cried into the evening, fell asleep on the floor, and woke up sobbing in the morning. In desperation, I called the Salvation Army and had them bring back her old youth bed and banged-up dresser. She slept in that awful bed until she went to high school, while some lucky second-hand shopper wound up with a very expensive bedroom set.

"Wow, Ma. Different from the old house. Nice, though. Way small." Annie hoisted her backpack higher on her shoulder, not yet willing to set it down and acknowledge these new digs as home.

"True," I said, following her into the living area. "Small, but comfortable. Easy to clean; no more hotel maid service." Smiling, I pulled out a chair from the dining table. "Put your pack down, honey. We're home." A surge of elation shot through me. I had despaired of ever saying that to my daughter again.

She hesitated, then shrugged the bag off her shoulder and dumped it on the chair. As soon as that ratty pack was empty, it was going straight down the garbage chute along with that dreadful black sweat suit. I couldn't wait to obliterate those filthy reminders of her life on the run.

Across the room on my bedside table, the red light on my answering machine blinked. Ignoring it for the moment, I shooed Annie into the shower, then sat down on my bed to call her father. I didn't want to be accused of failing to notify him immediately.

Upon hearing his daughter was safe, Frank launched into a torrent of questions. I answered as best I could, but soon reached the limit of my information.

"Annie and I have barely begun to talk, Frank. As you might imagine, she's a bit touchy."

"Let me speak with her," he demanded.

"Not right now. She's in the shower."

"Then have her call me when she gets out. Meanwhile, I'll book a flight over. I'll be there Monday."

That was the last thing I wanted. "Please, Frank. Give me some time to reconnect with her."

"That's exactly what I'm worried about, Laura. After all, she ran away on your watch."

I inhaled sharply. "Yes, but look who she came home to."

Frank swore. "You have her call me the minute she's dressed, you hear?"

"I'm sure she'll do exactly that." I took great satisfaction in hanging up without telling him he was soon to be a grandfather. Annie could let him in on that little surprise.

Fighting my irritation over what should have been a joyful sharing of Annie's return, I pushed the button to retrieve my messages. I hate my answering machine. It rules my life in diabolical partnership with my phone. Between them, they keep me in a perpetual state of anticipating bad news.

Diana's breathy British voice gushed forth. "Darling. How is that little muffin? Give her a big pinch for me, will you, for staying away so long and driving her Mum crazy. Listen, love, you're going to clobber me. I told the other agents you had a family emergency, which was true, and that you told us to carry on with the showings on our own. Okay, so I lied a bit, but they didn't mind. They gave me the addresses and met us there on schedule. The listings were a bust, though, especially the one in Kula. The neighbors must have mobs of teenage kids. Beat-up cars and trucks parked along the road in every direction. But listen, darling, along the way we found the house of the century. Remember I mentioned a friend had spotted something? It's in Haiku, For Sale by Owner. I know you hate FSBOs. But it's the most—" *Beep.* The message cut off.

Before I could react, the machine beeped again and spewed out the next message.

"Darling, how can you operate with such a short interval on your message tape? At any rate, it's Diana again, as if you didn't know. What I meant to say is, it's the most incredible house, and the yard is a tropical fantasy. This is it, Laura, this is the house we want. I made an appointment with the owner for Jerry and me to see the interior tomorrow afternoon. Call me when you can. I'm delirious your daughter is home." *Beep.*

An emotionless male voice intoned, "End of messages."

Just as I had feared: Bad news. I ran my fingers through my hair, trying to sort the situation out. You can't blame a seller for wanting to sell a home by himself and save the commission, or a buyer wanting to deal directly with the seller for the same reason. However, they lose the benefit of having a dedicated negotiator and chief problem-solver in a complex legal transaction. Most For Sale By Owner sellers (FSBO, pronounced *fizbo*) cooperate with a buyer's agent and pay half the commission. I hadn't thought it necessary to execute a buyer's agency agreement with Diana and Jerry, as they were such good friends. Without that agreement, however, they were free to proceed on their own. Saving money can be a powerful trump over friendship.

Behind the closed bathroom door, Annie turned off the shower. My hopes for a quick, uncomplicated sale to the Colemans swished down the drain with the last of her soapy water. As much as I disliked FSBOs, half a commission was better than none, especially when suddenly faced with supporting an adult child and grandchild into the foreseeable future. But Diana and Jerry would have to agree.

I replayed Diana's messages, straining to detect a word, a tone of voice, the slightest hint that she and Jerry still wanted me to represent them. Nothing, just a cheerful request to call them back with no sense of urgency. I felt sick to my stomach.

"Ma, you got anything clean I can wear?" Annie called through the half-open bathroom door.

Grateful for the distraction, I pulled an oversized olive-green T-shirt from a dresser drawer and handed it in to her. "Do you want me to get anything out of your backpack for you, sweetheart?" I asked.

Barreling out of the bathroom, she almost knocked me down as she streaked toward the dining table. "Don't touch my fucking backpack," she screamed. "Leave my fucking stuff alone." With one hand tugging the shirt down over her wet belly, she made a grab for the wretched thing and hugged it to her chest as if it contained the crown jewels. Facing me, her eyes shooting icy sparks, she spat, "Don't touch my fucking things."

I recoiled as if I'd been slapped. A million resentments burst loose like a floodtide crashing over a breakwater. "Listen, young lady. Put that awful thing down and sit." I pointed to the couch. "I don't know where you've been or what you've been up to, but we're going to get a few things straight."

In a pout, she sank onto the cushions, still clutching the grimy bag above her stomach.

Three years of unrequited anger surged through me. "I've been as gentle as I know how with you so far today. Please note that it hasn't been easy. You drop out of our lives for three indescribable years, leaving your father and me sick with worry, and now you prance home and start acting like a piece of street slime. If you're going to live here with me, you need to know that I will not tolerate filthy language and being yelled at in my home. *My* home, Annie, *mine*. I work hard for it. I earn the mortgage payment and maintenance fee and taxes all by myself. I will not be subjected to that kind of disrespect in my home or anywhere else."

Glaring at me with disgust, she dumped the offending article on the carpet by her feet. Not daring to think what might be in it, I glared back.

She crossed her arms and stared out the glass doors at the mountain. "Shit, everyone talks like that."

I stepped forward and put a firm hand on her shoulder. "Not . . . in . . . my . . . home."

Flopping back against the sofa pillows, she picked up the TV remote control from the coffee table. She jabbed it at the set, frantically punching the buttons until she hit the power switch. CNN jumped to life with President Bill Clinton giving a press briefing at the White House. She clicked the channel button again and again, too quickly to comprehend what she was seeing. It was a gesture of pure defiance.

Shaking with fury, I reached over, grabbed the remote from her, and punched the off button. "That's another thing. I won't have the TV on continuously day and night, especially on your favorite trashy stations. You can watch whatever you want when I'm not home, but I can't take nonstop mindless noise in the background. Peace and quiet are important to me after a long day of dealing with clients. Do you understand?"

She shrugged her shoulders, stuck out her chin, and fastened her eyes on the blank screen. With her wet hair dripping onto the shoulders of the olive-green T-shirt, her pregnant stomach bulging beneath it, she looked so fragile, so vulnerable in spite of her hard-bitten insolence.

Was it Annie? Was it me? Or some kind of cosmic misalignment in which we were both hopelessly stuck? I had gentle, harmonious relationships with her brothers, not to mention zillions of friends, many of whom dated back to my childhood. Buyers and sellers loved me. Why was life so difficult with Annie?

My anger burned toward the real issue. I took a deep breath and sat down beside her. "Where have you been, Annie? Why did you run away? Why no word for three godawful years? And what are you expecting of me now that you're back?"

The muscle in her jaw tightened as she clenched her teeth. This was nothing new. That defiant bearing, that refusal to speak—both were as ordinary as breathing for Annie. I shook her shoulder.

"Can you possibly imagine what it feels like to know your child is gone and likely in danger? Your body goes into a kind of shock. You live in a state of underlying anxiety that never goes away. You're reduced to the level of an animal—all you can think of is how to get that child back to safety. We had no idea where to even start, Annie. And here you come prancing home again, expecting everything to be normal? How do you plan to care for yourself? How do you plan to care for your child?"

She glared at me. "Shall I just leave again? Would that make you happy?"

"Don't be ridiculous," I answered through gritted teeth. "I just want an explanation."

"Well, I'm not ready to give you one yet." She turned her back to me on the couch.

God grant me patience. I knew I'd get nothing from her until she was ready. Annie's stubbornness knew no bounds. Once she'd refused to go to school barefoot like the rest of the kids. She insisted on wearing pink sandals. Pink! She didn't even own pink sandals. For two days I dragged her into the third grade classroom barefooted as usual. Both days the principal called me to pick her up at morning recess because she sat cross-legged and cross-armed in a corner and refused to join the class. Where she got the notion, I never discovered, but if pink sandals would buy us peace, so be it. I caved in and bought her a pair. It was part of our pattern, established early. No matter how hard I tried to discipline her, or hold out against her stubborn obsessions, I could only win by putting the entire household into a state of siege. I had the boys to consider, and Frank. None of them deserved to come home to such an unpleasant atmosphere. It was better for all to give in and move on, or so I thought at the time. It never occurred to me that these episodes might have been symptoms of a deeper problem.

What we needed now was not pink sandals but space, emotional space for Annie to adjust to being home, and for me to come to grips with her return. Was I willing to just let her move in, to support her and eventually the baby? She had no job skills, hadn't even finished high school. I could help her, if she did her part, but I wasn't going to be a pushover any more.

Physical space was another thing we didn't have. My bedroom had originally been separated from the living room by sliding *shoji* doors, but I had removed them when I moved in. My office in the alcove off the living room didn't have a door, either. Living by myself, I enjoyed the open arrangement, much like living in a hotel suite. The only thing missing was room service.

I decided to take the high road for the moment. No good would come from mutual hostility. "I imagine you're tired," I said. "I'll make us a salad. Afterward, you might want to take a nap. For now you'll have to sleep on the hide-a-bed in the living room. As soon as I can, I'll rearrange my office and see about getting you a bed in there."

She sighed and rolled her eyes at the television. "Sure, Ma. Whatever." Not exactly affable, but we were over the hump. Why did I not gather her in my arms, assure us both that everything was going to be okay? Wisely, I settled for a quick pat on her leg.

"You and I have lived apart for a long time, Annie. We're going to have some major adjusting to do, both of us."

She darted me a quick, noncommittal glance.

"By the way," I continued as I walked toward the kitchen. "I called Dad while you were in the shower. He's overjoyed you're home. He wants you to call him right away. The number's by the phone."

She sat up. Her blue eyes widened. "Is he angry?" Frank's temper was legendary. He had a long fuse, but when it blew, everyone ran for cover.

I took stock for a moment. "Yeah. Basically, he's angry at me for letting you run away." I watched her to see if she had any comprehension of the deep damage her behavior had inflicted.

She shrugged, passing on the opportunity to make amends. "He's not mad at *me*?"

I shook my head. "He's just glad you're home, kiddo. He's flying in on Monday. For better or for worse."

CHAPTER 4

Against my better judgment, I left Annie napping that first afternoon. I felt too keyed up to read or nap myself, nor could I just sit there waiting for her to wake up. I had to get back to the Colemans, but felt I could concentrate better at my office. In her exhausted, pregnant condition, I was sure Annie would sleep for hours. Now that my daughter had returned, I had to start letting her go again.

My real estate office, Blue Rock Realty, sat in the middle of a small strip mall, the likes of which clutter South Kihei Road between condominiums like dice tossed haphazardly out of a shaker—no rhyme, no reason, no planning to speak of. In the 1970s and '80s, developers got their hands on a piece of land, built whatever would bring in the highest return, and we lived with the results. Unlike the island's meticulously designed resorts, Kihei nevertheless has a certain charm if you love it as I do.

I complimented Peggy, our thirty-something receptionist, on yet another outlandish hairstyle. A chunky woman with a popcorn nose, Peggy's claim to fame was the most spectacular auburn hair on the island. The aging stylist in the salon next door worked it over once a week for free, provided Peggy didn't complain about the results, and didn't mind a bit of sensual neck massage in the process.

Peggy was always very protective of her agents, and I was very fond of her. Feeling too raw from our first few hours together, however, I couldn't bring myself to tell Peggy or anyone else at the office that Annie had returned. Not just yet. The entire staff had been unflaggingly kind and supportive when she ran away. My broker, Kathleen Cowan, had been particularly patient. I knew they would all cheer to hear of her return, but I wasn't sure I could hold myself together. My emotional reserves hovered just above empty.

I headed past the computer bank and the sales and listings board, where my name was conspicuously absent, and straight to my cubicle. Perhaps if I could set aside my conflicted feelings about Annie, even for an hour, I'd gain a better perspective. Somehow I had to push past my anger, fear, and confusion.

I clamped on my mental blinders and sat down to puzzle out what to do about the Colemans. My most loyal, or so I had thought, clients were about to jump ship and swim with the sharks alone, leaving me with nothing to do but wave from the deck. In their best interests—and my own— I had to stop them.

Before I picked up the phone, I worked out my approach. The real estate business depends on what you say and how you say it. It's widely known as salesmanship. My skill during my next conversation with Diana or Jerry was worth approximately $9,000, my share of the commission in their $500,000 price range—provided they agreed to carry on with me as their agent. It was not an amount to take lightly.

Since my divorce, I had learned to live modestly within the framework of a profession that required me to dress well, drive a nice car, attend costly community events, and treat my clients to coffee, drinks, or meals whenever it would expedite a sale. With Annie on my hands, I feared all my hard-learned personal economies that made this lifestyle possible would fly out the window.

As an independent contractor, which most Realtors are, I don't get paid a penny until a sale closes. There's no base pay to keep a body afloat during lean periods. Months of hard work often go by with no commissions at all. Then suddenly several sales close, showering me with gold. Most of the money pays down maxed-out credit cards. Add a few well-deserved treats to celebrate the windfall, and there I am, back to zero with rarely a dollar put by for the next round. Saving for such absurdities as income taxes or retirement? Forget it.

I've learned to handle such unstable finances by living lean, thinking about money as little as possible and hoping for the best. It's a precarious lifestyle, certainly not recommended for a person with no spouse or alternative income, but it keeps me from getting hog-tied over every little disappointment. Now I *had* to think about money. Frank and I were hugely in debt to the detective we hired to find Annie, never mind that he hadn't found her. He didn't care which of us paid his bill. Our contract stated we were both fully liable for the entire amount. Neither of us had made a payment in the past four months. The man's dunning letters were getting more and more unpleasant. No doubt I was his prime target. It's well known all Realtors are rich.

In spite of my prodigious full-time efforts, I hadn't closed a sale in three months. I had only one modest deal in escrow, the Schultzes, due to close next week. My commission would be enough to bring my mortgage current and scatter modest payments to the detective and my other creditors. Having no idea how I would manage beyond that, I simply had to make this sale to the Colemans.

Girding my mental loins, I rang the familiar number. Diana answered, breathless as usual. We got through the preliminaries about Annie. Not for the first time, I was grateful my cubicle afforded me some degree of privacy. Unsure what to say about the baby, Diana coughed to cover her embarrassment and rushed on about the house.

"Darling, I simply get shivers thinking about it. This is *the* house. It's a miracle!"

I waited to see if she would volunteer anything important, such as my role in helping them make the purchase, but she paused for me to gush right back at her. I tried.

"It sounds wonderful, Diana. Truly, it does. Your message said you have an appointment to see it tomorrow?"

"Yes, we positively can't wait. I just know it will be even more fabulous on the inside."

"And the price?"

"Quite a bit higher than we'd anticipated, but Jerry says we can handle it. Isn't he a love?"

I sank a little lower in my chair. "I'm thrilled that you've found some-thing you both like." A miracle indeed. "But I have to ask you, Diana, where do I stand in all this?"

Tension crackled over the line. I kept my mouth shut and pictured her impaled like an iridescent beetle on a brass pin. "Uh, well . . . Jerry's not home right now," she finally managed.

"Come on, Diana. You and I have always been straight with each other. We've been friends for a long time. This is an important decision for all of us." I was relieved that Jerry wasn't home. He was too logical. If I could hook Diana into the obligations of our longtime friendship, I had a chance. Then she'd go to bat with Jerry. "You know, even though it's For Sale by Owner, I can still act as your agent. Having a trained negotia-tor who is not emotionally involved often results in a better price." I hoped I didn't sound like I was reading from a script. I was. I'd picked it up at a recent sales seminar.

"Well . . ." Diana faltered.

"And there are lots of pitfalls between acceptance of an offer and closing of the sale. You could end up in a lawsuit if the seller decides you've breached even the most fiddly detail of the purchase agreement." Unable to read her face and body language, I could only hope the word *lawsuit* made an impression.

"Yes, but . . . but the commission . . ."

"The brokerage fee may seem high, Diana, but haven't I always earned it in the past?" The commission stood out as the most formidable figure on a closing statement, but referring to it as a brokerage fee took out a bit of the sting, or so the theory went.

"Yes, of course you've earned it. You know we've loved having you as our agent. And you're a *dear* friend. But Jerry worked out the commis-sion, Laura. We could save oodles by dealing directly with the seller. Six percent of the asking price would buy us a trip around the world, and then some."

"Not quite," I hastened to disillusion her. "It would probably only be three percent. FSBOs who agree to work with a buyer's agent usually pay only half. See, I've already saved you a bundle." I waited for her to laugh at my Blondie and Dagwood logic, but she didn't. This was going to be harder than I thought. Time to change my tactics. "Do you want me to look up any information on the property? Size of the lot, dimensions of the improvements, names on title, seller's existing loan?" Every little bit she asked me to do for them was another toe over the threshold. All that data was at my fingertips. I would happily share it with them if they committed to using my services.

She began to backpedal. "Gee, do we need to know all that right now? We're not even sure we're going to buy it."

My eyebrows shot up. "You were a moment ago."

"Laura, I don't know what to say. Jerry really wants us to do this on our own. Saving all that money is a real turn-on to him. You know how stockbrokers are." Yes, I did. I also recognized her avoidance technique: blame it on the other guy.

I fired my last salvo. "The truth is, Diana, that a FSBO seller thinks *he* is going to save all that money. He's not selling it by himself so *you* can get it for less. He's selling it by himself so he can save the *entire* commission." Of course, they could compromise somewhere in between, but they would have to tumble to that on their own.

"I . . . never thought of it that way." Good, she was weakening. Diana was not the ultimate decision-maker, but if I convinced her, she just might convince Jerry. It was known as the "black negligée" close: convince the wife, then turn her loose on the husband.

"It's true," I continued. "But look, I know you and Jerry want to do the right thing. You have to admit I've put a great deal of time and effort into getting you this far. We've eliminated dozens of properties you don't like. I've educated you on the market so you're able to make an informed decision. Wouldn't you agree that I've earned a good part of that brokerage fee already?"

I had her squirming on the brass pin. "Look, Laura, I can't commit to anything without Jerry. Please . . ." Her conscience was in overdrive. Perfect. It was time to back off and let her better instincts take over.

"Will you do this for me, Diana? Will you discuss it with Jerry to-night, and give me a decision by ten o'clock tomorrow morning? I'm wildly distracted with Annie, and I need to know whether to drop this entirely, or to keep on trucking for you. Can you do that much for me? If you do decide you want my services, I'll go with you to see the house tomorrow afternoon."

"Sure, Laura." Her voice softened a bit. "You know this isn't any-thing personal."

That's what they always say, but it always feels personal to me. "I know. I also know you'll do the right thing. Get back to me by ten in the morning, okay? I'll wait for your call."

"Of course, darling. Kiss, kiss to Annie."

My hands were shaking as I put down the phone. All around me the office buzz pressed in like a swarm of midges from the nearby Kealia mud flats. I was much more upset by the potential defection of my friends than I'd realized.

Over the years I'd worked hard at learning to handle the disappoint-ments inherent in the real estate business. So often, just when I thought I'd sewn up a deal, the phone rang and everything came crashing down. A seller might refuse a totally reasonable offer because the buyer said some-thing offensive about the purple walls in the master bedroom. A miffed father might refuse to come through with the promised down payment because he hates his daughter's live-in boyfriend. Sometimes, after weeks of legwork on my part, a buyer might bow to family pressure and ask doddering but licensed old Aunt Harriet to write the offer despite me clearly being the procuring cause of the sale. Sure, I could fight it, but it wasn't usually worth the time and effort. Rejection was a daily tonic: bitter, harsh, and hard to swallow. The disappointments never stopped hurting, but I thought I had mastered the ability to weather them without visible dam-age. Apparently not.

And what about luck? It's one thing they don't tell you about in pre-licensing school. The luck to be on floor duty when the million-dollar-listing call comes in. The luck to find a client, like Diana, who buys and sells repeatedly and recommends you to all her friends. The luck to have an uncle who has a 25-acre oceanfront parcel he wants to develop and sell with you as his broker. You need luck to survive in the business. You can be ready for your luck, educated to recognize it, beat the bushes for it, experienced enough to grab it, but you can't create it. Luck happens, or it doesn't. I'd had my share, but never enough to get me above the level of daily drudgery.

So why do I persist in such a difficult business? To be honest, there is no rush like scoring a sale after a long, hard contest with balky buyers or stubborn sellers, or a desperate battle against a competing agent to sign a prime listing. It's exciting, exhilarating, fascinating, addicting. In short, I love it.

Flying into action, I gathered the facts on Diana's FSBO, just in case; took care of a few other business items, then decided I might as well make a clean sweep of nagging matters before I went home.

Calling my healthcare provider, I asked about Annie's status regarding medical insurance. As I suspected, a nineteen-year-old child who was not enrolled in school full-time was not eligible for coverage under my group plan. She could take out an individual policy, but it would not cover her pregnancy and delivery, which are considered pre-existing conditions. As for the baby, if it became my dependent, I could add it under my policy as soon as it was born, but coverage would not be effective until thirty days after the birth. If the baby were premature or otherwise distressed, we were on our own until coverage kicked in. This was worse than I feared. I needed a distraction to cope with such sobering news.

Spending money when my finances are gurgling down the drain always cheers me up. I poked into the tourist boutique three doors down from the office and picked out a couple of sassy short muumuus for Annie. I was determined she would never wear those black sweats again. God knew what other rags she had in her backpack.

Sleeveless, scoop-necked, high-waisted, and generously gathered under the bust, the muumuus looked cool and comfortable. One was pink, splashed with raspberry hibiscus, the other yellow with green-and-red parrots. Ridiculously garish, they'd cheer us both up. At the drugstore, I found bikini panties that would stretch under her belly; a toothbrush, comb and brush, rubber slippers in her small size, and deodorant. Certain things I was willing to share, others I was not.

I found Annie on my bed, propped up against the pillows, legs crossed under her stomach, an elfin toad in that oversized olive T-shirt. Her lemon sherbet hair drifted over her shoulders. A few soggy Cheerios floated in half an inch of milk in a bowl that tipped precariously beside her. She'd removed my grandmother's antique quilt from the bed and folded it neatly on the pink velveteen loveseat that backed against the sliding glass doors. My heart swelled at this small gesture of thoughtfulness.

Annie raised her eyebrows in greeting and lowered the television volume with the remote.

Setting the shopping bag on the floor, I moved the cereal bowl to the dresser and sat on the edge of the bed. "Hi, sweetheart. Did you have a good nap?"

"Yeah, Mom. I feel much better. Sorry I yelled at you. And the language . . . I'll try to keep it clean."

Tears sprang to my eyes. An apology from Annie, especially one that sounded quite grown-up and sincere, was a noteworthy event. Maybe there was hope for us after all. She looked at me shyly through her blonde eyelashes, waiting to be forgiven. I rubbed her thin ankle.

"It's okay, honey. I was wrong, too." No, I wasn't, I thought. I've got to get out of the habit of thinking everything is my fault. Pausing for a moment, I wondered how to convey my genuine concern for her. "It's not just the language. It's . . . everything."

She hugged me fiercely. "I know, Mom. I know." When she pulled back, there were tears in her eyes, too.

"You'll tell me when you can, won't you?"

She looked down at her hands and whispered, "I promise."

Determined to prolong the peace, I steered us into safer waters by picking up the shopping bag and upending it onto the bed.

"Look what I bought you." I held up one of the frocks. "Surprise! Muumuus!"

"Oh, sh . . . shoot. Wild colors, Mom. Totally tourist!" She reached for them and started to laugh. She dove for the bikinis and raised her fair eyebrows at me again. "How did you know I need underpants?"

I grinned. "A mother knows these things. You know what Grandma always said . . ."

We chanted together, "Always wear nice underwear in case you get into an accident. You don't want to disgrace yourself in the emergency room." Together we dissolved into giggles.

"Thanks, Mom, and for all the rest of this stuff, too."

"You're welcome. Listen, how about we scoot down to the beach? You won't feel like you're really home until you've gotten your feet wet and sandy. With the volcano on the Big Island spewing up so much ash, we've had glorious sunsets lately."

"Great idea," Annie declared. "Just let me change."

By the time I fell into bed that night, I felt I'd been beaten against the cliffs by a day-long emotional typhoon. The sunset had indeed been spectacular. Annie seemed genuinely affected by it. She looked adorable in the yellow parrot muumuu, if you could call someone at seven months adorable. I sat on the rocks while she waded in the surf, the breeze flapping the soft fabric against her slim thighs. No one who grew up in the Islands could be immune to the pull of the South Pacific. Perhaps she had been near the ocean, maybe in Los Angeles or San Francisco or Seattle, but it wouldn't have been the same. Our ocean was warm and sparkling, soothing and welcoming, everything Annie needed right now. I prayed it would work its healing magic on my little girl.

When we got home, Annie called her brother David in Provo. He was ecstatic with the news and wanted to come home right away. She told him not to be stupid, that she'd see him at Christmas. She promised to write Damien in El Salvador tomorrow. And tomorrow we'd call my parents in Honolulu.

With all of that on my mind, plus the uncertainty with the Colemans, I surprised myself by falling asleep quite easily, lulled by Annie's amused chortling at "Saturday Night Live." We had one more day alone before her father arrived.

CHAPTER 5

I'm an early riser, always have been. In my childhood, Mother had me up and moving before the stifling midday heat set in. We rested or read after lunch, waiting for things to come alive again when the cooling afternoon clouds settled into Nuuanu Valley. It was part of the rhythm of the Islands. The habit had stuck—minus the naps, of course.

Beset with nervous energy, I waited for Diana and Jerry's Sunday morning call. By eight o'clock I had read the newspaper, drunk three cups of coffee, and was desperate to get moving, but Annie was still sound asleep across the room on the hide-a-bed. No telling how late she'd stayed up watching TV, nor how long she would sleep. My computer in the alcove office beckoned me. My bank statement had arrived the day before, and needed to be balanced so I could buy groceries without fear of overdrawing. However, the clicking keyboard was a mere five feet from Annie's head. There was nothing I could do without knocking about and waking her up. The pale mint drapes were pulled across the sliding glass doors of the bedroom and living areas to soften the blast of the morning sun. They formed a perfect screen for a pair of rice sparrows who hopped along the balcony railing like Indonesian shadow puppets, chittering and pecking at each other in silhouette.

I refreshed my coffee, fluffed up the bed pillows and picked up a novel. The phone rang almost immediately. I started at the noise and upset my cup, spilling scalding hot coffee onto the sheet. As I jerked out from under from the spill, my "Hello" sounded more like a moan.

"Laura? It's Diana." She pronounced it "Dian-er," in true Brit fashion.

"Ahh, good morning," I managed.

"I can hardly hear you."

"Sorry, I just spilled hot coffee on my leg." Why had I mentioned it? It was as good as admitting my extreme anxiety, never a smart strategy when a client has your life in her hands.

"So sorry, love. You did say to call. Are you all right?"

"Sure. But I'll have to keep my voice down so I don't wake Annie. She's asleep on the sofa just across the room."

"Good, then I'll talk and you listen. Jerry and I discussed things at length last night. At great length, as a matter of fact." She paused for a moment. "There's something a bit off about this seller."

"Off? What do you mean?"

"Peculiar. Weird. Dodgy. First of all, there's no way we can reach her directly. We have to leave a message on her machine, and she gets back to us."

"That's not too strange. Sounds like *my* life." The spilled coffee was cooling, but my leg still stung. I rubbed it with the damp sheet, then straightened the pillows with my free hand, settled back, and braced for a disappointment.

"There's something else," Diana continued. "When I spoke with her yesterday, she said that when we come today, we're to park the car down the road, around the bend and out of sight. She'll meet us at the gate. If she's not there, we're to wait at the gate, but under no circumstances are we to go onto the property without her."

"That doesn't sound too unusual. Maybe she has a big dog."

"That doesn't explain the 'leave the car around the bend' bit, does it?" Diana asked.

"True." Would she get on with it and put me out of my misery? Was I, or was I not, involved in this purchase?

"And here's more," Diana went on. "We drove up again yesterday afternoon, just to cruise by and make sure we weren't over-exaggerating our first impression. And you'll never guess—the For Sale sign was down."

"Fallen over in the bushes, or gone?"

"Gone. What kind of person puts up a For Sale sign, gets one interested call, and takes it down right away?"

"Maybe she had more than one interested call," I ventured. "Maybe someone else beat you to it altogether." Wouldn't that solve my problem nicely. We could go on looking and find a nice, normal, listed property. One with another agent to handle the seller and my commission as buyer's agent guaranteed. My spirits began to rise.

"Someone else can't have beaten us to it!" Her voice rose on the British "*cahn't*."

"So . . . on second look you're still interested? If it's still available?"

"Ever so much. It's even better than we thought. In the late afternoon the sunlight filters through the trees and gives the entire property a sort of . . . mystical sheen. And we figure from the master suite—at least we think it's the master suite—you get the full panorama of sunset from the Paukukalo side. You simply won't believe it until you see it."

They were goners. I leaned forward and gripped the soggy spot on the sheet, wrapping it around my fist like a boxing glove.

"So . . . that means I'll be seeing it today?"

"Yes," she hissed, as if squishing the commitment out of a rotten bread-fruit. "We decided we do want you to represent us, darling, provided the seller agrees to pay your commission. We argued over it long and loud, let me tell you. Jerry was a bastard, but bottom line, we think this seller is going to be difficult. You'd know what I mean if you'd spoken with her. We'll likely pay a higher price, but we don't want to lose it because we're amateurs. We want your expertise."

I sank back into the pillows, weak with relief. Hooray for the black negligée close. I didn't care how difficult the seller was. Most sellers, and buyers, too, get difficult at some point during a sale. I'd get that house for Diana and Jerry, and the commission for myself, whatever it took. The money would go a long way toward shaking that detective off my back. Say what you will about the ethics of putting the client's best interests first—it's almost impossible not to consider one's own interests as well.

***

We parked precariously on the narrow country road that hair-pinned through Haiku, two wheels of Diana's red Bronco on the ragged-edged pavement, the other two on the soggy grass shoulder. We could only trust the vehicle was far enough over to avoid being swiped by oncoming cars as they careened around the bend.

During the drive Diana told me what little she'd gathered about the property owner. From the greeting on the answering machine, it appeared she was a physician of some sort. She'd sounded stressed and secretive during their one short conversation. My search of the public records and the phone book had revealed more.

Dr. Randa Entwistle was an anesthesiologist at Maui Memorial Hospital. According to the county tax assessor's records, she was the sole owner of the property, had owned it for eight years, and was unmarried. She had purchased the vacant land in 1984 for cash. Four years later she took out a mortgage for the construction of the home. We'd need a title search and some hometown gossip to find out anything more.

As a professional courtesy, I had called her and left a message saying the Colemans had engaged me to represent them, and that I would accompany them at the showing this afternoon. I stated that I'd like to discuss a commission agreement, but she hadn't returned my call.

While we cooled our heels at the chained and padlocked gate, I began to feel the spell that had enchanted Diana and Jerry. The property ran five acres along a deep gulch, bordered on the road by a white wooden fence behind a mock orange hedge. Clusters of tiny white blossoms doused the humid air with sweet citrus fragrance. Beyond the wooden gate, the gravel driveway swooped downhill and curved to the left. Following the contour of the land, it doubled back and looped in front of a stunning, two-story white stucco house with a Chinese-green ceramic tile roof. Modern in design, the house perched on the edge of the spectacular gorge. From our vantage point, we could see the lush jungle growth cascading down the far side of the gap.

The landscaping enhanced the natural flora and dramatic lava outcroppings of the acreage. Silver-leaved *kukui* trees, orange African tulips, and fringed acacia palms towered over clumps of white spider lily, purple bougainvillea, green tree ferns, and red torch ginger. The lawn was perfectly mown, right to the edge of the ravine. Whoever had designed the landscape had created a tropical paradise with intense passion.

Diana vibrated with excitement. In pleated tan slacks, a tweedy beige pullover, and ivory sandals, she looked strictly Junior League. Add to that her crinkly, dark blunt-cut bob and flawless complexion, and she presented the picture of exactly what she was: the pampered wife of a wealthy husband.

"See how private it is?" she said. "Unless you stand right here at the gate, you can't see the house at all. And the neighbors are completely out of sight." This was true, one more important feature that met their criteria.

Eventually, a figure emerged from behind the house and waved at us, then started up the driveway. The woman was tall and bony, probably in her mid-fifties, with elbows that poked out sideways in a jerky rhythm as she trudged toward us. She reached the gate, fiddled with the padlocks, then pushed it open. She shoved a hand out to Jerry, nodded solemnly at Diana, and ignored me.

"Randy Entwistle," she declared in a low, raspy voice.

The term "long in the tooth" might have been coined for Dr. Randa Entwistle, although it had nothing to do with her age. Her brief greeting revealed a glimpse of dentition that only an endodontist could love. Purplish receding gums showed an alarming amount of exposed root, and the space between her two front teeth would easily have accommodated a nickel. They splayed out over her bottom lip, creating a permanent indentation the shape of two Chiclets.

She wore a long-sleeved plaid shirt, faded jeans, and muddy rubber boots. Her sandy hair, peppered with gray, had probably never had a good day in its entire existence. Short, wavy and bushy, it had an unruly life of its own. In an earlier era she might have been described as a rawboned old maid of undistinguished character. In our liberated day, I guessed she was brilliant at her work and intensely antisocial.

I identified myself as the Colemans' agent, per the message I had left on her machine, to make sure she understood that I represented them. She nodded curtly, an improvement over being ignored. Certainly better than being asked to leave.

"What do you want to see first, the grounds or the house?" she asked Jerry abruptly. "Whatever it is, we have to hurry."

This woman needed an agent. Her sales skills were appalling.

"Oh, I'm dying to see the interior," Diana exclaimed. "Let's not wait another minute."

I tried to catch her eye to convey that she should curb her enthusiasm, allowing me a little bargaining room, but she grabbed Jerry's hand and together they bounded up the steps ahead of the doctor.

The interior more than lived up to its promise. The light-filled entryway was floored in the same glossy jade green as the roof, the ceramic tiles laid diagonally to draw the eye across the room toward a stunning koa wood double staircase, its polished steps rising in twin crescendos of rich brown planks alive with golden highlights. The softly grained banister, a work of art in itself, curved up, crossed the landing at the top, and flowed down the other side. Outside of Iolani Palace in Honolulu, I had never seen a staircase of such overwhelming magnificence. Backing the stairs, a semi-circular bay of floor-to-ceiling windows overlooked the ravine. We simply stood and gaped.

Oblivious to our astonishment, Randy Entwistle urged us on to the right, into a sunken living room carpeted in off-white Berber. The furnishings, understated and expensive, included an intriguing mixture of modern designs and Oriental antiques. A deeply-veined green marble fireplace dominated the far wall, flanked by panels of clear glass etched in a bird-of-paradise motif. All along the left-hand side of the room, a series of French doors opened onto a wide flagstone terrace extending to the gulch's edge.

"Oh, Jerry, do come here immediately!" Diana beckoned to him from the open French doors. "Can't you just see it? Mai tais in the hot tub every night." Smiling, Jerry put his arm around her. They strolled toward the redwood tub at the edge of the terrace, clearly entranced.

Certain a sale was imminent, I took Dr. Entwistle aside in the living room so we could clarify our relationship. "I understand your intention is to sell the property yourself," I began, striving to sound amiable but businesslike. "Would you consider signing a listing agreement? If things don't work out with the Colemans, I'd be able to market the property for you through the Multiple Listing Service and attract another buyer." I wasn't about to cut my fee in half without at least trying for the full commission.

Frowning, she reared her shaggy head. Every short untamed hair quivered with indignation. Her gray eyes were cold as lead. "You Realtors are all like. Give you an inch and you take a mile. No, I am not interested in signing a listing agreement. I don't want anything to do with Realtors. You muck everything up, and you don't look out for anyone but yourselves."

As if I hadn't heard that before. Still, it smarted. Disdaining to reply with my opinion of a medical system that denied my daughter and her unborn child insurance coverage, I kept my voice smooth and sympathetic.

"I'm sorry if you've had a bad experience with a Realtor in the past, Dr. Entwistle. I hope that won't prevent you from working with me solely as the Colemans' representative. They've been steady clients of mine for years. They're adamant that I act on their behalf. As you can see, they may be interested in the property. It would be a shame to let them get away. I'm willing to work for the buyer's half of the commission. You'll handle your issues, I'll handle theirs. It's not something I routinely do, but because the Colemans have been such loyal clients, I'm willing to make an exception. Would that work for you?"

By definition, FSBOs are independent thinkers, which can make them tough to manage. My few previous forays into FSBO territory had left me frustrated and wounded, with nothing to show for my efforts. Dr. Entwistle wasn't the only one who'd had a bad experience. She squinted, as if evaluating my sincerity, but remained silent.

I plunged ahead. "I have a commission agreement right here. It means you pay me only if you and the Colemans actually close the sale. Beyond that, you and I have no relationship. If for some reason this deal with the

Colemans doesn't work out, you are free to sell the property on your own to someone else. Does that sound a little more acceptable?"

She stretched her upper lip over those livid gums and stained teeth, while studying me in silence. Nervous sweat slid down my armpits. She was not making this easy.

"What it means, Dr. Entwistle, is that I'll guide the whole transaction. I'll be helping you, too, but only as a customer, not as a client. I represent the Colemans and my loyalty is to them. However, I still owe you a duty of honesty and fairness. Does that make sense?" I couldn't have done a better job of reading her Miranda rights.

She shoved her fists into her pockets. Finally, she blurted, "So who writes up the offer?"

I dared not blink at this sign of capitulation. "I do, according to the Colemans' instructions. Then I'll bring it to you. I'll explain every detail and answer all your questions. I'll make sure you understand all the terms and conditions before you sign anything. I'm going to be working double duty on this, Dr. Entwistle, while only getting paid on one end. But I'm willing if you are."

Smiling, I waited for her assent. At a time like this, the first person who speaks loses. Although she hadn't demonstrated much of a bedside manner, I felt sure we could work together, provided she followed my lead, did things according to the rules, and respected my relationship with the Colemans. I'd bend over backward to make it easy for her. Half the commission on a sale this size would be more than worthwhile.

"This isn't how I expected it would be," she began, rubbing a finger across her upper lip. Finally she walked over to the fireplace and kicked a brass andiron. A shower of cold ashes puffed onto the hearth. She turned abruptly, both hands in her pockets, elbows jutting out. "All right, I'll do it. But we've got to move fast. Time is of the essence. You bring me an acceptable offer right away, and I'll sign whatever you like."

A secret zing shot through me. We had jumped the first hurdle, but the race wasn't over yet. Until she signed a commission agreement, she and the Colemans could still make a deal behind my back.

"Great," I said. "Let's take care of our own arrangements. How 'bout the kitchen table? We can spread out—"

She raised a hand to stop me. "Look, you bring me an offer. If it's a good one, I'll pay your fee. Beyond that, no go. I need to sell right away. *Right away.* You're not the only agent who has been pestering me. I got so many calls I had to take the sign down."

"Have you received any other offers?"

"Ah . . . no, not yet."

"Expecting any?"

"That's none of your business."

True, from her point of view. My gut said that if she had another offer pending, she'd have crowed about it. But Diana and Jerry needed to act quickly, just in case. Besides, there was always the chance that my clients, given more time to think, would decide the doctor wasn't so formidable after all and proceed without me.

"May I ask why you need to sell so quickly?" I queried in my mildest manner, hoping it would open an avenue of sharing. Knowing her motivation would help me guide the Colemans in making their offer and, if necessary, apply pressure on the right spots during the negotiation.

She gave me a long, studied look, as if deciding whether or not she could trust me. Evidently, it was too early for that. "Let's just say I have compelling reasons. Bring me an offer. As I said, timing is critical." Her eyes hardened, her expression turned bleak.

"Will you be home this evening if they come to a decision? I'll drive back up to present the offer."

Her eyes widened in shock. "No! Don't come up, for God's sake. Leave me a message on my machine. I'll get back to you. A message, that's all."

Startled by her vehemence, I asked, "Isn't there any way to reach you directly? Your pager, for instance?" I pointed at the device on her belt.

She pulled it off, glanced at its face, and quickly clipped it on again. Her eyes darted from side to side behind me, as if she expected someone to burst into the room. A pathetic sense of entrapment lurked in those deep-set gray eyes. I sensed she was caught on a dilemma that baffled as well as frightened her. Her raspy voice cut with a sharp edge.

"Forget the pager. It's for hospital emergencies only. Just leave a message. I'll get back to you." She spun around, strode to the French doors, and called out to Diana and Jerry rather roughly. "We have to leave. Now."

Over Diana's objections, she hustled us out of the house and herded us up the driveway like a gaggle of confused *nene.*

Who was this Dr. Randa Entwistle, I wondered as I scrambled uphill after Diana and Jerry. How did such a graceless person graduate from medical school and come to own this grandly designed, tastefully appointed home? Nothing about her matched the property. For sophisticates like Diana and Jerry it was perfect, but I couldn't imagine Randy Entwistle calling it home.

The doctor's odd behavior gave things a dicey edge that fueled Diana and Jerry's excitement about the property. They were smitten. Knowing an offer was certain, I closed my eyes in the back seat of the car, leaving them to chatter about it unimpeded.

Randa's all-fired hurry to sell presented ominous questions. Why was the doctor so nervous? Why had she shooed us off the property so rudely? And why so adamant that I not contact her directly?

With these questions unanswerable for the moment, my thoughts turned to the other conundrum in my life. Annie had set off for the beach with a towel and suntan lotion before Diana and Jerry picked me up that morning. She assured me she'd have no problem walking the two blocks back to my apartment when she'd had enough.

I still didn't begin to know what kind of life my daughter had led for the past three years, although I had read enough about runaway girls to take an educated guess. She could find the same kind of trouble right here at home. Kihei is no stranger to drug dealers and sexual predators, whose escapades and infractions are reported regularly in the *Maui News.* Was I worried about Annie hooking up with all the wrong people? Darn right. She'd been no saint in high school. If my imagination was even half accurate, she'd survived as a runaway by becoming an expert in all the wrong things.

Anxious as I was to get back to her, however, I had two deliriously eager buyers on my hands. I didn't dare put them off, for fear they would go behind my back and take action without me, or another buyer beat them to the prize. When a property's time comes to sell, multiple offers often materialize out of the woodwork. We would all be unprotected until I delivered the Colemans' offer and Randy Entwistle signed it, along with an agreement to pay me a commission.

We studied the comparables back at the office—similar homes that had sold recently in the same area—and wrote up an offer for fifteen percent less than the asking price. Even though I warned them that the seller might be insulted by such a lowball offer and refuse any further dealings with them, Jerry, like most buyers, insisted on giving it a try.

CHAPTER 6

I splurged and took Annie to dinner at The Four Seasons that night. My earlier fears about her day had proved groundless. Safely at home when I arrived, she stood sun-kissed and showered, combing her wet hair at the mirror above my bedroom dresser. When she turned to greet me, the hem of her pink hibiscus muumuu, pulled up by her belly, hung a good three inches higher in front than in back. As fetching as she looked, this would take some getting used to.

Our table hugged the edge of the pool terrace overlooking the rippling bay. Darkening waves danced under a turquoise and salmon sunset sky. Pulled up behind her ears with butterfly clips, Annie's tresses cascaded over her shoulders like quicksilver. As the changing light played across her face, she took on the beguiling glow of a young Mona Lisa, her secrets held tightly within.

While I mused on the puzzle that was my daughter, I fought down prickles of irritation over the Colemans' offer. I had called Dr. Entwistle as soon as Diana and Jerry left my office, hoping to take it to her right away and get an answer before anybody changed their minds. A hot offer tends to cool down if not delivered immediately.

As it turned out, all I was able to do was leave a message. I took a long shower, ran a load of wash, and straightened up the apartment with one ear cocked toward the maddeningly silent phone. Annie dozed through the late afternoon. After she awoke, she began to pace, obviously wishing she were anywhere but cooped up in a small apartment with her mother.

From time to time, she stopped at the front door, as if considering how soon she could escape me.

She'd had a penchant for wandering as a small child. I'd never been able to let her out of my sight. When she got older, wandering turned to running away from discipline. We often found her hiding in a closet, or up a tree, or at a friend's house, knowing we'd be so relieved to find her that her offense would be forgiven. As a teenager she'd tried hitchhiking to Hana after a particularly nasty argument over my refusal to buy her a car. Hitchhiking had been declared illegal on the island shortly after the invasion of hippies in the early 1970s. The police picked her up and held her at the station until I got there. In a way, her skipping off three years ago was just her normal pattern raised to a grander scale.

I finally gave up on Dr. Entwistle, glad I didn't have to make the long drive to the country after all. Neither did I want to spend the evening cooped up and listening to the sighs of a bored teenager. Randy Entwistle could bloody well leave a message on *my* machine.

I chose the picturesque hotel restaurant thinking the familiar surroundings would relax Annie a bit, help her open up to me. We'd often eaten at the Four Seasons as a family when Frank wanted a break from his own hotel. I also thought we'd both feel more comfortable there than in my apartment, less likely to flare into overheated displays of emotion. Still far from calm about her three-year escapade, her precipitous return, and her bold lack of contrition, I knew it would be counterproductive to lose my temper. It was also our last chance to be alone before her father arrived the next day to shatter whatever peace we managed to establish between us.

Even if she persisted in her refusal to talk about the recent past, I yearned to know how she felt about the baby. So far she had shown no interest in her impending motherhood. Did she plan to keep the child? Put it up for adoption? *My grandchild!* Surely she felt some warmth, instinctive if nothing else, that would erase from my mind her one short, devastating comment on the subject as we drove home from the airport: *keep it, kill it, or give it away.*

As we perused the menu, a young Hawaiian man strode to the rim of the outdoor dining area, bronze-sculpted, clad only in a red loincloth. With a conch shell tucked under his arm, he posed nobly, swept the terrace with his gaze, then settled on Annie with open interest. She met his eyes with a flash of contempt and turned away. Not for the first time I wondered about a world of which I knew nothing, the world of beautiful women who attract men for all the wrong reasons. Whatever men wanted, Annie had it. She'd acquired a woman's body at thirteen: shapely legs; narrow but rounded hips; and high, full breasts. Add blonde hair in a society of Asians and Pacific Islanders, and she was irresistible. As the boys began calling, Frank bristled with protectiveness. I watched warily. To her credit, Annie never seemed terribly interested, always more focused on surfing and soccer. That very lack of interest seemed to encourage them.

Sufficiently disdained, the young man threw back his magnificent Polynesian head and blew three deep throbbing blasts on his shell trumpet. Having gathered everyone's attention, he exchanged the conch shell for a flaming brand and lit the nearest tiki torch, then loped across the terrace, igniting one torch after another. That done, he sprinted through the hotel grounds, lighting the torches along the waterfall, pool, garden, and beach walk. Then he disappeared behind a cluster of cabanas at the far end of the lawn. Annie had not bothered to follow his progress beyond the terrace. What thoughts, I wondered, go through a young woman's mind when a man shows such blatant interest?

"You look lovely tonight, honey," I commented. "The pink muumuu suits you as well as the yellow. Did it feel good to lie in the sun today?"

She laid her hand on her belly. "Fantastic, except that every time I got comfortable, it decided to move, and I had to adjust. I had to dig a *puka* in the sand if I wanted to lie on my stomach. They like it their way, don't they?" She still wouldn't refer to "it" as a baby.

"I'm afraid that's how it is for the better part of eighteen years." I smiled, waiting for an acknowledgement of the universal bonds of motherhood. Turning back to the menu, she ignored my comment.

We gave the waitress our orders. I waited a little longer to see if Annie had anything further to volunteer on the subject of babies. Evidently not, so I plunged on.

"You haven't said much about the baby, Annie. I can't help but wonder how you feel, now that you're safely home."

She closed her menu, but continued to stare at its cover. Without looking up she said in a small voice, "I don't feel much of anything, except fat and tired all the time."

I reached across the table and put my hand on hers. "I sure remember the fat and tired part. David and Damien were so active, they never gave me a moment's rest when I was carrying you."

She looked at me accusingly. "But you had a normal family. You had Dad."

"True. And you were planned and wanted. I'll never forget how thrilled we were when you were born, not only a perfect baby, but with female equipment. Dad passed out pink-ringed cigars at the hotel for a week." I smiled at the happy memory.

Annie pulled the damp cocktail napkin from beneath her soda and began picking it into soggy white bits. "Mine won't be like that."

"Like what, honey?"

"Everyone happy and celebrating." Her eyes remained on the sodden napkin pieces.

I hesitated, wanting to be supportive, but still clinging to remnants of my own upbringing. "One doesn't exactly celebrate in your circumstances. But, sweetheart, I'm here to help in every way I can. It's not like the olden days, you know. We're not going to keep you hidden behind closed drapes and pretend you went on an eating binge." I smiled, but she didn't.

"Does Dad know?" Her eyes were wary.

"Not unless you told him when you called him last night."

"No." She fell silent for what seemed an eternity. I watched the torches flicker against the darkening sky. The sun had disappeared into the sea, pulling over us a deepening canopy of purple-gray clouds. A Hawaiian trio on the far side of the terrace strummed soft guitar, ukelele, and bass over the hum of conversation at nearby tables.

When she looked at me again, the tension around her eyes had re-laxed a bit. "You've been good, Mom. Thanks for not yelling at me. About the baby, I mean."

This small praise glowed in my heart. "I may get yelled at myself. I haven't called Grandma yet."

Annie stuck out her glistening lower lip, a sympathetic gesture that hid a smile. She was well-acquainted with her Honolulu grandmother's rigid view of the world. A stickler for the proprieties, Margaret Wildethorne Henderson knew her place in Island society with unshakable certainty. She played her role to the hilt.

"What do you think Grandma will say?" Annie asked. In spite of her quirks and prejudices, Mother loved her grandchildren to distraction. She relaxed with them as she never had with me. Of course, there was always a servant hovering in the background, ready to step in when Mother de-creed the fun was over, but when it struck her fancy she'd been uproari-ously entertaining with Annie and her brothers.

"I don't know," I replied. "I keep putting off the call. I'm afraid she and Grandpa will rush right over, and suddenly I'll have my mom and your dad on my hands at the same time. You know how they are, each of them nattering at me with conflicting advice." I rolled my eyes in mock horror.

She ventured half a smile. "I'm really sorry to put this all on you, Mom."

In the beguiling torchlight, I believed her. I reached across the table and patted her arm. "What would really help, sweetheart, is if you could tell me where you've been and *why*, Annie, why you ran away. What happened to make you so unhappy?" I asked sincerely, allowing no anger or fear or bitterness in my voice.

With a sigh, she flipped her hair back off her shoulders. "It's compli-cated, Ma. So much has happened. So much I'm ashamed of. You'd never understand."

"Try me, sweetheart. I'm all you've got right now. Dad's on his way, but he'll leave again. Grandma and Grandpa will come, but you know how they are. They live in their own little world. I'm it. You've got to tell me so I can help you."

Her eyes glittered in the torchlight. She dashed the tears away with an impatient hand—a tough, gritty gesture. The waitress arrived with our dinner, a filet mignon for Annie, fresh *opakapaka* sautéed in lemon butter for me. Annie took a bite of steak and closed her eyes, relishing the sensation. I wondered how often she'd had a decent meal lately. Finally she spoke, looking at me earnestly.

"Do you have any idea how hard it is to be a blonde *haole* girl at a public high school on Maui?"

"Well, yes . . ."

"No, you don't. You went to a private school on Oahu where you were sheltered with kids like yourself. Sure, they had local kids there, too, but they were different. Their parents were either rich or made huge sacrifices to send them there. Either way, they weren't about to see their kids shine it off. You had rules on campus, enforced rules. The parents backed the teachers up. Didn't you tell me once the girls went on strike to get permission to wear Roman sandals?"

"Well, it wasn't exactly a strike."

"Whatever. That's the kind of stupid issues you had. Big deal. My high school was a jungle, Ma. Have you got any idea what I went through every day?"

"You were only there for a year! We tried to give you the best education we could. We sent you to that nice little private grade school—"

"Yeah, Ma. You know what went on there? They let you learn whatever you want, at your own sweet pace. I just played and copied the other kids. I never learned anything but how to cheat. I went into seventh grade barely knowing how to *read*."

I didn't believe her. "That's impossible. We read together every night."

"Yeah. I looked at the pictures and memorized what you said. Then I picked out the books we had at home when I had to read aloud at school. I was cute. I fooled everyone. I could B.S. my way around all the teachers. But it got old. I was always afraid I'd get caught. By middle school I was totally behind—and scared."

I felt like I'd been hit by a cane-haul truck. "Annie, I did all kinds of research before we decided to enroll you in that school. We knew you wouldn't be able to handle the confinement of a traditional classroom. Afterward, we had endless conferences with your teachers." Yes, and they had told us Annie roamed the classroom, interrupting the other students, keeping the place in a ferment, day after day. The only reason the school allowed her to stay was that they needed every live body to make ends meet.

I tried to help Annie at home, but she refused to cooperate. Frank and I were at our wit's end. When we had her tested for learning disabilities, they labeled her borderline so she didn't qualify for special education services. She was capable, they reported, but unwilling.

"So you switched me to Grady Hall in ninth grade." What she didn't know was that Grady accepted her only after her grandparents made a sizeable contribution to the school's endowment fund. "That was a total disaster, Ma. I hated every minute of it. I couldn't do the work."

"We gave you the best," I repeated, feeling as small as the bits of parsley in my mashed potato, and about as impotent.

"Like I said, it was horrible," she continued. "I could barely add and subtract, never mind do fractions, decimals, and percents. I didn't know an x-squared from a square of baking chocolate. As for reading, sure, I can read a menu, newspaper headlines, short articles, easy stuff like that if I feel like it. I know the words. But as for history, science, literature— you have to totally concentrate. If you don't get the beginning part, you lose it. I could never keep the stuff in my head long enough to make sense of it. I just couldn't absorb it. It got so that I hated even trying. So I did the only thing I knew. I acted up and got kicked out."

I remembered the call from the Grady Hall headmistress. Frank had left only months before. I was still in terror mode over my own situation. I lost my temper and lashed out at Annie. When I calmed down, I hired a tutor to get her through the end of her freshman year.

"Those correspondence courses you took to finish ninth grade . . .?" I asked.

"Get real, Ma. The tutor did the work. He just told me what to write in the booklets, and I passed."

My fish had gone cold. A pair of capers drowning in butter stared up at me accusingly. "Why didn't you tell me? Annie, I'd have done anything to help you, anything at all."

"I hated school, Ma. Don't you get it? Having a tutor was cool, a real cruise. Remember I asked if I could finish high school that way?"

"Good thing I said no. From what you're telling me, you still wouldn't have learned a thing." Not to mention that the tutor had become a little too interested in her personally.

She grinned. "Yeah, but no pressure. That was smooth. Lots of time to surf. Besides, you were hassling long distance with Dad over the divorce. If you weren't crying, you were out doing real estate. It's, like, I don't know . . . I just couldn't talk to you."

I tried to grasp the torment my child suffered while I had been trying to get my own life sorted out. Those months after Frank left remain a black hole in my mind. I felt scared, angry, and put-upon. It was all I could do to set one foot in front of the other and make it to the end of each day. Keeping the children fed, sheltered, and getting them to and from school were major accomplishments. After Frank lost his fancy job in New York, there was no hope of child support beyond help with school tuition payments. My attorney tried to tap into Frank's unemployment insurance, but the laws on mandatory child support were still full of loopholes; the mechanics of enforcement between Hawaii and the East Coast a joke. Once he became self-employed, there was no point in pursuing it further.

As for earning a living myself, employment opportunities on a neighbor island for someone with a degree in medieval French literature were severely limited, to say the least. I'd been a stay-at-home mom with a smattering of part-time real estate experience. My résumé was a one-liner.

With Frank's departure, real estate became my only viable option. When I told my parents of my plans, Mother had snorted, "Realtors are nothing but a bunch of unethical shysters. You can't possibly mean it."

"Mom! What else can I do?"

"Well, someday all this will be yours," she said, making a dramatic sweep of my childhood home overlooking Honolulu and the ten magnificent acres on which it stood. Someday, yes, but in the meanwhile we had to survive. Never once did Mother offer an early manifestation of my inheritance to ease my chronic financial crunch. In my most desperate moments, I imagined that faraway day, never wishing for my mother's demise, but knowing that if I could just hang on, my later years would be secure. It wasn't much help.

"I don't know why you have to bash yourself bloody in such an ugly profession," Mother had concluded. "You haven't the gumption to succeed in that business. Why can't you be a teacher in a nice private school for young ladies?"

Her searing observation stuck in my throat like a lump of sticky rice. Every listing I took, every sale I made became one more validation that proved her wrong. It was mighty powerful motivation. While Annie struggled with schoolwork, I struggled to keep the family afloat and establish myself in a life-eating business. She was absolutely right. I was either crying or chasing after sales every waking minute.

"I am so sorry, Annie. I knew you were having a tough time, but I had no idea it was that bad. No matter what my own problems were, there's no excuse for having been so out of touch. As bad as that was, however, I still don't understand why you ran away."

She sucked in her lips and nodded. "You're right, there's more." She swallowed one more bite of steak and gurgled the dregs of her soda through a straw. "So, sophomore year I went to public high school. No choice, totally unprepared. The classrooms were a zoo, the teachers had no control. They couldn't discipline the students without going through a dozen stupid procedures. Security guards patrolled the campus. Did you know that? Nobody wanted to learn anything except for a small group of honor students in advanced classes. And of course I didn't qualify for any of those.

"So I was dumped in with all the *titas* and *blalahs* who only wanted to smoke in the bathrooms or make out in a car. I'm not kidding. It was a battle zone. You heard about Kill Haole Day? It was Kill Haole Day every day at that school, not just once a year. And speaking of bathrooms—

they were staked out by big *titas*. If a *haole* girl like me tried to use the *lua*, they'd pound you. No lie, I couldn't go to the bathroom all day. I had to eat lunch with no drink so I could hold it 'til after school. Even if I raised my hand in class to go when nobody else was there, the teachers never let me. Remember I always got urinary infections? That's why. My bladder couldn't take it."

I'd heard about Kill Haole Day at public high schools in the state—a day when it was actually dangerous for *haoles* to go to school. And I'd heard rumors about the bathroom situation at Annie's high school, but never quite believed it. Damien and David had attended the island's only Catholic high school, where *haoles* were more accepted. And of course they were boys, so I'd never had to deal with *titas* in the bathrooms. Antibiotics had cured her recurring infections, but I never suspected there was a deeper cause.

"If you couldn't tell me, why didn't you report all this to the principal?"

"Yeah, Ma, get real. You think they didn't know? They never did sweet squat. They were just running out the clock so they could retire with fat pensions. Trust me, anyone who blabbed to the principal got punched out the next day. I know, I saw it happen."

"But, still . . ." There had to be more, and there was.

"Yeah, so get this." Her face hardened. "There was one gang of local boys who targeted *haole* girls. Blonde was best. They never left me alone. Before school in the parking lot, in the corridors walking to class, sitting behind me in the classrooms and assemblies, even following me home sometimes. That's how it was, always hanging around, staring at me, licking their filthy lips, making gross kissing sounds, and whispering disgusting words at me. Another *haole* girl was getting the same treatment. She told me their secret gang pledge was to screw every blonde *haole* girl on campus. Ma, it was disgusting. I hated it. It got worse and worse. I couldn't take it."

I gasped. "And still you didn't tell anyone?"

"Yeah." The flickering torchlight in her eyes reflected deep pain there. "I finally did."

"And?"

She bent over her stomach and hugged it with both arms. "And then I ran away."

I was utterly demolished. How could my child have suffered so much with me in total ignorance? How could a mother love her child enough to jump in front of a runaway truck or spear a shark to protect her, yet be so completely unaware of her private struggle?

"Did your brothers know?" I asked in a very small voice.

She shrugged. "Damien was already in college. David was at St. Anthony. What could they do?"

I pushed my plate away and stared out into the darkness. The vicious snake of self-incrimination gnawed at my entrails. "Well, if not your brothers, who did you tell?"

She looked away, but not before I caught the fresh shine of tears in her eyes. She crumbled her napkin into a ball, threw it onto the table and stood up abruptly. "It doesn't matter. Let's go."

"But—"

"I don't want to talk about it anymore. Thanks for dinner. Let's go home."

The atmosphere was tense on the short drive from the resort. Annie rebuffed any further questions, making it clear there would be no more revelations that night. I helped her open the hide-a-bed and smooth out the sheets. She submitted to a goodnight kiss, but quickly turned away.

For me, sleep was impossible. For all those years I had believed the nightmare of raising Annie was entirely my fault. I had blamed myself for everything that went wrong in her life. For the first time, I began to realize there were parts of the nightmare she'd lived in her own silent dimension, things that couldn't possibly have been my fault. I began to think that Frank's arrival tomorrow might be a blessing. If he were as ignorant of Annie's struggles as I, perhaps I could let up on myself just a bit.

CHAPTER 7

There was no message from Dr. Randy Entwistle when we returned from The Four Seasons, only a frantic plea from Diana to ring as soon as I heard the merest scrap, no matter how late. There was no point in calling her back. I was stymied until the seller contacted me. I was emotionally incapable of dealing with the Colemans' business, in any case. My restless mind mulled over what Annie had told me, searching for solutions. The harassment by the high school boys and *titas* in the bathroom was appalling. Annie surely needed therapy to deal with the scars, but I doubted she would agree. I'd suggested seeing a family counselor toward the end of ninth grade to sort out our relationship, but she'd flatly refused. A year later she ran away.

What about her school work? Was it too late for her to learn to read properly? Get her GED? I'd have to approach it in stages. She might accept such guidance from Frank. Even at her most rebellious, she sometimes cooperated just to please her daddy.

As I sprawled on my bed, my thoughts circled round and round like a cat chasing its tail. The night was impossibly warm. The sweaty sheet draped my body like a dentist's X-ray shield. I kicked it off, but found no comfort in the humid night air. Exterior lights from the condominium next door, reflecting off my white ceiling, could have lit a Broadway stage. Within and without, everything conspired to keep me in a state of wakeful agitation.

The Colemans' offer would expire late tomorrow afternoon. Would the doctor make contact before the deadline? If so, would I somehow muster the strength to present it convincingly? With a glance at Annie's sleeping form across the room, I stabbed on the TV and tossed fitfully to CNN's coverage of the civil war in Somalia until I finally fell asleep.

The first order of business Monday morning was to get Annie to a doctor. I called my ob-gyn, Dr. Lily Fujikawa, only to be told she was booked solid. When I begged, they agreed to work Annie in if we came early and waited. Annie put up a fuss, but I refused to budge. I may have failed her in the past, but there would be no compromise on her remaining prenatal care.

On the way, we stopped at my office to leave a key to the one listing I had in escrow, the Schultzes. The buyer's final walk-through was scheduled for later that day, with closing on Friday. I had planned to attend, but it was more important to take care of my daughter. The buyer's agent, Al Madrid, would have to handle it on his own.

A Valley Isle real estate legend, Al was a man of great local-style charm and considerably less integrity. Despite his shady reputation, he had an unshakably loyal clientele, due to his plantation roots, his support of the Democratic party, and his huge extended family. I had learned early that if I were romancing a prospect who mentioned Al Madrid, it was wise to back off and cut my losses. The minute Al smelled a sale among his wide circle of influence, he scooped them up and bagged another big one. I was very leery of him.

Al and I had done one previous deal together—my buyers, his listing. At the final walkthrough, I'd discovered the new top-of-the-line refrigerator-freezer had been removed and replaced by an old apartment-sized model that didn't even have an ice-maker. Adding insult to injury, three expensive ceiling fans had been replaced with cheap, garden-variety models. I was steamed.

Al only chuckled when I called him on it. "Check the contract, sweetheart. It says 'all built-in appliances, including a refrigerator and three ceiling fans.' It doesn't say which refrigerator or which ceiling fans."

"Al, that's blatant fraud," I countered. "You know it means the ones that were in the house when the buyer made the offer."

"You can't prove what was there, baby."

"Oh, yes, I can, Al. The buyers took photos the day they made the offer to send to their kids on the mainland. We can prove the items in question were replaced with ones of lesser value. You'd better put them all back, or you'll have a lawsuit on your hands."

He hung up on me in a great huff, but the next day the original refrigerator and ceiling fans were back in place. If I knew Al, he was waiting for an opportunity to get even with me.

While I waited for Annie in the doctor's reception area, I mentally reviewed the progress of the Schultzes' sale. As far as I could tell, it was solid. I should get paid a week from today.

When Annie came out of the examination room, I stood and asked, "Is everything okay?"

"Yeah," she replied, holding up a sheaf of paper. "I guess I have to have some fucking lab tests, though."

I inhaled at her language. "Annie!"

"Okay, okay. Some f-ing lab tests."

"You can do better than that. Just plain 'lab tests' will do."

She rolled her eyes. "Okay, just plain lab tests."

"Thank you. What did Dr. Fujikawa say?"

"She said I'm fine."

"That's all?"

"Yeah."

"You haven't had any medical care during your entire pregnancy, and all the doctor says is you're fine?"

She flipped her bangs off her forehead. "Well, aren't you happy?"

Once more, I was thrown by Annie's changing mood. This was not the young lady who had dined with me in sophisticated splendor last night, who had opened a bit of her heart and shared some of her most painful moments.

I bit back a retort and pointed her in the direction of the lab. "Go."

When she turned the corner, I went back to ob-gyn. "Excuse me," I said to the Tongan clerk who was clicking her computer keys with annoying concentration. "I'm Mrs. McDaniel. Dr. Fujikawa just examined my daughter, Annie. She's seven months along. This is her first pre-natal visit. May I please speak to the doctor? I want to know if she's really all right."

Without looking up, the clerk poked a pen into her bushy black hair, punched a more few keys, and pointed to the screen with a chipped red nail. "Your daughter is over eighteen, yeah? We cannot give you any information without her permission. You have to ask your daughter." She looked up at me as if I should be satisfied.

"But she won't tell me anything."

"I'm sorry. I cannot help you." She lowered her gaze and repositioned the pen in her hair. The chipped red nails resumed their relentless clicking of the keyboard.

I spoke to the top of her frizzy head. "You don't understand. This is not a normal situation. She's a runaway. She's been gone for three years. She might have AIDS or . . . hepatitis or . . . or . . . *worms*."

She looked up, shaking her head. "Cannot." Even the worms hadn't made an impression.

I refrained from jumping over the counter and running into the examination rooms to accost Dr. Fujikawa myself. Who knew what diseases Annie might have picked up, never mind the neglect of her pregnancy. Lily was a personal friend as well as my doctor. In fact, I had helped her buy a house several years earlier. Surely, she'd want me to know if Annie had any worrisome condition.

I thrust my business card at the clerk. "Look, please tell Dr. Fujikawa to call me this afternoon. Here are my phone numbers."

The young woman nodded, accepted the card, removed the pen from her hair, and stabbed the button to answer the next phone call.

Annie was quiet and preoccupied on the way home. Perhaps the reality of the baby had finally hit. I could only hope. While raising my daughter, I had learned to leave her alone when she was so self-absorbed. I remembered only too well that trying to communicate with her while she was in one of her moods usually spelled disaster. At best, she would retreat deeper, remaining withdrawn for hours. At worst, it triggered a full-blown tantrum that went on until she stormed out, or fell asleep, or I gave in.

My best friend Barbara Jaworski had urged me to see a counselor shortly after Annie ran away, thinking I could at least come to terms with my side of things. We worked on my relationships with my mother and Frank. When the counselor pushed, we worked on my relationship with Annie. But I didn't tell the counselor everything. My nights with Annie as an infant lay deeply buried. Even now, I was unwilling to go there.

On my bedside table the red-eyed monster was blinking madly. Wishing it would self-destruct, I hit the play button much harder than necessary. No such luck.

"Laura. Frank. I'm in San Francisco, leaving in about an hour. It's one o'clock here, must be ten in the morning there. I get in around four p.m. United flight seven-three-two. Tell Annie her Dad's on his way." Her knight in shining armor, his voice implied.

Beep.

"Yeah, Randy Entwistle. Uh, yeah, the offer. Uh, let's see, uh, I . . . okay, Taco Bell. Taco Bell in Kahului. Meet me there . . . four-thirty this afternoon. Bring the offer."

Beep.

"Laura, this is Al Madrid. Look, baby, we got problems. That Schultz house is fucked. No way this thing's gonna close on Friday. The rafters are shot with termites, and it needs a whole new fucking roof, *confunnit.* My buyers are shitting all over me. Call me, baby."

Beep.

"Laura? This is your mother. We didn't hear from you over the week-end, dear. Is everything all right? Call when you can. I'm at bridge this afternoon, but home this evening. Dad says aloha. 'Bye-bye."

Beep. Beep. Beep. "End of Messages."

You see why I call it the red-eyed monster? Nothing but demands, bad news, and scoldings. Everyone and everything crashing in on me at once, none of them having any consideration for the trouble that might have been conveyed by the messages before theirs.

I sat on the bed and jabbed the erase button. Annie clicked on the TV. I walked over to her, snatched the remote control from her hand, and clicked it off.

"Did you hear all that? I have to think."

She flopped onto the couch in a pout. "What about Dad?"

"He expects me to pick him up at the airport, but I can't. That Dr. Entwistle, the one I've been trying to deliver an offer to, can meet me today at four-thirty. I've got to be there. The offer expires at five o'clock."

She clicked her tongue in disgust. "Always the sale. When does the family come first with you, Ma? This is, like, *déjà vu* already."

Fists tight at my sides, I stood above her and glared. "Look, young lady. The sale, as you so scornfully put it, is what is going to feed you, house you, pay your hospital bills and support your child until you can get your life together. Not to mention that I still owe a bundle to the private detective we sent after you. Can you even begin to guess how much that cost? And for what? How dare you complain that I have to go out and earn a living?"

She hung a leg over the edge of the couch and scuffed her toe on the white carpet, then looked up at me sheepishly. "You hired a detective to find me?"

"Well, of course we did. What did you expect, we just sat here, hoping you were happy somewhere and had simply forgotten to call us for three years? Of course we hired a detective, for all the good it did. We had visions of you dead in a cane field or on a slab in some mainland morgue, for God's sake."

Her little chin quivered. "I never thought you'd hire a detective."

I pulled over a dining chair and sat down facing her, hands clasped between my knees.

"It seems like there's a lot of stuff you never thought about, Annie. Maybe you ought to. Your father and I were literally disabled with worry.

We had no clue where you were for three years. The only comfort we had was feeling certain you hadn't been kidnapped, but took off deliberately. Some comfort that was! How could you have done that to us?"

Annie looked at me intently. "That's awesome, Ma. A detective?"

I wanted to shake her. "Annie, don't you get it? You came close to destroying us! It was all I could do to make it through each day, hoping against hope you'd turn up with some kind of reasonable explanation."

"Gee, Ma. Okay. I get it. Chill."

Was I communicating or just howling in the wind? "I'm waiting for an apology, Annie."

"Okay, so I'm sorry." She spat it out as if a fly had blown into her mouth.

"That's it? You're sorry?"

"Yeah. I am sorry. It didn't turn out the way I expected. That's what you wanted to hear, isn't it?"

"I want to hear you're sorry for the agony you caused your father and me, not for how it turned out."

She clicked her tongue. "Okay, Ma, sorry for that, too. Okay?"

God give me patience; it was a start. I took a deep, trembling breath. "Okay. You're home. Our prayers have been answered, but it's going to take some getting used to . . . for both of us." I paused, not sure where to go from there, how much more to say. Safer to change the subject.

I stood up, reached over and stroked her hair. "I really do have to deliver this offer, so I won't be here when Dad arrives. He'll have to rent a car. I have no idea where he's staying. If you go with him, be sure to call and leave the name of the place and the phone number. I'm really on a thin edge, Annie, and I want to know where you'll be." I brushed a shimmery lock behind her ear. The boundary between concern and smothering was beset with land mines. It would be so easy to trip one off.

She shook her hair away from my fingers. "Yeah."

I leaned forward and hugged her. She softened for an instant in my arms. With a tentative smile, I chucked her under the chin and went to my phone to dial the number for Al Madrid. Better get it over with.

His condescending voice oozed through the receiver. I held it away from my head, as if the ooze would soil my hair. "Eh, you saw the termite report?" he asked without any opening pleasantries. "The rafters look like Swiss cheese. The bank won't fund the loan with that kind of structural damage. On top of that, we're walking the boundary today, see, checking the survey pins, and my buyer trips on a wooden shake, *confunnit*. We look around and there's fucking shakes all over the place, behind, you know, in the grass where they never mow. So we climb up a ladder and find out the whole roof is chop suey. Must be from that Kona storm last week."

My heart sank. "Didn't you do a roof inspection during the buyer's discovery period?"

"Nah. I figured no need, yeah? The seller's disclosure says the roof is okay."

"Well, I'm sure it is. If there were any problems, my sellers would have disclosed them."

"Well, they got major disclosures now, baby. Unless the sellers put on a new roof, with new rafters, the buyer's gonna sue."

"A new roof and rafters? Al, that's absurd. It would eat up my seller's equity. They'd have nothing left for the down payment on their new home." I rubbed a hand across my forehead. It came away glistening with perspiration. Not only was this deal threatened, but the next one as well.

"Not our problem, baby. You go check. The thing is no good. Termites eating up the rafters, and shakes all over the place except where they belong. The bank already sent instructions to escrow to hold up the closing until they get it fixed. I sent a copy to your office."

"Al, you don't understand. Without a down payment for their new home, my sellers have no reason to sell."

"Sorry, baby, my buyers want that house . . . with a new roof and rafters. They'll sue. Your folks should have disclosed. Bad scene. They're in default, big time, baby, and you know it. They cannot bail out. No way."

"But Al—"

"Later, baby." He hung up.

My stomach was shredding. Dooley and Anita Schultz has sold their house on a lark. For the first time in their married lives they had a good income and thought it would be fun to buy a brand new home, but they were not strongly motivated. Although they had found the home of their dreams in a new hillside development with ocean views, they refused to sign a purchase agreement until this sale closed. They planned to rent while the new home was built. Was that why they wanted to wait before committing to the new home—to see if they got away with undisclosed issues in the old home?

They'd freak at the idea of sacrificing their equity for a roof and rafters they would never live under. They'd be left high and dry, back to renting on a permanent basis. I rifled through the stack of overdue bills on my desk. The Schultzes were the only light on my horizon. I had to get them closed.

Although they wouldn't be home, I needed to run over to look at that roof right away to see if Al was bluffing. Hopefully it was all *shibai*, and we'd just need to replace a few shakes. If he was telling the truth, however, and the sellers were unaware of the situation, I might somehow be able to wiggle them out of it. For the moment, I couldn't think how, but there had to be a way. But if Dooley and Anita were pulling a fast one, they'd better be prepared to replace the rafters, buy a new roof and join the ranks of the renters. I wouldn't have much pity for them in that case.

I had just enough time to take care of this before meeting Dr. Entwistle with the Colemans' offer. Returning my mother's call would have to wait.

Sure enough, the roof was a mess, and there were enough wind-blown shakes in the weeds behind the house to make a bonfire. I was certain they hadn't been there a week ago when I checked the staking myself. Dooley and Anita had to be aware of the damage. That Kona storm, with its contrary winds from the south, had been fierce. My only question was how they could have been so stupid with the evidence so obvious. But they were my clients. I had to give them the benefit of the doubt.

I dashed to my office to pick up the lender's instructions to halt escrow. The damning termite inspection report was waiting for me, too, as well as a personal letter from the buyers to the Schultzes, demanding they replace the roof and rafters and complete the sale. Insurance would cover part of the storm wreckage, according to their deductible, but not the termite damage. I quickly called several roofers and carpenters to get ballpark estimates.

As much as I dreaded a confrontation with Dooley Schultz, I knew I'd better deliver this news in person. My willingness to fight for them would hinge on what they knew about the situation and how straight they were about it. It's much easier to determine if people are telling the truth face-to-face. Body language speaks volumes.

I made it to Glittering Sands Art Gallery in less than three minutes. Fortunately the showroom was empty of customers. Anita climbed down from a stepladder where she had been hanging one of her husband's paintings and greeted me cheerfully. I said I needed to speak with them both, preferably in the privacy of Dooley's studio out back. Puzzled, she led me past the display of his latest work and the counter where she assisted customers with framing. We found Dooley at his easel in his messy, sunlit studio, one paintbrush clenched in his teeth, another in his hand, stroking in a stormy sky on a large canvas.

Dooley's light, lively style with acrylics belied his bear-like appearance. His claim to fame was a method of applying layers of sand to a canvas with clear-drying glue to create a bas-relief beach in the foreground. He then painted seascapes or sunsets in the background to quite a glitzy effect. The sand appeared meltingly soft with glints of light sparkling off the glue. He had a devoted following among tourists, making his gallery a popular visitors attraction. No *kamaaina* would dream of setting foot in there.

I summarized the termite report and the roof issue as succinctly and unemotionally as possible.

Dooley spat out the one paintbrush and loomed over me, teeth bared and eyes popping. His hairy, freckled calves bulged above his straining leather sandals.

"A new roof. Are they crazy? Here's what I think about a new roof." He sliced the air in front of me, zip-zip-zip, with the other brush, purple-tipped and lethal.

"They're pretty upset, Dooley," I replied, jumping out of the danger zone.

"*They're* upset? If they walked in here this minute, I'd give them something to be upset about." He stamped his foot and shook his head like a wild animal, sending his long, stringy, sandy hair flying around the rim of his bald pate. "Why should I buy them a new roof?" he demanded. "They had two weeks to do their inspections. They never said anything about the roof. They can't get away with that."

Anita, his one-woman public relations dynamo, shop manager, and reality-checker, interrupted with a hand on his beefy arm. "Dooley, Dooley, let's listen to what she has to say."

I bobbed her a grateful nod. If I could get her on my side, we had a chance of getting out of this without being dragged into court. Anita fascinated me. She charmed the customers, kept the books, swept the gallery, and made sure Dooley's name and work appeared regularly in a galaxy of tourist publications. Her husband's opposite in every way, she was petite, soft spoken, practical, and diplomatic. Half Japanese, half Irish, in contrast to his barbarian *haole* physique, she was an ivory-skinned, exotic beauty. She'd twisted her long, straight black hair into a loose knot atop her head and anchored it with a lacquered chopstick. Wispy tendrils trailed on either side of her face, adding to the charming effect.

Plunging on, I said to them, "The termite damage in the rafters is so extensive it constitutes structural damage. The bank won't close until they are replaced. Maybe you didn't know about that, because the rafters are hidden in the ceiling, but when the buyers did their final walkthrough this morning, they found shakes in the bushes. They climbed up on the roof for a better look. I checked it myself on the way over. It looks pretty bad." I dared not use Al's phrase, "chop suey." That would inflame Dooley even more.

He planted his sandaled feet firmly on the paint-splotched concrete floor, crossed his Popeye arms over his barrel chest, and glared at me. "That's ridiculous. The roof is just fine."

Despite the air conditioning in the gallery, perspiration collected between my shoulder blades. My blouse stuck, clammy and uncomfortable. Dooley's defensive stance convinced me he was lying. If I couldn't get him to admit the truth and make good on his deception, we'd all get dragged through the mud. I reached deep inside for all the finesse I could muster.

"It's not fine, Dooley. All I had to do was stand on the bumper of my car and peek over the eaves trough. The roof looks like a checkerboard, and shakes are blown all over the back yard." I paused and waited.

We breathed through a long, tense moment. Then Anita broke. "See, Dooley, I told you."

"Shut up, Anita."

She bit her lip but didn't flinch. Not for the first time, I wondered what she saw in this unattractive, temperamental man.

Dooley swiped his hands with a paint-smeared rag, obviously stalling while he assessed his position. I let him stew for another long moment, then stepped in slowly and deliberately for the kill. "You may not have known about the termites, but you knew about the roof, didn't you, Dooley?"

He glared at me, his bushy eyebrows bristling with fury. I refused to blink. The silence did its work.

"Fuck." He turned back to his easel and began slapping in more furious purple sky. He knew he was dead meat.

Anita turned her back on him and quizzed me earnestly. "Do you have any idea what all this would cost?"

I shared with her the rough figures I had obtained from the roofers and carpenters. From the corner of my eye, I saw Dooley's hand erupt in circular motion. Violent charcoal thunderheads massed on the canvas in the purple sky.

"Wow," Anita said. "We have a pretty high insurance deductible for storm damage. That, plus the rafters, will wipe out our down payment for the new house."

I nodded. "If I'd known, Anita, I'd have counseled you take out a home equity loan, make the repairs and stay put."

She pulled the chopstick out of her topknot, twisted the hair tighter, and anchored it again. "Can we get out of the sale now?"

"That was my first thought, but you can't cancel the contract without the buyer's consent, and they seem determined to proceed. They want the house and they want it in good repair, as is their due. You're clearly in the wrong, Anita." I handed her the letters from the bank and the buyers, plus the termite report.

She scanned them quickly. "We're stuck, then?"

"As far as I can see. That roof is a major disclosure, Anita. Why weren't you guys up front about it?"

Anita glanced at Dooley, his back to us, still painting furiously. "I begged him, Laura. How many times did he climb on the roof and nail back the shakes after a big wind. But last week—I guess he never got around to it. I told him we had to disclose the whole situation. He said the buyers could discover it on their own, or find out about it after they moved in. I knew it was wrong, but with Dooley, what can you do?"

It all made sense. "That's why you guys wanted to sell, yeah? Because you knew about the roof *and* the rafters, and wanted to get out without replacing them so you'd have enough money to move on."

Anita pursed her lips. She didn't have to reply. I knew it was true. That explained why their motivation for selling had seemed so flimsy, why they had held back on contracting for a replacement property. They were holding their breath until this one closed, just to be sure.

Anger propelled me beyond any desire to avoid more confrontation. They had broken the law and lied to me, exposing all of us to possible legal action. I turned toward the easel, fired by righteous indignation.

"Dooley, please put down your brush. You lied on your disclosure statement, and again just now when I asked you about it. I won't put up with that. The buyers will force you to make the repairs and close. If you refuse, that means a lawsuit. And I get dragged into it right along with you." I looked from one to the other, daring them to contradict me. I hoped like hell things would not go that far, but I had to impress upon them the possible consequences.

Anita lowered her head, refusing to meet my eyes. Dooley bristled with defiance.

"You have a fiduciary duty to us," he declared. "You explained that very carefully when we signed the listing contract. You can't tell them we knew about the roof. You'd be giving away confidential information."

"I've got news for you. My fiduciary duty ends the moment you ask me to commit an illegal act. Covering up for your lie is an illegal act. I'll have no part of it."

His massive chest heaved several times, but he'd apparently run out of macho rejoinders. "So, what are you going to do?"

"Nothing until eight o'clock this evening. Call your insurance guy and a couple of roofers. Get your own estimates, and find out how soon they can do the work. Then call me and let me know what your plan is. I'll keep quiet until eight, but not one minute beyond."

Anita appeared to crumble. Her hair, falling out of the knot, straggled in a dismal curtain down one side of her face. I felt sorry for her, but not sorry enough to keep from walking out the door looking much sterner then I felt.

Damn them, I thought, speeding down the Psychedelic Road toward my rendezvous with Dr. Entwistle. I should have been rehearsing how I was going to handle her. Instead, I was still furiously replaying the scene with the Schultzes.

How dare Dooley and Anita mislead me so blatantly and think there would be no consequences? But they weren't the first sellers I'd had who believed the rules didn't apply to them. Had I been too harsh on them? My clients had blown it, deliberately and fraudulently. I had every right to sound off. But I still had to retain their confidence to get things resolved. My commission would be delayed, but I could live with that. If they got right on it, the job could be done in three weeks.

The tranquilizing *wiliwili* shadows flickered across my windshield as the sun arced over the West Maui Mountains. In the hot, dusty afternoon, my anger began to subside. Knowing that the buyers were determined to close the sale, my job was to get the Schultzes to comply with the least amount of collateral damage. Yes, they would be left without a down payment for their next home. I felt sorry for them, but, as my mother would say, they made their bed and they could sleep in it. Leaving them to ruminate was the best thing I could have done. By the time I rounded the curve at the Puunene Sugar Mill, I began to feel better.

CHAPTER 8

Taco Bell was surprisingly crowded for mid-afternoon. Moms with kids and teenagers in groups filled the room with noisy chatter. Dr. Randa Entwistle waved her lanky arm at me from a corner booth in the back. I eased onto the bench opposite her and set my file on the table. At least we were somewhat out of the racket.

"How are you, Dr. Entwistle? Thanks for making time to meet me."

As tall and rawboned as I'd remembered, Randa Entwistle strained toward me, elbows on the table, without acknowledging my greeting. She wore a multi-colored rayon aloha shirt and khaki shorts. Parchment skin stretched tight across her beakish nose. A fistful of ginger-gray hair, bound tight by a red rubber band, bristled like an old-fashioned shaving brush on one side of her head. With those alarming teeth and gums, she could have been a poster girl for periodontal disease. Maybe she thought nobody noticed, since her professional life was conducted behind a surgical mask.

I tried once again. "Nice to see you, Dr. Entwistle."

"Call me Randy. What's the offer?"

I'd planned a little small talk, to build rapport, to remind her I was a nice person, and that we both had the same goal: selling her house. Her abruptness unnerved me.

"I have it here," I said, placing my palm on the closed manila folder. She would have to contain her curiosity until I covered some important preliminaries. "It's a very good offer, Randy. My buyers are well qualified. But before we look at it, we need to go over a few things. You and I don't know each other, yet if you and the Colemans come to an agreement, we'll be working together very closely. I want to make sure we both understand the parameters of our professional relationship." I smiled, encouraging her to lighten up.

She looked straight at me with no hint of warmth. Her sunken cheeks and darkly circled eyes suggested serious sleep deprivation. Then, as it had when we met at the property, her glance darted nervously from side to side behind me. Maintaining eye contact was going to be a project.

"What's the price?" she demanded.

Again, I forced myself to smile. This was not going well.

"All in good time, please, Randy. Before we discuss the offer, you'll need to sign a commission agreement, as we discussed yesterday. You told me you would be willing to pay half our usual commission and represent yourself. My loyalty is to my clients, the Colemans, but I will provide you with fair, honest, and ethical guidance as a customer. Agreed?"

She cleared her throat and remained silent, glancing once again into the space behind me. I pulled the commission agreement from the manila folder. It was simple, just one page.

She took a few moments to read the document. Without comment, she pulled a pen out of the pocket of her aloha shirt and signed both copies. I gave her one and let out a deep breath.

"Thank you," I said, tucking my copy safely into the folder.

Randy leaned forward, gripping the edge of the table, as if ready to snatch me by the collar. "Tell me now. What's the offer? How much?"

It went against all my training to present the offer cold, without first finding out why she was so desperate to sell. However, in the face of such agitation, any probing for information would have to be done bit by bit during the course of the presentation. Randy looked panicky enough to flee if I didn't get on with it.

I set the offer on the table facing her, being very accomplished myself at reading real estate documents upside down. I pointed to the center of the top page.

"They're offering $616,000. That's less than your asking price, but the buyers are—"

Her face collapsed. She exhaled a veritable gust of wind through those gate-like front teeth. Her knuckles, still gripping the edge of the table, turned white. "I told them I wanted $725,000! That's my price, especially if I have to pay you a commission. This is preposterous! Why are you wasting my time?" She propelled herself to the end of the booth and gathered her crane-like legs beneath her for takeoff. My heart dropped onto the floor beneath me.

"Dr. Entwistle! Randy. Please, listen." She stopped at the edge of the bench, poised to fly right out of my life. Fighting to be heard above a gaggle of giggling girls at the next table, I raised my voice.

"There are many more considerations than price, Randy. As I said, these buyers are well qualified. The offer is clean, with no contingencies. They don't have another house to sell, and they can probably close in four weeks. Isn't that what you want? A fast closing?" She had been emphatic about the need for haste yesterday at the house. It was the only clue that might help me reach her. Four weeks was wildly optimistic, but I was willing to gamble.

She turned around but remained at the edge of the bench. "I've got to get it sold. As soon as possible, but that price is no good!"

"Then we counter. Buyers always start low and expect to negotiate. It's part of the process. Let's review all the terms and conditions of the offer." If I could get her to do that, chances were she'd relax and keep the dialogue open instead of turning the whole thing down. She didn't make any move to rejoin me in the booth, but she didn't get up and leave, either. Feeling I was gaining, I continued my pep talk.

"You know, Randy, a first offer is often the best offer. You don't want to turn down what might be your prime opportunity. Bear with me. I promise we'll get back to the price later. When we do, I'll show you the comparables on which they based their offer." I'd seen it many times— sellers turning down a good first offer simply because they were insulted by the lowball price. They also thought if it were this easy, a better offer would come along right away from someone else. Two years later, they would still be waiting for that better offer.

Eyeing me warily, Randy slid back into the booth. We spent the next hour and a half grinding through the contract, line by line. Once she resigned herself, she was an attentive listener. Along the way, she loosened up and gave me some sketchy background.

She had built the house for her parents, who had retired and come to live with her eight years ago. Her mother was an interior designer, her father an architect who loved puttering in the yard. That explained the magnificent edifice and park-like grounds. When her father passed away five years ago, her mother returned to the mainland, leaving Randy to rattle around alone.

She asked intelligent, insightful questions and accepted most of my answers and explanations, unlike some physicians I've worked with who believe that handling life and death on a daily basis somehow makes them experts in real estate. Begrudgingly, my respect for her increased as we went along. I can't say that I was on the verge of liking her, but I did feel we were laying a thin foundation of trust between us.

By the time we got to the last stultifying term on the sixteenth page, we were both wilting with fatigue. Randy rubbed a drooping eyebrow and poked for remnants of ice in her glass with her straw. Anything solid was long gone.

"Look, I appreciate that this is a decent offer," she said. "If you're right, maybe the best I'll get. But I have to have more money."

"May I ask why the precise amount is so important? Do you plan to buy another property right away?" If so, did I sniff another sale?

"Trust me, it's critical. I need to net a certain amount and not a penny less."

"And may I ask why?" I persisted. Sellers often get hung up on PFTA numbers, "Pulled From Thin Air," that had nothing to do with reality.

She blew her nose into a paper napkin and dropped the crumpled wad under the table, hitting my instep. I winced and kicked it away, wondering where this woman had learned her manners.

"All right. I don't see why I can't share this much with you. My mother has Parkinson's disease. Right now she lives near my sister Karen in California, but it's becoming more and more difficult for Karen to cope. We found a retirement home that my mother likes. It's very expensive. Mom can manage the monthly fee, but I need to buy in for her. Her name is at the top of the waiting list. It could happen any day. I've got to be ready."

That much made sense. I believed her, but considering her almost pathological reticence yesterday, she'd shared it too easily. I had a strong feeling she was throwing out a red herring to distract me from her real reason for selling the house.

"Okay. But surely you have savings? You're single, obviously well paid. The buy-in for your mother can't be entirely dependent on the proceeds of this sale."

Her face closed. Despite the glimmer of camaraderie she had allowed while talking about her mother, we were still on an upwind tack.

"I have no savings," she finally said.

"Why? Surely a successful physician . . . ?"

"Forget it! My finances are none of your business."

"Okay. I understand the urgency of having the money in hand when your mother's unit becomes available, Randy. But something tells me there's more than that driving your need to sell."

She sighed, deeply and soulfully. Something certainly weighed heavily upon her, something she was unable to shrug off. I was dead certain it was more than just getting her mother settled in a retirement home.

Once again her eyes darted around the corners of the room, then fastened on me for a long moment. She wanted to trust me, I was sure of it. While I tried to think of something to say to ease her mind, my thoughts turned to Frank and Annie. Had he arrived and safely connected with our daughter? A run to the pay phone outside the restaurant was out of the question. That would break the mood with Randy, destroying whatever confidence she might be working up to share. I pushed aside all thoughts of family, forcing myself to concentrate on matters at hand.

"Have you ever," Randy asked, looking at me seriously, "been in a situation where you are stymied at every turn? Where your whole future hinged on breaking a logjam in a way that the logs don't come crashing down and destroy you?"

I nodded sympathetically, thinking again of Annie. "Yes, I have." I wasn't about to share the details of my personal life with her, but I could admit that much.

She nodded, acknowledging the common thread. "I'm an intelligent woman, highly educated, professionally secure. Yet about four years ago I got myself into an unbelievable muddle. I'll be the first to admit how stupid I was. All I want is out, with my medical license and professional dignity intact." Her husky voice wavered on the last three words. She lowered her face into her hands, a picture of abject despair.

"And this has to do with the house?"

She looked up, her eyes pleading with me to understand. "About a year after my mother moved back to the mainland, I met a woman on the beach."

My own eyes must have narrowed, or perhaps my head quirked slightly. She slapped her hand on the table.

"Hey, I'm not talking about a pickup. God forbid. It's just that I love to sketch. I was sitting under a *Kiawe* tree, idly doodling, waiting for inspiration to strike, when I noticed this woman lying face down on the sand maybe a dozen feet away. She had the most outrageous scar on her leg. Really, I was fascinated. I couldn't imagine why she wasn't completely crippled. Most of her upper calf was gone, just carved right off. I encounter these things in the OR, but I rarely get to see the results after the patient heals. Without thinking, I began to sketch it. It was really incredible. Mottled, wrinkled, shiny. Great texture for a drawing exercise." Her face lit up as she remembered her fascination with the woman's deformity.

"All of a sudden, don't you know, she pitches herself upright and hobbles over, sand flying in every direction, to see what I'm doing. 'How dare you make a mockery of my injury,' and all that. Wildly hostile. Accuses me of invading her privacy, ridiculing her in public, that sort of thing. When I told her I was a physician, she calmed down a bit. We got to talking.

"It turned out she'd had a boating accident. Got caught between a dinner cruiser and Ma'alaea Pier. Ghastly. She was still in physical therapy, experiencing a great deal of pain. To top it off, she'd been kicked out of her rental cottage that morning. Her landlady gave her forty-eight hours to get out, which is illegal. She had a copy of the state Landlord-Tenant code with her and was studying up on her rights. I felt sorry for her, with her injury and all. She could barely walk. Without thinking, I offered her a room in my home, temporarily, of course, until she could find something else. God knows, there was enough space for both of us."

I wondered what the woman had done to get kicked out of her digs on such short notice but didn't want to interrupt the narrative by asking. Randy seemed reluctant to go on, however, as if she had already revealed too much.

"I take it things haven't been all sweetness and light?" I suggested.

She snorted. "For a while it worked out fine. I hadn't realized how lonely I was. She was lively . . . and fun. Except when she got angry. But I learned how to keep her steady. Mostly by agreeing to whatever she wanted, I'm sorry to say."

I cringed. That sounded exactly like me and Annie. But no more.

Randy continued. "I was rarely home. My shifts at the hospital last ten to twelve hours, and then I get called back on emergencies. We went days without seeing one another. She kept the place neat and tidy. She's a meticulous housekeeper, in spite of her disability. She did wonders with the yard, too. It went to pieces after Dad died. She was passionate about it, always picking up new plants, trimming, pruning, fertilizing. We have a Samoan crew, of course, to weed and mow. Between the gardening and housekeeping, she more than earned her room and board. I had no quarrel on that score. In fact, I was grateful to her. It was excellent therapy for her, too, all that moving about. Then things just kind of disintegrated about a year ago. I've got to get her out, but she won't go."

"What happened a year ago?"

Randy hesitated, then cased the room behind me again. "It's a mess. I just need to get her out, okay?" Her face warned me that if I pursued that line of questioning, she'd clam up for good.

"So why don't you just ask her to leave?"

"Hah. She won't go," Randy spat. "She refuses. I've tried everything. Begged, pleaded, offered her money. When none of that worked, I packed all her stuff and put it in storage. She hauled it all out and had it back in the house within hours. I changed the locks and tried again. Same thing. I forgot to lock the upstairs bathroom window. She climbed up the trellis and got in that way."

I raised my eyebrows.

"Oh, she's quite nimble now. There she was when I came home, propped up in *my* bed, eating a bowl of chocolate chip ice cream. I haven't slept there since."

The image was ludicrous. "She kicked you out of your bedroom?"

"Yup."

I'd dealt with uncooperative housemates before, but this was extreme. "You must have been fit to be tied."

Randy snorted. "I was. I detest her. I want her out of my house and my life. Now."

"What about consulting an attorney?"

"Yeah, right. I went to an attorney. He wrote her all kinds of stern letters, to no avail. Finally, he told me that selling was the only surefire way to get her out."

"That sounds pretty drastic, selling your home to get rid of a housemate."

"The attorney said that if I tried to evict her any other way, the court would likely find in her favor, at least in the short run. Even though she's more of a guest than a tenant, he felt they'd probably bend over backward to accommodate her, since she's legally disabled, unemployable, and has no resources. She plans to stay that way, I might add. She's become an expert at milking the state disability system."

"So not only has she taken over your house, but you support her, too, more than just room and board?"

She sucked in her lower lip and nodded. "Yup."

"Still?"

"Have to."

"Why?"

She clicked her tongue and quickly scoped the room behind me again. That obsessive behavior had stopped briefly during the intensity of relating her story.

"So that's where it stands," she said, leaving my question unanswered. "Now you know why I really have to sell. I do need the money for my mother, but, bottom line, I want her out. I appreciate all your work. Please tell the Colemans—is that their name? Thank them for the offer, but they need to pay my price."

I was losing my legendary patience. Visions of Annie and Frank's reunion kept breaking through my concentration. I refused, however, to leave without a counteroffer.

"Look, Randy, psychologically, it's really hard to go back to buyers with a rejected offer and expect them to try again. I'll admit their offer was a bit low, but they need some encouragement. I know you want to sell, and here's your chance. Let's do a counteroffer that works for you. They love the house. And once the Colemans decide to buy, they always plow straight ahead and close the sale. You won't have any problems with them during the escrow period." I paused for a moment, wondering if I was getting anywhere. She remained silent.

"Do you have any idea how much trouble buyers can cause if they get cold feet along the way, Randy? It's called buyer's remorse. It happens all the time. The Colemans aren't like that. You've got serious, qualified buyers here." She looked at me warily, still not about to cave in. I switched to one last tried-and-true tactic. "Let's check your bottom line. You've got a firm figure in mind—the price of your mother's retirement home— in terms of net proceeds. Let me do a quick calculation, based on the buyer's offer, and see how far off the offer really is."

She shrugged and scanned the room again. I could see she was losing interest. I had to work fast, show her she could accept less than her asking price and still walk away with the sum she needed. Sometimes it worked, sometimes it didn't. But I was down to my last bullet.

Randy grudgingly verified the amount of her outstanding mortgage and told me what she needed to net. I added in the likely closing costs, including an estimated $2,500 for a complicated survey into the gulch.

"Look," I said, turning my notepad toward her. "At this price, we stay under $700,000 to make the buyers feel like they got a deal, and you walk away with what you need."

She looked at me with interest, but her voice was hesitant. "What if you're wrong?"

"I'm not wrong. I work out figures for clients every day. At $699,000 the Colemans get something to feel good about. It gives you what you need, and we may have a deal."

She crumpled her empty straw casing into a wrinkled white pellet. "This isn't what I'd planned. Getting a lower price, and paying a Realtor, to boot."

"I know," I said, anxious to deflect that line of thinking. "But it's your ticket to getting that woman out of your life—now. Isn't that the point?"

She stared at me, rolling the compact white pellet between her fingers until I thought I would scream. "You don't give up, do you?" she finally muttered.

I knew I had her. "No." I nailed her with a killer smile.

She shot the white pellet across the room with her thumb. "Six hundred and ninety-nine thousand, eh?"

"Your mom gets her retirement home and you get that woman out of your life." I held my breath and prayed.

With a groan, she pulled the pen out of her pocket. "Where do I sign?"

I wrote in the new price with the speed of light, tightened the closing to four weeks, and slid the counteroffer toward her, pointing my pen at the signature line. Even if we couldn't close in four weeks, there was a standard provision allowing either party to extend for another thirty days, given a legitimate reason. I hoped we wouldn't need it.

She scribbled her indecipherable physician's scrawl. "This had better work," she declared.

CHAPTER 9

By the time I gave Randy Entwistle her copy of the completed counter-offer in our cozy little corner at Taco Bell, it was well after sunset. The sky had darkened outside the window; streetlights glowed. Traffic streamed by with headlights blazing. I'd been explaining, coaxing, and wrangling for over three hours. Demolished with fatigue, I slipped off the bench, stood, and offered her my hand. "I'll call you as soon as I have their answer. Wish me luck."

She gripped my palm. "That I do." Her voice was serious, yet her eyes flashed gratitude and hope. For the first time I saw that, relieved of the mind-shackling stress she was under, she might be lively and entertaining. Perhaps if one enjoyed tatting or pressing flowers.

"Oh, one more thing," I added, picking up my file. "How can I contact you directly without having to leave messages on your machine?"

Her face clouded as she shook her head. "You can't."

"So that's it—just leave a message?"

Looking out the dark window, she nodded. "Yup, for now."

That wouldn't do. Success in my business depended on swift, definitive communication. "Is there a time of day when I can reach you directly at the hospital, then?"

She snapped back to attention. "No, for God's sake, don't do that. Don't ever try to contact me at work, by phone or in person. You'd ruin everything." The very idea set her to frantically scanning the room again, bringing to a halt our brief exercise in camaraderie.

Beyond frustration, I had to keep trying. "How about at home in the evening? Do you screen your calls? Will you pick up if you hear it's me?"

She looked at me as if she had never seen me before. "Just leave a message," she muttered from behind clenched teeth.

Her abrupt switch from manic scanning to barely there threw me. "Well, how often do you check for messages?"

She gazed out the window again. "Whenever."

Dropping my bag and folder on the table, I leaned toward her. "Randy, that's not good enough. Offers and counteroffers are time-bound. I need to know how soon you'll get back to me if I leave a message. Will it be hours, days, weeks?" My voice ended in a high shrill. I took a deep breath. We'd gotten through a difficult afternoon. I didn't want to blow it now.

"I'll get back to you," she answered, her eyes glittering. "That's the best I can do, okay?"

Leaving the restaurant with a reasonable counteroffer in hand, I should have soared triumphant. Instead, I felt beaten to a pulp. How do you deal with someone who begs you to get her out of a dreadful entanglement but holds back on necessary information? Gives you her full attention one minute, then slides off into her own haunted world the next, all the while denying you the most ordinary means of communication?

Whatever was bothering Randy about her housemate went much deeper than the meager details she had just revealed. All I wanted to do was to make the sale. How deeply into her tangled affairs would I have to delve to get the job done for my clients?

Heading straight for the phone booth, I called my apartment, praying to connect with Annie or Frank. Receiving no answer, I punched the code to retrieve my messages. For once, there were none. My spirits sagged even further. Of course Annie was with Frank, but where? The uncertainty left me edgy.

Driving toward Kihei, I decided to go directly to the Colemans, make short work of delivering the counteroffer, then find my daughter and ex-husband. I was nervous about seeing Frank again. It had been almost three years. Part of me hated him for walking out, for remarrying, for having another child. Yet as I drove, a familiar sense of excitement crept up on me. Was it possible to still have feelings for a man who was so clearly finished with me?

Frank and I had met in college our senior year. A sorority sister asked if I would tutor a friend of hers in first-year French. He had failed it once and needed the foreign language credit for his international economics major.

Awed by his good looks, I couldn't help laughing at Frank's antics in the library where we met to study. He was a complete cutup. Soon, however, he drove me wild with frustration because he wouldn't take my beloved French seriously. Finally, during our third session, I told him I refused to waste any more time trying to help someone who wouldn't cooperate.

"Fine," he said. "Let's go have a beer."

To my great surprise, he seemed to enjoy my company. I'd never had a real boyfriend, certainly no one as handsome or as much fun as Frank.

We dated casually once or twice a week for the rest of the school year. He quickly became my all-consuming passion. I wept many a tear when he failed to invite me to his fraternity formal in the spring. A little sleuthing by my sorority sisters uncovered another coed, about whom he was apparently more serious. I saw them together in the student lounge one day, sipping Cokes and holding hands while they gazed into each other's eyes. She was a flashy blonde with breasts like cantaloupes. Devastated, I vowed never to see him again. But when he called that night, as smooth and suave as if nothing had happened—and from his point of view, nothing had—I was a pushover.

Now that I know a lot more about men, I suppose he must have been sleeping with her, and dating me just for fluff. In those days nice girls "didn't;" in fact, we still worried about whether a goodnight kiss on the first date was too "fast."

Graduation weekend Frank was most attentive. Apparently Cantaloupes, who was only a junior, had already gone home. His parents and mine came for the festivities, but we took them back to their hotels early. Amid exaggerated tiptoeing and whispering, Frank sneaked me into his fraternity house where he seduced me in the most patient, loving manner. In a state of wonder, I surrendered my virginity, a thrilling finale to my college career. Awash in tears on the plane home the next day, I was certain I would never see him again.

Diploma in hand, facing a blank slate with regard to my future, I returned to muggy, dull Honolulu. Girls in the early 'sixties still went to college for something to "fall back on." No one ever suggested I would actually use my degree. Besides, what possible use was a bachelor of arts in medieval French literature in Hawaii? Not having accomplished my real mission, obtaining a "Mrs.," I felt a dismal failure.

What a letdown to wake up every morning in the overripe splendor of Pua Olena, my mother's ancestral home high in Nuuanu Valley, with no plans, no interests, no future. Most of my high school chums had met men in college, married right after graduation, and lived jazzy lives on the mainland. A few had struck out on their own as department store buyers, teachers, or flight attendants. A career held no appeal for me, especially in Honolulu, which seemed hopelessly provincial and boring. Nor did I have the enterprise to join my friends on the mainland where life might be more exciting.

Mother did her best to keep me busy with her never-ending charities, but somehow I couldn't get excited about saving Honolulu from billboards or serving peanut-butter sandwiches to the homeless.

In truth, I was pining for Frank. Leaving him had sucked the life out of me. I'd had so little experience with affairs of the heart that I simply didn't know how to pull myself out of it. In high school, where you would expect to learn these things, teenage life was different in the Islands. Although no one blinks at interracial relationships these days, in the 'fifties and 'sixties they were still considered daringly beyond the pale, at least by people I knew.

About a third of my private high school class was Caucasian, *haole*, which reflected the Island population in general. That put two-thirds of the boys off limits. Most of the *haole* boys I knew were creepy, pimply, and weird, in my exalted opinion. The few who were acceptable—the tall, handsome campus leaders and football heroes—wouldn't have dreamed of asking me for so much as an answer in algebra class, never mind a date. They had their pick of any girl on or off campus. Most often, they chose to bestow their hearts and athletic medals on willowy, exotic *hapa-haole* types.

These girls were part-Caucasian, part-Hawaiian, with perhaps a dollop of Chinese or Portuguese, and simply knock-down gorgeous. I never understood why it was perfectly acceptable for the *haole* boys to date the *hapa-haole* girls, at no risk to their futures. My Uncle Ransom had a part-Hawaiian wife. We were all crazy about Aunt Noelani. But for a *haole* girl to date a *hapa* boy—well, that was the end of her reputation. And reputation was still all-important in the 'sixties.

So, although there were a good number of "steady" campus couples, my friends and I simply didn't date. We poured over *Archie and Veronica* comic books, wondering what it would be like to walk into a sweet shop full of teenage boys and girls just like ourselves, bantering and laughing over ice cream sodas, and then walk down the street, hand in hand with a fella to the movies or a sock hop. The comics seemed so normal; a slice of mainland life I could only dream about.

My entire high school experience on the subject of dating was a last-minute invitation to my senior prom. Even though I knew he had asked and been turned down by two other girls, he was tall, *haole*, and on the football team, albeit third string. I am to this day eternally grateful that I wasn't reduced to sitting home that night in a blue, embarrassed funk. I saw him years later at a high school reunion and thanked him.

When Frank and I parted the day after college graduation, he made no promises except to write. I devoured his letters in the privacy of my bedroom at Pua Olena, reading them over and over until I had memorized every nuance. I scrutinized his handwriting, finding in each stroke and slash and curl feelings never intended by his words. He wrote about life on the farm in Iowa, helping his Dad harvest the fall crop before setting off to the city to begin his career as an aide to the state secretary of agriculture. The Vietnam War was raging, but his future employer had finagled him a deferment based on agriculture as an essential industry. He wrote nothing intimate, certainly no declarations or even hints of love. No mention of Cantaloupes, either.

In the depths of missing Frank so desperately, I began to fear I might be pregnant. Lying in bed one night, wide awake and drenched in cold sweat while the mountain rains pelted the moss-softened eaves outside my window, a small glimmer of hope ignited my soul. Yes! As soon as I wrote Frank the news, he would drop all his plans and dash over to marry me. We'd fly back to Iowa after a Tahitian honeymoon and begin life as Mr. and Mrs. Frank McDaniel. With the morning sun, my burden lightened and life seemed bearable again.

My immediate problem was to find out if my suspicions were correct. I couldn't go to our family doctor. The doctor's wife played bridge with my mother every Monday afternoon.

A physician unknown to the family would have eliminated that problem, but I worried he'd feel duty-bound to pick up the phone and inform my parents. Teenagers had no right of privacy back then. In either case, the visit had to be paid for. Where would I get the money without being interrogated? Mother gave me mad money, but asking for the price of a doctor's visit and lab tests would surely have raised eyebrows. If I put it on our insurance, the claim would have shown up on my parents' monthly statement.

The free pregnancy clinic run by the Catholic diocese was also out of the question. My mother and her chums were the backbone of the volunteer staff. I couldn't risk it. Being "in trouble" would be the ultimate disgrace. The library became my only safe source of information. I gleaned from my reading that if I passed the time of my second period, I could be pretty sure I was expecting. There was nothing for it but to wait. Until Frank was actually on his way, it would have to remain my closely guarded secret.

Over and over, I composed "the letter" to Frank in my head, not daring to put it on paper until I was sure. It always began, "My Darling Frank, I have the most wonderful news . . ."

The week my second period was due, I awoke in the night with horrible stomach cramps. I bit the corner of my pillow to keep from crying out. Lying there curled up and moaning, I prayed for appendicitis. Around two in the morning, I got up to use the bathroom. As I stood, warm liquid gushed down between my thighs. One fast flick of the bathroom light revealed streams of blood spattering the white tile floor. I had read enough to know I was having a miscarriage. I stayed in bed for the next few days, feigning the flu. Double sanitary napkins soaked up the flow. I hid the blood-soaked pads in the back of my closet in a brown paper bag. Mother and Tami were attentive, but not suspicious. On the next burning day I took the bulging paper bag out to the back yard incinerator and watched my dreams go up in smoke.

I continued to lose weight, and became more and more lethargic. By mid-October my parents were truly concerned. In this day and age, they would have whipped me off to a psychiatrist, but again, in the 'sixties, this was not done by people in our circles. Instead, they sent me to my Uncle Ransom's ranch on the Big Island for some healthy outdoor therapy. Soon the horses, fresh mountain air, and my rough-and-tumble *hapa-haole* cousins, together with my Aunt Noelani's unquestioning love, began to turn me around. I returned to Pua Olena the week before Thanksgiving, revived but still aimless.

On the day after Thanksgiving, I stood in the kitchen making myself a leftover turkey sandwich for lunch. The servants had been given the day off for the holiday. I will never, as long as I live, forget the puzzled tone of my mother's voice as she stood in the kitchen doorway announcing, "Laura, you have a visitor."

My stomach flipped over. The mayonnaise and cranberry-smeared bread slid out of my hand and landed face down on the linoleum floor. That soft plopping sound remains with me to this day. I couldn't possibly have known, but I did.

Frank stood just inside the open French doors on the far side of the living room, framed by white porch pillars against a backdrop of palm fronds and yellow plumeria blossoms. Hands in pockets, he stepped forward, hesitant in approach, yet eager in expression. His deep, open gaze never left my face.

Rooted in the hallway, I stood dumbfounded. My brain simply couldn't make sense of him being there. I had never written, much less mailed "the letter."

I caught sight of my mother in the corner of my eye, and could only think that whatever was happening was too intensely personal to share with her. My mind began to stir with desperate thoughts of how to get her out of the room. Good manners bailed me out.

"Mother, you remember Frank McDaniel. You met at my graduation." My voice was so weak and wobbly it sounded as if it were coming from beyond the palms and plumerias. Mother and Frank shook hands politely. I turned to her and silently implored her to leave. Flicking her glance back and forth between us, she assessed the requirement to chaperone against her daughter's unspoken request for privacy.

"Well, do sit down, you two," she finally said. "I'm sure you have lots to talk about." Then she was gone.

My heart thrummed wildly. I sidled onto the nearest sofa, completely at sea as to what to say or do. Frank removed one hand from his pocket, nervously tossed a small box into the air, then strode across the room toward me. He knelt at my feet, took a ring from the box and asked me to marry him.

The dust motes in the warm air took on a surreal shimmer. The gentle rub of palm fronds rose to a pattering crescendo. The sweet fragrance of plumeria wrapped itself around me in a smothering cloak. As every sense heightened, my skin tingled until I thought it would burst. The room swirled around me. Frank's anxious face faded into nothingness.

The next thing I knew I was stretched out on the couch, too dizzy to move. Mother frantically sponged my forehead with a damp washcloth while Frank rubbed my hand and looked worried. We were married two weeks later at the old stone church across the street from my high school.

What a Cinderella story, I mused as I pulled into the Colemans' driveway with Randy's counteroffer face-up on the passenger seat. But wasn't
that what girls were brought up to expect? The story always ended with
the prince slipping on the glass slipper, or the diamond ring. Nobody ever
mentioned that real life began the next day. Well, as soon as I finished
with Diana and Jerry, I'd find Frank and Annie and see what kind of real
life that tarnished prince and our daughter were up to.

"Six hundred and ninety-nine thousand! Laura, that's wonderful," Diana
squealed when I presented the counteroffer to them. Dressed in a white
silk caftan that hugged every curve in the soft evening breeze, Diana
glowed with elation. "Jerry, she's practically giving it to us!"

Jerry rolled his long-suffering eyes at me, but didn't say a word. Their
acceptance of the counteroffer should have been a slam-dunk, but Jerry
obviously had some thinking to do. By the impassive look on his face, I
could see he was going to put me through my paces before making a final
decision. Given my anxiety to connect with Frank and Annie, the thought
set my teeth to grinding.

We stood on their lanai beneath a jewel case of glittering stars. This
house, which I had sold and closed three months ago in anticipation of
their next move, had provided my most recent commission. It perched on
a low hill overlooking the ocean. When Diana and Jerry had bought it, the
view was unimpeded, but there were no covenants protecting their view
corridor. Not only had Diana run out of decorating ideas, but their downhill neighbor's new second story with a Spanish tile roof now blocked a
good slice of their view. I'd been lucky to find them a buyer from eastern
Oregon who was thrilled with the bit of ocean that could still be seen, and
who was willing to rent back to them until they found another home. That
transaction had been easy.

Jerry frowned at me, Mr. Cool to the max. He was not going to allow
himself to become excited. "What else did the wretched woman change?"
he asked.

"Nothing serious," I assured him. "Just a shorter closing, four weeks,
which we can extend if it takes longer to get your loan approved. She

explained that she needs the money to buy into a retirement home for her mother."

"Let me see that thing," Jerry growled. He whipped the papers out of my hand and stood under a yellow bug light to study them. *Here we go again*, I thought. Another battle of egos. The counteroffer was too easy, too smooth, too acceptable. There was nothing to fight about. Jerry loved a good contest before he gave in and snatched the deal. I looked at Diana for commiseration, but she was still bubbling with triumph.

"Four weeks! That's marvelous, Jerry. We can start packing right away!"

Now was the time to tell them what I had just learned about Dr. Entwistle's battle with her housemate and the potential difficulty ahead of us in evicting her. So help me, I knew my duty, but I couldn't face it. I wanted to get home to my family. The place on the back of my neck that tingles when I'm in the wrong went into spasms. In my exhaustion and frustration, I ignored the warning.

Jerry continued to read through the document, picking at a few obscure terms. I reassured him on every one. If he'd asked anything about the housemate, I'd have blurted out what I knew, but he didn't.

Finally, Diana said, "Come on, Jerry. Except for the price and the closing date, the doctor accepted it exactly as Laura wrote it. The price is great. If we can close in four weeks, it's better than we hoped."

Ignoring her, Jerry fired off a few more rat-a-tat questions, all things we had covered before. The man was not new to the business of buying and selling real estate. It was all I could do to stand still and answer him. He knew it was a good deal but couldn't accept it without a verbal fencing match. Since the seller wasn't available, I was the only possible sparring partner. I had no patience for that role tonight.

"Come on, darling." Diana finally exclaimed. "Let's sign. It's exactly what we want. And the price is soooooo righty-o." She moved over and snuggled against him. I had to look away. Settling onto a chaise lounge, I closed my eyes, praying for one more iota of endurance. This was an opportunity for them on a silver platter. The house was everything they had dreamed of and extensive enough to keep Diana occupied with decorating and landscaping for years. And because of the higher price, the commission was considerably more than I had expected when we began looking. *For Annie and her baby, dear God, please let them accept.* Tomorrow we'd deal with the housemate.

Sunk in that brief respite while Diana and Jerry cooed, I lost my struggle to keep thoughts of Frank and Annie at bay. Had Frank picked Annie up? How had he reacted to her pregnancy? Was he being gentle with her? Annie and Frank had generally gotten along well. It was mother and daughter who rubbed each other like fingernails on a blackboard. My eyes sprang open at that disturbing thought, pushing aside my anxiety about the sale. I could not sit still another moment. I perched on the edge of the chaise lounge and gathered my things. I had to get home.

At that moment Jerry nuzzled some nonsense in Diana's ear. She giggled into his shirt. He looked over at me and cleared his throat. "We'll call you tomorrow."

I narrowed my eyes. "Why on earth? This is what you want! It's as smooth as silk. Let's sign now and be done with it." Fear rose up to bite me. They weren't going to accept the counteroffer. The letdown knocked the wind out of me.

Jerry moved behind Diana and wrapped his arms around her, indicating the audience was over. "We need to sleep on it, Laura. We'll call you in the morning. The counteroffer expires at noon tomorrow, right?" He raised his eyebrows at me.

It did, indeed. I should have tightened it to tonight, but I hadn't been sure they'd be home. "As you wish, Jerry. We'll get together in the morning. Let's all meet in your office, say, at nine o'clock? Or would ten be better?" If he agreed to a meeting instead of a mere phone call, he was as much as admitting he had decided to accept, or at least keep the ball rolling with a new offer.

He nodded. "Ten works for me." His condescending smile told me he knew exactly what I was up to. I had quietly exposed his posturing. By the gleam in his eye, I could see that his esteem for me as a fellow salesperson hitched up a notch.

***

My apartment was empty when I got home, the red message light pulsing in its dark corner. I gave it a weary stab, hoping for news of Annie.

"Laura, this is Anita Schultz. It's okay about the roof repairs. We don't want any trouble. Sorry Dooley was so prickly. Let's talk in the morning." *Beep.*

Ah, problem solved by letting Anita and Dooley stew in their own juices. Good strategy. Closing likely. Paycheck in sight. Could I please go to bed on this upbeat note and not listen to any more messages? Of course not. Please let the next one be Annie, telling me she's safely with Frank at his condo. Don't let it be Dr. Entwistle, canceling the counteroffer. If she got cold feet after I left her, she could cancel just by leaving me a message because Diana and Jerry hadn't signed the counteroffer. My stomach tightened as the tape hit the next message.

"Laura, this is Lily Fujikawa. You must be so thrilled that Annie's home. I understand that you have some questions regarding her health. I really do have to respect her confidentiality. But I can assure you she seems fine. Her pregnancy appears to be normal, but I'd like to see her in a week when we have the lab results. No apparent signs of disease. I gave her a prescription for prenatal vitamins, which she should start right away. Better late than never. The best thing she can do is get plenty of rest and nourishing food. I'll look forward to seeing her then. Take care." *Beep.*

Thank you, Lily, for that much reassurance. The tape rolled on.

"Mom, I'm with Dad. He looks great. You should see his hair. He has a ponytail!"

A muffled Frank groaned in the background. I tried but failed to picture the clean-cut Frank with long hair.

"Anyway, Dad's taking me to dinner, then I'll come back to your place. He's at Maui Shores, unit three oh eight. By the way, Grandma called. She and Grandpa are flying over first thing tomorrow morning. See ya."

Beep. Beep. Beep. "End of messages."

Disaster by answering machine. I threw myself on the bed and groaned.

CHAPTER 10

My mother's fabled ancestor, Jacob Dashton Wildethorne, had arrived in Honolulu in 1846 on a whaling ship. His father, a dour Connecticut preacher, was set on the lad following him into the pulpit. Taking the simplest course available to a rebellious, penniless fellow of his time, Jacob ran away to sea instead. He was eighteen when he first laid eyes on the Sandwich Islands and succumbed to their charms.

The first boatload of New England missionaries had arrived only twenty-eight years earlier, its occupants bent on converting the lascivious natives to their straight-laced view of Christianity while destroying every vestige of their pagan culture.

The whaling industry, which supplied the world's finest oil for lamps, spermaceti for candles and perfume, lubrication for the burgeoning Industrial Revolution, and baleen stays for women's corsets, was booming. By way of its location, Hawaii was a perfectly positioned provisioning station in the vast Pacific expanses. As many as 400 tall-masted ships anchored daily in Honolulu Harbor the year of young Jacob's arrival.

A daily ration of rum was issued aboard the ships to keep the whalers happy. By the time they arrived in the Islands after several years at sea, the rum barrels were cracked and empty. Having set foot on land with a prodigious thirst, Jacob quickly sized up his opportunities. Foremost was the slaking of his own thirst, then eventually that of the entire Pacific merchant fleet.

Jacob hired on at a pub in Honolulu, where he earned his room and board and learned the fine art of distilling sugar-cane juice into strong spirits. He soon became the chief supplier of rum to the grateful port of Honolulu and to the royal household.

When the American Civil War ended in 1865, soon after the discovery of oil in Pennsylvania, the Pacific whaling industry settled into its death throes. Kerosene, cheaper and easier to obtain now, replaced whale oil in lamps and lessened dependence on spermaceti candles. Heavier petroleum products were soon brought into use to grease the machinery of the Industrial Revolution. Of no less importance, lightweight flexible steel found its way into the stay pockets of women's corsets, allowing baleen to revert to its natural duty: the sieving of krill and plankton in the mouths of the whales. Too late to benefit from these positive changes of fortune, the Pacific leviathans had become fewer and farther between. Many whaling ships had been confiscated by the North for war duty, or simply sunk to blockade Southern harbors. Sea captains who persisted in the dying trade now sailed what vessels remained as far north as Alaska to fill their barrels. Wretched, four-year journeys became the norm.

Meanwhile, Jacob diversified. While keeping his hand in the rum trade, always a thriving business in a port town, he opened a general merchandise emporium. In addition, Wildethorne Carriage supplied horse-drawn transportation to the royal court and most of upper-class Honolulu.

He married along the way, the daughter of a penniless Lutheran school teacher who was helping the missionaries codify the unwritten Hawaiian language. Mazie Lindholm was only too happy to elope with him, tainted though he was by the pursuit of filthy lucre. Their exchange of vows aboard an inter-island packet caused a scandal that rocked the censorious town.

During the reign of Alexander Liholiho, King Kamehameha IV, Jacob became one of the king's advisors, and Mazie a confidante of his beloved Queen Emma. Our only tintype of them shows Jacob sitting on an upholstered divan staring with great dignity and fuzzy mutton chops at the camera. Mazie stands behind him, her dainty fingers on his shoulder, a gardenia in her fair hair. She grins mischievously, unheard of in the staid portraiture of the time. They were known about town as the Wild Wildethornes.

While cutting a wide social swath, Mazie and Jacob reproduced in good order. Also in good order, their children and grandchildren enjoyed and dissipated much of their progenitor's hard-earned wealth.

By the time my mother, Margaret Wildethorne Henderson, received her inheritance, there were only two significant items left: a cattle ranch on the Big Island, which went to my uncle Ransom, and the estate in Nuuanu, our family home for five generations.

Mother inherited Pua Olena along with half the trust that contained old Jacob's remaining assets. The income from her share of the trust supported my parents in old-world style, which my mother considered her due. So had I, until I found myself married and living outside the velvet nest. As Mother often reminded me with that dramatic sweep of her arm, "All this will be yours someday, my dear, every bit of it, but meanwhile you must make do. Once you're married, don't come crying home to me."

She was overly generous with gifts to me and the children, treated us like royalty whenever we visited Honolulu, but rarely would she part with cash. She was absolutely stuck on the benefits to my character of "making do" until "all this" became mine. The few times I did beg a handout, she extracted blood in return. The experiences were so unpleasant, I vowed never to ask again.

Eccentricity and stubbornness weave through my family all the way back to Jacob and Mazie and beyond, I mused as I undressed for bed, hoping Annie would return soon from her visit with her father. In spite of all our mutual hurts and frustrations, my heartstrings were and always would be subject to my daughter's errant plucking. I fell asleep wondering how we would manage my parents' visit in the morning.

Annie must have tiptoed in on feet of felt. I heard nothing until the mynah bird chorus burst forth at dawn in the banyan tree off the corner of my lanai. Panicked, I threw off my covers and was halfway out of bed before I saw that she was safely snuggled up in a crocheted afghan on the couch.

I never failed to melt at the sight of that troubled child in sleep, so tranquil in repose. What a sweet face she had when free of the confusions of her young life. Tipped-up nose, pixie chin, and that shimmery blonde hair. All my children had started out as towheads, but my sons had turned dark when they reached adolescence. Only Annie retained her silver-blonde tresses, thanks no doubt to the Scandinavian Mazie Lindholm. Two days at the beach had brightened it to a magical sheen in the filtered morning light. A faint sprinkling of freckles peeked through again on her cheeks.

When I looked at Annie, I often saw Mazie in that elfin face with its stubborn pointy chin. Had Mazie been in Annie's situation, the rules would have been harsh and unbreakable. A hasty marriage would have been arranged and life would have gone on. For Annie, things were much more complicated. Girls these days tended to keep the child, raising it with varying degrees of ineptitude while growing up themselves. Looking at her now, I allowed myself for the first time to face the notion that had been seeping in since the moment I laid eyes on her at the airport: it's often the unwed girl's parents who end up raising the child.

Frank didn't wait much beyond the mynah birds to call. "Laura, how are you?" That smooth, all too familiar baritone—a lure toward traps into which I mustn't fall.

"Well enough, and you?"

He ignored my stiffness. "Fine, fine. Just so goddamn relieved the nightmare is over. She looks great, eh?"

"If you don't count borderline malnutrition and a near-term pregnancy."

"Come on, Laura. What's the matter? You don't sound excited." His voice rose with accusation.

Excited? No. Relieved, of course, but wary of where Annie's return would lead. I deliberately lowered my voice to disguise an attack of cynicism. "Frank, it's awkward to talk while she's sleeping right across the room."

"Well, come on, then. I'll buy you breakfast. I'm at the Maui Shores, just down the road from you. You can be here in five minutes. Let Annie sleep."

I needed time to call my parents. The best thing to do would be to head them off until I had dealt with Frank and put the Colemans safely into escrow. Mother would be mortally wounded that I hadn't called her the minute Annie returned. There would be major recriminations. As with Frank, she would somehow make everything that had happened to Annie all my fault. I wished now I hadn't chickened out last night, but I couldn't avoid them any longer.

"Give me thirty minutes," I told Frank. "I'll be there."

To avoid disturbing Annie, I drove down the road to my office. First, I called a furniture store and ordered a bed to be delivered for Annie as soon as possible. Then I called my parents. Tami, Mother's ancient Japanese cook and housekeeper, and the woman I loved best in the whole world, answered at Pua Olena. I was too late.

"No, Laura, you mom and dad already leave for airport. Long time now. You pick up Kahului nine-thirty plane. She say tell you when you call. So nice Annie come home, yeah?"

Good old Tami. I could see her enigmatic smile and her gray hair tucked in a bun at her neck. She was the mother of my heart. When my own mother was off tending to her charitable duties, Tami watched over me. As a toddler I had followed her everywhere. I napped on a mat in the kitchen and drove her wild with my endless questions. But she was always there for me, while my mother, a veritable dragon of benevolence outside the home, was not.

Tami had been wonderful with Annie, too. Nothing that girl did ever put her off. Calmly and firmly, Tami corrected her over and over again when we visited, never running out of patience. No matter how I tried, I never attained that same sense of serenity and certainty in dealing with my daughter.

Smiling at her fondness for Annie, I assured Tami my parents would be picked up at the airport. The timing with the Colemans could not have been worse. Frank would have to do airport duty.

"Are you kidding?" Frank exploded when I announced his assignment. "I haven't seen them since we split up. They have no aloha for me at all."

We were seated at the terrace restaurant on the ground floor of his condo, at a table for two along the outside railing. Visitors dressed in bathing suits, T-shirts, and rubber slippers strolled along the sidewalk beyond a low jasmine hedge. Sporting a turquoise polo shirt, white Bermuda shorts, and loafers without socks, Frank looked more settled and mature than I had ever seen him. His thick brown hair, which he'd always worn short, was now shoulder-length and indeed pulled back in a wavy ponytail. Forewarned by Annie's remark on the answering machine, I had expected it to be an affectation. Instead, he looked second best to Mel Gibson.

I had always been mesmerized by Frank's dark good looks, and never understood why he had found me the least bit attractive. No one had ever accused me of being pretty, not Frank, and certainly never my parents. Of course, they could have neglected to mention it, but I doubt it. I suppose I'm nice-looking when I'm dressed up, bejeweled, and coifed, but nowhere near Frank's category of gorgeous. So help me, this new veneer of maturity, ponytail notwithstanding, only added to his appeal. I realized right there on the spot that I had never gotten over him. We'd been divorced for six years, and he had hurt me terribly. Why did I find him more attractive than ever?

"No, Frank. Oddly enough, my parents still adore you. If you'd bothered to write to them, to bring things to closure, you'd know they hold no ill will for you at all. In fact, they have nothing but nice things to say about you. My mother blames me for our divorce."

"No kidding?" He sat back, amazed. Looking across the table at him, I was equally amazed. I couldn't believe I had once been married to this man, that he was the father of my children. He seemed a complete stranger, a devastatingly attractive stranger. The Frank I knew, as recently as three years ago when he flew over to help sort out Annie's disappearance, was a brash, high-energy guy, handsome, oh, yes, but always joking around and never quite serious except on the job. The man across the table from me was subdued, serious and mellow, as if all his irritating qualities had leached out and left behind the essence of the man I had fallen in love with. Perhaps he'd been tamed by the tragedy of his young son Georgie.

"They've always liked you, Frank. My mother still thinks it was some kind of a miracle that I snagged you, as she puts it. She asked me, several times, in fact, how I could possibly have let you go." I paused to let him come up with a diplomatic answer to that, but he was stumped. I pressed my advantage. "Look, I have an appointment with a client to wrap up a deal at ten o'clock. I can't be in two places at once. You have to pick them up. Take Annie with you. Obviously they're dying to see her."

"Do they know . . .?"

"No, not unless she told them on the phone yesterday. I rather doubt it, but we haven't talked. As you know, I left her sleeping—she looked so blessedly innocent—so I don't know."

"So I have to handle the whole thing?" he asked. "What if they freak out on me?"

"Come on. My parents are too dignified to freak out on you in public. They'll wait until they're alone with me. Then my mother will let me have it. I can give you her speech, word for word, right now if you like."

He threw back his head and laughed. He knew Margaret Henderson well. "Never mind, never mind, I'll do it," he said. He was even more gorgeous when he smiled.

"*Mahalo*," I replied. Frank would handle it just fine. He was an expert in smoothing out difficult situations. That's what hotel managers did.

I filled Frank in on everything I'd learned about Annie, including her near-illiteracy and the harassment she'd experienced in high school. He took it all in with surprisingly little castigation toward me. I suspected his own guilt was doing a number on him. Then he dropped the bombshell he had unearthed.

"Sounds like she spent her years away in the Far East," he told me, stirring sugar into his coffee.

"The Far East?" I gasped. "How in God's name did she get there? Those countries are scary. Did she say where?"

"Thailand."

"Thailand? That detective spent all his time looking on the mainland! How could he have been so clueless? We owe him all that money, and he wasn't even in the right hemisphere?"

"She disappeared without a trace," Frank reminded me. "You know how hopeless it was."

During those terrible years I had tried to comfort myself by picturing Annie in places on the mainland where they treated her kindly, small towns where a nice family took her in as a nanny perhaps. But Thailand, where they sold children and ate rats? What other dreadful things didn't we know about our daughter?

"Did she say who she was with, or why she ran?" I asked.

Frank shook his head. "We never got that far. She opened up for a little bit, and then she didn't want to talk about it anymore."

"Thailand," I repeated. "My God, she was half a world away, and we had no idea. Did she say what she did there? How she lived?"

"We never got to that part, either."

I looked at him obliquely. "You know what happens to young blonde girls who have no money in the Orient."

"What are you implying?" His eyes narrowed, ready to defend his daughter against unsavory accusations by her mother.

"Frank, attractive young girls living on the loose like that usually end up doing more than waitressing to make ends meet. Especially in the Far East. A young blonde *haole* girl? Come on."

"You mean you think she was dealing drugs?" he asked hopefully.

"Worse, Frank."

"You mean a . . . a prostitute?"

"It's possible, isn't it? In fact, highly likely. She obviously had men in her life. She doesn't know who the father of her baby is."

He gasped. "She said that?"

"Yes. She's barely educated, Frank. What else could she do?"

"My God. My own daughter." He looked down at his runny eggs and greasy Portuguese sausage, then pushed the plate away.

"Wake up, Frank." I wanted to kick his shin under the table to make him face reality. Is it only mothers who see their daughters in the light of truth? "You've got to help me convince her to get some counseling. Whatever happened over the past three years, she needs help getting over it. Maybe she'd agree if it came from you."

He took a long sip of coffee and looked up at me. His eyes were deep and dark and puzzled. "But it's over. She's home."

"She's like a moonbeam, Frank. Shining into our lives, but always out of reach. I can't get a grip on her. She sits in my apartment like a dog with a broken leg, staring out the window, yearning to get back to chasing cars as soon as the cast is removed. She's in limbo right now, waiting for the baby to be born, counting the days until she can get back into action. Believe me."

He ran a tense hand over his smooth, tight hair. "What a dreadful thing to say about your own daughter."

"I'm only reporting what I've observed, Frank. I've had two more days with her than you have. She needs help." I squeezed a wedge of lime over my papaya. My nose wrinkled at the tangy spray. "And what do you think she intends to do with the baby?"

"What do you mean?" he asked.

"Is she going to keep it? Can you see Annie as a mother? She never refers to the baby except as 'it' or 'this.' She seems to think it's only a temporary impediment to her comfort. I don't think she's connected with the fact that the . . . the . . . impediment is a human being."

"But surely when they put the baby in her arms . . . ?"

"That's a myth, Frank. Wake up! I'm praying with all my might that I'm wrong. But I can't see her cooing and gurgling over the little tyke, cheerfully giving up her freedom for round-the-clock feedings and dirty diapers. Can you?"

"You sound so crass!"

"Come on. I'm just trying to be realistic. Because if Annie doesn't bond with the child, then what?"

Frank looked at me, long and deep.

"Yeah, you got it," I said, feeling as if my miserable soul had been stripped bare. "And I'm not sure I'm up for that."

"What about adoption?" he whispered, as if it were a dirty word.

"I don't know. Seems like girls keep their babies nowadays, whether they ought to or not. Several of my friends' daughters have brought children home, and it's my friends who are raising them. Oh, Frank, that's not what I want to do for the rest of my life!"

What could he say? He wasn't in any position to take the child himself. He and Holly had their hands full with Georgie. I felt myself flushing, ashamed of sounding more concerned about my own life than that of my daughter and grandchild. I waited for Frank to call me on it. I hated him seeing me at my selfish worst, but who else shared my concern? He didn't respond, perhaps chagrined that he himself had so little to offer. I changed the subject, relieved to have spoken my fears, even if we couldn't resolve them on the spot.

"Tell me about life in The Bog," I said, making a conscious effort to relax. We needed a break from serious matters, matters that would take time to resolve.

He took a sip of guava juice. "Man, I had forgotten how good this tastes. A nice change from cranberry juice. Hmmm, life in The Bog, as you insist on calling it. It's . . . different. We're way out in the country, privacy to the max. Really quite beautiful. I must admit, I enjoy the change of seasons. Reminds me of Iowa. Very different from this year-round summer." His gesture took in the shimmering beach and glittering ocean across the street.

"And Holly?" I asked with trepidation, knowing we would have to acknowledge her existence sooner or later.

He shook his head slowly and responded with admiration. "She's a wonder. I never knew a woman could have such depths."

I had depths, I thought, depths of despair when you left me. His sincere tone and the honest look on his face told me he truly loved her. I might not be over Frank, but he was obviously over me. Fighting off a wave of sadness, I gathered my gumption and plunged deeper into the danger zone. "While we're being honest, may I ask the one thing that has always been a puzzle to me?"

He grinned a grin that could disarm an entire regiment of ex-wives. "Go ahead."

Framing the question took every ounce of courage I possessed. When

Frank had proposed, that Friday after Thanksgiving, he told me only that the department of agriculture job had not materialized, and that he realized he really did care for me. He decided, he said, to make a dramatic gesture by flying over unannounced to ask for my hand. If I refused, he would enlist in Honolulu and take his chances in Vietnam. At the time, I was too overjoyed to question him further. Cantaloupes never entered the conversation.

When he left me twenty years later, he was equally as reticent. In the months that followed, I'd been too wounded to ask many questions by phone. The few times I did, Frank was not forthcoming. He kept repeating, "It's over. I'm in love with Holly. That's all I want to say."

Seated with him in the open-air restaurant, I had a panicky feeling that this might be my last chance to get an honest answer, an answer that, whether I liked it or not, would finally let me put our marriage to rest.

"Did Holly just happen like a *coup de foudre,* a clap of thunder, or were you tired of me and vulnerable to the next woman who chanced along?"

"Whoa, that's a big question," Frank replied. He took a sip of coffee, gazing at me through the steam, then put the cup down and interlaced his fingers around it, as if to anchor himself against whatever violent reaction I might have to his answer. I braced myself, heart hammering, already regretting having asked.

"I knew the day I married you it was wrong," he said thoughtfully. "Standing at the altar with the priest, watching you float down the aisle on your father's arm . . . I knew it was wrong, right then and there."

I grasped the sides of my chair for support. Anger and humiliation rose up to choke me. "My lord, why did you propose in the first place?"

He shook his head. "The romance of the Islands, maybe. Loose ends? I cared for you, Laura. Don't get me wrong. We had a good life. But it was never the real thing."

A hot flush crept up my neck. "Three children and twenty years weren't the real things?"

Rubbing the back of his neck, he looked extremely uncomfortable.

He knew how much this must be hurting me. He picked up the credit card slip and signed it. "Look, we'd better get Annie up and moving, or we'll miss your parents' plane. Don't want to give Margaret and Jack any reason to be annoyed with me at this point. And you'd better get that big deal taken care of." He smiled and put a hand over mine on the table. The gesture was so intimate. "I'm truly sorry for the hurt I've caused you, Laura. You deserve every happiness."

I wanted desperately to be furious with him, but Frank had always been a master at apologies. I could never stay angry at him for long. I realized I was still susceptible to his charm, like it or not.

He gave me a hug in the parking lot. "It's all old stuff, Laura. Let's not drag it up again."

I squinted against the morning sun. Backlit, his face was in shadow, but his eyes were bright. "No, Frank. You're not off the hook. I want the full story. I know there's more." As shaken as I was, I intended to complete this conversation before he returned to Maine, not stopping until I had all the answers. My pride demanded it.

"You owe me that much. And I'm going to get it."

CHAPTER 11

Jerry Coleman kept me waiting almost half an hour while he handled a complicated stock transaction on the telephone. Sitting in his reception room, I thumbed through a magazine, not absorbing a single written word. Diana was nowhere to be seen. That could only mean they were rejecting the counteroffer and not bothering to make a new one. Still smarting from my conversation with Frank, my spirits sank lower.

I supposed this was what I deserved for withholding important material information from them last night concerning the recalcitrant housemate. I'd woken up several times during the night, castigating myself for skirting my duty to my clients. But I'd been so tired, so anxious about Annie and Frank, and so annoyed with Jerry's shilly-shallying. I planned to disclose the full story immediately, provided they were still interested.

By the time Jerry finally hung up and gestured through the glass partition for me to come in, my nerves were strung as taut as ukulele strings. He reached across his desk to shake hands. "Sorry, Laura, you know how it goes with a demanding client."

"Only too well."

My dig rolled right off him. He picked up his copy of the counteroffer from his desk and frowned. "I'm still not sure what to do here."

"What exactly are you unsure about?" I asked, hoping to flush out his objections and overcome them handily. At least he hadn't rejected the counteroffer out of hand.

He motioned me to a chair. "The one thing we didn't discuss last night was the seller's motivation. It could influence what we do. Did you find out anything more?"

He gave me the perfect opening. Mentally crossing my fingers, I told him exactly what Randy Entwistle had told me about her housemate, her numerous unsuccessful efforts to evict her, and her lawyer's ultimate advice to sell the house out from under her. I also conveyed the sum Randy needed to buy into her mother's retirement residence.

"Why the hell didn't you tell us this last night?" His face was grim, his confusion showing plainly.

There was nothing for it but an honest apology. "I'm sorry, Jerry. No excuse, except that I was exhausted and very concerned about my daughter. If you'd been ready to accept the counter last night, I would have. But since you wanted to sleep on it, I figured I could tell you today. I really do apologize."

He steepled his hands, put his fingertips to his chin, and narrowed his eyes. After a long moment, he sighed. "So what's your gut feeling? Should we go another round?" Apparently he was willing to overlook my sin of omission.

"My true gut feeling? I hope to heck I never end up on an operating table with Dr. Entwistle at the gas controls."

Jerry barked with laughter and slapped the contract on his desk. "You got that right. Jesus, what a fucked-up broad. Now, listen. If we make a new offer, try to beat the price down again, she's skittish enough to change her mind about the whole thing. Who knows, she and that housemate could even patch up their feud while we're still trying to negotiate."

"Or someone could make her a better offer," I said. "She took the sign down, remember, because she got so many calls."

"Hmm." Jerry scanned the contract again, deep in thought. "I hate to just cave in."

I stood up and walked to the expansive window that looked out over the tops of Monkeypod trees in the parking lot below. At Kahului Harbor two blocks away, an inter-island cruise ship had rounded the breakwater.

As I watched, a black and white tugboat moved into position against the giant ship's bow to guide her into her berth.

"Your call, Jerry."

"Diana really loves that house," he finally said, joining me at the window. The tug nudged the ship toward the pier. The floating palace towered over the outdated docking facility.

In my softest voice, I replied, "And you don't want her to lose it over a few grand. Why don't we just go ahead and accept?" I picked up the counteroffer from his desk and handed him a pen. The places for his initials and signature were highlighted in blue.

Diana, as it turned out, was at the hairdresser downstairs having her roots touched up. She jumped out of her salon chair the moment she saw me enter, nearly knocking the brown dye brush from her startled beautician's hand. "Darling." she cried. "What did Jerry say? Are we buying it?"

"I have his signature right here. All I need is yours."

"Marvelous! Let me at it." She hitched the pink cape over her shoulder, grabbed my pen and scribbled on the remaining blue lines.

"All right, Diana." I exclaimed. "Congratulations! You've just bought a fabulous property!"

Diana danced and swirled around the beauty shop, her mud-anchored hair spikes jiggling madly. The bemused beautician backed away, holding the touch-up brush over her cupped hand. The other customers cringed at the nasty stuff flying off Diana's hair.

In the lobby of Jerry's building, I found a pay phone and dialed Randy's number. Once, just once, I prayed, let the woman answer. But, no. That was asking too much. I left a message saying the Colemans had accepted her counteroffer, that we needed to make an appointment for a property inspection, and that she needed to fill out a disclosure form. I stepped out of the building to face the glorious day. The Monkeypod trees shading the parking lot were shot with spidery pink blossoms in the brilliant sunshine. Their tiny leaves dappled the asphalt with myriad dancing shadows.

I, too, wanted to dance, jump, trip the light fantastic in wild circles of glee. The rush of making a sale is an all-time natural high. My every nerve was zinging. That was what I lived for, the intense thrill of clinching a difficult deal, walking away with all signatures in place. That glorious moment of acceptance—the meeting of the minds—validated all the grunt work that went into every transaction. That was the moment of sweet aloha.

My broker Kathleen flipped back to the first page of the contract and signed her approval at the top, the last step before opening escrow. She looked up at me and beamed.

"Good job, Laura. You're back on the sales board." Then she paused, tapping a French-manicured fingernail on her desk. "You know who has the skinny on this place? Your pal, Barbara Jaworski at South Shore Realty. She sold the vacant land to the doctor, before he built the house. Better give her a call, see what she knows. There was something wacky about it." That wasn't what I wanted to hear.

Kathleen stretched five feet, two inches in three-inch heels. Her ex-husband was a cosmetic surgeon. Every year at Thanksgiving she took a vacation under his skillful knife, as stipulated by their divorce agreement. On New Year's Eve, she appeared a little more tucked, sculpted, suctioned, smoothed. The process had peaked about five years ago, however. The worldly eyes, the over-stretched shiny cheeks, the knotty veins on her hands gave clues to her true age that no surgeon could alter. Regardless of her obsessive vanity, Kathleen packed more professional knowledge and common sense in that tiny, enhanced frame than most people could wheel around in a trunk. She never failed to provide rock-solid direction to her agents through the twists and turns of a tight transaction. I considered myself extremely fortunate to have her.

With a quizzical look, I asked, "So Barbara was involved in the original sale to Dr. Entwistle?"

Kathleen had a prodigious memory, another thing that made her a crackerjack broker. She remembered more about her agents' transactions than they did themselves.

"Barbara and I sat on the same nonprofit board at the time. We shared the occasional glass of wine after meetings." She nodded her head as the details came into focus. "Yeah, that was a humdinger. Call Barb and ask. She might give you a few clues so you can avoid trouble later. You'll have your hands full, working both sides of the deal."

She turned to her office safe, spun the dial, and pulled out a stash of earnest money deposits for offers that were still under negotiation. She clipped the Colemans' check to their contract and handed them both to me.

"By the way," I said. "Your ex is an MD. Do you think he might know anything about Randy Entwistle, professionally, I mean?"

"He knows her very well. He never lets anyone else pass the gas for him in the OR. She's put me out . . . well, let's say more than a few times."

"Good reputation?"

"The best. I wouldn't let any other anesthesiologist on this island get near me. I can't speak for her personal life, though."

"Well, at least that's something."

"Good luck," Kathleen said, turning to the pile of papers on her desk. "Hopefully this sale will speed right on through."

By the time I pulled into my condo parking lot, it was blazing mid-afternoon. I'd delivered the Colemans' contract and check to escrow, then stopped by the Schultzes' gallery to have them sign an addendum to their contract regarding the roof and rafters. Once they had accepted the inevitability of the situation, Anita and Dooley wanted it over and done with. I couldn't have agreed more. My commission was assured, but at the moment I was too hot, sweaty, and tired to appreciate it. All I wanted was a quick dip in the condo pool and a few minutes alone with my feet up and eyes closed before I tracked down Annie, Frank, and my parents.

There is, as they say, no rest for the weary. My immediate circle of nearest and dearest were all gathered in a nattering clutch in my living room when I pushed open the apartment door. Mother launched herself at me like a buzzing hornet. "Oh, Laura, how could you? Look at this girl. How could you not have told us? Our own dear Annie finally returns to her family, and just look at her. We're the last to know she's *hapai*."

"Hi, Mother. Nice to see you, too." I dumped my briefcase on the dining table, covered now with my office paraphernalia in preparation for the delivery of Annie's bed.

My father heaved himself from the couch and came toward me with hefty arms outstretched. "Laura, sweetheart, such a scramble. Don't pay any attention to your mother. We're just thrilled that Annie's home."

I sank into my father's safe embrace. Oh, blessed haven. I closed my eyes and drifted back to Pua Olena, to the wonderful Sundays of my child-hood when my father was mine all day. Mother may have been the driving force who kept the household, not to mention the entire non-profit sector of Honolulu, functioning, but my father loved me like a big fuzzy teddy bear.

"Daddy." I snuggled against his chest and inhaled the scent of Bay Rum. Such an old fashioned after-shave, but I loved it. Bay Rum meant Daddy was home.

Mother interrupted us with an insistent tap on my shoulder. "Laura, we've got to get things worked out. This child needs help. Your father and I will take her home with us and see what's to be done."

I pulled away from Dad and turned to look at her. As usual, she was the picture of impeccable taste. For the trip to a neighbor island she wore a raw silk beige shirtwaist, accented with an emerald-green sash. Mag-nificent emerald and diamond earrings peeked out from beneath her soft platinum waves, matching the emerald and diamond wedding rings on her left hand.

"Mother, please. Annie and I have things under control. There's no need for you to become involved." When would she understand that I was a grown woman, capable of functioning, even solving a problem, on my own?

"Involved? She's our grandchild! Let's get one thing settled right now, Laura. This girl is not giving birth on Maui. It's far too . . . too . . . primitive

over here. What if there are complications? We can't have them helicop-
tering her to Honolulu at the last minute while she's hemorrhaging to
death."

Annie unscrunched herself from a corner of the couch, belly to the
fore, and blew her bangs off her forehead. "Grandma, that's gross."

Mother put her hand on Annie's shoulder. "Precisely, my dear. At
least *you* understand."

"For goodness sake, Mother. Stop scaring her. I took Annie to my
own ob-gyn. She gave her a complete examination, with blood tests and
everything. All is well. She's on prenatal vitamins and has nothing to do
but eat and rest until delivery." I didn't mention that the test results
were not back yet, nor that I had not yet picked up the vitamins at the
drugstore.

Annie twisted away from her grandmother, crossed her arms over her
stomach, and sat down again on the couch beside her grandfather, no
doubt wishing herself back in Thailand, regardless of how dreadful it
might have been. "I'm not going to Honolulu," she stated.

Dear Frank sank lower and lower in the sofa chair, crossed his legs,
and tried—not very hard—to hide a grin behind his hand. He never
argued with my mother, preferring to let her rant on until she ran out of
steam, then swoop in for the kill. It was clear he wasn't going to change
his tactic now.

Mother turned to me and sniffed a haughty sniff. "But I don't know
this doctor. Who are her family?"

"Mother, for God's sake. I've been seeing Lily Fujikawa for years.
She's perfectly qualified. We do have real MDs on Maui, you know."

"But . . . Fujikawa . . . don't tell me she's local?"

"She's as local as you and I. Grew up in a plantation camp on Kauai.
What difference does that make?"

"Humph," Mother replied. "That just won't do. And that hospital. Really, Laura, nobody has babies on the outer islands. Annie simply has to
come to Kapiolani. The sooner she's safely with us on Oahu, the better."

Kapiolani Women and Children's Medical Center in Honolulu is the premier maternity hospital in the Pacific. I was born there. So was my mother, and everyone who was anyone, in her stilted view. A mere county hospital, even one as thoroughly modern as Maui Memorial, was beyond contempt. She conveniently ignored, of course, that her grandchildren had been safely born there.

I still knew so little about Annie's years away, about the anguish she suffered prior to leaving, and the dark life she had led on the run. Against all that, the decision to deliver at Maui Memorial or Kapiolani seemed ludicrously unimportant.

Behind his former mother-in-law's back, Frank stared at the ceiling. If I hadn't been so irritated, I would have joined him in a good laugh. This was Margaret Wildethorne Henderson to the core. Her snobbishness was legendary, and she never made any apologies for it. In her ossified circle of Island society, the highest credential one could have was a missionary or whaler ancestor. In the early 1990s nobody gave a rip, but Mother had carried the antiquated torch all her life and wasn't about to set it down anytime soon.

"Please, Mother, let it go," I pleaded. "Annie is *my* daughter. We'll handle it. She's healthy. The baby's kicking. It's only a matter of time."

My Catholic mother winced at the earthy reference to the unborn child. The wheels spun in her brain as she switched to another track. "But this place . . ." She swept her arms in denigration of my compact apartment. "The three of you can't live here. How will you manage with a baby in this tiny space? With all the nursery equipment? It's . . . it's impossible."

Father spoke up in the commanding tone he reserved for Mother at her worst. "Margaret, I'm sure Laura and Annie can manage on their own. Really, my dear, let it go."

Annie stood abruptly, brushed past her grandfather's knees, and faced us all, her eyes blazing.

"Quit talking about me as if I'm not even here." She flounced out onto the lanai and slammed the screen door behind her. With her thin back to us, she gripped the railing, head lowered, shoulders quivering. Was she crying?

Suddenly I flashed on two-year-old Annie, throwing her doll through a tenth-floor hotel balcony railing and trying to squeeze through after it. She'd been as slithery as an octopus. I'd caught her just in time. I ran to the screen door. "Annie! Come back inside. You're frightening me."

She turned her tear-stained face toward us. "Leave me alone! All of you, just leave me alone!"

My blood was boiling. Annie and I had barely begun to reestablish our relationship, and there was Mother, setting us at odds again. I had played right into it. As far as Mother was concerned, the prodigal child had returned, "Annie as Project," desperately in need of her prodigious organizing ability. Mother failed to realize that Annie would never submit to her industrial-strength management style. The best thing I could do for my child was to thank her grandparents for coming and send them back to Oahu. Annie, Frank, and I needed this time together without Mother's interference. Before I could speak, Frank finally got the message and stood up. We were still a team.

"Margaret, this is upsetting Annie," Frank said. "Look at her. She's ready to jump over the railing. You've got to let the three of us work things out. I know you're thrilled to see her. We all are, but I think the best thing you and Jack can do is go home and let her settle in with Laura. I'm sure they'll visit you soon. Come on, we'll stop for an early dinner on the way to the airport."

Mother began to sputter, but Dad stepped in with a firm hand on her waist.

"Frank's right, my dear. Things are way more complicated than we realized. Annie's safely home. Our prayers have been answered. Let's be on our way. I'm sure Laura will keep us informed, won't you, sweetheart? If there's any reason to bring Annie to Honolulu, you'll be on the first plane, eh?"

"I promise, Dad." God bless my father. Although a bit portly these days, he was still handsome in a Cary Grant sort of way, complete with a cleft chin. His thick hair had grayed in a distinguished manner, and his charming smile could stop a tsunami at high crest. He strolled onto the lanai, put a protective arm around Annie, and guided her back into the living room. "Come on, sweetheart. We all love you. We just want to help."

In spite of Mother's guilt-inducing protests, we all piled into Frank's rental car and headed for a restaurant near the airport. Frank and my father kept the conversation light and impersonal, bantering back and forth about the nonsense that went on in the hospitality industry. Even Annie laughed at some of their tall tales. Mother was unusually quiet. While she may have lost this battle, she was regrouping to win the war.

CHAPTER 12

Annie spent the next few days with her father. It was the best gift I could give them. I tidied my apartment, enjoying the respite of being alone. I accompanied the Schultzes to their closing on Wednesday. Their sale would record as scheduled, with escrow holding the money to pay for the roof repairs after the buyers took possession. I often experienced a feeling of letdown, even loneliness, after a closing, when clients who had occupied such a huge part of my life moved on without me. In this case, I was just glad it was *pau*. Dooley, Anita, and Al Madrid were out of my life, and my check was forthcoming.

Meanwhile, I waited for Randy Entwistle's call to acknowledge the Colemans' acceptance of her counteroffer. Her lack of communication was outrageous. Diana and Jerry called me three times a day, wanting to know when we could schedule the inspection. None of us could understand the seller's lack of enthusiasm. She'd gotten what she wanted, a quick sale at a good price with highly qualified buyers. For me, it was one more sinking sign that all was not well in Haiku.

Randy finally made contact Thursday afternoon. Of course, I wasn't home. Annie had stopped by to pick up clean clothes and took the call. I came home to an empty apartment and a childishly scribbled note: *Dr. Ant Something—tomorrow at 9. Don't be late. Meet you there. Wait at the gate.*

I ripped the message off the notepad and stared at it. What else might Randy have revealed if she'd spoken into the tape instead of to Annie? I made a mental note to remind Annie not to pick up the phone unless she was certain the call was for her.

Then it hit me—nine o'clock tomorrow? There were only two residential house inspectors on the island, both perpetually busy. I'd have to beg to get one out there with so little notice. I called the one who lived closest to Haiku, hoping he could squeeze us in. No answer. Left a message. Same with the second inspector. I could only pray that one of them would get back to me by evening.

I called Diana at home and Jerry at his office, told them both we had an appointment tomorrow at nine. Even if I couldn't get an inspector by then, we could give it a good once-over ourselves and send the inspector later.

As I'd expected, neither inspector was available until early next week. Giving them another three days to complete the report would bring us right up against the buyers' ten-day approval deadline. We'd be pushing it, but it was workable. I booked Carlton Tanimoto for Monday morning. The Colemans and I would go up alone tomorrow.

Once again, the white wooden gate was chained and double padlocked. Diana, Jerry, and I cooled our heels on the road for fifteen minutes before Randy finally pulled up behind us in her dented maroon van. She fumbled repeatedly until her trembling fingers got the numbers on the padlocks lined up correctly and the locks fell open.

As we pushed through, Jerry muttered, "First thing, I'm going to put an automatic opener on this gate." Randy peered at him as if he'd announced he was going to install an underground nuclear reactor. The woman was as jumpy as a sand crab away from its hole.

"Come on, come on," Randy urged, trotting down the driveway ahead of us. "We have to do this quickly." She darted a glance back up at the gate. I hastened to join her, while Diana and Jerry, hand in hand, paused on the hill to take in the lush scene below.

"Are you expecting anyone else?" I asked as I caught up with Randy. I pointed to two old cars parked alongside the garage. They were typical

Maui cruisers, rusted-out and patched with duct tape, capable of getting from A to B, but just barely.

"No, no, at least I hope not. Definitely hope not. But we have to be quick." She stopped, beckoning for Diana and Jerry to speed up and join us.

"Why?" I asked, hoping to recoup a bit of the rapport I had worked so hard to establish at Taco Bell.

"Uh, well, she might be back. I don't know, but she might. Or she might not."

"Sorry? I'm lost. Who might be back?" I asked.

"Moana. She might be back. Maybe."

"Moana? Your housemate?" She hadn't mentioned her name before. I was surprised she was Hawaiian. Somehow that didn't figure. From Randy's account of her aggressive behavior, I imagined her a sharp-nosed *haole* with heavy makeup, thin lips, and helmet-shellacked hair.

"Yup, well, sort of. Housemate. Housekeeper. Gardener. Bookkeeper. Bitch. You name it. Claws into everything." The words sluiced through her spread-eagle teeth.

"Hey," I called up to Diana and Jerry as we reached the bottom of the drive. "You go on into the house. Have a good look around. I have some business to discuss with Dr. Entwistle. We'll be out back." Whatever was going on with Moana, I had to get Randy to tell me more before she deteriorated completely.

I gestured her to follow me around the house to the terrace, where we could sit at a table in the shade. My breath caught as we rounded the corner, struck by the view across the gulch. Every hue and intensity of green glowed in the vibrant morning light. A wedge of aquamarine ocean, framed by the ravine, glittered and teased in the distance. Beauty, tranquility, privacy—this property had it all.

I pulled a fistful of papers out of my file and laid them on the glass-topped table. "Here's your copy of the signed counteroffer, Randy. I need your acknowledgement that you received it. A signature, right here." I offered her a pen and pointed to the yellow highlighted line on the original. "I've opened escrow. We're moving ahead." I waited in vain for a hint of gratitude.

Ignoring the pen, she squirmed in her seat and started plucking at the place on her faded gray slacks where a crease might have been if they'd been ironed. A flush of trepidation arose on my chest.

"Randy? We're under contract now. Your acknowledgement is merely a formality." My fist clenched the pen. "You're not having second thoughts?"

She wouldn't look at me. "Uh . . . second thoughts? Not exactly. But I'm not too sure . . ."

I pushed for a straight answer, all the while dreading what it might be. "What exactly is it you're not sure about?"

"That I should sell."

That was about as straight an answer as you could get. The flush crept up my neck, hot and bothersome. "But you *are* selling. You and the Colemans have signed the contract. We're in escrow."

"Yeah, well, maybe that's not such a great idea." Her gaze raptly followed the flight of two white pigeons as they coasted between the verdant banks of the ravine.

By extreme effort, I cleansed my voice of panic. "Why not? What's happened since the last time we talked? You seemed so determined to sell, so eager for a quick close. Time is of the essence, and all that." I flicked my pen against the rim of the table to wrest her attention away from the birds. "Have you and Moana worked things out, by any chance?"

She jumped out of her chair and barked at me, rapid-fire. "No, no, nothing like that. God forbid. But . . . she won't like it. She won't like it at all. I don't know what . . . what I should do." She turned and stalked from the table to the lava rock wall at the edge of the terrace, rubbing the side of her head until her hair stiffed out like dried seaweed.

The woman, abysmally unattractive to begin with, became more so with each close encounter. Her personal life was overwhelming. I truly resented being pulled into the role of counselor here, but somebody had to take her in hand, or I'd be left with a broken contract and litigious buyers. I joined her at the wall, hoping the sympathy in my voice didn't sound forced.

"What's happened, Randy? Please tell me, so I can help you sort it out."

She put one foot up on the wall and began to assault her slacks again. If she worried the non-pleat with much more vigor, she's soon have one thigh clad in shreds. "She's been traveling, you know."

"Who?"

"Moana. Flew off with her . . . her . . . boyfriend. That damn Prakash." She spat out his name.

"Wait a minute. A boyfriend? What's a boyfriend got to do with it?"

She looked at me with utterly tired eyes. "Everything. Things were just fine until she took up with him last August or September, maybe. Now he's set her against me. That's when all the trouble began." She nodded her head resignedly. "Yup, that's when it all began."

Oh, how I hated to hear about boyfriends. I took great satisfaction in working with single women, empowering them to become homeowners on their own. As often as not, however, a boyfriend muscled in and started to call the shots, even though he wasn't a party to the transaction. Or perhaps *because* he wasn't a party to the transaction. I'd seen it too many times—the boyfriend, pure sour grapes, doing everything in his power to mess things up, pretending all the while to help. It was strictly a control issue, exacerbated by the fact that she was moving ahead in the world and he wasn't.

In this case, however, things were different. Moana wasn't involved in the sale. More than likely the two women had gotten along reasonably well, at least in Randy's perception, until the boyfriend came along and upset the balance, leaving her out of their cozy new arrangement.

"Does he actually live with her in the house?" I asked. "Is he also going to be inconvenienced by the sale?"

"Huh. He moved in months ago. Just for a few nights, I thought. But ever since she kicked me out, he's been sleeping upstairs with her. Wait 'til you see their bed. They gave mine to Goodwill. He has all kinds of fancy furniture. Moved it all in. Now he acts like he owns the place."

"What does he do for a living? Is he a furniture dealer?" I needed to get a feel for this disturbing new presence who could influence the outcome of the sale. "Judging by the pieces I saw in the living room, he knows his way around Oriental antique bazaars."

"Don't know for sure. Something that involves a lot of traveling. He uses the garage for a workshop. He's got a bunch of fancy equipment in there. Keeps it locked up. When he's in town, the rural route mailman picks up boxes. Little boxes, you know, bunches of them about this big." She made a figure with her thumbs and forefingers. "I can't figure it out. It's very hush-hush. Moana helps him, but she won't say a word."

My mind raced to the worst-case scenario. "Do you think he's manufacturing illegal drugs? If he is, the federal government could confiscate the property overnight, with no compensation to you. Both you and the Colemans would be up a very dry creek."

Her face went white. "Illegal drugs?" she echoed. For a moment she struggled to speak. "That . . . that sounds a bit farfetched. He wouldn't be sending illegal drugs out in broad daylight by U.S. mail."

"I don't know," I replied. "In the movies, the more you do something right under the law's nose, the more likely you are to get away with it."

She stared at me, biting her lower lip so hard I thought her teeth would mash right through it. "It can't be," she finally muttered. "I kinda thought they were stringing beads—you know, big, clunky hippie beads. Moana wears them all the time. She has oodles of them. Selling them in Paia, sending them to shops on other islands, and California, maybe. They have lots of hairy-legged, granola-crunchy types there, too, you know. Maybe that's why Prakash travels—to buy beads from all over the world." Her eyes begged me to believe this simplistic scenario.

Her naiveté amazed me. "Why would everything need to be so hush-hush under lock and key for bead necklaces?"

"Uh . . . maybe the beads are really valuable? Or they have unique necklace designs they don't want anyone to copy?"

"Oh, please. Wouldn't it be great if that's all it is? You'd better find out, Randy. If he's manufacturing or selling drugs out of your home, you could lose it any day. The federal laws on the subject are cut and dried. I've seen it happen. They do a bust, and the landlord loses everything, even if he lives off-property and doesn't have any knowledge of the illegal activity."

"That's not fair," she exclaimed.

"Fair or not, that's the law. I attended a workshop on it just last month. There's new legislation pending that would allow an innocent landlord defense, but so far it's still hung up in Congress."

"Then we *have* to get them out of here," she declared, balling her hands into fists. "Thank God I put that For Sale sign up. Good riddance to bad rubbish." She looked at me again with those bitter, smudgy eyes. "Things were just fine until he entered the picture, you know. Prakash ruined everything."

I refrained from comment, feeling quite certain things had spun out of control way before Prakash stepped into the picture. I let her keep talking, hoping to get a richer sense of what was really going on.

"Moana told me they'd be gone for a month. I figured I could get the house sold and closed before they got back, see. If they came home and found a new owner in residence, what could they do? Then Monday I ran into Prakash. That slime! Smack dab in the doorway of Hisamoto Store. Scared me half to death. Thought I was seeing a ghost." With each pronouncement, her voice got raspier. Spittle gathered in the corners of her mouth as she continued.

"Maybe they never left at all. She's here on Maui somewhere. Just hasn't come home yet for some reason. I don't know what to do. She'll try to stop the sale, I know it. I just know it." She began her obsessive scoping of the scene behind me again. Whatever Prakash might be up to, Randy appeared to be much more frightened of Moana.

From above, Diana's excited voice drifted down. ". . . right here, Jerry, by the window. That four-poster I showed you in the catalog last night . . ."

I frowned at Randy. "I don't quite understand. How can she stop the sale? She doesn't have any interest in the property. According to the real property tax office, you're the sole owner." County records had been known to be inaccurate, however, and the more reliable preliminary title report would not reach my desk for another week.

Randy refused to look at me.

"Aren't you, Randy?"

"Yeah, yeah, I own it, I own it. It's mine, mine alone."

"But . . .?" Icicles shivered down my backside.

"She . . . she . . . may *think* she owns it . . . or part of it." She was following the pigeons again, watching them swoop and circle in an updraft.

"Randy, why would she think she owns part of it?"

She winced. "Maybe . . . because I told her . . . she did."

"You told her? What does that mean? Did you sign any papers?" Lord, let me get her attention away from those everlasting birds.

"Yes . . . no . . . maybe . . . I'm not . . . sure."

This was the woman who administered anesthesia in the operating theater. I could just hear it: *"Doctor Entwistle. The patient is turning blue. Are you there? Earth to Entwistle. Shouldn't you adjust your dials, Doctor?"*

"Yes . . . no . . . maybe . . . I'm not . . .sure."

Perhaps my mother was right about Maui Memorial Hospital. I tugged at her sleeve. "Randy. Why might Moana believe she's a co-owner of the property?"

She turned to face me, shoulders hunched in despair. "She . . . uh . . . she made me sign something."

My iron clamp of self-control flew off. "What kind of something? A deed? What?" My voice shrilled up a whole octave.

Randy pushed her chair back from the table, her eyebrows raised in alarm, her mouth firmly shut.

"Randy, just tell me what kind of paper you signed!" I tapped my heel on the flagstones, forcing myself to calm down.

"We . . . we went to a notary. I do remember that. Moana's big on notaries."

"Was it an official document drawn up by an attorney? Typed out in legal format, stapled to a blue backing, maybe?"

"I don't think so. It was in her own handwriting . . . on a yellow legal pad."

"All right. What did it say?" This shouldn't be so hard. The woman had a medical degree, for heaven's sake.

"Something about . . . giving her half a share of the property."

"Something about giving her half a share of the property?" I could only parrot her statement while I grappled with its possible repercussions. If Moana was adamantly against selling, and she had a legitimate ownership interest, we were dead in the water. None of this mattered, of course, if the boyfriend Prakash got the place confiscated first. My mind was reeling. "Where is this paper, Randy? Can you show it to me? So I can see if, in fact, it gives her a legal stake?"

"I don't know," she whimpered. "I never saw it again."

"Aha. So you don't know if it even exists." An optimistic thought, quickly dashed.

"Oh, she has it, all right. She reminds me of it every time I tell her she has to leave."

What kind of woman was this Moana? And what kind of wimp was Randy to become such a pawn in her manipulative hands? My patience snapped. "Okay. So where do we go from here? Do you want to sell the house? One word: yes or no? No more games." I could not allow myself to get sucked any further into her personal drama. My job was to get this house for the Colemans, or get them out now before we ended up in a legal battle. It was time for Randy to dive or get off the cliff.

"I really—"

"No, Randy. Do you want to sell or not? One word: yes or no."

Her eyes brimmed with tears. Fresh out of sympathy, I waited while she got hold of herself. I did not avert my gaze. Finally, she nodded her head, slowly and pathetically. She spoke through those awful clenched teeth. "Yes. I do want to sell. I need to sell. Especially if Prakash is up to no good. I want them both out of my life, damn it, once and for all. If you're right about the drugs, we'd better get moving."

I let out the breath I'd been holding. "All right, we're agreed. We'll proceed with the sale. Until I see that yellow piece of paper, I can't be sure what, if anything, Moana can do to stop us. You've got to get your hands on it. Then we can run it by an attorney. If the deed doesn't exist,

we need to know that, too. You're on your own. I can't help you there."
She shuddered, but I refused to let up. "We also have to find out what
Prakash is doing in the garage. I suggest you call the police. Don't go
snooping around and put yourself in danger."

"No, no," she shouted. "No police! I don't want any police involved. Let's
just get the house sold. That will take care of everything. Just get it sold."

Her violent reaction frightened me. She knew more than she was admitting. I didn't like it one bit.

"Randy, I insist you call the po—"

She grabbed the contract from me. "No. Where do I sign?"

Not waiting for an answer, she ruffled through the papers, found the
last page, laid it on her knee, and signed the acknowledgement.

I was speechless.

"Where's the disclosure form you mentioned when you called me?"
she asked as she thrust the contract back at me.

Functioning like a robot, I gave her the blank form and went over the
instructions to disclose every material fact, past or present, known to her
about the property that might impact the market value or the buyer's decision to buy, including Miss Moana's claim of ownership. And the clan-
destine business operation in the garage.

As she tucked the sheaves under her arm, Diana and Jerry sauntered
onto the terrace. Randy and I waited uneasily in the shade while they
stood, hand in hand, marveling at the pristine view. My mind moved on
to damage control. How would they react, I wondered, to these desperate
new developments? They could cancel on either of them. At the moment,
that wasn't a bad idea.

The sound of a diesel motor broke through our reverie. We turned to
see a beat-up white pickup truck squeal around the corner of the house,
leaving ugly brown skid marks in the grass. We all gaped. The truck stopped
abruptly, muddy front tires smearing the terrace flagstones. A tall, thin,
middle-aged woman dressed in a multi-colored tie-dyed T-shirt, chunky
beads, and a swirling red broomstick skirt jumped out. She slammed the
truck door with both hands, then whipped around to face us, arms akimbo.

"Who the hell are you?" she roared.

CHAPTER 13

The swirling red fury barged across the terrace, her mud-caked leather sandals slapping the flagstones like shutters in a windstorm. Coils of long gray hair quivered in a free-flying frizz as she bore down on our stunned little group. In spite of a noticeable limp, she moved with the agility of a dervish. If this was the dreaded housemate, she was no more Hawaiian than Randy or me.

Jerry tightened his arm around his wife and edged her back a few steps. Silly me, I glanced at Randy, expecting her to step forward and take charge. Instead, she sidled up against the low wall behind us in sheer terror. With one more step backward, she'd be ass over teakettle into the ravine.

Reluctantly remembering my professional role, I stepped forward, held out my hand and forced myself to say, "How do you do? I'm Laura McDaniel, with Blue Rock Realty."

The woman punched her fists into her hips and glared. She exuded a faint essence of sandalwood. "Yeah, I know who you are, Little Miss Real Estate. I see your picture in the newspaper. What the hell are you doing here?"

While I blinked in surprise, Randy recovered her few remaining wits. "Mo. What are you doing back? I, uh, thought you were in Burma. Or Singapore . . . or Indonesia." Brave speech for someone still cowering behind me, as if I could, or would, protect her.

The woman elbowed me aside and turned her full wrath on Randy.

"You shut the hell up. You knew damn well I was home. You saw Prakash at Hisamoto's yesterday. Don't bullshit me, Randy."

"Sorry, sorry, sorry, Moana, don't get all upset, please, please. These, uh, these people, uh . . . they're here to see the house . . . uh . . . the yard, the yard. I met them, uh, on the beach the other day, you know how I meet people on the beach. I was telling them about all the fabulous landscaping you did here—all the ferns and heliconia and ginger you planted. They asked if they could see it, and, uh, I invited them up. Didn't I?" She ventured a step farther from the protection of my shoulder, her eyes begging Diana and Jerry for confirmation. She was literally hopping up and down in distress.

Increasingly alarmed, I could only hang tight and see if the Colemans would play. Diana opened her mouth. Jerry tightened his grip on her shoulder. Then he let go, stepped in front of her and extended his hand to Moana.

"Hey, there. You've done an incredible job here. I understand you planted every one of these colorful exotics." Quick on the draw, that boy. I was sure his neglect to mention his own name and Diana's was deliberate. The less that woman knew about them, the better.

Moana's necklace rose up and down on her heaving breast. The carved wood and amber beads were strung on thin black grosgrain like *kukui* nuts. They were actually quite beautiful. Maybe Randy was right about the bead business in the garage.

Moana touched Jerry's hand with the tips of her fingers, then immediately withdrew as if his palm were smeared with excrement. She jerked her head toward the driveway. "Well, you've seen it. Now get the hell out. And you, Miss Prissy Realtor, don't let me catch you on my property again. Or you'll answer to me personally."

Jerry, Diana, and I darted unbelieving glances at one another. No one said a word. Randy stood there, hanging her head, shuffling one foot back and forth on the flagstones. At an unspoken signal, the three of us took off and marched up the driveway double quick.

"Whew," Jerry exclaimed as we careened onto the road in the red Bronco. "What planet did she come from?"

"And how did Randy let herself get in so deep with such a witch?" Diana wondered.

"Two dykes, they deserve each other," Jerry muttered. "Lessies, all the way."

I was incensed. "Oh, come on, man. Just because two women live together doesn't mean they're lesbians."

"Did you see how they fight? How one bosses the other around? Give me a break. I can spot lessies clear across the Molokai Channel."

"For God's sake, Jerry," I countered. "That's ridiculous."

"Oh, give over, you lot," Diana exclaimed. "Whatever their relationship, we're going to have to deal with it. Now listen, Jerry, do we really want to go through with this?"

Go, Diana, I silently cheered, bracing myself as Jerry spun the wheels around another of Haiku's infamous hairpin turns. Through the open window, I could almost touch the huge philodendrons that draped the eucalyptus trees crowding the narrow road. The air smelled moist and earthy from the morning rain, so reminiscent of Pua Olena.

"Honey, it's your house," Jerry replied. "Speak now or forever hold your peace."

Diana stared out the window as we hit Hana Highway. Bearing left, we cruised past the windsurfing beach at Hookipa. Colored sails zipped fearlessly up and down the waves in a stiff off-shore breeze. I tried windsurfing once and nearly drowned. It isn't a casual sport.

At this point, I didn't know what to think about our fearful Dr. Entwistle and her unlikely property. I'm a real fighter when it comes to closing a sale. In fact, I've pulled off some miracles in my day while relishing the battles. There are bloody ankles all over town where I've dug in and refused to let go. Buy or die, as the saying goes.

The need to advise one's clients to fight or pull back isn't always clear, however. Because an agent is a benefited party to the outcome, the process sometimes becomes ethically derailed. More than once I've found myself in the squirmy position of urging my clients to close, even when, in their best interests, I should have advised them to cancel. I will never be comfortable with the push and pull of my conscience in such murky situations. I consider myself an ethical person. I know the rules, and I follow them. But from time to time, I find myself nudging—for no other reason—in the direction that results in a paycheck.

I rolled my window all the way down, closing my eyes to the stream of fresh ocean air, hoping it would clarify my thinking. The dynamics of Dr. E. and her housemate were beyond me. Who knew what depths of nastiness that lurked behind this introductory encounter with Moana? I'd have given the moon to be able to discuss the situation with my broker Kathleen and get her solid guidance, but she had left for a camping trip in Alaska the day before. Since I didn't have much confidence in the bro-ker-in-charge during her absence, I decided to forge ahead on my own until Kathleen returned. If the Colemans wanted to call it quits once they knew the full story, I wouldn't object. I'd find some other way to take care of my daughter and grandchild. Selling timeshares, perhaps.

Once we passed the windsurfers, Diana revived a bit. She launched into plans for redecorating the house and re-landscaping the yard. She envisioned an English country garden, with the tropicals dug up and dis-carded. Better not let Moana get wind of that, I thought.

Jerry remained annoyingly neutral, nodding and agreeing with ev-erything she said. The farther we got from Haiku, the more Diana's spirits lifted. We stopped for lunch at Mama's Fish House in Paia. By the time we ordered, she had begun to glow again. Her sculpted cheeks regained their classic blush; her dark eyes snapped with determination.

"I don't care how awful that woman is," Diana declared, stirring sweet-ener into her iced tea. "She can't stop us from buying the house. We have a signed contract. The property is absolutely perfect. Laura, wait until you see the kitchen. It's a dream. And the master suite! How dare she!"

Jerry winked at me. I kept forgetting he was a salesman. Suddenly I understood. He had quietly been letting Diana sell herself all over again. He wanted the property as much as she did, but wanted Diana to think it was her decision. To my chagrin, I had allowed myself to become so caught up projecting the endgame that I forgot the basics. One up for

Jerry. They were both emotionally attached to the property. Moana's little scene had backfired, strengthening their resolve instead of turning them off. As for me, I just plain hated to lose a sale, no matter what the difficulties. Throw me a challenge and watch me fight, especially against someone as outrageous as Moana.

The waitress set down a fresh swordfish salad for Diana, and seafood curry for Jerry and me. Helping myself to mango chutney and chopped peanuts, I relaxed for a moment, enjoying a few spicy mouthfuls while half listening to their ongoing decorating discussion.

Now was the time to tell them about Moana's claim of ownership and her boyfriend's hidden business in the garage. Prior to these revelations, all we'd had to worry about was getting rid of a clever freeloader. If either of these two new possibilities was true, however, things had escalated to a whole new level. There were ways of dealing with them, but we had to be prepared for combat.

I took comfort in the fact that Diana had found the property on her own. She was the one who had spotted the sign, called Randy to set up the initial appointment, and then told me about her marvelous find. No matter how they reacted to the forthcoming news, the Colemans could not blame me, not that they wouldn't try. When things go wrong, it's always the Realtor's fault.

"There's more you need to know," I said, hoping the excellent meal and their enthusiastic homecoming visions had mellowed them. It was a tossup which disaster to mention first. I crossed my fingers and picked what I judged to be the least toxic. "While you were in the house, Dr. Entwistle told me she signed some kind of paper giving the housemate a share of the property. There's a possibility Moana's actually on title."

I sipped my iced tea and watched Jerry's face, waiting for that tidbit to sink in. The color rose on his neck like mercury in a thermometer. "What is that bitch trying to pull?" he bellowed.

"Ssh," hissed Diana. "The whole restaurant is looking at you."

Diners at nearby tables froze as if we had clicked the pause button on a VCR. All noise ceased except for a tinkly cascade of ice water pouring from a pitcher at the far end of the room. All eyes snapped from Jerry to the oblivious waiter. He looked around in confusion. Then, as if someone pushed the play button, everyone in the room lost interest, reanimated, and turned back to their own conversations.

"Don't shush me," Jerry spat at his wife. Ignoring us both, he speared a succulent curried shrimp with his fork and popped it into his mouth. "I don't like to be fucked with," he declared, enunciating around a half-chewed mouthful of greenish seafood mush.

"I know," I said, wincing at the unsavory sight. "I don't like it, either."

I explained that until we could get an attorney to examine the actual document, which Randy hadn't seen since the day she allegedly signed it, I couldn't make a call on it. Even if the title report, based on a thorough search of the public records, showed Randy as the sole owner, Moana's unrecorded deed could still be legitimate.

Jerry snapped his fingers at a busboy and signaled him to remove our plates. "What are our options?" he asked me.

"You can pull out right now, based on the disclosure of a possible co-owner who has not signed the contract. In fact, if she is a legitimate owner, the contract is null and void."

"Oh, no," Diana exclaimed. "Jerry, oh, darling, I desperately want that property. We've got to fight for it!"

He gave her an exasperated look and turned back to me. "But if Moana's not on title, and we can prove it . . ."

"Then our girl can sell it to you unimpeded. Provided, of course, she can get the poacher out prior to closing."

Diana grinned. That label suited our red-skirted nemesis perfectly.

"And if she *is* on title?" Jerry asked, waving away the waitress who was hovering with the dessert tray.

"Randy could offer to buy her out," I replied, wishing he hadn't done that. The chocolate macadamia nut torte looked particularly tempting. "The woman's angry as a gaffed shark right now, but a thick wad of green might soothe the gaping wound."

Jerry snorted. "Or . . .?"

"Randy could sue for partition. One partner can force the other to sell. It would involve a court battle, cost a bunch of money, take forever. To be honest, Randy doesn't look like much of a fighter, especially if pitted against what we saw of Moana."

"You're right," Diana said. "Did you see how flat-out scared Randy is of her? Fat chance Randy'd take her to court. I can't see anything of the sort. We'd better go for the buyout." As if it were that simple, I thought, or their choice. Even though her proceeds from the sale would be considerable, they were earmarked for her mother's retirement home. Randy had admitted she had no savings. Was she just a poor money manager, or had Moana considered skimming one of the perks of doing the books? In any case, it sounded unlikely that Randy could offer enough to impress the woman.

"There's more," I continued. "You heard Moana mention someone named Prakash. He's Moana's boyfriend, according to Randy, as of about a year ago. He apparently caused the final rift between them. He's moved in with Moana and is operating some kind of secret business in the locked garage. Worst-case scenario, it's an illegal drug lab."

"What?" they both exclaimed at once.

"Right. Randy's not sure what's going on there. She thinks they're stringing hippie beads to sell. We should be so lucky. If it's drugs and the law gets wind of it, the property could be confiscated. Of course you could always buy it afterward from the U.S. Government, but who knows how long that would take."

Jerry said, "Fuck." Diana just stared at me. Then Jerry asked, "How can we find out, about the drug lab, I mean?"

"I told her to call the police. She refused."

"Is there any proof?"

"Only the double-locked door, the window covered with cardboard on the inside, and the postman who picks up piles of small boxes when the man's in town."

Jerry threw his napkin down on the table. "Oh, Laura, for Pete's sake. You're crazy. He wouldn't be operating a drug lab in a country mansion and mailing it out via the U.S. Postal Service."

"Something's going on in there," I said. "Randy said he has all kinds of equipment. That doesn't exactly square with stringing beads."

"I just can't believe it would be drugs," he said. "You've got to be delusional."

"Your choice, Jerry. I've told you what I think."

"I think you're a raving alarmist. No offense, but after what you've been through with your daughter, I'm not surprised."

Go ahead, I thought, throw in PMS, too. He refrained, but I knew he was thinking it. Maybe he was right, not about the PMS, but that I was jumping to irrational conclusions. I was the one who had suggested drugs, not Randy. And that postal service business *was* pretty farfetched. But something was going on in Randy's garage. Jerry seemed willing to brush it off, but it worried me plenty.

The Colemans agreed we'd play it one day at a time. Regarding Moana's purported deed, we'd give Randy a chance to locate it, or convince us it was all a mistake. Meanwhile we'd see what popped up on the title report. As for Prakash and his drug lab/bead-stringing operation, maybe the inspector would be able to get into the garage on Monday and allay my fears. Of course, I'd have to warn him of my suspicions, in which case he might refuse the assignment altogether.

Clearly Diana and Jerry wanted the property, all the more so because it dangled just out of reach. Diana was smack dab in love with it, while Jerry wasn't going to let a woman outfox him. Certain now about their separate but equal motivations, I felt my juices gathering for a battle royale.

Chapter 14

When I got back to my office, I sent a fax to the escrow company placing a rush on the title report. Fifty dollars well spent should have it in my hands by Tuesday. With the threat of Moana's interest and my other suspicions, we couldn't afford to waste any time.

I left a message for Randy, telling her the inspector would be there on Monday at ten o'clock. I reminded her to fill out the real property disclosure form and get it back to me beforehand in case there were any concerns to share with him.

Still at my desk at Blue Rock Realty, I remembered Kathleen's suggestion that I get some background on Randy's purchase of the property from Barbara Jaworski. Barb and I had been good friends for several years, although I hadn't seen her much lately. She must have been driving at the edge of her newfangled car phone's broadcast area, because her voice crackled and jumped when she answered my call. I filled her in on Annie's return, accepted her felicitations regarding the baby. Then, enunciating clearly, I asked if she had once sold a vacant lot to Dr. Randy Entwistle.

"Oh, yeah," she replied with a chuckle. "The never-ending saga. Why do you ask?"

I had to tread lightly. Because Barbara had originally sold Randy the lot, she had every right to expect Randy to list it with her if she ever decided to sell. Randy was under no obligation, of course, but that was always an agent's hope and expectation. Buyers eventually become sellers, and the business rolls on. I didn't want Barbara to take offense. Even between good friends, the business can be uncomfortably competitive.

"Well, she stuck up a FSBO sign last week," I replied. "One of my clients saw it. We're in escrow, Barb, and it's getting weird."

Either Barbara or the phone spat. "Ptaw." Then she continued, her words pocked by static. "I saw that sign when I was showing property up there last week. It was only up for a day. I wouldn't go near that place again with a ten-foot pole. Those two are as loony as they come." At least she wasn't offended that she didn't get the listing. In fact, she sounded pleased.

"What's the skinny on the housemate?" I shouted over the static.

"Aha. The infamous Corey Sue. Or Moana, as she styles herself."

"Tell me more!"

"Look, I'm rounding the curve at the Pali. We're gonna fade. My next few days are ghastly. What say breakfast on Tuesday? Before Brokers Caravan. Meet me at the little café on South Kihei Road around the corner from my house. The one that makes that great sour cream coffeecake. Seven o'clock."

"I'll buy," I yelled into a blast of electronic crackle.

When I finally got home, the only sign of life was the rude intruder. For a wild, frenzied moment, I was tempted to jab the erase button and catapult the recorded messages to never-never land. I got a grip on myself just in time and threw a towel over the machine instead. Whoever wanted my attention could just wait.

Annie was undoubtedly with her dad. If not, I couldn't cope with any more disasters today. As much as I'd tried to sound optimistic about Moana's claim of ownership, I knew how serious it was, and what an ugly battle it could become. Even if she didn't show up on the title report, the possibility of an unrecorded deed hung over us like a guillotine. As for the locked garage, I truly hoped Prakash was nothing more than a mooching bead merchant. Moana's necklace had been intriguing. Too flamboyant for my taste, however.

For someone who owned so few clothes, Annie certainly knew how to spread them around. I picked up her things and threw them into the washing machine—shorts, muumuus, T-shirts, and underwear. Forget the luxury of separating colors and whites, sturdies, and dainties. Annie would never have granted them that favor.

As I scanned the apartment for anything I might have missed, her crumpled backpack caught my eye. Stuffed into the space between her new bed in the den and the computer credenza, one strap hung out in full view. For a long moment I stared at it, remembering Annie's overly protective behavior at the airport and again later when I offered to get some clothes for her. What was she hiding? Did I really want to know?

In the few days she had been home, I had seen no signs of drug use. But then, would I even recognize them? Annie's brothers had been arrow-straight, totally involved in sports and other school activities. As far as I knew, drugs were never an issue with them. Annie may or may not have been involved before she left home. By her own account, I had been oblivious to much of what she'd struggled with. Was it now or never, I wondered, one last opportunity to cast the scales from my eyes, to face something that scared me witless?

Memories of my mother rooted me to the spot. She'd been an inveterate snoop throughout my childhood. She considered it her Catholic duty to poke through everything I brought into the house, part of her one-woman crusade to keep her daughter pure. Most of her scouting forays were for naught, except to irritate me.

On one daring occasion, however, I had snitched a photo of a boy I liked from the high school yearbook layout table and hid it in my underwear drawer. The following afternoon when I came home from school, Mother met me at the back door, pale and shaken. From her demeanor, I leapt to the assumption that my father had had a heart attack. Gulping for air, I fought back tears as I followed her rigid back through the kitchen and down the hall. Our bare footsteps rasped on the *lauhala* mats in a discordant rhythm. She ushered me into my father's den where she launched into a tongue-lashing absurdly out of proportion to the size of the offense.

"Don't you know what happens to young girls who chase after boys?" she cried, her face pinched with anger. "How disgusting to put that boy's picture in the drawer under your . . . your . . . panties. Mother Nature only cares about one thing, young lady—the propagation of the species. And you must never, *ever,* be her willing handmaiden."

Overwhelmed with relief that my father was okay, I accepted a two-week grounding. Her tirade left me confused and wary over my burgeoning interest in boys. Never again did I allow myself so much as a thought about the opposite sex in my mother's presence. And I vowed that if I ever had children of my own, I would respect their privacy. So far, I had honored that promise.

But this was different. My grandchild was at risk. I gingerly picked up the filthy pack and peered inside. It was empty. I searched through all the zippered pockets, inside and out. Nothing. Whatever she had been so intent on protecting was no longer there. Had she hidden it somewhere else in the apartment? As I stood there considering possible hiding places, the idea of snooping in my own home gave me pause. How very demeaning. I would observe Annie carefully, I decided, but not dismantle my entire apartment looking for contraband. If her hiding place was obvious, I would stumble upon it soon enough. If Annie really wanted to hide something from me, her clever little brain would easily outsmart mine.

I washed the dishes she had left on the coffee table, then cleared out the remainder of my office gear from the den. Her bed had arrived the day before. My mother, I hated to admit, had not been far off base. How were three of us going to manage in this tiny space?

Once I had restored things to a semblance of order, I rang Frank's room, but got no answer. Thinking he and Annie might be relaxing by his pool, I changed into a swimsuit and T-shirt, and drove over to his condo.

Struck by the cool shimmer of the turquoise water beyond the encircling red hibiscus hedge, I paused at the pool gate to savor the tableau. Children splashed and shouted in the clear afternoon sunlight. Parents looked on indulgently. Adult singles stretched languorously on recliners, their slickly oiled bodies radiating pheromones of availability.

Pretending to be oblivious to their true mission, they casually flipped the pages of paperback spy thrillers and romances.

I wondered for a moment what it would be like to see Maui through fresh, untroubled eyes. For some, their vacation on the Valley Isle was a once-a-year reward for winter survived in a frigid clime. For others, it was a once-in-lifetime dream come true. For *kamaaina* residents like myself, it was a constant push to be productive in the debilitating heat and humidity while everyone else was having fun.

Amid all this delight and good cheer, I spotted my daughter reclining cross-legged on a chaise lounge in the full sun, a blonde Buddha in a purple bikini. Her naked stomach bulged over a miniscule triangle of fabric in the most vulgar way, her *piko* protruding obscenely. I winced at yet another display of her casual attitude toward her pregnancy. Sure, I'd seen *hapai* young women at the beach wearing bikinis right up to delivery—granted not in my day—but this hit a little too close to home.

As I stood there gripping the gate, the truth struck me, the truth I had been dodging since the moment I'd spotted Annie at the airport. This young woman was a stranger to me. She was not the child of my heart, the child I had lost and longed for so anxiously. In her place was another creature, forged by her years on the run. I hadn't gotten my daughter back at all. My Annie was gone forever.

For a staggering moment I could only cling to the bars, rocked by the searing revelation. The happy sounds of children in the pool took on jagged, hurtful edges. Each joyful shout, each carefree splash stabbed me, smote the very fiber of my being. The unspeakable fear that had haunted me these past three years was indeed a fact. My child was gone, lost irretrievably. I was left with a stranger and no proper way to mourn the loss. If I'd had the will to turn around at that moment and walk away, I believe I would have. But I could only hang on to the pool gate until the wave of despair ebbed. I hadn't thought I was capable of feeling any more hurt over Annie. At some point before her return, when I began to believe things were truly hopeless, I felt myself reluctantly begin to let go. One can carry negative emotions for only so long before the human body's natural defenses take over. The wound never disappears, but scar tissue builds over it, allowing one to laugh again. Seeing Annie at the pool stretched out with such barbaric disregard for the proprieties ripped that scar wide open. In some ways this new loss was more difficult than death, which at least brings finality and closure. A mother is vulnerable to the vagaries of her child's behavior for as long as she lives, even when the child sheds her known persona and becomes a stranger along the way. Motherhood is a lifetime sentence.

Frank spotted me, and waved gaily for me to join them. Tears welled, but I forced them back. Not now. I would somehow have to come to grips with this new pain. God grant me the strength to accept and do the best I could for the young woman who was no longer Annie.

Frank sat up on his chaise lounge and shaded his eyes. Wearing only swimming trunks, his body was as trim and lithe as ever, albeit pale from his recent years in Maine. It wouldn't take him long to regain the golden tan he'd sported in the past.

He stood to greet me. "At first I looked right past you, Laura, standing there by the pool gate. I almost didn't recognize you. You seemed lost in another world." There was an open invitation to confide in his voice.

I shook my head, not wanting to go into it. I said "Hi" to Annie, asked how she was feeling, told her I'd wrapped things up with the Colemans, at least for the moment. Grinning, she made the Hawaiian *shaka* sign with one hand, a non-contact pat on the back. I began to feel better.

For the rest of the afternoon we relaxed by the pool, getting up from time to time for a cooling dip, all three of us quietly occupied with our own thoughts. I shut out all speculation about the Colemans and Dr. Entwistle. There was nothing more I could do about them for the moment. The sensual pleasure of lying in the sun near Frank and Annie, suspended in a momentary lull with no rancor between us, helped me begin to accept my earlier realization. There was nothing I could do about that, either. Acceptance brought a small degree of peace.

I abandoned myself to the curative powers of the sun and water. By the time the shadows of the red hibiscus hedge lengthened across the pool deck, I felt refreshed and able to carry on in spite of the sadness that would always be with me.

As we stood to leave, Frank announced to Annie that he was taking her mother out to dinner that night. Annie acquiesced, shrugging her shoulders and saying she was tired anyway. It pleased me that Frank wanted time alone with me, even if it was only because of our mutual concern for Annie.

Dressing for the occasion gave my morale an unexpected boost, not to mention my stomach a few butterflies. I hadn't been out to dinner with a man other than clients since Frank left me. Certainly nothing that resembled a date. Of course, this was only my ex-husband, now married to someone else, but just the same I found myself caught up in a deliciously heightened sense of awareness. The swing from despair over Annie to what can only be described as excitement took me by surprise. I decided to go with the flow. I deserved a pleasant evening for a change.

I flipped through a dozen outfits in my closet before settling on a clingy, spaghetti-strapped number that was just a bit dressy, just a bit sexy, just a bit fun. The bias-cut skirt swished delightfully around my calves with every step. Topaz and pearl earrings set in gold, a long-ago gift from Frank, complemented the soft green-and-beige bamboo print. I gave my hair a couple of twirls with the curling iron, and stroked smoke on my eyelids. Luckily I was able to indulge in all this foolishness behind the closed bathroom door, away from my daughter's street-wise gaze. Emerging, I suddenly flushed with embarrassment at having gone to such trouble to please the man who had discarded me.

Annie quirked her head at me and grinned. "You look great, Mom," she said. I kissed her goodbye—she reluctantly let me—and almost made my escape. As I fished for my gold sandals amid the clutter of footwear at the front door, she called out, "Too bad it's hopeless."

I slipped through the apartment door and fell back against it, feeling wildly exposed in my flimsy frock and minimal underwear. Why hadn't I chosen something more modest, with a high neck and sleeves at the very least? But I couldn't go back in and change. That would confirm to Annie that she'd read me one hundred percent. Mortified, I made up my mind to keep the evening on an impersonal level, to focus on helping Annie, and not let one iota of my feelings for Frank show through.

Pacifica had always been one of our favorite restaurants. Polynesian in decor, understated and classy, it offered a superb selection of Pacific Rim specialties. Tucked in with minimal signage between a drugstore and a bank in a strip mall near my office, Pacifica had a steady local following that freed it from the seasonal ups and downs of resort restaurants. It was impossible to get in without making a reservation days in advance, but the owner/chef, now a globetrotting culinary celebrity, had once worked for Frank.

"She's not our Annie any more," I began as soon as we were seated, still smarting from the child's stinging remark.

"What do you mean?" he asked, accepting menus from the waiter.

"Our Annie has disappeared and won't be back. The girl who sat with us at the pool today is another person, with Annie's looks and memories, but with a whole new layer to her that we can't tap into. I realized it this afternoon, watching her through the pool fence. Remember you said I looked like I was in another world? I was. I had to retreat for a moment emotionally. I was just . . . overwhelmed with sadness. She's not the Annie who ran away, Frank. I never dreamed that her return would be like this. It all seems so . . . flat, so . . . meaningless."

He handed me a menu and nodded. "I think I know what you're saying. I feel it, too. For some crazy reason it makes me think of the reunification of Germany. It was one country and one people before the Second World War. After it was partitioned, the East and West Germans spent forty years thinking of themselves as different. Suddenly with President Reagan's 'Mr. Gorbachev, tear down this wall,' the country's back together again. The people on both sides suddenly found themselves struggling with the very change they had prayed for. They were strangers to each other and didn't know what to do about it."

I had to shake my head. Frank was an avid television documentary watcher. This made him a fascinating conversationalist, a riveting raconteur, always a hit at dinner parties. It was so like him to put our personal struggle with our daughter into global terms. In a way, aggrandizing it kept Annie's situation at a safe distance, made it a bit more manageable for him. It also made me wonder, not for the first time, if we were really going to be able to communicate about her.

"I don't know what to do, Frank. She's so closed off, won't tell me any more. Is she that way with you?"

"Yeah. But I don't see any great need to probe and ask too many questions. She's home, Laura. That's what counts. I'm not sure I really want to know what she was up to while she was away."

"Just let it go?" I was incredulous. I didn't think that was right, nor that I could do it. "Her health and the baby's health could be affected by how she's been living."

"Do we have a choice?" he asked. "If you obsess on trying to get her to talk, she'll shut down even tighter."

I hated his "father knows best" tone. I hated even more that he was sometimes right. "She needs counseling, Frank. Did you broach that with her?"

"No, not yet. Give me time."

"I can't even get her to tell me what she plans to do about the baby," I said. "If nothing else, don't we have a right to know that?"

"A right?" he asked in his patronizing manner.

"Well, yes. You'll waltz on home to Maine while I have to deal with it. If she keeps the child, which girls seem to do these days . . . why, I can't picture it. She's immature and disinterested, to say the least. What kind of a mother will she be? And what will I do—stand by watching, ringing my hands, trying not to interfere when her lifestyle is anathema to me?"

Frank busied himself slathering roasted red pepper pâté on a paper-thin square of *lavosh*.

"Then there's adoption," I continued, determined to get this all hashed out. "If she puts the child up for adoption, that'll be a staggering emotional loss. Even if she doesn't seem to care, *I* do. It's my grandchild. If she's going to give it away, I need to prepare myself, Frank. I already love that little one." My eyes teared up. I couldn't continue.

"What's the third option?" he asked gently, breaking off another piece of *lavosh* while the waiter served our drinks, a Corona Light for Frank, a Margarita for me. I took an icy, reviving sip.

"What if she keeps the baby, then can't—or won't—cope? There I'll be, picking up the pieces. Frank, I've raised three children, part of the time by myself. God help me, I don't want to do it again."

"Give it a rest, Laura. You're tying your underwear into knots without giving Annie any credit at all. She's an adult, for God's sake. She's taken care of herself for three years without any help from you."

"Yeah, and how?" I asked.

"Please, Laura, let's not go back to that again. We don't know, do we? Honestly, think about it for a minute. We don't know. You've assumed the worst, that she sold drugs, prostituted, I don't know . . . what's worse than that? She probably did something totally ordinary, cleaned hotel rooms or worked in a store, kept herself afloat in a perfectly acceptable way. We just don't know. We may never know. Let it go."

I looked away, unable to respond. The chef waved at us from his charcoal grill behind the cocktail bar. I smiled back, but didn't return the wave, hoping that would stop him from coming over to chat.

Taking my silence for acquiescence, Frank plunged on. "As for her plans for the baby, maybe she hasn't made any yet. Maybe she really doesn't know what she wants. Maybe all this time she's concentrated on keeping herself together and getting home. That must have been hard for her, don't you think? It's probably hard for her to get used to living with a parent again after all that time on her own, too. Cut her some slack, Laura. Let her work things out at her own pace now that she's safe and being cared for. She'll come 'round before the baby's born. Don't put so much energy into looking for trouble."

I hate noble sentiments, particularly when they aren't mine. Was he right? Annie and I had been on a collision course since the day she was born. Could I step back now and allow her to be an adult? Of course, but it would be nice if she met me halfway.

"Tell me, Frank, why did you marry me in the first place?"

His head jerked at the abrupt transition.

"At breakfast the other day, I asked you why you married me. You skirted the question. It's time you gave me a complete and honest answer." My emotions churned just below the surface. If they were going to erupt, let them erupt on my behalf for a change, not Annie's.

Staring at me intently, he pushed his chair back and crossed his legs. Dressed in navy-blue slacks and a light-blue oxford-cloth dress shirt, open at the neck, sleeves rolled halfway up his forearms, he looked like a television anchorman two minutes before camera time. Folding his napkin, he set it on the table beside his plate. "You really want to hear this?" he asked.

I stuck my chin out defiantly. "I do."

He looked at me earnestly, as if preparing to report on an earthquake in Bangladesh. His fresh-shaved cheeks were sleek and smooth. Not a tied-back hair on his head was out of place. "Okay." He picked up his napkin and wiped his perfectly clean mouth. He glanced away for a moment, then returned my gaze with a disarming degree of uneasiness. "Well, you probably didn't know at the time, but I was seeing another girl our senior year." He paused to see how I sustained the blow. If I had been in a more generous frame of mind, I would have said he looked acutely discomfited.

"Cantaloupes," I stated.

"What?" He uncrossed his legs and leaned forward, elbows on the table.

"Cantaloupes. I knew all about her."

"Cantaloupes?"

"She was stacked, as we used to say in those days. They looked like cantaloupes. I assume that was the attraction?"

"Jesus, Laura. Give a guy a break. Do you want to hear the story or not?"

"Sorry. Go ahead."

"Her name was Angela." Frank's voice softened as he said it. My sorority sisters and I had been so charmed by the sobriquet, "Cantaloupes," that we had never sleuthed out her real name. Angela. I hated it.

"She was from Ames, Iowa, just like me. We knew each other in high school, although not very well. We connected up at college, and by the end of my junior year it was pretty serious."

The first bites of my lobster and mandarin orange salad were doing funny things in my stomach, but it was too late to stop now. "I suppose you spent your junior summer together at home?"

He pushed back and balanced on the two rear legs of his chair as he had every morning of our married life at breakfast while reading the newspaper. "Yes. It was the most fantastic summer of my life. We were both working, me on my dad's farm, she in a shop in town. Our evenings together were golden. Right out of a movie." His eyes drifted into the past. Coughing, he hastened to add, "Don't forget, you and I hadn't met yet."

I flashed on Sandra Dee and Troy Donahue, naked on a beach blanket in a cornfield. Not a pretty picture. I could barely force myself to ask the next question. "Why did you bother with me, when you were obviously in love with someone else?"

"Honest to God, I met you for tutoring with nothing else in mind. I figured you could get me a D in that wretched French class. Period."

"Until when?"

He chuckled, then nodded at the waiter who stood by with bowls of lemongrass consommé. "You were the most puzzling girl I'd ever met. So serious, so earnest, so goddamn determined to get me through all that *parlez-vous*-ing if it killed us both." Grinning, he added, "I guess it became a game to see how far you would go."

My eyes stung. "Until you scored graduation night?"

"No, please, Laura. I meant with the French. I really enjoyed your company. Please don't believe I was trifling. I wasn't."

"But what about Can . . . gela?" I could barely speak her name.

"You've got me there. We were actually planning to get married."

Steel bands constricted around my chest. "All along?"

"All along." He studied the lemongrass slivers floating in his soup.

"How could you have led me on so, while you were seriously committed to her?"

"Honestly, in my own defense, I don't believe I did lead you on. You and I went out to a movie, a walk, a soda in the student union maybe once a week. Some phone calls in between. Not much more than that."

"But for me that was a big deal."

"Laura, you were such an innocent. In some ways, you still are. That's a large part of your charm. I'd never met a girl who was so totally trusting and . . . and . . . *grateful* for the smallest amount of attention."

I was mortified. "You make me sound pathetic."

"Not at all. You were young, innocent, delightful in your very own way."

"But it was Angela . . ."

"Yeah." He looked off into the distance again. "So after graduation I went home to Iowa. You know that. I worked on the farm until we got the fall crop in. After that, I intended to go to the city and start with the Bureau of Agriculture. Angela had one more year of college, and then we'd get married."

"You wrote to me in Honolulu that summer. A number of times. How come you didn't tell me?"

He looked chagrined. "Chicken, I guess. I sensed it might hurt you."

"Well, you were right about that. Did you ever plan to tell me? Were you just going to keep me dangling?" My sense of outrage grew. How could I have been such an idiot?

"I didn't know you were dangling. Your letters were just as friendly as mine. Nothing more. I figured we were buddies, that eventually the letters would peter out and we'd be done with it."

"Even after we made love that last night at college?" I whispered.

He looked deeply into my eyes. His were soft and sincere, with little lines I had never noticed radiating from the outer edges. They added to Frank's new look of maturity. "Do you want me to tell you I regretted making love with you that night? No way. And I don't think you did, either. It was fantastic. But it didn't mean I was serious."

"But *I* was! Totally serious! You were my first, Frank." As if that pulled any weight with a guy.

All those years, I had kept to myself that I had gotten pregnant that night. The secret lodged in a deep part of my soul, a place I'd never opened to anyone. I hugged that secret close. It was mine, only mine, a part of myself I would never share with Frank.

"So what happened?" I asked, anxious to focus on a less threatening part of the past. "How did you end up on my doorstep with a ring in your hand?" An unpleasant detail occurred to me. "I hope it wasn't the ring you bought for her. That would be unbearable."

We both leaned back to allow the waiter to remove the soup bowls and serve our main course, fresh mahi mahi for both of us, his with an oriental glaze and mine with citrus and champagne *buerre blanc*.

"Give me a little more credit than that," he replied as soon as the waiter retreated. "No, I bought that ring for you after Angela told me she'd fallen in love with one of her professors. She'd decided to return to the West Coast to be with him."

Aha. Now we were getting to the good part. The part where Frank got hurt, too. Things were looking up. "Go on," I said, a note of smug triumph in my voice.

He raised his hands in a gesture of hopelessness. "It destroyed me. I simply had no idea she was seeing him. Apparently it had been going on for some time. She was sleeping with both of us that whole last semester. He must have known about me, because at the end of the school year, he told her she had to make a choice. She came back to Ames for the summer, acting as if nothing was amiss. We banged each other senseless from June through September, if you really want to know. Then she told me. And she left."

"So you threw caution to the wind and looked up poor little Laura." All those years I had walked so proudly as Frank's wife, when in truth our marriage had been second best. I realized then that an instinctive caution had kept me from questioning Frank's arrival on my doorstep. I'd accepted things at face value and thanked God every night for the miracle of this man in my life. Throughout our years together, I'd been secretly afraid that if I delved too deeply into his past, the miraculous bubble would burst. I hadn't dared ask. Now I knew why. With nothing more to lose, I let anger propel me on.

"Was that it, then? You felt sorry for me?"

"Don't, Laura. It wasn't like that. I had to get away. Every inch of Ames reminded me of Angela. I couldn't stay around. As for my city job, I was doing it for her, so we'd have a home set up with some money in the bank by the time she graduated. None of it mattered anymore. I was completely lost."

A woman at the next table threw back her head and laughed at something her companion said. How dare she find anything amusing here.

"About five days later," Frank continued, "here comes another letter from Laura. Sweet, uncomplicated Laura in Hawaii. About as far away from Ames as you could get. This time, without anything different being said, the tone of your letter changed. It seemed more than just a friendly letter. Somehow I understood that you were waiting for me. It seems crazy in this day of ten-cents-a-minute long-distance phone calls, but back then we only called overseas if somebody died, remember?"

I nodded.

Frank continued. "Besides, if I picked up the phone, I was afraid you'd tell me my impression was mistaken and not to come. All I could think of was getting away from Iowa and starting a new life, in Hawaii yet. I thought you'd be a kind and loving person to start that new life with. If you'd turned me down, I'd have enlisted right then and there, volunteered for Vietnam."

My eyes sought his. "Even though you didn't love me."

"I did love you, Laura, in a different way. You were easy to be with. I thought we could make a go of it. And we did."

I straightened up in my chair, tightening my anger around me. "Until you got tired of me."

"It happened gradually, Laura. In the beginning, I found you enchanting. You were so refreshing, so eager to please. So bloody different from Angela. She was—if you really want to know—demanding, moody, and downright selfish. I soon realized what a favor she'd done me by breaking things off. With you, I could think about other things, like my work. I wasn't always turning myself inside out to keep you happy, like I was with her. I never seemed to be able to please her, no matter how hard I tried. You, on the other hand, seemed delighted to be my wife and the mother of our children. You kept a lovely home, entertained magnificently, got the children to their ball games and hula lessons, did their homework with them. You left me free to climb the ladder at the hotel. That became all-consuming. You remember. Once I found my niche, I burned with ambition. Part of my strength was knowing I had a loving wife and blessed tranquility to come home to." His eyes slid away into memories again. This time I knew they were nostalgic ones of the five of us together. He'd never guess the price I paid for that tranquility.

"I loved it, Frank. I was deliriously happy. It was just the kind of life I'd dreamed of. A real family, surrounded by friendly neighbors, pot-lucking back and forth. So different from growing up all alone at Pua Olena . . . until it ended."

The waiter removed our plates. Frank pulled out his credit card. I beckoned the waiter back and ordered a Keoki coffee. No matter how much it hurt, we weren't finished yet.

"Holly," I prompted. "We aren't leaving until you finish the story."

Frank flashed two fingers, signaling the waiter for a Keoki coffee for himself, too.

"How to explain Holly. She happened. I was a goner the moment I sat down next to her on that flight home from San Francisco. One chapter of my life slammed shut, and another one opened. There was no going back. I'm happy with her, Laura, in a very different way. She's an intellectual challenge, not that you aren't smart, but she's got a mind like a laser. And she's fanatically devoted to Georgie."

"Not that *I* wasn't devoted to *our* children."

"Of course you were. But the need wasn't the same, was it?"

My thoughts flew to Annie. "Maybe it was, Frank. Maybe we just didn't know it at the time. Is it possible Annie's autistic, too? Not to the degree Georgie is, but it would explain some of her behavior. I did some research when I heard about Georgie's problems, and discovered that autism has many manifestations and degrees of severity. What if Annie were on the near end of the bell-shaped curve, 'borderline,' as they call it? It could explain why she was such a non-responsive baby, why she was so fearful of change, why she never learned to read effectively."

I expected him to be shocked, but he only stared at me for a long moment, considering carefully before he replied. "I don't know. It could certainly be possible. And it *would* explain some of her behavior, now that you mention it." He paused, as if finally absorbing the full impact of what I had said. "You're right—autism does have all kinds of variations, from very mild to severe. She was so different from the boys, wasn't she, and so difficult. In some ways she's like Georgie, although nowhere near as extreme. It's all so puzzling, isn't it? All the more reason for her to get counseling. Maybe if we can get a correct diagnosis, it won't be too late for constructive therapy, if there is any. I'll definitely pursue that angle. I'm sorry, Laura. I've been so focused on Georgie that I never took my thoughts any further regarding Annie. Perhaps some of the things Holly has learned will help." He looked at me in a sincere, compassionate manner. "You did the best you could with her, Laura. I'm sorry I left so much of it up to you. We had no idea what we were really up against. None of this is your fault."

That meant more to me than he could possibly have known. For a moment I simply looked away. Then I smiled and said, "Thank you. It means a lot that we can share this, and that you understand. Now go on with your story. I still want to hear it."

He took a long drink of beer. "All right, if you're sure." I nodded.

"Meeting Holly made me realize I'd become bored. Both at home and on the job. I'd worked up to general manager of the best resort hotel on Maui. There was nothing more to strive for in Hawaii. I was at the top of my profession, and not yet forty years old. Holly presented a challenging escape on several levels. Sophisticated, fascinating, a world traveler, an international journalist. Italian, of all things, a real New Yorker. And me, a farm boy from Iowa. Add to that the opportunity to try my skills in

New York—Mecca for a hotelier. Of course, I didn't see it in such clear terms then, but basically that's what it was all about."

"Well, you certainly found your challenges." When I'd first heard that Frank and Holly suspected their son Georgie was autistic, I experienced a secret shot of satisfaction. Life swings around and slaps you nicely if you get too far out of line. But when I learned how serious it was, I experienced genuine compassion. Frank and Holly were just beginning to face the seriousness of Georgie's condition when Frank and I hit the skids with Annie. Nobody deserves that kind of double jeopardy.

My voice softened. "How is Georgie?"

Sadness clouded his face. "Some days I feel we're making progress. Others, I truly believe it's hopeless. I hate to see Holly beating herself up so much. She's relentless in seeking out experts all over the country. All those journalistic investigative skills laser-focused on one quest—finding a cure for autism. Being self-employed, not much of it falls under our medical coverage. Of course, if she finds a solution, it'll all be worth it. But it's taking a toll on her, big time."

"I'm really sorry, Frank. It must be every bit as hard on you."

"I love him, Laura, as much as I love our three. It's just so sad he'll never enjoy the simple pleasures of life, at least, as we know them."

He paused to sign the credit card slip. "So now you know the tawdry story of my love life, past and present. Satisfied?"

"Not at all. But at least I know. There's some comfort in that."

He reached across the table and put his hand over mine. "I never meant to hurt you, Laura. I hope you know that."

I closed my eyes, feeling the warmth of his palm for a moment, then withdrew mine, picked up my napkin from my lap, folded it and placed it on the table. "Well, you did, Frank. You hurt me a lot. I hope *you* know *that*. But we've both moved on. So be it."

He flashed me a grateful smile. As we exited the restaurant, he put his arm around me. I felt defused, as if a huge emotional charge had been released.

***

The mellow, bitter-sweet mood of shared confidences lasted only as long as the drive home. Serenity deserted me the moment I opened my apartment door. It was dark and Annie was gone. Her bed in the den was mussed; a damp towel was draped across my office chair. She couldn't have taken my car. I'd driven it to meet Frank at the restaurant. Wherever she went, she must have walked.

I pictured her among the navel-pierced, dreadlocked teens sauntering up and down South Kihei Road, half dressed and looking for action. If that's what Annie was after, I had no doubt she would find it a short two blocks from home. Annoyance fighting with panic, I called Frank, begging him to go with me to look for her.

"Laura, for Christ's sake, leave her be. We're not going crazy over this. She's nineteen. She knows how to take care of herself. Besides, where would we even start looking?"

"But what if she's gone for drugs?" I pleaded.

"Are you going to keep her locked in every minute of every day? You'll drive yourself nuts. Leave it be. Go to sleep, Laura. The next thing you hear will be Annie letting herself in, clean and sober, I promise. She probably went to a movie."

Right. When would Frank begin to understand his daughter?

The next thing I heard was not Annie letting herself in, but the phone shrilling on the bedside table near my ear. The red numerals on the clock said 3:04 AM. My heart began pumping like a bicycle racer's pedals. *Oh, God, don't let this be the police . . . or the hospital.*

I scrambled for the receiver. It was Frank, sounding horribly shaken. "Laura, get over here, now. I know where Annie's been."

I clutched the sheet to my heart. "Is she hurt? Is the baby okay?"

"No, I mean . . . I don't know. I mean, I don't know where she is tonight, but I know where she's been these last three years. Get over here, fast. Don't waste a minute."

I heard the television murmur in the background, followed by the sound of Frank vomiting.

CHAPTER 15

Frank opened the condo door immediately at my knock. His face was drawn and pale. I recoiled at the smell of his breath.

"You'd better sit down," he said. He pulled a rattan chair in front of the TV for me. The set was on, the screen a solid blue. Before I could ask what in the world this was all about, he sat on the arm of the chair and clicked the VCR play button.

At first I couldn't make out what was happening. There was a lot of fuzzy, flesh-colored movement, with oddly dissonant piano music in the background, banging away in mini-crescendos. Then the camera focused in a little tighter on something that seemed to be pumping up and down. As the camera pulled away, I saw that it was moving in and out. That was enough for me. I arose from the chair, highly indignant.

"You got me all the way over here in the middle of the night to see a porn flick? How dare you?" I was incensed, betrayed by our honest exchange at dinner, assuming he had deliberately softened me up for a clumsy seduction attempt.

He grabbed my arm. His voice was like cement. "Sit down and be quiet. You'll see in a second."

Still seething, I did as I was told. The camera panned back from the close-up . . . and there was our daughter . . . our daughter. Stretched out unclothed on a messy bed, wrists chained above her head to an ornate brass headboard, being simultaneously slapped and fucked by a naked madman wearing a checkered Middle-Eastern headdress. The man was old and dark, gray-bearded and disgustingly hairy.

I catapulted to my feet. My hands flew to my mouth, but not soon enough to stop a deep-throated scream. Frank jumped up and snapped off the VCR. My mind went blank. I staggered backward, lost my balance, and fell toward the chair. Frank leapt forward to steady me.

"What does this mean?" I asked, grasping the chair arms for support.

"What do you think it fucking means?" he shouted. "Isn't it obvious?"

Frozen, unable to compute, all I could do was stare, hunched over, at the empty blue screen. With all my might, I willed it to come alive again with *our* movies of Annie, running on the lawn with her brothers at Pua Olena, or frolicking in the surf at Kamaole beach. I could not look at Frank. Lost innocence, gone forever. A full body slam could not have hit me harder.

Finally I managed to rasp, "Where did you get this tape?"

"Annie left some of her shit here. I surprised her, I guess, when she was looking for a hiding place. She stuffed it in the bathroom cabinet, behind the towels." He gestured wildly down the hall. "I was getting a clean one and the fucking thing fell out on my foot."

The memory of Annie at the airport and later at my apartment angrily guarding her backpack flashed through my mind. "The backpack. That must have been what she had in her backpack. She wouldn't let me get near it. But why? Why would she keep such a piece of filth?"

"Why would she be *in* such a piece of filth?" he countered.

"My God, do you think that's how she lived? Making porn films? Maybe she *was* kidnapped, forced into it." If she'd been an unwilling victim perhaps my mind could cope.

Frank was ready to commit murder. "I don't give a fuck." He paced the room, back and forth. "Who are those mother-fucking bastards? How could they do this to my daughter?"

I could only shake my head. There had been no clues to its origin at the beginning of the tape. The empty sleeve was on the coffee table. I saw none there, either.

Stabbing the air with the remote like a latter-day Don Quixote, he fast-forwarded the film, looking for some kind of identifying information. I turned my back, unable to look. I didn't need to. Annie's image beneath that monster was seared on my brain, her eyes so terribly vacant. If I hadn't see them blink, I might have thought her unconscious. Surely she'd been drugged.

"Aha!" Frank shouted, pointing at the TV screen. "There it is. DreamSeed Tours, with a Los Angeles P.O. box number." He scribbled it on the condo's courtesy notepad. Then he grabbed the phone and started in on the unfortunate long-distance operator. "If it's not in L.A., try Hollywood, Bel Air, Santa Monica, you dumb bitch! All the movie guys live there!" He kept bellowing the name, DreamSeed Tours, as if the operator could find it if he shouted loud enough.

Finally, I began to focus again. "Frank, for goodness sake, you'll never find them in a directory. This is obviously an underground operation. The L.A. post office box is probably just a front."

Shooting me an icy look, he yelled, "You can't get a goddamn mainland phone number anywhere now that they've deregulated the fucking long-distance carriers!" With that, he ripped the phone from the wall and hurled it across the room. He fumed and fussed, threatening to kill them all before sunrise if he could just get his hands on the dirty bastards. Finally he gave the phone a swift kick that sent it ripping through the lanai screen door. He threw himself onto the couch, his face buried in a pillow, his entire body shaking with rage.

I sat beside him and put my trembling hand on his shoulder, to let him know I was still there, that I, too, was dying inside. The next thing I knew I was in his arms. We held each other on the couch and cried. Oh, God, how could our little girl have come to this?

I stayed with Frank for three nights. I wanted to be held and comforted by the one person who shared my pain, my bewilderment, my guilt. I didn't give a damn that he was married to someone else. He was my husband first and still would be if I'd had anything to say about it.

God help me, I did not want to see Annie. The truth was too big, too monstrous. I didn't know what to do with it, nor how to face her. The implications of the video were so devastating that I could only retreat into the circle of Frank's arms. We made love with an abandon I'd never experienced as his wife, a passion that startled and thrilled me. We drowned in shared sensations, animal feelings that blotted out the horror. In the end, however, nothing could erase the stark image of our chained, spread-eagle daughter copulating with a hairy, dishtowel-headed sadist.

We called the hospital every morning, and the police, to inquire if Annie had been injured or arrested. No news. The police promised to keep an eye out for her, but we agreed that an all-out investigation was not warranted yet. Combing the streets would only alienate her further, as word circulated that her parents were looking for her. Our best chance of finding her was to allow her the freedom to come home on her own. When she did, we would somehow come to grips with the nightmare video that played and replayed in our minds.

Frank went to my apartment daily to see if Annie had come home. I held my breath each time he returned. There were no signs of her. Her bed remained mussed, the dried towel draped on the back of the chair. Each time, I was conscience-stricken with relief.

Frank had planned to stay on Maui only a week, but he postponed his return so he could see this through. I was grateful beyond words. Because it happened on my watch, I had carried the entire burden of responsibility for Annie's disappearance. It seemed the height of luxury to sink into Frank's arms, lay my cheek against the soft hair on his chest, mentally detach and let him take charge. Some deep, inner self-protective instinct swamped me, allowing me to forget that my lonely responsibilities were the result of Frank leaving me in the first place. It didn't matter. I needed him. Would I be sorry later? This was now. Frank was the only reality.

Two days passed in a golden haze. All burdens lifted from my shoulders. I drifted in the lightness of not being in charge. Helpless until Annie chose to surface again, I floated along in a foggy limbo, leaving Frank only to conduct essential business.

Late Sunday afternoon I dragged myself to the office. Randy Entwistle caught me by phone while I was sorting through my mail. Was it only two days ago that hearing from her meant life and death? I forced myself to pay attention.

"I'll be at the property for the inspection tomorrow morning," she said, "but only if I can get Moana out."

"What do you mean?" That familiar knot tightened in my stomach. "Haven't you told her the house is sold yet?"

"Not . . . exactly." I pictured Randy twisting the phone cord around her index finger, caught like a mongoose snared between her actions and her fears.

"Well, for heaven's sake, when do you plan to tell her?"

I heard a whistling intake of breath through the gap in her teeth. "Uh . . . when the time is right. Yeah, I'll tell her when the time is right. Don't push me."

"Don't push? Look, you've got to tell her—right away! She's the key to this whole thing. What about her deed? Any luck finding that? And the tenant's business in the—"

"Stop. I said don't push me." She hung up.

Thoroughly exasperated, I hurried home to Frank. He pulled the drapes around our third night together.

Carlton Tanimoto met me at Randy's gate Monday morning, as planned. He was short, bowlegged, and an avid fisherman. His great joy in life was setting four or five long-line fishing poles on the beach in the evening, then stretching out on the sand beside them, snoozing to the slap of the shore break until he heard a strike bell ring. Today he wore wrinkled orange shorts, a faded purple Nagasako Fish Market T-shirt and rubber slippers. Dry sand dusted his feet, a dead giveaway of his nocturnal activities.

"So, what? Catch anything last night?" I asked while scouting the driveway below for signs of life. The property appeared to be deserted—no cars, no people, no activity. The only curious item was a mid-sized cardboard box, top flaps tucked in but not taped shut, sitting outside the closed garage door. Was this my opportunity to sidle up to the carton, take a quick peek inside, and discover what was happening inside the garage?

Carlton slapped the oversize white cooler in the back of his pickup truck. "Yeah, I caught one big *ulua*," he answered in Pidgin. "Sold 'em to the fish market on my way over here. Plenty tourists gonna eat good tonight." His Oriental eyes sparkled with triumph. Was it the thrill of the catch, I wondered, or the considerable sum he received for his effort? Probably both, I suspected.

"One thing I need to tell you before we begin," I said to him, pointing down the hill, "the garage is locked. One of the residents is running a business from it. Nobody knows what it is, but there's an outside possibility it's a drug lab. Check out that box down there by the garage door. It could be filled with contraband. I'm gonna take a look." I bent down, put one leg through the horizontal bars of the fence, and slid through.

Scowling, he said, "Try wait one minute. Dangerous, Laura."

I straightened up on the other side. "Nah, I'm only going look inside the box."

He regarded me skeptically. "You better not. What if the guy hear you and come out with one gun?"

"And what about you w'en you go inspect? Same t'ing."

"I can handle. If the garage stay locked, I no go in. Period. I make one note of it inside my report, and *pau*. Believe me, I never take no chance. And mo' bettah you no take chance, too. Jes in case."

I squinted into the sun to study his face. Every trace of humor was erased. "You're the first person who takes me seriously about this."

"Sure, I take you serious. But I jes do my job. That's it. No sked 'em." He grinned, unable to remain somber for long. "*Ulua* running again tonight, you know. I no miss that, no matter what."

I could only shake my head. At that moment, the mailman pulled up in his red, white, and blue truck. Leaving it running, he got out and eased himself through the fence bars a few feet from me. He jogged down the driveway to the garage, picked up the cardboard box, and trotted back up the driveway with it. As he squeezed through the fence again, he jerked his chin in greeting. Then he tossed the box into the truck, climbed in the cab and took off down the road. There went my chance to play girl detective.

I turned to Carlton. "You see? I'm not making this up. Something's cooking in that garage."

"I jes going do my job, okay? I let you folks worry 'bout dat."

As the mailman's truck disappeared around the corner, Randy arrived in her old maroon van. The three of us crunched down the driveway to the house, where Carlton got to work immediately on the exterior. Randy and I slipped out of our shoes at the front door and went inside. Finally, I thought, I'm going to have an uninterrupted opportunity to see the entire house. My two previous visits had been disconcertingly brief. As we walked down the hallway toward the kitchen, I mentioned the mailman and the box pickup.

"That's exactly what happens," she replied. "Prakash sets the box out, takes off for the day—God knows where—and the mailman picks it up and off it goes. It's just too casual an arrangement to be drugs, Laura."

I shrugged my shoulders, not knowing how to respond.

They say a woman will buy a house if she loves the kitchen. Diana had done cartwheels over this one. Now I saw why: stainless steel appliances, granite counters, and polished koa wood cabinets, some with showcase glass fronts. A comfy breakfast table nestled in a bay window overlooking the terrace and gulch. What staggered the eye and tugged at the heart, though, was the huge brick fireplace at the far end of the room, with antique copper pots lining the mantel and two easy chairs fronting the hearth. It was right out of a colonial mansion.

"My heavens," was all I could say, momentarily transported to another time and place.

"I know," Randy said, stopping beside me. "Everyone goes nuts over this kitchen. Mother is a pioneer fanatic. This was her dream. She loved sitting by the fire, reading all that westward-ho stuff. She shipped crates of U.S. history books with her when she moved back to the mainland."

"I can't think of anything cozier during the rainy season," I marveled. "It's perfect."

"Yeah, we practically lived in this room. Dinners on our laps . . ." Sadness crept into her voice, as she remembered happier times when her parents shared her life. I wondered if the cozy little dinners had continued with Moana. Somehow I couldn't picture it, but you never know. Reluctant to break the spell, I gestured toward the breakfast nook. "Let's sit down. There's lots to go over."

We sat on opposite sides of the table with the full panorama of the gulch visible through the bay window. Moving aside a bunch of purple bougainvillea in a ceramic vase, Randy handed me her completed disclosure statement, which included mention of the mystery business in the garage and Moana's claim of ownership. She had indicated the house was in good repair, that there was nothing, at least to her knowledge, of concern. We'd have to wait for Carlton's confirmation. I thanked her for her diligent effort and slipped the disclosure into my file.

I informed Randy that the buyers had performed on all their contractual obligations so far, including applying for their loan and contacting their insurance carrier. Randy listened attentively but showed no emotion. Was she pleased that matters were progressing? Apparently it was going to be her secret.

"What about Moana?" I asked. "Does she know?"

"No, no, not yet. I've been too busy. Mastectomies, hip replacements, hysterectomies, tummy tucks. It never stops." Randy started pinching off the bougainvillea blossoms, one by one, and shredding them into a little pile on the table.

My bare toes curled in sudden awareness of the chilly slate floor. "Where is she today?"

Randy glanced toward the door. "Yesterday was her birthday. I gave her a gift certificate to the Green Rose Trellis and told her to go buy a new outfit this morning."

"How could you be sure she'd go?"

"I couldn't. We lucked out." Relief showed in her tired gray eyes. Inwardly I groaned. What if Moana had not gone along with her flimsy plan?

Before I could work up an answer to that, Carlton walked in and stopped dead on his unshod feet. His stocky bare legs looked like a pair of black-haired daikon radishes. "Holy mahi mahi," he exclaimed. "Some kitchen."

Randy and I laughed. The pressure eased a bit. "Seriously, you folks could cook one whole cow inside that fireplace."

"We tried once," Randy replied. "A hind-quarter, actually. Huge mess. Barbecuing outdoors on the propane grill works much better."

I could picture that—a chance to get her hands on the meat, while also manning the gas.

Carlton grinned, scratched his head, then glanced at his notebook. "So, I know the garage stay locked, but I cannot get inside the bedrooms, either. You folks got the keys?"

Randy looked chagrined. "Ah, keys . . . to the bedrooms?"

"Yeah, the doors stay locked, all three down here and the master upstairs. I need for get in. What you want me for do?"

She simply stared at him.

"Randy?" I inquired. "Why would all the bedroom doors be locked?"

"Ah . . ." She squirmed in her chair and let loose another rain of shredded bougainvillea blossoms.

"Randy?"

"She . . . she rents them out."

"Who rents them out?"

"Moana."

"She rents out the bedrooms?" I tried, but failed, to keep the surprise out of my voice.

"Yeah, at least . . . the three downstairs ones. I guess . . . I guess the tenants have their own keys."

"You mean there are other people living here besides Moana and Prakash?" That explained the two Maui cruisers I'd seen parked near the garage on Saturday. My problems had just multiplied exponentially.

"A-Apparently."

"But it's your house."

"Ah . . . I guess . . . I guess she wants the money."

I glanced at Carlton for help. He only stared, eyes as wide as Japanese eyes can get.

I turned back to Randy. "Wait a minute. You mean she rents out the three downstairs bedrooms and keeps the money? In your house?"

"Yeah." The last remaining blossom fell from her fingers onto the pile of purple debris on the table in front of her. "They aren't here much. When they are, they pretty much keep to themselves."

For the moment, I was speechless. Carlton licked his pencil, peering at Randy as if she were a newly discovered alien species. While I appreciated his unspoken validation of my own opinion, my scattered thoughts began to focus on getting him out of the room as quickly as possible. Right now I needed to help Randy save face, even though she didn't deserve it. Allowing Carlton to witness any further humiliation might cause her to shut down, eroding any hope of meaningful communication.

I switched on my most ingratiating smile. "Carlton, sweetie, could you find something else to inspect for the moment? Like the toothbrush racks and toilet-paper holders in the bathrooms? Randy and I will figure out what to do about the bedroom locks and come find you."

Scratching his salt-and-pepper crewcut, Carlton shrugged and sauntered out of the room. I knew exactly what he was thinking: *Haoles . . . what can you expect?*

I turned back to Randy. "Let me get this straight: Moana collects the rent, keeps the money, and you pay the mortgage?"

"Yeah." She sank lower and lower in her seat, too embarrassed to look at me.

"And what about the master bedroom? Why would that be locked?"

"Uh, Moana sleeps there, with Prakash . . . when he's in town. They've locked me out." She lifted her jaw, daring me to take issue with that.

"All right, then. May I ask where you're sleeping?"

She winced. Her gaze darted out the bay window toward the ravine, then back to the kitchen, flicking from fridge to island chopping block to fireplace—anything to keep from looking me in the eye. Finally she focused on the pile of decimated purple blossoms in front of her. She swept them off the table with one swift hand and watched them drift like confetti onto the uneven stone floor.

"Oh . . . here and there," she finally said, her voice thick with defeat. "Wherever."

"What do you mean, here and there?"

"Mostly on the beach."

"I'm sorry?" I gestured wildly to include the house and the acres beyond. "You own this huge fantastic property, and you sleep on the beach?"

She broke a twig from the denuded bougainvillea and began to snap it into tiny bits. "Yeah, well, you've seen what Mo's like. I told you, that's why I put the house on the market. She's dug in like a tick, Laura. She's destroyed my life." Her weary eyes begged me to understand. I found it difficult.

"Sounds like she's got a good thing going here, Randy." That was the understatement of the year. "But, look. Those three extra evictions could blow the closing date clear out of the water. You'd better get your attorney working on them, pronto."

She looked unhappy, but nodded her head.

"Not that it's any of my business," I continued, "but with such tenuous sleeping arrangements, how do you manage to function at the hospital every day?"

"Most of the time it's okay. I can sleep anywhere. You learn that during residency."

"What about showering and staying clean?"

"There are showers in the locker room at the hospital. No sweat." She raised her eyebrows, as if expecting praise for this clever arrangement.

No sweat, indeed. I'd be terrified to find myself on the operating table at the mercy of an anesthesiologist who spent her nights on the beach.

"Do any of your colleagues know you're in such a pickle?" I asked.

She leaped up and thrashed out of the breakfast nook, jolting the table with her knee. I grabbed the vase of naked bougainvillea twigs as it tipped. "No!" she shouted. "For God's sake, you keep your mouth shut. Not a word to anyone. I'd be ruined. My career is all I have left."

"All right, all right, simmer down." Gingerly, I set the vase back on the table, vowing to make sure I didn't need an operation any time soon.

Gripping the edge of the table, she leaned toward me. Her words sputtered through her shingle teeth. "Just get this place sold, that's all I want. Get it sold, and get Moana out of my life."

I gathered my papers and slid them into the folder. I only signed up to help my clients purchase the house. I didn't bargain on having to deal with the seller's abysmal personal life as well. But if that's what it took to close the sale . . . . "Okay, but what about those keys?" I asked. "How are we going to get Carlton into the bedrooms?"

The windows to the tenants' rooms were open, so Carlton only needed to jimmy off the screens with a screwdriver, with Randy's permission. It occurred to me that we might be trespassing on the tenants, but I banished that troublesome thought in the interests of expediency.

Leaving him to clamber in, Randy led me back into the house and up the magnificent, curved koa stairway. She stood on the second floor landing and rattled the knob on the master suite's double doors. It was definitely locked. Undaunted, she strode to a window at the far end of the landing, deftly removed the screen, and scissored over the windowsill onto the roof. I stuck my head out and watched, astounded, as she shuffled her way expertly along the steeply sloping green ceramic tiles, hugging the exterior wall like a gecko.

"Don't worry, I've done this before," she shouted as she disappeared around the corner. "She never shuts the bathroom window."

I held my breath until I heard a crash and a thud, followed by a curse on the other side of the wall. Bathroom windows are not noted for their convenient height. Rubbing her elbow, Randy opened the massive double doors and ushered me in. Her eyes gleamed with triumph. "Moana doesn't win every time," she declared, stepping back so I could enjoy the impact of the impressive suite.

The focal point was a hand-carved teak bed of extraordinary beauty, set diagonally in the corner. Mosquito netting, tied back with lavender silk bows, draped the four posts. I ran my hand over the gracefully curved footboard and sighed. A stately armoire and two matching dressers stood against the opposite walls. If Prakash had brought this furniture from the Far East, the man had taste plus the means to indulge it.

Randy had stepped out of sight. I wandered into the master bathroom, a discovery in itself. Everything was set on white marble, with the commode tucked discreetly behind a curved, glass-block wall. There I found Randy standing on the toilet in a state of high agitation, trying to replace the window screen she had knocked out during her precipitous entrance. Her hands shook so badly, she dropped the screen each time she tried to fit it into the frame.

"Moana will kill me if she finds out I got in," she whimpered, fading into a crouch on the toilet seat. I shooed her away, picked up the screen, climbed aboard, and snapped it in with one easy thrust.

CHAPTER 16

Driving home, I puzzled once again over Randy Entwistle's crippling paranoia. Here was a respected, if quirky, physician, who was unaccountably terrified of her middle-aged, semi-disabled housemate. Randy had all the money, all the possessions, all the power, yet she was reduced to sleeping on the beach and sneaking in and out of her own home, which Moana ran as a rooming house for her own exclusive profit. The farther I got from the lush ravines of Haiku onto the arid central plain, the more ludicrous it seemed. The situation would have been downright comical if Randy weren't so visibly frightened. The whole thing just didn't add up.

Far across the wind-swept cane fields, the sun had burned the morning clouds off Haleakala. Light-green patches of pastureland on the mountain's upper slopes gleamed like fields of jade. Emerald groves of trees shimmered here and there in dark relief. Above it all, the sky outlined the peak in clear powder blue—innocent, uninvolved, serene—everything my life wasn't.

My thoughts turned to Annie. Pray God she had come home while I was away, safe and unharmed. Frank and I would have to face her sooner or later with the video and somehow reconcile that knowledge with the person who was our daughter.

Once again I found myself caught in the old familiar state of emotional ping pong. Just when I got a handle on the ups and down of my business, concern about Annie overwhelmed me. Then I'd come to some kind of temporary emotional truce about her, and business worries would

close in again. I was acutely uncomfortable in this agitated state, yet no
matter how I twisted and turned, there was no relief in sight. Neither
Annie nor the business was likely to change.

Frank had promised to stay by the phone, and to check my answering
machine by remote every hour. At my knock he opened his condo door,
shaking his head. "Still no sign of her," he said. Worry lines radiated from
his velvet brown eyes.

Feeling terribly let down, wanting to blame him, I marched about his
living room from the sliding doors to kitchen pass-through, back to the
doors, again and again, wearing a path in the ghastly shag carpet. "What
are we going to do, Frank? I can't stand it any longer. It's so hard to
pretend she'll show up any minute and everything will be just fine."

Having satisfactorily vented his rage the night we discovered the video,
he was once again the sensible one. "Give her another day, Laura. We
agreed. I checked with the hospital and the police again this morning. If
she hasn't shown up by noon tomorrow, I'll report her as a missing person. You know if we send out search and rescue too soon, we'll do more
harm than good."

Thinking the mechanics of preparing a meal might settle me down, I
made sandwiches, which we took to the lanai with iced sodas. Beyond the
railing, the ocean glittered through the tops of Hong Kong orchid trees lush
with amethyst bloom. Somewhere on the property a lawnmower buzzed.
Sitting down on a white plastic chair, I closed my eyes and took a deep
breath. The scent of fresh-cut grass wafted me back to Pua Olena, a child
again, alone, running barefoot across the rain-soaked lawn. Recalling the
feel of soft mud between my toes, the mist-laden air on my face, I began to
relax. A deep sense of protective isolation seeped through me like a drug.
My disconnect was almost complete when Frank quietly asked how things
had gone with Dr. Entwistle's inspection. Lazily, I opened my eyes.

"The woman is a wreck," I told him, calmer now and ready to bring
real life back to the foreground. "She's a physician, for goodness sakes,
yet she gets the willies every time I mention her housemate's name. She
was wildly concerned that we leave no evidence of our visit. Before we
left, she dragged me on a complete sweep through the house."

"What about the garage? The nefarious den of iniquity?"

"Go ahead, tease me about it. Carlton said it was locked tight. It still makes me nervous, even though no one else seems to care. The one small window is covered with cardboard on the inside, so nobody can see in. Don't you think that's suspicious?"

"Could be. You'd better get this sale closed and get those people out of your life."

"I'd like nothing better, believe me."

Frank tipped back his chair and crossed his feet on the railing. "This Moana must have some kind of serious hold over the doc. Something besides claiming she has a deed and refusing to move."

I swallowed my last bite of sandwich. "Like what?"

"Dunno. That's your job." He smiled. It didn't erase the sadness that was Annie in his eyes.

"Thanks a bunch." I felt strangely beaten. Learning about the downstairs roommates had knocked me sideways. In addition to the shrew upstairs, we now faced three other evictions. And what about Prakash? He was much more than the boyfriend who had upset the equilibrium between the two women. What was his stake in the outcome?

My head spun with potential complications. Sensing my overload, Frank put his empty plate on the coffee table, stood behind me and began to massage my shoulders. I sighed and gave myself up to his caressing hands.

Drifting in and out of sleep in Frank's arms the following morning, sated from a decadent night of lovemaking, I regretted my early appointment with Barbara Jaworski at the coffee shop. For a few more lazy moments I snuggled deeper into Frank's embrace. His chest hair tickled my cheek like tiny meadow flowers.

The ringing phone, repaired and functional again, jangled me out of my reverie. Frank reached for the receiver. "Annie?"

My heart took off like a herd of galloping mustangs. Please let this be her! Frank shook his head and dropped back onto his pillow, one arm still tight around my shoulders. I wilted against him in disappointment.

"Holly? Honey?" He squinted at his watch. "Yeah, it's only six o'clock here, but no problem. I'm awake. No, really. Sun's up, birds are chirping." As he paused to listen to his wife, I pulled away, feeling as alone as if I were on a moonlit beach with no friends for a hundred miles. "Yeah, baby, Annie's fine. Little pistol! She stayed out last night, but she's okay. I thought you might be her."

Another pause. I rose up on an elbow and looked at him. Frank's dark hair, loosed from the ponytail, spread out in seductive waves on his pillow. Only the breeze caressed my naked breasts.

"Of course, sweetheart, I miss you, too," Frank continued into the phone. "Like crazy. It's lonely as hell out here. I can't wait to get home. How's Georgie?"

At the mention of his son, I wondered again about Annie and borderline autism. I sat up. Pieces of the puzzle clinked into place in my mind. If we could have her tested, maybe, just maybe, we'd at least know.

Oblivious, Frank listened to Holly's reply regarding Georgie. He smiled and gestured that I should rejoin him. Nothing doing. Suddenly I knew it was time to wise up and admit things were truly over between us. Had been for years. We'd had a sweet, sensual interlude, based on a shared concern for Annie. He'd used me. And I'd used him—a shift of the load I'd carried alone; a brief, resumed partnership after all these years. That's all it was. Time to move on. I grasped a lock of his hair, twisted it between my fingers, and gave it a good yank.

"Ouch," he yelped, frowning like a hurt puppy.

Good, I thought. Let him explain that to his wife. I picked up my clothes and walked out of my ex-husband's bedroom, head high, never to return.

The entwined aroma of hashbrowns and suntan lotion greeted me as I wove through the café courtyard filled with happy tourists enjoying an early breakfast before a taxing day of snorkeling and sunbathing. Barbara waved from an outdoor table against the white picket fence. She looked great. Aside from a dash of lip gloss and mascara, a few twirls of the curling iron was all she needed to perfect her looks. Almost six feet tall, lean, taut and tanned, she was a raving beauty with high Slavic cheekbones on which you could land an airplane. Men were crazy about her— a gorgeous ex-cop who spoke their language and could keep up with them physically. She wore her usual T-shirt, jeans, and rubber slippers, a contrast that only added to her allure. Her blasé attitude toward fashion didn't hurt her business a bit. Rather, her Salvation Army couture helped build trust with clients who resented paying for an agent's flamboyant designer wardrobe and flashy jewels.

At the stand-up counter I paid for a piece of sour cream coffeecake, chock full of macadamia nuts, along with a double shot of espresso. A dual blast of caffeine and sugar was just what I needed. The hell with Frank.

By the time I slipped into a chair across the umbrella-shaded table from her, Barbara was well into her *loco moco*. You've got to be local, or almost, to love it: a heap of sticky rice topped with a hamburger patty, brown gravy and a sunny-side-up fried egg.

"So sorry I'm late," I said, setting down my plate and mug. "Annie's been giving us fits."

Her eyebrows shot up. "Us? That means you've been with Frank. This early in the morning? I heard he was back. You're not sleeping with him, are you?" Her hazel eyes drilled into mine, challenging me to deny it.

I looked back defiantly. "So?"

There was no stopping her. "The husband who left you for a New York Italian? You idiot!" She bit the tip off a jalapeño pepper with surgical precision. Only Barbara knew me well enough to draw a conclusion from a single flimsy inference.

"Annie took off again three days ago. Not for good, mind you. She's got to be on-island somewhere. But after everything I went through alone the first time, it was nice to have Frank around to share the burden. Who's to argue?" I lifted my chin and stuck out my lower lip.

"Well, far be it from me." She bit off the rest of the pepper and discarded the stem on her plate. "Men just fuck, you know; it doesn't mean anything."

Formerly with the LAPD, Barbara pulled no punches. She'd left the family farm in Illinois the day she graduated from high school. The eldest of twelve, she could shoe a horse, drive a combine, and dance the legs off any man she cared to ask. She was tough, street-smart, and more fun than anybody I knew—when she wasn't using her cop skills to probe an open wound.

"You're right. But it's over. Finally. He's been a big help in dealing with Annie," I added in my own defense. "But listen. You know his young son is autistic. It occurs to me maybe autism—or something like it—is what's been going on with Annie. Sounds crazy, but it would explain so much, Barb."

She cocked her head to one side. Her sun-streaked brown hair fell in loose, shiny curls over her shoulder. "Go on."

"I got some books when I heard about Georgie. He's my children's half-brother, so I wanted to know what they'd be dealing with in their relationship with him. I began to glimpse Annie in those pages but just couldn't deal with it at the time. It's a baffling disorder with a range of symptoms that go from mild to severe. Obsessive-compulsive, difficulty in relating to people, things like that."

I filled her in on some of Annie's puzzling behaviors, including my trials in caring for her as an infant, her constant running away, and her completely off-the-wall response to coming home from school to the surprise of a new bedroom set.

"And you know," I continued, "any time I bought her new clothes, she'd throw a tantrum when I tried to get her to wear them. I finally figured out that if I draped them around her room and left them there for a week, she'd get used to them and allow me to dress her in them. It worked. I did that for years. In high school she had five favorite outfits, one for each day of the week. And she always wore them on the same day every week. That's not normal, you know."

"No, it's not," Barbara responded. "You may be on to something."

"So maybe the way Annie's life has turned out isn't all my fault," I ventured. "I did my best, but I just didn't have a clue."

"So maybe you can forgive yourself?"

"Yeah, I'm working on that. Thanks. This presents a whole new way of looking at things."

"Meanwhile, no word from Annie, going on three days?" she asked, spooning up the last of the egg-yolk-slick rice from her plate. "Of course you sent out the cops?"

"We've called them every day, and the hospital, just checking. We'll ask for an all-out search if we don't hear from her by noon today. It's the same nightmare all over again, Barbara. Only this time she has to be on-island. She'd be insane to try to leave in her condition. I don't think they'd let her on the plane." I couldn't tell her about the video. I might not survive the telling.

Barbara tore four bags of sugar into her coffee, stirring with a vengeance. "You know she could be in a cane field somewhere."

Ouch! I shut my eyes, willing away the possibility Frank and I had so carefully avoided discussing. Bodies are often found stabbed, strangled, shot, and raped in our picturesque sugarcane fields, a perfect camouflage for evil deeds. "I know. That's the image I was trying to block out in Frank's arms."

"Sorry, Laura. Guess I always expect the worst. That's why I got out of the cop biz. Saw too much bad stuff."

I nodded. Her experience on the L.A. beat made Barbara a crack Realtor. No detail was too small to escape her notice. Immediate corrective action, no matter how distasteful, was automatic. Long, hot hours showing property all over the island? Piece of cake, she often said, compared to driving a patrol car on a ten-hour shift with the possibility of life-threatening danger lurking around every corner.

Anxious to veer away from images of Annie's body dumped among the cane stalks, I asked, "So what about this Entwistle business, Barbara? What do you know that would help me out?"

"Hah! That's one crew I wish I'd never butted heads with. What a dweeb. That Randy Entwistle—totally incapable of making a buying decision until her parents arrived and took over."

"Papa designed a fabulous house," I prompted. "Fit for a movie mogul."

"Papa killed himself over the yard," she replied. "Literally. Dropped dead of a heart attack chopping back the jungle one day."

"How sad. Kathleen tells me you lived across the street from them."

"Yeah, before I moved to Kihei. Done in by rain and mildew, not to mention spiders, centipedes, and those characters across the street."

Barbara now lived just around the corner from the coffee shop. In addition to her own modest, three-bedroom house, she had two detached rental units, both illegal, a gaggle of messy geese that lived in a storm ditch running the length of her property, and a hunky *hapa-haole* boyfriend, the crime reporter for the *Maui News*. She may have gotten out of law enforcement, but she still lived with it every day.

"And you met Grant," I added.

"Yeah." Her eyes sparkled. "What can you do when the guy needs to live in town so he can respond to police calls in the middle of the night? I'm just glad it's not me anymore."

I brushed coffeecake crumbs off my lap. A trio of mynah birds hopped over and began pecking them off the cement floor. It cheered me to know that someone as independent as Barbara could be subject to accommodation when it came to a man.

"So what about this Moana?" I probed. "Dr. Entwistle tells me she put the house on the market to get rid of the woman. What kind of deal is that?"

"Yeah, the housemate from hell. I only had two actual encounters with her. She got me over there one day to help unload her truck. She'd been out to Hana. Dug up a whole bunch of tree ferns for the yard. Cockroached from Haleakala National Park. She bragged about it, called it 'drive-by landscaping.' Oh, I itched to slap some cuffs on her for that."

I chuckled at the thought.

"The second time was after her car accident, a big pile up at Five Corners. Really nasty. The doctors had to decide between amputation or a really heroic save. Same leg she smashed earlier in a boating accident. The day I went over with some cookies, she was in a cast, hip to ankle, laid up on a couch in the living room, a full-time nurse in attendance. Paid for by Randy, of course. I felt sorry for her until she lit into me about all the jerks who messed her up in the hospital. That woman can cuss. Even though she was in a lot of pain, it seemed to me she should have been grateful they saved her leg."

"And that she had such luxurious surroundings in which to recuperate for free," I added.

"Really. When she started telling me about the lawyer she'd hired to sue the hospital and half the staff, I told her I had to go water my lawn."

"In Haiku?" I laughed. "With all that rain?"

"Exactly. She didn't even get it. Fully self-obsessed bitch. The kind you don't want to tangle with."

"Well, I'm pretty tangled, unfortunately. And Dr. E. is still less than useless." I eyed my last bite of coffeecake, wishing it weren't. "Say, Moana can't be her real name. She doesn't appear to have a Hawaiian bone in her body. Certainly not in her belligerent attitude. On the phone the other day you called her 'the infamous Corey Sue.'"

"Her *real* name is Corrine Suzanne Urquhart. How's that for a handle? She's from Arkansas, if I remember correctly. Went by Corey Sue until one day she decided to grab herself a Hawaiian name. The nerve. Then she dropped the Urquhart and started referring to herself as Moana Entwistle."

"Why?" I asked, popping the last nut-filled piece of perfection into my mouth.

"It opens doors around town. You know, related to the doc and all."

"Well, whatever her name is, she claims to have an ownership interest in the property."

"No kidding? Hold on a sec." Barbara signaled to a waitress who was circulating with a glass coffeepot.

"Randy bought the property in her name alone," Barbara stated as soon as our mugs were full again. "Have you seen a title report?"

"Not yet. I put a rush on it."

"Well, it's possible she cut Moana in later. They were pretty cozy there for a while. Lonely people do strange things."

"Yeah," I muttered, my thoughts flashing back to Frank and myself. "How come Randy's so dead set against her now?"

"You mean she hasn't told you about Prakash?"

"Ah, Prakash. The boyfriend who blew the happy girlsome to bits. Randy mentioned him. What do you know about him?"

Barbara pushed her chair a few inches back from the table, turned sideways and crossed her lanky legs, showing off her deep-scarlet toenails . "Well, first of all, his real name is Charles something or other. He moved here some years ago from the mainland to lie back, live on the beach, eat bananas, heal from the bruises of a former life. You know *da kine*. Grew a beard, rented a shack down the country in Paia, drove a duct tape special."

"How did he go from Charles to Prakash?"

"Got into Zen, took an East Indian name—Paia is full of those types. Prakash! What a joke! He's no more Indian than Moana's Hawaiian. Sucked up welfare, grew pot in his back yard. Big money if you can dodge the law."

I nodded, knowing only too well. Maui Wowie—*pakalolo*—is powerful stuff, sought after worldwide.

"Anyway, sooner or later the free and easy lifestyle must have paled," she continued. "So he shaved off his beard, took a bath, and got a real job."

"How come you know all this?" I asked.

"Shit, it's a small island. Besides, Grant's been asking questions about him."

I set down my coffee and leaned toward her. "About Prakash?"

"Yeah, something's coming down. He won't tell me squat. Not one bloody thing. Drives me crazy. I could strangle him!"

My heart constricted. "I knew it—there *is* a drug lab on the Entwistle property!"

She abruptly uncrossed her legs and turned to face me, elbows on the table. "What?"

Could I trust her with my suspicions? Something warned me not to, but her cop read on the situation would be invaluable. I decided to chance it.

"According to Randy, Prakash has some sort of hush-hush enterprise going on in the garage. It's double dead-bolted, and the only window's blocked with cardboard on the inside. We couldn't get the inspector in yesterday. You don't think there's any possibility of the property being confiscated, do you? Under the federal drug law?"

"Back up a tad. You think he's manufacturing illegal drugs?"

"Randy says he's installed a bunch of equipment in there, and the mailman stops to pick up boxes when Prakash is in town. Unsealed boxes, with smaller boxes inside. What if he's making crystal meth or something, and mailing it out right under everyone's noses? It's a logical jump from growing *pakalolo*."

"Through the U.S. Postal Service? Get real!"

"Why not? Who would be suspicious? The greatest capers have been pulled off in the most audacious ways, at least in the movies. Nobody suspects a thing if you act all normal."

"Well, this ain't the movies, dearie," she said with a derisive snort. "But I do know Grant and the MPD are watching him. Son of a gun, you might be right. Do you have any concrete evidence?"

I shook my head. "Just a hunch."

"How 'bout Randy? Has she seen anything definitive? Other than the locked garage and the mailman picking up boxes?"

"No. Randy thinks they're stringing hippie beads."

She clicked her tongue. "Yeah, and the Pope's not Catholic. Until we know for sure, you stay away from the place. Let Dr. E. deal with Moana and Prakash. Just do what you can on your end to keep the sale moving. Leave Moana and Prakash alone."

"Easy for you to say. They're the key to getting this deal closed, and getting me paid." A noisy truck growled by on the other side of the picket fence. In that moment, I realized my friend now had the power to sabotage my sale completely. "Barb, you've got to promise not to tell Grant any of this. He'll pass it on to the police, and my deal will be sunk. If the police figure it out on their own, that's one thing, but Randy Entwistle doesn't deserve to have her property snatched. Nor do the Colemans. As soon as Prakash finds out the property is sold, he'll pack up his stuff and disappear into the night if he's really doing something illegal. There's no way anyone with half a brain would hang around waiting to get caught. Promise me."

"No problem. I'm so pissed at Grant for not sharing, I wouldn't tell him what day of the week it is if he asked."

"Good. Thanks." I studied her in her T-shirt and jeans, trying to picture her in a blue serge uniform with badge on her chest and a pistol on her hip. She'd have done Charlie's Angels proud.

CHAPTER 17

That mangy kid was sprawled on the sofa as casually as if she had just come in from a morning stroll. I tossed my file case onto the kitchen counter and rushed toward her. "Annie, where have you been?" Anger once again wrestled with relief at seeing her safe and sound.

Languidly, she twisted toward me, eyebrows raised in wonder that I should ask such a dumb question. "Hey, Ma." For an instant the scene shifted. I saw her, limbs outstretched, breasts exposed beneath the pummeling Arab. I backed up a couple of steps, repelled by the image.

Her feet were caked with dirt, her hair clumped and fuzzy. Her new yellow muumuu was bunched up and soiled, the hem partially ripped. The coffee table next to her looked like a picnic after a dog had rummaged through it: candy wrappers, a ripped-open chip bag, and a half-eaten tin of caramel popcorn. Her bland expression showed absolutely no concern for the recent panic she had caused Frank and me. Cold fury triumphed.

"What are you doing, lying there with your dirty feet on my couch and food all over the place? Look at all those chips on the carpet! The ants are at them already. And that soda can sweating on my table. And that dreadful music blasting down the hall. Turn it down, for heaven's sake."

Groggily, she pushed herself upright, slid her encrusted feet over the side of the couch, and stared at me as if I were crazy. I was. But not crazy enough to miss her dilated pupils, her unfocused gaze. My reaction rose swift and visceral. I snapped off the TV and pointed toward the bath-room. "Look at you. Get up and wash those feet. Then get back out here. We're going to talk."

I paced until Annie emerged nonchalantly from the bathroom dressed in clean shorts and a T-shirt, a towel slung around her neck. She padded back to the couch, leaving a trail of soggy footprints on the white carpet. I clenched my teeth. She sat down and bent over her stomach to dry her feet. Her voice was giggly. "Sorry, Ma. Can't reach my feet too good."

That made me even angrier. I spoke through clenched teeth. "All right. You've been gone for three days. Each one of those days was like a year for your father and me. If you were not *hapai*, young lady, I'd turn you out immediately and let you fend for yourself."

She straightened up, trying her best to focus. "Ma, chill. What's the big deal? I have friends here, you know. I'm not gonna stay holed up all day, every day. Boring to the max. I've got six weeks of freedom, and then what? Diapers, bottles, and all that crap. Don't tell me I can't have my last bit of fun."

"Your father and I were frantic! We spent three years agonizing over you, and then you disappear again, without so much as a note or a phone call? It's obvious you've been smoking dope. I can tell by your eyes and these munchies." I gestured toward the mess on the coffee table. "You may not care about yourself, but I won't sit by and watch you do some-thing that's deliberately harmful to your child."

She gave her feet a final flourish and dumped the towel on the floor. "Leave me alone. Just leave me the fuck alone."

"So I'm supposed to feed you, clothe you, shelter you, pay your medi-cal expenses, give you spending money and leave you alone? And not worry my silly little head about the harm you may be doing to my grand-child? Is that it?"

She took a loud gurgling sip from the dripping soda can. Her eyes as cold as the deepest ocean currents, she replied, "You don't own me. Or the baby."

For a moment I could only stare. How was it possible to have such warm and loving thoughts of a person when she slept or was out of sight, such soul-grinding concern when she was lost or in trouble, yet be so overcome with antagonism face to face? I slowly sat down on the chair kitty-corner from her, clasping my hands around my knees, trying to hold myself together.

"That's true. But I won't stand by and watch this, Annie. It rips me apart. I love you. I love your baby. If you are going to live here, and I am going to support you, you have got to follow my rules. That means no drugs of any kind. Period. You will also get your GED, now, before the baby is born. And you will make plans for what you intend to do after the birth. I'll give you six weeks from when the baby's born. That's all. Then you'll be on your own, whatever it takes. Do you understand?"

Abruptly she flopped around on the couch, tart and clumsy in the same motion, slid down on the pillows, and clamped one arm across her belly. Damp feet elevated on the armrest, stubborn chin set, she stabbed the air repeatedly with the TV remote. A nauseating chorus of twanging guitars, played by spastic gargoyles in green spiked hair, drowned out my plea.

"We've got to get tough with her, Frank. I won't take her insolence and her complete lack of interest in her baby's welfare." I had fled to Frank's condo. I had to get away from Annie to regain my perspective. At the news she'd returned, he wanted to rush to her immediately. I forestalled him, wanting first to prepare a united front.

"How much of this am I supposed to take?" I asked. "She tells me to chill out, that I don't own her."

"And you don't." He sat on the couch opposite me. A heap of damp towels and dirty clothes blocked the hallway to the bedroom. Through an open door, the bed was a distasteful jumble of unmade sheets.

"No, but I have some right to know where she is and what she's up to. To intervene if she's using drugs. Somebody has to advocate for her baby."

"Perhaps. But she is nineteen, and it is *her* baby. Parental rights and realities can be two different things."

Was I explaining color to a blind man? "How would you feel if you were in my shoes? If she had shown up at The Bog instead of here, and inserted herself into *your* real life?"

Frank looked amused. "Isn't that an interesting thought. Maybe Holly could have done something with her."

He might as well have slapped me. I blinked back tears. "That hurt."

"You asked."

I lashed back. "I've told Annie she has to get her GED before the baby is born. And that she needs to be out of my apartment by the time the baby is six weeks old. I refuse to just let her veg around feeling sorry for herself. She's in a very serious situation, and she needs to grow up."

He raised his eyebrows. "Sounds like you really laid it on the line. Good for you."

"Yes. And no more drugs, not even *pakalolo*. You need to back me up, Frank. She carries on as if she's harming only herself."

"Any harm she might have done to the baby has been done by now. Aren't the early months the most dangerous? That's what Holly learned in her research for Georgie. We have no idea what Annie did to her body when she first got pregnant. We can't fix it now."

"What kind of reassurance is that?" I asked. "I know she's smoking dope . . . maybe worse. I'm worried sick about the baby, Frank."

"Then find a bigger place to live now, where you two can at least have your own privacy. Maybe if you don't have your face rubbed in it all day, it'll be okay."

"Make sense, Frank. It's not okay for her to smoke dope when she's pregnant, whether I witness it or not. And besides, who's going to pay for a bigger place? I sure can't. Even if I rent out my condo, I'd run a negative. Unless . . . you could cover her share?"

He picked up the newspaper sports section, snapped it open, and scanned an inside page. "I'm struggling, Laura, just as you are. The Bog, as you so lightly call it, barely breaks even. And Georgie's medical bills are fierce, let me tell you."

"You've had success with your book," I ventured hopefully.

"Yeah, well, it has a very specialized audience. Hotel managers and colleges that teach hotel management. It sells steadily, but not by the crate. Two thousand dollars in royalties is a big quarter."

That wasn't too encouraging. "Can you at least *help*?"

He stood and began prowling the room. "What about Margaret? It's damn silly for you to be so strapped when she lives like an East Indian tea baroness." He practically spat it out. My mother's tightness in the face of her own personal excesses had always driven him wild.

"My mother is my mother. For as long as I live, I'll never understand her attitude toward money. She sends outrageous gifts, treats us like visiting potentates when we're in Honolulu, but I can't shake loose any cash. God knows, Frank, I've tried. These last years haven't been easy."

He stood in front of me, legs apart, arms crossed over his chest. Springy little gray hairs frizzed out above his ears. Why hadn't I noticed them before?

"Try again," he suggested. "Maybe she'll loosen up for her granddaughter."

Maybe she would, for Annie. An immediate change in our living situation was the one thing I could do to ease the tension between us. Should I call now, and let Frank witness my humiliation? Or wait until I got home, and risk losing my nerve? You never make a sale by procrastinating. I turned my back to Frank and picked up the telephone. My stomach did a flip-flop at the sound of Mother's voice, imperious as ever.

"Mom? How are things?"

"Laura! You refuse to return my calls. I'm positively distraught. What's going on over there? How's that precious girl?"

I grasped the receiver with both hands and spoke through gritted teeth. "Annie's fine, Mom. She's lying on my couch, resting and watching TV. But I need your help." I scrunched my eyes shut and grimaced. "Annie and I aren't doing too well in my little space."

Her voice got real prissy. "I told you it was foolish to buy such a tiny apartment."

"Mom, listen. I bought it. I'm stuck with it. It works fine for one person and occasional guests. I never dreamed anybody would move in with me."

"Sell it. You're a Realtor."

"Mom, I refinanced recently, took out the equity for David's tuition. I owe more than I could get for it. I'd have to take cash to the closing table, cash I don't have."

"Humph." Her thoughts were as loud as a football game broadcast: *You had to go into real estate, but you can't even manage to buy a good investment.*

"Mom, I need to rent a larger place, or find Annie a place of her own. But I can't afford to do either. Could you please help me out?"

She didn't miss a beat. "Send her over here. We discussed it last week when your father and I were on Maui. It's the perfect solution. She'll be right here when it's time to have the baby. You won't have to bother with that dreadful county hospital. Just send her here, and I'll take care of everything." She almost trumpeted with satisfaction.

"No, Mom, that isn't the solution. For eight hundred a month I can find her a small place, maybe even in my own building. Then we'd be close. I could look after her. We'd both have our freedom. Please, Mom, it would make all the difference in the world, to both of us." I glanced at Frank. He pulled on his ear and nodded encouragingly.

"Eight hundred a month! That's a small fortune!"

I groaned. "Mother, it's for Annie, not me."

She paused for a moment. "And how long would this have to go on?"

Ah, a positive buying sign. "I don't know. Some girls go to work six weeks after giving birth."

"What? Six weeks? Why, that's criminal. Of course she can't go to work in six weeks. You send that girl over here. I won't have it any other way."

"Mom, please!"

"Not another word. Send her over right away. Oh, wait a moment. Your father and I are going to Molokai for a few days. You'd better hold off until next week Wednesday. I'll send you a little something to tide you over. That's my final offer."

"Final? It's your only—"

"Aloha, dear. Let us know her flight time. I'll send Calixto to pick her up." She rang off.

Furious, I turned to Frank. He sat on the couch, grinning, the bastard. I plunked onto the chair and grasped my knees until my knuckles turned white. "It has to be her way, or she won't budge an inch," I muttered. "She has to be in complete control."

Slowly, with the studied stealth of a lion slithering across the savanna toward his unsuspecting prey, Frank leaned over on one elbow and stretched his other arm toward the end table. Continuing the sinuous movement, he grasped a hand mirror that was lying near the table's edge. In one final elegant movement, he eased toward me and held the mirror to my face.

"Like mother, like daughter," he said.

Thrown hard, a hand mirror will shatter on an avocado shag rug.

CHAPTER 18

Frank made his point, damn him. Somehow Annie and I had to learn to live together in the short run on mutually accommodating terms. But there was one more issue Frank and I had both studiously avoided.

"What about that video, Frank? It haunts me day and night. I look at her and see her spread out . . . We can't just pretend we didn't see it. What are we going to do?"

He rasped his hand over his chin. "God, where do we even begin? Murder would be good." He shrugged one shoulder and rotated it several times, as if easing an ache.

"But what do we *do*? What do we say to Annie? When I look at her, all I see is my little girl and that . . . that big gorilla with the dishrag on his head."

"Yeah." He bit the inside of his cheek, too overcome for a moment to speak. "I don't know. If we act all upset, we'll just alienate her." He picked up the unmarked video case sitting atop his television. "Look, it's my turn. Let me talk to her. We need to know her side of the story before we can determine what to do about it. If this thing was filmed before she turned eighteen, we've got a serious case of child abuse on our hands. We can report it to the authorities and let them pursue it."

"But it happened in Thailand. The local police don't have any authority in a foreign country."

"You're right, but we can't just let it go. Somebody needs to be punished."

"What if she was eighteen and consented?"

"Then I guess there's no crime, at least by the book."

"But what has it done to her soul, Frank? That's what I'm worried about. I told you what I felt that day at the pool. She isn't our Annie any more. I'm beginning to understand why."

"Look, let's see what she has to say. We'll let her know we're truly on her side, that we want to help her, whatever the circumstances were. Can you line up with that?"

"What choice do we have?" I asked. "We have to do something."

Frank's delight in seeing Annie safely at home lightened my heart. For a long moment he sat next to her on the couch, holding her, not saying a word. She responded to her father like the Annie of old, allowing him a level of familiarity she steadfastly denied me.

"Baby? Are you okay?" he finally asked, caressing her hair.

She closed her eyes and nestled closer. "Tell Ma to chill. She won't leave me alone."

Frank glanced at me over Annie head. "Your mother loves you, honey. She only wants what's best for you and your baby."

She pushed herself out of Frank's arms. "Then tell her to leave me alone. I can take care of myself. I'm not using. I'm just smoking a little dope. It relaxes me."

I rolled my eyes. Frank shook his head in warning. Gently he turned her shoulders until she was unable to avoid his eyes.

"Look, sweetie, I don't like it anymore than Mom does, but we have something more serious to discuss." He picked up the video he had placed on the coffee table when we walked in.

"What's that?" she asked.

"I think you know. I found it with the gear you stowed in my linen closet."

Her eyes darted to me, bristling with hostility. "You've been going through my stuff?"

He held up his hand to silence her. "I was looking for something in the closet. It fell out and hit me on the foot. I could hardly ignore it. What in God's name is this all about?"

Annie hid her eyes with her hands and shrank into the cushions. Frank pulled her hands away and gently grasped her chin. "Baby, talk to us. We want to help."

Still, she sat there, silent and remote. At least her eyes had cleared. She appeared to be down from her high.

"For parents to see their daughter in such a . . . such a . . . a compromising position, well . . . I can't begin to tell you how it feels," Frank continued. "I'm horrified . . . frightened . . . and sad. What in the world is this all about, Annie?"

Frank's control astounded me. He had slipped into his professional demeanor as the consummate hotelier. Only the strained, precise enunciation of each word and the slight tic of an artery on his right temple betrayed his surging emotions. No father should ever have to have a conversation like this with his daughter.

Annie tried to respond but only managed great gulps of air. Her breasts heaved above her bloated stomach.

Frank put a hand on her shoulder. "It's okay, baby. Your mother and I love you. You're safe. Please tell us what happened. Whoever did this to you needs to be in jail."

She twisted away from Frank, shouting, "No, no, not that! No, I won't tell you anything. You can't do that! He'll kill me."

"It's okay, Annie, it's okay," he said. "We won't do anything you don't want us to do, but please, can't you tell us why you're so frightened?"

Frank held her while she sobbed, rubbing her back and smoothing her hair. It was the first time she had cried since her return, at least to my knowledge. My heart ached, but I forced myself to remain seated while Frank comforted her. She'd finally cracked. Now perhaps we'd learn something that would enable us to help her.

Tears still spilling, she looked at me, her face guarded and resentful. Yet when she began talking she sounded as if she were glad things were finally out in the open. "You . . . you remember I told you the boys were hassling me at school?"

I nodded. "Dad knows, too."

She flashed him an inquiring look.

"It's okay, baby. Mom brought me up to speed. Go on."

"You . . . you asked me if I . . . if I told anyone, tried to get . . . help."

I nodded again.

"So I did, yeah, I found help. My social studies teacher." She swiped her nose with the back of her hand. "The boys cornered me one day in the hallway, stupid little shits. Mr. Campbell came around the corner and saw what was happening. He . . . he . . . told the jerks to get lost and . . . and . . . and he put his arm around me and . . . and . . ." She broke down into hiccuping sobs, hugging her belly.

Frank and I exchanged alarmed glances while she tried to collect herself. The memories were apparently still raw, in spite of everything she'd been through since. I squirmed as I watched her relive the pain, knowing I had let her down tragically at the time by being so engrossed in my own problems. But I knew she'd stop talking if I made a fuss.

"He . . . he . . . he put his arm around me and . . . and . . . walked me into his classroom, and . . . and . . . shut the door . . ." Her attention drifted off. The fear and anger left her visage, leaving a softness she rarely exhibited. She turned away from us, lost in that distant memory.

Frank sprang up off the couch. "Don't tell me the bastard seduced you."

She turned back to her father, answering in a breathless voice. "No, Daddy, no, it wasn't like that. Chaz was wonderful. He let me come to his room any time I needed to get away from those boys. I went there every day. I felt safe with him. Safe. He was so sweet. After a while we started going to his house after school. I felt like he was the only person who really understood me. He was kind and tender and gentle. I . . . I loved him."

"And you thought he loved you?" Frank asked in a hollow voice.

"Yeah. Yeah, I did." Her eyes went flat as she said it.

"What happened then, sweetheart?" I asked. "Were you . . . lovers?" I could barely say the word.

She began gulping air again, fending off new tears. She squeezed her eyes shut and nodded her head.

"Couldn't you have come to me, Annie? I'm your mother. Somehow we could have worked it out."

Annie shot me a pitying glance. "There was nothing to work out, Ma. I loved him."

Frank frowned at me, then asked her, "Is he the one you ran away with?"

Again she nodded. "Just before school got out in June, Chaz said he was going away and wanted me to come with him. At first I said I couldn't, that you'd never let me go. But he kept talking about it. I couldn't bear the idea of him going without me. He was my whole life."

Her whole life, and I'd known nothing about him. Just as I'd known nothing about Frank's plans to marry Angela. "Well, you were right about one thing," I said. "I certainly would not have let you go."

"Duh." She glared at me as if I were a complete idiot. "So he convinced me to just take off, without letting you know. I had my passport from when Grandma took us to Italy, so it was no big deal. I wanted to be with him. I hated school. What a drag. All I did was look at the trees outside the classroom window and count the minutes until I could be with him again."

"But the misery you put Dad and me through—"

"Laura," Frank cautioned, raising a hand.

"Okay," Annie said, hard-eyed again. "I'm sorry. Is that what you've been waiting to hear? I'm sorry I hurt you. If it makes you feel any better, I'm very sorry I went. It didn't turn out the way I expected. No way, no how."

"What happened, honey?" Frank asked softly, entreating me with his eyes to keep quiet.

Annie's face clouded. She pulled the ribbed neck of her T-shirt over her mouth as if to filter the words she was going to say.

"We went to Thailand. I thought it was going to be just him and me, a romantic summer together. Instead, it was a charter flight full of men. Horny men. Disgusting men. They were going to Thailand to 'sample the feminine pleasures of the Orient.' Assholes." She blinked her eyes rapidly as if to erase the disturbing vision. "Chaz used me as bait. A little blonde *haole* girl, the only female on the plane. He told me to 'friendly up' with the men, get them excited about the delights waiting for them in Bangkok. He told me to sit on their laps, wiggle around, tease them . . . assholes."

"Why did you do it?" Frank asked.

"Because he asked me to. I'd have done anything for him at that point. I kept hitting on the *pakalolo* in the bathroom. That was one thing about Chaz—he always had a good supply of weed. That made everything tolerable, at least at first. But those men were creepy. Barf."

Glancing at Frank's face, drained but determined, I felt us sliding down a slippery slope with an open abyss at the bottom.

He asked in a frigid whisper, "What happened when you arrived?"

"He had this whole fucking business going." She spat it out. "DreamSeed Tours. I had no idea. He'd been building it up while he was teaching, see. With Christmas vacation, spring break, and summers off, he has lots of time for traveling. But that was his last year at school. He'd finally gotten DreamSeed solid enough so he could quit teaching and run it full time. He rented a fabulous house in Bangkok, lived like a king. He brought in tours from all over—the West Coast, Hawaii, Japan, the Middle East, Australia."

Frank and I exchanged glances. DreamSeed Tours, the name on the video. "My God. What happened when you found all this out?" I ventured.

She shrugged. "For a while I really didn't get it. He kept me out of it, except for the plane ride. I told him not to ever do that to me again. So I stayed at the house. It was kind of like being at Grandma's—servants and stuff. No pressure, just lazy days. We spent mornings together. He went off to work every afternoon. There were some American kids around. I hung out with them, explored the city. It was great. Until . . . ."

"Until what?" Frank prodded. I gripped the edge of my chair, not certain I could take any more.

Her voice hardened. "Until one day he came home and told me I'd had enough of a free ride. Just like that. Not nicely, not asking if I would help. He just told me I had to start working right away. The next after-noon he took me to a hotel room. An ugly, fat Japanese man sat on the bed. You should have seen his rotten-toothed smile when I walked in." At this point Annie stood up and began a frenetic pantomime of the encoun-ter. She made an exaggerated bow. "'Ah,' says Mr. Fujisake, "'you have brought me a leetle blondie.'" Annie turned to her father and me. "That was it. The men from those places—Japan and Saudi Arabia and like that—wanted 'a leetle blondie,' just like the fucking local boys back home. It's a curse, I tell you. A curse." She jerked on a hank of her blonde hair.

She sat down again, arms crossed above her belly, and continued. "So, he set up a video camera in the corner. He charged them extra for filming them with me. Gave 'em bragging rights. Didn't matter who else they fucked. They wanted the 'leetle blondie' to show their buddies back home. Assholes."

Frank was momentarily speechless. Seeing the video had been bad enough, but to hear her describe it . . . . I, too, could only sit and stare.

Frank recovered first. "Is there more?" he asked.

"Oh, yeah. Chaz changed completely. No matter what I did, he acted all cold and shut off. He suddenly had no interest in me except as a bloody prop. I was expected to do these fucking videos, two, three, sometimes four a day. He had a muscleman, twice my size, who escorted me to the hotel and took me from room to room. It was horrible. I took every kind of shit to get through it. It's easy to get high in Bangkok." She wadded the crew neck of her T-shirt and stuffed it into her mouth, creating a momen-tary gag, as if to keep from throwing up.

"You still lived with him?" Frank asked.

She spat out the gag, wrinkled and soggy with saliva. "Well, yeah, like where else could I go? But he had no use for me at home. He'd brought in this other woman, see. A Cambodian woman, Nok. She moved into the house, into his bed. Suddenly I had to sleep in a maid's room downstairs. Like I was dirty now that I was making those videos with other men. From then on he pretty well ignored me, except for making me work."

"Why didn't you just come home? Or call?" I asked, unable to con-tain myself.

She looked at me, her face ravaged with dried tears. "Sure, like I didn't beg him to let me come home? Begged, day after day. He just laughed in my face. You know what he said? 'You're making a fortune for me, leetle blondie. You're staying right here.' When he found out I was *hapai*, he beat me so badly I couldn't work for a week. Then he found out the men liked me even better that way. The perverts thought it was sexy. That did it. I made up my mind I'd get away or die trying. I couldn't take any more."

Frank and I listened, spellbound in spite of ourselves. "Is that when you phoned?" I asked.

"Yeah."

"But you hung up."

"I choked. I couldn't talk. I was too ashamed."

"But, Annie, we'd have come immediately."

"I wasn't . . . I wasn't sure."

"Drop it, Laura. Baby, how did you finally get home?"

"He . . . he had my passport. I had no money. I was stuck, or so he thought. I started scheming. I was really mad. Every afternoon when he left, Nok had a masseur come in. That was my time to prowl if I had a break from the hotel. I turned the house upside down looking for my passport. One day I lost track of time. Nok caught me. When I leveled with her, she said she knew where my passport was. She got it for me. She was willing to do anything to get rid of me. Fine with me, I didn't give a rip. I just wanted out. Meanwhile, I was snitching money from him at night while they slept. A few bucks here, a few bucks there, so he wouldn't miss it. The assholes paid him in U.S. dollars, cash. He brought his stash home every night. It took a while, but eventually I scammed enough to buy a ticket. Nok helped me get it."

"Is this dreadful Chaz the father of your baby?" I asked.

She gave me a scathing look. "No," was all she said.

A familiar numbness crept over me, exhausting, numbing, enervating. I knew it well. It had saved my sanity between bouts of anxiety while Annie was gone. While I had learned to welcome the smothering mantle in the past, I struggled now to fight it off. This was no time to sink into protective shock. Annie needed both of us, present and accounted for.

"We've got to do something," I demanded. "This Chaz is an arch-criminal. After everything he's done to you, we can't just let it go."

She jumped up and flung herself across the room at me. "Ma, he'll kill me. He comes back to Maui all the time to organize his tours. If he finds out I've reported him, he'll kill me. I know it. I saw him do it to one of the girls who worked for him. She ran away one day, and he sent a gang of thugs after her. Two days later they dragged her into our compound, kicking and sputtering. We were eating dinner on the porch. Chaz got up from the table, walked down the steps, picked her up and wrung her neck. Just like the cook with a chicken. She jerked a couple of times and *pau. Maké*, die, dead." Annie's face paled during the telling. Freckles stood out on her cheeks like acne scars. She continued in a whisper. "Chaz dropped her on the dirt, wiped his hands on his pants, came back up the steps and finished his dinner. After a while he looked at me and said, 'Don't you give me any trouble.'"

"My God," I gasped. "We're up against a maniac."

Frank said, "We won't do anything right away, I promise, Annie. This is too frightening. We'll have to give it some careful thought. We don't know whether he's on-island or not. But we have the tape, just in case. That's why you brought it home, isn't it, honey? In case you needed to prove your story, or to have something on him if he ever came after you?"

She nodded, wiping her eyes. "I didn't want you to see it, but I didn't think anyone would believe me." Her voice sounded so very small.

"We believe you, honey," Frank said.

She held her hand out for the tape. "Give it to me, Dad."

"Don't you want me to hold on to it for safekeeping?"

"No. I want it. Just to make sure you and Ma don't get any ideas about taking it to the police."

He inhaled sharply as if to argue, then apparently thought better of it. "Okay, honey." He handed her the tape. "We'll get past this, somehow."

Frank put his arms out and pulled her to stand with him. He held her for a very long time in silence. Then they opened their arms and welcomed me into their embrace.

CHAPTER 19

Holly called three days later with a crisis regarding Georgie. Frank left on the next available plane, obviously torn but anxious to return to his family despite his concern for Annie. I was not sorry to see him go. His presence had become more and more distasteful, less and less helpful.

In particular, we strongly disagreed on what to do about Chaz Campbell. I wanted to go to the police immediately, but Frank and Annie insisted we wait. Frank worried that once the local police got hold of it, my family name and his former prominence in the visitor industry would generate a media circus. Annie was no longer a minor, thus vulnerable to journalistic exploitation. Before we acted, Frank wanted to consult an old school chum, a New York attorney who specialized in international criminal law. Unfortunately, the man would be out of the country for another month. Reluctantly, I agreed to wait.

Frank took Annie to dinner alone the night before he left. I don't know what he said to her, but her behavior after that was subdued. She continued to hang out with the street kids, but didn't stay out overnight again. She enrolled in GED classes and appeared to be taking them seriously. Frank got her to agree to go to counseling, but at her insistence not until after the baby was born. Later was better than never, so we accepted the delay.

Annie and I fell into an uneasy routine. Although it was constantly on my mind, I decided not to ask any more questions about Chaz Campbell or her experiences in Thailand for the moment. I needed time to process the horror of her tale before I could talk about it unemotionally. To find out my daughter had been so abused by so many men—it nearly killed me to think of it. The image on the tape, the endless others my imagination conjured up, played over and over in my mind until I thought I would go mad. Then there were days when I could drum up no feelings for her at all. However much she had been a victim, I'd find myself looking at her and thinking, *you chose to go with Campbell in the first place*.

Of more immediate concern, because of the baby, was her use of drugs. She dug in her heels and refused to discuss it, except to swear she currently only smoked marijuana. "Non-negotiable, Ma."

My part of the bargain was not to bug her. It wasn't easy. My best strategy was to bury myself in work, which reclaimed my attention in any case. The Coleman transaction was at a critical point. Diana and Jerry signed their approval of the disclosure statement and the inspection report. The fact that the inspector couldn't access the locked garage didn't bother them, as the rest of the home was in fine condition.

As for my suspicions of illegal drug manufacturing, Jerry continued to shine it off, repeating that Annie's situation had made me overly suspicious. He insisted we get on with the evictions and close the sale, ASAP. I wasn't convinced, but if they were willing to chance it, so was I. To cover my *okole*, I updated my notes in the Colemans' file, making sure I had a detailed log of all our conversations by phone and in person. If Barbara's reporter boyfriend was asking questions about Prakash, no detail was too small to be ignored.

The appraisal came in at $10,000 above contract price, thanks to the surprise closing of a comparable property just down the road to a Hollywood rock star. Being a non-MLS sale, I'd had no idea it was pending. Needless to say, the Colemans were thrilled. All we needed now on their side was final loan approval.

All the holdups were on the seller's side. I verified that Randy's attorney had sent out eviction notices to all the tenants. There was nothing to do but wait. I felt like a frigate becalmed in the doldrums—fitted out for a swift journey with no wind to fill the sails. With a transaction that depended on aggressive monitoring of every detail, the wait was excruciating. Once again, the only cure was distraction.

I switched into high gear with two new buyer prospects. I squired them about in the relentless September heat until they both found properties they liked, one a modest starter home on the windy north shore; the other a condo near mine. Between them, I spent a week in frantic negotiations, a process complicated by the condo buyers waiting until just before their return to the mainland to make their offer. Adding to the three-ring circus, the condo seller had defected to the natural life in the *ohia* forests of the Big Island. Typical of Big Island dropout mentality, he was laid back almost to the point of being comatose. His agent seemed just as useless.

The final counteroffer came through the morning of the buyers' flight home to Louisiana. When I called, they had already checked out of their hotel. Although we could have carried on long distance, a mainland buyer's enthusiasm usually wanes once the airplane door slams shut and Paradise fades into the sea behind them. After all the running around I did for them, they were not going to get on that plane without accepting the counter.

My one shot at finalizing the deal was to catch them in the terminal. I sped to the airport, located their flight on the departure board and ran down the concourse toward the gate, hoping they hadn't boarded yet. Happily, there sat Betty Le Boeuf beside a mountain of carry-on luggage, jiggling a pair of rolled-up beach mats on her golf-tanned knees. Her husband Jim walked toward her, holding two steaming paper cups of coffee. They were both greatly surprised to see me, having nowhere near my sense of urgency over finalizing this little matter.

We exchanged hugs and a bit of small talk while I caught my breath. Then I showed them the counteroffer.

"The seller only deleted the requirement that the appliances be in working order at closing, because they're old and he didn't want to warranty them," I explained. "But you're planning a complete renovation, so that doesn't matter. And he raised your offer by five grand.

That's peanuts—it only adds thirty-nine bucks to your monthly payment. He agrees to the rest of the terms and conditions. Isn't that great?"

Betty lowered her false eyelashes and blew on her coffee. The aroma made me melt. I'd dashed off with nothing but toothpaste foam for breakfast.

"How 'bout it, Betty? We can manage that." If anyone ever had a name that matched his physique, it was Jim Le Boeuf. A beefy fellow with a bulbous nose, bristly ears and foul tobacco breath, he'd retired as an ocean platform oil driller. His monthly pension exceeded any income I ever hoped to earn.

Betty pouffed her strawberry-blonde curls with her carmine fingernails, and glanced at the jeweled watch on her other wrist. She scanned the passenger lounge impatiently, raising her perky nose at the milling confusion of sunburned passengers. Raised in New Jersey, she laid on a fake southern accent as thick as *filé* gumbo. "If we don't get in line, we gonna get bumped," she drawled. "These airlines overbook every chance they get."

Jim rolled his eyes. "Come on, Betty. This is important. Do we want this condo or not?"

I held my breath, waiting for the boss lady to speak. Seeking a distraction so they wouldn't sense my anxiety, I fastened on a young family two rows away. Mom, Dad, and toddler, so beautiful in their mixed-blood, *hapa haole* way. Dad held the child; Mom carried a string-tied bakery box. Some lucky relatives on another island were due for a gift of Komoda Bakery's famous butter rolls or crème puffs. For an indulgent moment, I imagined Annie and her baby in that happy scene, knowing it was impossible.

"Oh, for goodness sake, Jimmy," Betty exclaimed. "Let's buy the durned thing. Where do we sign?"

Fifteen minutes plus a flurry of signatures and initials later, I hugged Jim and Betty goodbye and sashayed out of the airport, signed contract tucked safely in my file case. All I needed was my broker's approval, and I could open escrow. I floated out of the terminal on a cloud of euphoria. My senses soared as I sped back to Kihei. The sky looked bluer, clouds whiter, coconut trees greener, jasmine on the breeze sweeter. I loved it. I lived for it. Making a sale sent me spinning—body, mind, and spirit.

Maybe my luck was turning. Maybe I could handle Annie's and the baby's expenses after all. I burst into song, happier than I'd felt in days. I was as hooked on selling as Annie was on pot.

I stopped at the office, completed the paperwork, got the broker-in-charge's signature, and walked the contract, together with Jim's earnest money check, to Valley Isle Escrow at the far end of the mall. With great satisfaction I plunked a fat envelope on Nadine Freitas' desk for the second time that week.

"Gee, you're really going to town," she said, smiling graciously. A few years younger than I, Nadine was beautiful as only Portuguese women can be. Dark wavy hair, flawless creamy skin, shapely body, and eyes fringed with lashes so lush they had to be real. Last year she had discovered colored contact lenses. Today her irises were lavender.

"I wish I could do this every week, or even every month," I replied, transfixed by those surreal eyes.

"I hear your daughter's home," she said. "You must be very relieved."

Nadine had four children, one of whom was currently awaiting trial at Maui Community Correctional Center for breaking and entering. She smiled, but her lavender eyes remained flat. This time I didn't think it was just the color.

"Yeah," I replied. "Kids . . . they sure put you through it, don't they?"

She nodded, began to reply, then apparently thought better of it.

An escrow officer acts as a neutral third party, making sure every term and condition of the contract is satisfied prior to closing. She verifies all deposits are correct, delivered on time, and disbursed accurately at closing. Many's the time Nadine caught an unresolved detail and saved the day by calling my attention to it before it was too late.

"I'll get cracking on this one right away," she said, rapping her knuckles on the envelope. "Enjoy your daughter. You never know what they're going to do next."

I thanked her, feeling I'd gotten the lighter burden regarding our children's problems.

Still buoyed by the Le Boeuf sale, I called Annie and told her I'd pick her up for lunch. It's bad luck to celebrate a sale before it closes, but I didn't care. Flying high, I wanted to share my success with my daughter.

"Honey, would you like to shop for baby clothes?" I asked her as we drove out of the condo parking lot. "We could have lunch at Kaahumanu Center and pick up a few little things." I glanced at her, hoping I hadn't pushed too far. "Just to get you started," I added.

She looked out the window for a long while. From the corner of my eye, I saw her rub a slow circle around her stomach. With five weeks to go, was she at last feeling and believing the baby was real? Was it possible to bond with a child conceived under such horrendous circumstances?

"Sure, Ma. Lunch first, though. I'm starved."

Once again, she threw me for a loop. Strangely docile all afternoon, she willingly went along with whatever I proposed. I told her about my sale that morning, describing the scene at the airport with the Le Boeufs. She laughed as I dramatized big rough Jim Le Boeuf being bossed around by his tiny strawberry-coifed wife. Did I imagine a hint of admiration in her eyes for the way I handled a touchy situation and scored the deal?

Still smiling, we shared a piece of coffee ice cream pie, then moved along to gather a basic layette. As we shopped, Annie seemed interested, fingering the soft fabrics, holding the little garments up as if imagining them on her baby. By the third shop I could see she was tiring, so we called it quits.

On the way home she surprised me by telling me about her visit to the doctor the previous day. "I had a sonogram, Ma. They gel you all up and slide this cold thing over your *opu*. I saw the baby on the monitor. Cute nose. Kinda like Dad's. I saw its hands and feet, too. When it kicked, I felt it at the same time I saw the foot move on the screen. Pretty bad, huh?" Her voice held hints of wonder.

How I would have loved to witness that. "Any idea if it's a boy or a girl?" I asked, trying to sound casual.

"I never asked. I don't care either way." Most expectant mothers finish that sentence with, "as long as it's healthy." *Oh, Annie. I do despair.*

"What about childbirth classes? I'm sure they have them at the clinic. Labor's no picnic. I'd be thrilled to be your coach."

She looked at me in disgust. "Lame, Mom. No way."

"But—" I bit off my rebuttal. For a few blessed hours we'd been an ordinary mother and daughter, sharing the joys of her impending childbirth. Time to count my blessings.

When we got home there was a message from Jerry on my answering machine. Sensing doom, I returned his call. Without preamble, he launched into me. "Look, I want this settled. My earnest money is sitting in an escrow account, earning zero interest, when it could be riding the market. Do you know what the Dow hit yesterday?" As a stockbroker, Jerry was constitutionally opposed to idle money.

"It's out of our hands," I reminded him. "You know Randy's attorney sent eviction notices, personally delivered by the sheriff's deputy. By law, they have forty-five days from the date of delivery to get out. Technically, they can stay right up to the very last day."

"And if they don't leave?"

"You could take the property with Moana and the others in residence and evict them yourself after you take possession."

"Yeah, and what if you're right about that drug lab? Wouldn't that be just peachy if it got busted before we got them out and the Feds confiscated the property? No way."

"Just thought I'd mention it."

First thing Monday morning I drove to Maui Memorial. I wanted to know exactly what Annie's uninsured childbirth would cost me. I had asked Lily, but like most physicians, she wasn't up to speed on the monetary details. Seated at the hospital admissions desk, I tried my best not to melt down at the dollar amounts the clerk so casually tossed my way. I'd have to make a sale a day if Annie's delivery were anything but routine.

The clerk must have sensed my distress. "Have you considered registering your daughter with Ohana Care?" she asked.

"What's that?" I replied.

"It's the state-sponsored healthcare program for people who can't get health coverage any other way."

Never did I imagine a child of mine would have to rely on government assistance. But pride is an expensive indulgence. "Will they take her in the last months of pregnancy?"

"I think so. A lot of their clients give birth here. Why don't you go see them? They're just down the road."

I drove right over, still reeling from the financial reality of an uninsured birth. My pregnant daughter was as unprotected as a street person. This was not a good time to let family dignity stand in the way. The lowrise Ohana Care Clinic opened off a large parking lot shaded by mango trees. Half a dozen plastic lawn chairs flanked the front door, to which a sign was taped:

WELCOME TO OHANA CARE CLINIC.
IF YOU HAVE A RASH, PLEASE STAY OUTSIDE
AND TELL THE PERSON WHO ACCOMPANIED YOU
TO COME INSIDE AND GET A NURSE.

I glanced nervously at the people seated in the lawn chairs, wondering what kind of rashes they might be guilty of. Varying shades of brown faces eyed me with disinterest. I spotted nothing alarming on any of them. Not terribly reassured, I stepped quickly past them into the clinic. More brown faces seated on couches and standing in line, predominantly attached to pregnant girls and women. I was the only *haole*. A familiar feeling of self-consciousness settled over me, as it had routinely throughout my life. As often as not, I was the only Caucasian at church, in the grocery store, or at my children's Little League games. You get used to it.

When my turn came, a young Filipina case worker invited me into a private consultation room, where I explained Annie's situation. She spoke excellent English with no trace of an Island accent. She must have gone to college on the mainland. Her friendly manner put me immediately at ease.

"That's exactly why we're here, Mrs. McDaniel," she said. "From what you've said, your daughter is indeed eligible for Ohana Care. If you'll fill out these papers, and have her sign them, she'll be covered as soon as you bring them back."

"And her hospital expenses? The baby's?"

"Both fully covered."

"What if the baby has serious complications and needs to stay in the hospital for days or weeks or even months?"

"All taken care of. And she'll have her choice of providers. Who has she been seeing?"

"Lily Fujikawa."

"Ah, good, Dr. Fujikawa's on our list. Just let her know your daughter is now under Ohana Care."

I sagged in my chair. "As simple as that?"

She smiled, putting her hand on mine. "Don't worry. You've come to the right place. We're here to help."

"Well, I certainly appreciate it." Then I remembered the rather sinister sign on the clinic door. "By the way, what kind of rashes do you keep outside?"

She smiled. "Measles. Rubella. We have so many pregnant girls in here, we don't want to take a chance of someone bringing it in. The nurse goes outside and checks anyone who might be suspicious. Has your daughter had rubella?"

"As a matter of fact, she and her brothers had it as children."

"So, we don't have to worry about that," she said.

No, I thought, we don't have to worry about that.

Vastly relieved, I returned to the office. And promptly wished I hadn't. A fax awaited me, fronted by a cover page from the lavender-eyed Nadine at Valley Isle Escrow. "Please advise," said her cryptic comment in perfect Palmer manuscript.

The faxed document, an innocent piece of white paper, was covered with a large, familiar scrawl that slanted up to the right.

I, Randa Corrigan Entwistle, M.D., do solemnly swear that I now realize selling the house at 1155 Kauhoku Road in Haiku to be a grievous error. I hereby instruct escrow to cancel the sale, and return the buyer's earnest money deposit in full.

Ms. Corrine Suzanne Urquhart, also known as Moana Entwistle, has the right to remain in residence, along with any companion(s) of her choosing.

Ms. Urquhart has the right to continue renting the three downstairs bedrooms and keep the rental income for her own purposes.

I solemnly declare that I will continue paying the mortgage and refrain from selling the property for as long as Ms. Urquhart wishes to remain in residence.

I myself will find other accommodations on a permanent basis.
Signed, Randa Corrigan Entwistle, M.D.

Subscribed and sworn before me this 30th day of August, 1993.
Attested, Caitlyn Rivera, Notary Public, State of Hawaii.

So . . . Moana had finally gotten the message.

CHAPTER 20

How in the world had the notary been able to keep a straight face when the ferocious Moana pulled Dr. E. in by the ear and made her sign that amateurish document? It was certainly not the notary's job to question the content of such a declaration, but she did have to verify the declarant's identity, and that she signed of her own free will. The handwriting was definitely Randy's. The free-will bit was highly questionable.

As evidenced by this latest caper, Randy was more bamboozled than ever by Moana. She danced a two-step every time Mo jerked the strings. But why? Perhaps Frank was right. There had to be more to it than Randy's neediness and the unequal balance of their personalities. I left Randy a message to call me, pronto.

As things stood, Randy couldn't just cancel the sale, no matter how much her housemate pressured her. The Colemans had a legally binding contract. Unless Moana actually produced her deed, the notarized hand-written instruction to escrow was worthless. It constituted clear notice, however, that Moana had donned her battle gear.

The spot between my shoulder blades that lets me know I'm headed for trouble began to tingle. Kathleen had returned from her vacation in Alaska the day before. It was time to run the latest developments by her and get some help in navigating the rapids.

No human being should wear chartreuse. On Kathleen, it turned her wind-whipped complexion the shade of curry stew. Blissfully unaware, she listened to me with her usual laser-focused attention. I brought her up to speed on the Colemans' transaction, including the fact that we were now dealing with multiple evictions and an alleged deed in the name of the housemate.

"This deed that Moana claims gives her an ownership interest—have you seen it?" Kathleen asked.

"No. Randy says she can't get her hands on it. The woman has hidden it well, if in fact it exists."

"And there's no mention of Moana, or whatever her real name is, in the title report? Randa Entwistle is listed as the sole owner?"

"Correct." The expedited report had arrived as requested earlier in the week.

Kathleen tapped her pen on the pile of papers on her desk. It had grown alarmingly since the last time I saw it.

"That might be the answer," she said. "The woman may very well have what amounts to a holographic, or handwritten, deed. But she obviously hasn't recorded it at the Bureau of Conveyances. Therefore, if you can close this sale quickly and record the Colemans' deed first, Moana's deed would be worthless. By law, a recorded deed for value, in other words, as the result of a bona fide sale, would prevail over an unrecorded gift deed, even though the gift deed was dated earlier."

Score! Kathleen had dredged up a wispy remnant I now recalled from real estate school. This little gem was one of the innumerable obscurities one memorizes for the licensing exam but never expects to encounter in actual practice. Once again, Kathleen's grasp of pertinent minutia amazed me. Which is why she was the broker, and not I.

"Do the Colemans want to proceed, knowing that at any moment Moana could wake up and secure her interest by recording her alleged deed?" she asked.

"Yes. It just adds to their determination. But I have a feeling the woman thinks hiding the deed beneath her mattress creates a stronger threat. Keeping the doctor guessing gives her more power."

"Hmm. Could be. You need to talk to escrow right away. See how they handle the possibility of an unrecorded deed. It could constitute a cloud on the title. Vague as it is, they may not be willing to close until it's settled one way or another."

I winced. Calling escrow to ask this kind of question is like examining your breasts for lumps. You know you have to do it, yet what if you actually find one? "Okay, will do," I said, bowing to necessity.

"Good." Kathleen turned to her computer and clicked open a file, effectively dismissing me.

"There's more," I said.

"Oh?" She answered without turning back to face me.

"I think there's something going on in the garage, maybe an illegal drug lab."

She snapped to full attention again. "What in heaven's name makes you think that?"

"Padlocks on the garage door. Window blacked out with cardboard. Totally hush-hush. The inspector couldn't get in. Even Randy doesn't know what's going on in there."

She looked at me incredulously. "Well, who does?"

"Moana's boyfriend, apparently. He's one of the people we need to evict. He travels a lot, but when he's here he's busy in the garage at all hours. The mailman makes regular pickups."

"Come on!" Kathleen relaxed against the back of her chair. "I was ready to believe you until you mentioned the mailman. Nobody ships out illegal drugs by parcel post in broad daylight."

"That's exactly what the Colemans said. And Barbara Jaworski. And Frank. But something *is* going on. Barbara's boyfriend Grant at the *Maui News* has been asking questions about this Prakash guy. Grant won't tell her what's up. The whole thing feels downright creepy. I'm afraid if it is drugs, the Feds could confiscate the property before we can close."

"That's pretty farfetched. This is real life, Laura."

"Yeah, and shit happens in real life. Just last month Realtor Caravan toured a fabulous estate in the wilds beyond Ulupalakua Ranch that had been confiscated and is now on the market, title held by Uncle Sam. The owners were big-time dealers from L.A. who moved their business to Hawaii and got busted. That story made front page news, remember?"

She nodded. "Okay. You've made your point. You'd better be scrupulous about how you proceed. And stay away from the place, you hear? Keep the Colemans away, too. Don't let me find out you guys have been poking around, trying to determine what's in the garage. Right now, today, put everything you've just told me in writing to the Colemans, every single detail, with your strong recommendation that they pull out of the deal. All they have to do is accept Randy's handwritten rescission, legitimate or not, and they'll get their deposit back. If they refuse, insist, and I mean insist, they hire an attorney. This situation is too sticky for a mere Realtor."

"You're right," I admitted, much as I hated the idea. When attorneys get involved in a real estate deal, all bets are off. They find trouble in every paragraph, including items that are not at issue. The next thing you know, the attorneys, who are likely weekend golfing buddies, get into a grand pissing match. At that point a lowly agent can only stand on the sidelines, grinding her teeth and ducking the spray. However, as Kathleen had pointed out, I was way out of my professional league. The time had come.

I thanked Kathleen for her counsel, went to my cubicle and started the letter, grateful that my notes were in order.

Even if the Colemans were determined to proceed, there were numerous ways they could lose the property prior to closing: Moana's purported deed, any one tenant's refusal to move out, and confiscation. Loss of the property would be a huge disappointment, to them and to me. But none of these factors constituted actual danger. Except the unknown: Prakash. If he were running a drug lab, he'd most certainly defend it from nosy intruders. More likely, however, now that eviction notices had been served, he'd pack up and slink away in the dark, knowing his location was no longer secure. In either case, I vowed to do as Kathleen ordered, stay away and keep my clients away. I began to feel better—almost—about recommending an attorney.

Before I finished the letter, I called Valley Isle Title. Nadine Freitas came on the line immediately. "I thought I'd be hearing from you," she said.

"What's the deal with this so-called rescission signed by Dr. Entwistle?" I asked. "Can a purported co-owner pop up, just like that, and force a cancellation without proof?"

"You'd be surprised. People try all the time. They think they have an interest in the property, or wish they did. Especially places down the country where family ownership goes back to the Great *Mahele*, the distribution of the king's land in fee simple to the chiefs and commoners in eighteen forty-eight. They didn't always bother with deeds in the old days, or if they did, they often neglected to record them. Now when some renegade descendant tries to sell, all kinds of claimants come out of the woodwork. As long as we're satisfied with the integrity of the title search, we don't take them seriously. This search clearly shows Dr. Entwistle as sole owner. I have my title people double-checking, but I doubt they'll find anything to the contrary."

"What if Moana really does have a deed but never recorded it?"

"She'll have to prove it to us. The onus is on her. If she brings us a legitimate deed, even handwritten, then of course we'll take it seriously and urge her to record it right away. Meanwhile, the Colemans can try to close and record first, thereby shutting her out. If they succeed, their recorded deed would prevail because they paid for the property and she didn't. That's how Hawaii law works regarding priority of deeds."

I breathed a little easier with this verification of what Kathleen had told me earlier. "And if Moana can't prove ownership?"

"Then she has no authority to cancel the sale."

"So what will you do?"

"We'll proceed under the assumption she has no deed. The burden of proof rests on the claimant. The cancellation came in by fax, with no follow-up. Naturally, we're trying to get in touch with Dr. Entwistle for some kind of explanation. Can you help me with that?"

I laughed. "Sorry, Nadine, no can do. Randy Entwistle is frustratingly unavailable. Leave a message. She'll get back to you eventually. Meanwhile, let me make sure I've got this straight: From escrow's point of view, Moana can't hold things up by asserting her claim via Dr. E.'s faxed, notarized cancellation instruction?"

"Not unless she produces the deed or gets a lawyer involved."

"Oh, God. Not more lawyers."

"But what does it mean?" Diana asked later that afternoon, as she set two glasses of iced tea sprigged with mint on her kitchen table. The faxed rescission lay on the polished wood surface between us next to a blue glass bowl of floating gardenias.

"I'm not quite sure." I crushed the serrated mint leaves with my spoon against the inside of my frosted glass, then sipped the fragrant brew. The piquant mint bathed and cooled my parched throat, as refreshing as a rain shower.

I had hoped to catch Jerry at home, too, but he'd had some errands to do in the late afternoon. I prefer to deliver difficult news to all parties at the same time, making sure everyone understands the situation in the same way, while steering their focus toward solutions.

"Surely Randy can't just opt out?" Diana asked.

"No. I checked with escrow. A contract is a contract. And unless Moana comes forward with an actual deed, she has no say. But here's the critical point: If she has a deed, even if it's crudely handwritten, she could record it at any time, and we'd be screwed. But if we can beat her to the punch by closing and recording yours first, we've got it. Both my broker and escrow confirmed that.

"But, even if she's bluffing, she can make life miserable for us by keeping her manipulative pressure on Randy. I have a call in to Dr. E., asking for an explanation. This whole business of not being able to contact her directly is driving me mad. Sometimes it takes days for her to get back to me. With a normal person, I'd call her at work, or just show up, but she's given me ferocious instructions not to do that. Not that I'm particularly comfortable barging in on an appendectomy."

Diana grinned. "You can't jump in your car and drop in on her at home in the evening, either. Heaven knows what beach she sleeps on."

"Believe me, I've been tempted. Can you see me shining a flashlight into every wind-surfer van parked on the sand?" We both chuckled at the notion.

Then Diana asked, "I don't suppose you can talk to Moana yourself, try to reason with her?"

I shook my head. "Reason with Moana? I'm not sure it's possible. She's the kind of person who would take everything I say and twist it to her own use. It's a trap I don't want to fall into. Besides, I've tried that with other people's tenants in the past, and it usually backfires. No, our best bet is to proceed as quickly as possible, and hope that the woman is either bluffing or keeps the deed hidden for her own purposes."

Diana's hazel eyes lit up. "So if we close quickly, we can beat her out?"

"As long as she doesn't tumble to the necessity of recording her deed. But you can bet she won't go without kicking and screaming."

Diana's eyes danced with delight. "Jerry and I will do some kicking and screaming of our own. We want that house!"

"I hear you. But something else just occurred to me about Moana. She lives in Randy's house more as a guest than a tenant. The Landlord-Tenant Code may not apply, specifically the rules of eviction. Even if it does, the courts in Hawaii generally bend over backward to protect the one who has no money and no place to live if she's turned out. With her injured leg, Moana can present a pretty desperate picture of herself, while Randy is a physician in a highly paid specialty. Moana wouldn't have to put on much of an act to get a judge's sympathy."

"That's outrageous! You mean we might not be able to get her out at all?"

"It's a grim possibility."

"And what about this thing?" She flicked the faxed rescission with a fingernail, setting it spinning on the table.

"I don't know if Randy really wants out," I replied, "or if she was coerced into signing. And if so, why? The fax just doesn't ring true. I've got to talk to Randy."

Diana took a sip of tea, then daintily picked a mint leaf off her tongue. "With an eviction that might not work, a cancellation that isn't a cancellation—oh, and your crazy notion that the feds could step in and confiscate the property at any time, we're in a bit of a muddle, darling, wouldn't you say?"

I nodded my head at her mocking understatement. "You've pretty well summed it up."

I felt like I'd fallen into a kettle of steaming *saimin,* that fragrant Japanese noodle soup flavored with green onion and ginger. No matter where I grabbed for support, I pulled up nothing but slippery loose ends.

Diana poked at the gardenias floating in the blue bowl at the center of the table, setting them in lazy motion. The air stirred with exotic perfume. I closed my eyes. For a brief moment I was a child again, running barefoot at Pua Olena, chasing butterflies along a gardenia hedge with a red fishing net.

Her next words dissolved my dreamy respite. "Maybe we'd better hire an attorney."

Once again, those dreaded words. I wiped my glass drips off the table with a napkin, then pulled an envelope out of my file case and handed it to her. "I'm one step ahead of you. I've summarized the situation in this letter, which also recommends you reconsider the purchase. Accept Randy's rescission and get out. If you insist on proceeding, you must seek legal counsel. That's the only way I'll remain involved as your agent. Things have gone way beyond my comfort zone."

Diana accepted the envelope and tapped it on the table. Then she narrowed her eyes and drilled into mine. "Whatever it takes, love, we want that property. Don't you dare desert us now."

CHAPTER 21

Of course I won't desert the Colemans, I thought as I pulled into my condo parking lot. Difficult as it was, however, letting go and allowing their attorney to take over would give me a welcome breather. From now on I only had to take care of routine details while the big boys tackled the hard stuff. I hated to give up control, but if everything exploded, at least it wouldn't be my fault.

I greeted Annie, who was watching TV on the sofa, crossed the living room to my answering machine, and hit the PLAY button. My private town crier fairly bristled with news as my punishment for being away all day. The small patina of serenity I'd talked myself into on the way home fizzled at the sound of an outraged voice.

"This is Moana Entwistle. I understand you have attempted to sell my home. This is outrageous and clearly against the law. I am an owner of the property. Your clients' contract is void without my signature. Dr. Entwistle is *not* interested in selling. She will refund the buyers' earnest money deposit in full. Dr. Entwistle has sent instructions to escrow to that effect. I'm sure you have a copy by now. Do not attempt to contact Dr. Entwistle or myself. You have done enough damage already." *Beep.* Furious, I poked the erase button, wishing it were Moana's eye.

I spent much of the evening in a restless ferment, tidying the apartment in jerky spurts while mentally conjuring up and then discarding various ingenious but impractical ways of getting in touch with Randy. Until I could confront her about her attempted rescission, I'd have no idea where things really stood.

When I couldn't contain myself any longer, I sat down and shared my frustration with Annie. From her usual prone position on the couch, she rolled her eyes and said, "Chill, Ma. You're stuck. Give up and relax."

I leaned forward with my arms crossed on my knees. "You don't understand. Our next few months of survival depend on closing this sale. I've got two other sales in escrow, but we need this big one to truly get back on our feet. Besides, look at all the time and effort I've put into it."

"But if everybody hires lawyers, like you said, the whole thing might bust up anyway. And you still won't get paid."

"True." I pushed out my legs and slumped against the back of the chair.

"So, do the Colemans want the house that badly?"

"Yes, they do." I sat up straight again. "The more difficult it gets, the more they want it. My job is to get it for them, whatever it takes. As long as it's legal, moral, and ethical, of course."

She ran her fingers through her flaxen hair, letting it drift like gossamer over her shoulders. "So what's more important to you, Ma? Getting the house for the Colemans, or closing the sale so you'll get paid?"

I stared at my daughter. She had nailed the Realtor's eternal dilemma right into my gut. Whose interest was I promoting? The clients', who would probably be better served by canceling now that things had gotten so dicey? Or mine, the agent's, who needed to close the sale to pay her bills and feed her family? I looked at my daughter, who was awaiting an answer with one fair eyebrow raised. I raised my chin and looked at her from a defiant angle. "Right now, today, getting paid is number one. This deal is consuming every waking moment of my life. I want it closed and the money in my pocket."

She grinned. "Okay. At least you're honest."

I kissed her on the forehead, feeling we were closer in those introspective moments than at any time since her return, closer even than on our shopping trip for baby clothes. She had glimpsed something of my inner struggle, seemed to understand my conflicted feelings. It was a comforting turnabout in mother-daughter relations.

Our unexpected intimacy took the edge off my restlessness. Gratefully, I settled down with a book. The last thing I anticipated was a call from Randy later in the evening. I was lying on my bed, dozing, when the phone jarred me awake. As soon as I recognized the doctor's gravelly voice, I motioned frantically for Annie to turn down the TV. Feeling as soggy as stir-fried *chow fun*, I pushed up onto one elbow and tried to collect my thoughts. Brusquely, Randy asked me if I had received her fax rescinding the sale.

"Yes, but Randy, you can't just bail out. You're under contract. The Colemans are hiring an attorney. They don't intend to let you out of it."

"But Moana doesn't want to sell." Her voice choked.

I was not moved. "You knew that when you put up the For Sale sign. Forgive me if I'm having a memory lapse, but you put up that sign specifically because you wanted Moana out of your life. Isn't that right?"

"Well, yeah, sort of . . . at the time."

"What do you mean? *Have* you changed your mind?"

"Sort of." She snuffed a big, sloppy sniff.

"Sort of? It's not a 'sort of' kind of thing, Randy. Selling a house is a big deal. There's no 'sort of' about it."

"But I've broken my word to her." That whine again.

"Which was?"

"To . . . to take care of her . . . forever. No matter what."

I rolled over onto my stomach with a groan. "When did you make that foolish promise?"

"It doesn't matter. The fact is, I did promise . . ."

"To take care of her forever? That sounds a bit extreme."

"Moana needs to be taken care of. She's got problems, big problems. She promised to run the household and handle my finances. I promised to take care of her. It seemed right at the time. In fact, she was a godsend. Working such long hours, coming home to that huge, empty house . . . She really took a load off me . . . for a while."

I could see the two of them having a glass of wine on the terrace at sunset, Randy feeling protective and grateful for Moana's presence in her life, making outrageous promises to her on the spur of the moment. Only, Moana had likely planned every step in advance, ruthlessly setting Randy up to get what she wanted. She knew a mother lode when she saw one. How could Randy, such an educated person, so highly respected in her field, be such a ditz? And how could she be so naïve as to believe she had to honor such a promise? Did she think all would yet be well if she just toed the line? She hated Moana. I was sure of it. What was this really all about?

"Tell me more," I said.

"For a while it was good. Hot dinner waiting, no matter what time I got home. House clean and tidy. Someone to talk to." Her voice sounded dreamy.

"And then?"

"Then it turned sour. Prakash. . . ."

"What about Prakash?" I sat up on the edge of the bed, gripping the phone. "Is he more than just her boyfriend?"

Randy hesitated, as if she'd already said too much. Then she sighed. "Prakash messed everything up. It isn't her fault she fell in love with him."

"Who *is* Prakash? Tell me something useful!" A moment ago I'd felt a vague glimmer of empathy. It is irritating when a man enters the picture and suddenly a gal pal is no longer available for Saturday night movies. But now my annoyance was seeping out sideways.

"What about Moana's claim of ownership? That's the biggie. Did Prakash have anything to do with that?"

"No, that happened before she met him."

"All right, so Moana had her little agenda all set up before he entered the picture. Were you able to get your hands on the deed you *think* you signed?" I waited for her to get defensive over my snide emphasis on "think," but it rolled right over her. Moana had trained her well.

"She won't give it to me. She says she has it in a safe place, that it's her insurance policy."

As I suspected. "Sure. Look, Randy, the simplest thing is for you to buy her out. Have you offered her enough money so she and this Prakash will walk away from you and the house forever?"

Randy began to sputter and moan. Her words spilled out between sobs. "It . . . it's not about money. I've tried, but she won't even listen."

"Maybe you need to up the ante. How much did you offer her?"

"Never mind. That's not what she wants." She launched into hysterical hiccupping, as if her shriveled soul were being wrenched out of her body, bit by bit. I did not sign up for this.

"Randy. Get hold of yourself. I can't help you if you—"

"Oh my God! She's home!" Bang, slam, went the receiver. My ear reverberated with the crash. I stood up and dialed Randy back immediately, but of course I only got her answering machine.

Too distraught to sleep, unable to concentrate on my reading, I lay there puzzling over our conversation. I had learned only one new thing: that Randy had promised to take care of Moana forever, and that she felt honor-bound to keep that promise. But why? And did this mean she really intended to wiggle out of the sale? Would she just show up with Moana's deed, record it, and end the game?

And what was Randy doing calling from the house at eleven o'clock at night? She didn't live there anymore. She must have snuck in, expecting to find the house empty, and freaked out when Moana walked in on her. Was she looking for the deed? Without direct access to Randy, I had no way of getting any answers.

I wanted to scream in frustration. I hated this helpless feeling, a feeling that was only too familiar. Stagnation hits at some point in every deal. Buyers or sellers have to make decisions or take action behind the scenes. The agent never knows which way they'll go. You sit at home, bite your fingernails, pray for a favorable outcome, and wait for the maddening phone to ring.

If I'd been invited to place a bet on the Colemans' outcome, I'd have had a hard time making a prediction. With Moana's propensity for buffaloing Randy into signing things, it was entirely possible that Randy had deeded Moana an interest in the property. Moana had likely prepared it in advance and presented it to Randy the moment she extracted the promise to take care of her forever. Or maybe Randy offered it to Moana after a spat to demonstrate her contriteness. I'd probably never know.

On the other hand, the more I knew about Moana, the more I believed this was a bluff, merely part of a bigger game. My frantic mind kept cycling through my dialogue with Randy, but no new insights revealed themselves. Before long, the predictable humor on the *Dave Letterman Show* and Annie's low bursts of laughter finally did the trick and put me out of my misery.

Before I could begin to wonder if Randy's attorney had received responses from any of the other tenants to whom he'd sent eviction notices, proof arrived in the afternoon mail:

> *We are the legitimate tenants of Bedroom A at 1155 Kauhoku Road, Haiku. Dr. Randa Entwistle and her agent Moana Entwistle are guilty of breach of contract, fraud, harassment, intimidation, misrepresentation, loud banging noises, and invasion of privacy.*
>
> *On July 7th of this year, we responded to a newspaper advertisement for rooms to rent at the above-mentioned premises. We gave Moana a $700 deposit for the room, and left a carload of our personal possessions in said room, preparatory to moving in the following day. We were not given keys at that time, as she said she had to make duplicates.*
>
> *When we arrived the next morning to get our keys, as agreed, the gate and house were locked and no one was there to let us in. We waited several hours, which caused us to miss our catamaran ride to Lanai, where we were to attend a company picnic.*
>
> *Those attending the picnic on Lanai will testify that our names were called to win valuable door prizes: a weekend for two on Kauai, com-*

*plete with hotel, airfare and a rental car. Since we
had to be present to receive our prizes, we lost
$1,047 in value.*

*In addition, we had to rent a hotel room
for two nights because no one showed up to let us
in, and we had nowhere else to live. The total for
that was $389, including meals.*

*Finally, we were so upset over losing our
prizes that we had a car accident driving into the
hotel parking lot the first night. That cost us
$420, which was not covered under our insur-
ance, which has a $500 collision deductible.*

*As you can see, our life has been a series
of disasters since agreeing to rent a room in this
house. We hereby demand of Dr. Entwistle the
sum of $1,856 to compensate for the damage to
our car, the cost of hotel accommodations, and
the loss of the prize, all actual damages that
resulted from her illegal treatment of us.*

*In addition, we were not informed of the
impending sale of the property until after we
moved in and saw the For Sale sign one day.
Then we received an eviction notice, contrary to
our lease which runs through July 9, 1994.*

*Dr. Entwistle has since harassed us by
beating on our windows and yelling at us to get
out. We have a legitimate leasehold interest in the
property, and the right to quiet enjoyment thereof.
All of this has caused us nervousness, fragmenta-
tion, and loss of sleep, just when we thought we
found a good place to live.*

*We will accept the above-mentioned sum
plus an additional $2,000 as hardship damages, a
total of $3,856 if paid within 10 days by way of a*

cashier's check or cash. We will move out the day
we receive the money. Plus the return of our $700
deposit, which Moana says she has already spent
and can't refund to us. Otherwise, we will stay
put.

Signed,
Buffy & Todd Krentz

That was the last straw. I couldn't sit around and wait until Randy called me again. Too many things were flying out of control. By her sworn statement, she was trying to stop the sale. According to the tenants, on the other hand, she was trying a little self-help eviction so she could complete the sale. Such crude methods left a lot to be desired. The Krentz's in Bedroom A had obviously taken exception, and could botch things all by themselves with no help from Moana.

What in tarnation was going on? I decided I had no choice but to storm the bastion and demand satisfaction.

CHAPTER 22

Maui Memorial Hospital sits on a hillside overlooking Kahului Harbor, perched above four levels of outdoor terraced parking. After snaking through the crowded lot several times, I found an empty space on the lowest tier, then hiked the steps through the tumbling garden to the lobby entrance. Half a dozen smokers sat on benches outside the main glass doors, creating a haze that aggravated my temporary shortness of breath. The views of the harbor and Haleakala were stunning, but I was in no mood to peek.

"Can you tell me if Dr. Entwistle is in the hospital?" I asked at the information desk in the lobby, still breathing heavily.

"Let me check," the clerk offered.

The lobby was calm, just a few children watching TV on ceiling-high sets in a cave-like alcove while their parents visited patients upstairs. In the gift shop across the way an elderly volunteer wearing a blue hospital auxiliary aloha shirt regaled a customer with the latest in institutional humor. Their laughter floated across to me, making me wish I could join them for a little comic relief.

"Ma'am?" The clerk called me to attention. "Dr. Entwistle is in surgery. Do you wish to leave a message?"

"No, thanks. I'll catch her later."

I found the elevator, located the surgical wing in the building directory, and pushed the button. The doors opened. I stepped aside for a mother and newborn infant in a wheelchair, obviously going home. An aide pushed the chair, followed by the beaming father, loaded down with flowers and a pink gingham diaper bag. The young mother gazed raptly at her baby, wrapped in a pink shawl and nestled tightly against her breast. Soon, I thought, Annie will be wheeled through this lobby with her baby. How I longed for a scene as lovely as this one.

Riding the elevator to the third floor, I exited to the linty ward smell of laundered cotton and dead skin cells. Toughing through a moment of queasiness, I found myself in what could only be described as a dismal enlargement of the hallway, lined with mismatched chairs, a sagging leatherette sofa, and a handwritten sign on a rectangle of cardboard that proclaimed, "OR Waiting Room." The sofa and all but one chair were occupied by members of a large Hawaiian family, large in the true classical sense. Not one of them, man, woman, or teenager, weighed less than three hundred pounds. In spite of uniformly faded T-shirts and baggy shorts, each provided an exquisite example of Island artist Madge Tennent's "rhythm in the round." With smiling eyes, sensuous lips, and graceful hands, they lounged with varying degrees of lassitude on the somber, stark chairs and sofa.

Corridors led off in two directions, but they didn't appear to be public-friendly. An elderly Japanese woman filing her nails at a nearby desk was the only other person in sight. Sporting the same blue volunteer aloha shirt I'd seen on the woman in the gift shop, she seemed semi-approachable.

"Is Dr. Entwistle available?" I asked, hoping I might catch Randy between procedures.

The woman shook her permed black hair. "She stay in surgery." In her Pidgin accent, she pronounced it, importantly, as "churg'ry."

"Can you tell me what time she'll be free?"

The woman ruffled through some dog-eared pages attached to a clipboard. "She finishing one gall bladdah. Could be one 'nother hour, unless they get one what-you-call-it . . . comp-li-cay-shin. You like leave one message?"

"No, thank you. I'll wait."

"If you give me you name, I tell her come see you. If it's im-paw-tan, of course."

I didn't want to give her my name, for fear Randy would do exactly the opposite. She had forbidden me to phone her here, never mind stop by in person. However, I owed her no duty of obedience. Perhaps if I inferred I was related to Dr. E.'s patient, the well-meaning volunteer would take it from there.

"When she's *pau*, could you just tell her she has a concerned visitor?" I asked.

"Concerned about the gall bladdah?"

"Yes, you could say that." I was, in fact, quite galled by the whole situation.

The volunteer scrawled out her version of my message, then bustled down the empty hallway to deliver it, obviously delighted she finally had something constructive to do.

I sank into the one remaining leatherette chair in the waiting area. Smiling briefly at one of the Hawaiian women, making minimal eye contact, I silently apologized for imposing on their space. I assumed they were related to the gall bladder, but refrained from asking. The woman smiled back, as if to reassure me they understood what I, too, was going through, waiting for a relative in surgery.

Niceties observed, I pulled my *Reader's Digest* out of my bag. I never travel without "an article a day of lasting significance." Hokey as it sounds, I spend half my life waiting for people. I'm content as long as I have something uplifting and non-taxing to read. I opened the magazine to a story about a man sailing around the world solo when he capsized in the north Atlantic. I enjoy reading about people whose problems are bigger—and colder—than mine. Try as I might to concentrate, however, I found myself distracted by an odd metallic clanking sound, not too loud, but vaguely familiar. Glancing about, I found no explanation for the noise. Chalking it up to the air-conditioning, I turned back to my magazine.

As the man in the ocean, gasping and sputtering between crashing waves, huddled under his overturned boat desperately radioing for help, the elevator doors bumped open. A young Hawaiian woman emerged, slim this time, carrying a huge rectangular pan covered with aluminum foil. Dressed in a lavender-and-white flowered muumuu, and dark hair flowing in gentle waves down her back, she resembled a goddess bearing a sacred offering. I recognized her as Haunani Tavares, head teller at my bank.

A teenage boy followed—his shorts slung so low on his hips they seemed in danger of falling off—toting a large brown grocery bag. Everyone in the room perked up.

"Eh, Sistah, we t'ought you nevah come back," one of the men exclaimed. "Where you wen' for da *lomilomi* salmon? Nort' Pole?"

Everyone chortled.

"Ah, shut up, you folks," she laughed. "I wen' bring um. No complain." She glanced at me and jerked her chin. "Eh, Laura, how you stay?"

"Good, good, Haunani, and you?"

"Real *poino*, bad luck, our uncle. They taking out his gall bladder once and for all."

She set the pan on the coffee table, not six inches from my knees, and peeled back the foil. The scrumptious aroma of fried hamburger patties and gravy suffused the air. My stomach did eager flip flops.

"Oh, wow, *ono* grinds," the other man exclaimed. He reached into the grocery sack and made great ceremony of pulling out paper plates, plastic forks, napkins, cups, and a dozen small cartons of passion-orange-guava juice, known locally as POG. To my astonishment, one of the women reached over the far side of the couch and pulled up an electric rice cooker, still plugged into the wall and steaming. That explained the mysterious clanking I'd heard earlier.

Their lively chatter transformed the waiting room from a dreary afterthought to a lively party pad.

"Come on, Sistah, make 'em fast. I stay hungry," the first man said.

"You always hungry. You jest wen' stop McDonald's drivin' ovah heah," said the older woman.

He feigned disgust. "How you know dat?"

"I stay right behind you, brah, inside da drive thru." Great guffaws of laughter and shaking stomachs. They were having a grand time.

Although I tried, I could not blend into the woodwork, nor move to another chair. I was trapped in the middle of their lunch. Mortified, I lowered my gaze and tried desperately to care about the shipwrecked man shivering in his upended sailboat. Hopeless. Out of the corner of my eye, I watched Haunani heap up a plate of sticky rice, two juicy hamburger patties, diagonal slices of fried hot dog, and drown them with a scoop of greasy brown gravy. She added a *lomilomi* salmon chaser in a little white paper cup. I swallowed repeatedly to control a rush of saliva.

With an irresistible smile, she turned and offered the laden plate to me. The man who had emptied the grocery bag handed me a carton of POG. Startled, I didn't know what to do.

"Come on," the man exclaimed. "You here, we here, we all gotta eat. No cafeteria inside dis hospital. Herry up. Bumbye da stuff goin' get cold."

Behind them the other folks smiled and nodded, encouraging me to take the plate. Haunani extended it closer until I had no choice. I took it, with the POG, and murmured my thanks. Nodding happily, they turned back to their food. The next plate went to the volunteer clerk, who needed no urging. She tucked into the rice and gravy before Haunani turned her back. The glum little group awaiting the outcome of their uncle's surgery became a happy family party in full swing. Having taken care of their guests, everyone grabbed a plate and began piling on the grinds, laughing and joking all the while. In their exuberance, I half expected them to rush down the hall with plates for the surgical team and the patient on the operating table.

The hamburger patties, sliced hot dog, sticky rice and gravy hit the spot. I cajoled myself into thinking the bits of fresh tomato and green onion mixed with the chilled raw salmon would scour out the epic load of cholesterol from the main course before it had a chance to snuggle up and attach to my arteries. Safe in my clever illusion, I savored every greasy bite. Upon finishing, we piled our trash in an overflowing wastebasket near the elevator. I thanked them profusely, feeling we were all great friends by now. The family settled in to wait again. One by one they nodded off in the huge uncomfortable chairs and sofa.

As my solitary wait for Dr. Entwistle dragged on, I began to feel ridiculous. For all I knew, Randy would strip, shower, re-gown, and scrub for the next procedure without paying any attention to the volunteer's note. Or, if she had a sixth sense about who her visitor was, she'd sneak out the physicians' private exit. She might have left the hospital by now. More and more, I felt on a fool's errand, but didn't know what else to do. I needed to see the doctor. Staking her out appeared to be my only hope. I had to admit I was enjoying the peace and quiet. No one knew my whereabouts. The clerk's phone never rang for me. Annie and Frank weren't around to irritate me. My snoozing comrades knew nothing of my business. Hospital personnel walked by, intent on their tasks, never looking in my direction. Picking up my magazine, I settled in to savor the solitude. Even if I missed Randy, which was entirely likely, I would enjoy a little eddy of self renewal. Such a luxury wasn't available at home anymore.

A peaceful hour passed. I enjoyed the delicious guilt until that familiar edginess crept over me once more. Finally, I arose and approached the clerk again. "Is Dr. Entwistle finished yet?" I asked.

She picked up the phone and punched four digits. She inquired, then nodded up at me. "She stay *pau*. Should be only few minutes. I went remind them for send her out here."

My stomach began a slow churn, partially due to the load of grease with which it was valiantly coping, partially because showdown time loomed.

Before I could return to my chair, the swinging doors to the surgery suite burst open. Randy barreled through, almost knocking me over. "S-s-sorry." She skittered sideways and arranged her gangly limbs, clad in blue scrubs, into a semblance of order. "Oh, it's you! What are you doing here? Damn it, this was supposed to be about the gall bladder. I told you *not* to come to the hospital."

Before I could respond, she grasped my arm and hustled me down the corridor. As we passed my chair, I snatched my bag and magazine. Several of the family had awakened, curious but placid. I waved them a wobbly farewell.

"How dare you come looking for me here?" Randy sputtered as we careened around a corner, barely missing a gurney with a frightened-looking patient strapped on it.

I tried to twist away from her. "Let me go. You're hurting me."

She tightened her grip on my arm. "Why can't you leave me alone? Is there no end to this aggravation?"

I wrenched my arm away and confronted her. "Have you forgotten? You're under contract with my clients. It's my job to keep you moving so we can close the sale. But you make it impossible when I can't even get you on the phone."

By now we were at the end of the corridor beneath a red EXIT sign. Randy pushed even with me and rammed open the door with her shoulder, precipitating us down two flights of concrete stairs. For all I knew, we were headed for murder and mayhem in the morgue. We crashed through another door at the bottom of the stairway and found ourselves on a cement walkway leading toward the emergency entrance. The sudden rush of sunlight and neon-green grass blinded me.

Randy thrust me toward a wooden bench beneath a *kukui* tree. Finally letting go of my arm, she plunked herself down on the bench and began kneading her hands in distress, all the fight suddenly leached out of her. I collapsed beside her, heart thumping, wondering what I was supposed to do. Against all odds, my instinct was to put a comforting hand on her back, but I refrained. Whatever her burdens, I couldn't afford to start feeling sorry for her at this late date.

"Apologies. Didn't mean to hurt you," she finally muttered. "I'm in crud up to my ass."

My heart sank. The last thing I wanted to do was play mother confessor to this troubled woman. But I had a job to do, especially if the crud concerned the sale of her home. I crossed my legs and leaned against the wooden backrest, feeling my adrenaline level begin to drop. The pale, star-shaped *kukui* leaves above us provided a shady oasis. "So tell me,

Randy, what's going on?" At last, I could question her in person. Now maybe the picture would begin to jell.

Randy shook her head. She remained hunched over, knees apart. "You don't know," she moaned. "You just don't know."

"No, I don't know. You're going to have to tell me. Don't you think it's about time?"

She straightened up and stared toward the harbor for a long while. Half a dozen surfers rode the waves surging along the breakwater. Finally she spoke, her voice defeated and flat. "She's got me by the short and curlies. There's no fucking way out." The doctor was still in OR vocabulary mode.

"You mean Moana?"

"Of course, Moana. Who else?"

"Why has she got you so tied up? It can't be that bad."

"Huh. You don't know Mo." She turned to face me, eyes pleading. "I told you part of it the other night on the phone, but not everything. If I tell you the rest of it, can you promise me confidentiality?"

"No, I can't. You're not my client."

"But you need to know the whole picture. I'm just not sure I can trust you."

"You've got to trust me, Randy. It's the only way I can help. But keep in mind I have a duty to inform my clients of anything you say that would affect their purchase."

She sat there for a long time, seeming to shrink within her wrinkled blue scrubs. A booming whistle sounded from the harbor. Across from the surfers, a tugboat was easing an inter-island freighter out of its berth prior to escorting it through the breakwater. I waited, rubbing my arm, which still smarted from Randy's vise-like grip.

Finally she cleared her throat. "I guess I'd better tell you anyway, because I don't know what else to do. Maybe you can help, maybe not." She turned to face me. "You've seen Moana's limp. She gets around amazingly well, but she's still in rough shape. Always will be." I nodded. "When we met, she was in a acute pain from her first accident. Her physician was trying to get her off some pretty strong painkillers. Narcotics. But Mo couldn't—or wouldn't—manage without them. After she moved in with me, I started writing prescriptions for her. She lied to her own doctor, told him she was off the stuff. But I continued to supply her. She was seriously addicted. It got worse after she had her car accident."

This was making me very nervous. "I don't quite—"

"Don't you see? I'm not her physician. It's illegal to write 'scripts for a controlled substance for someone who's not your patient. I can't believe I was that stupid, but I was. I just wrote her a new 'script the other night. I'd gone up to drop it off, but she wasn't home. I got in through a window. That's when I called you. With the house quiet, I figured we could talk. Moana's kept a copy of every 'script I ever wrote for her. While we were talking, I poked around in her desk, thinking I'd find them and destroy them. Then she walked in. Oh, God, what an ugly scene. She'll turn me in to the police if I don't back off on the house sale and continue supplying her. She's absolutely adamant."

I was appalled. "Lord, I figured she had some kind of hold over you, but I never imagined anything this serious."

Randy jumped up and began to pace. "So now you understand? I'll lose my license. I'll go to jail. At the very least, I'd be censured by my peers, have an albatross around my neck for the rest of my professional life. My work means everything to me. Everything! I'm damn good at it. I'll die before I give it up."

"Okay, okay." I tried to calm her down by refocusing. "You haven't mentioned Prakash. Where does he fit into this part of the picture?"

"Prakash." She pronounced it like a sneeze. "Until he moved in, things with Moana were manageable. She was nice to me because she needed the meds. But early on I made the ghastly mistake of letting her take over my income management. I work hard, make good money, but I just haven't got the energy or interest to deal with it beyond letting it pile up in my checking account. When Moana found out, she offered to take over, pay the bills, invest the rest for me."

"And you let her?" I stared at her, wide-eyed with disbelief.

"I'm ashamed to say I did. Another stupendous error in judgment. At first, it was a load off my mind. But she 'invested' my money in Prakash's business. Fat chance I'll see a penny of it again. When I found out, I closed my accounts and changed banks immediately, but the harm's done. I can't purchase a unit in the retirement home for my mother unless I sell the house."

"I see. Is Prakash still on Maui?"

"You never know with him. He comes and goes as his business requires."

"What exactly *is* his business? Do you know any more than when you first told me about him?"

"No. Last night, when I realized nobody was home, I nosed around the garage, thinking I could jimmy the window open. It wouldn't open. Then I got to worrying it might be booby-trapped, so I chickened out and left."

"Probably a wise move." I remembered the letter from the downstairs tenants demanding a payoff. I pulled it out of my purse and showed it to her. "I guess they sent it to me because they didn't have an address for you."

She read it quickly, then crumbled it up in disgust. "Jesus. What else can that bitch do to me?"

"These people can be dealt with, Randy. They're probably as anxious to move out as you are to get them out. The main thing is, are you willing to give in to Moana's blackmail? That's what this amounts to, you know, out-and-out blackmail. Can you continue living in terror of being exposed? It can't be very pleasant."

She balled her fists and struck her thighs. "It's pure hell. No matter which way I turn, I'm stymied. I can't live with her. We have no friendship left. She hates me, and I hate her."

"You can't live on the beach the rest of your life, either," I added.

"I know. I own that property. Why should she live in my house while I pay the mortgage? The whole situation is intolerable." She held out her hands, palms up, begging me for help. Her eyes were bloodshot, and her lower lip quivered, permanently imprinted by her dual-spade teeth. "I just don't know what to do."

The crud was definitely up to her ass. I didn't have a clue what to do, either. I gathered my bag, shoved the *Reader's Digest* into it, and stood up beside her. "You need to talk to your lawyer, Randy. Ask him to lay out your legal options, while protecting you and your license. Have you leveled with him about Moana's blackmail?"

"No . . . I was too ashamed."

"You'd better do it fast."

"Yeah. I had four messages from Mo on my answering machine this morning, each one more vicious than the last. She sure didn't like the sheriff knocking on her door with an eviction notice. The thought of returning her calls makes me sick."

I knew how she felt. I hadn't enjoyed my message from Moana, either. "Bottom line, Randy, are you willing to risk everything to get Moana off your back?"

She ran her hands through her gray-shot sandy hair, pulling so tightly her eyes popped and her mouth turned into a pumpkin grimace. "Yeah," she whispered. "I've run out of choices. I want that bitch gone. Proceed with the sale. Let the bloody chips fall where they may."

CHAPTER 23

Mother had promised "a little something to tide us over" until Annie joined her and Dad in Honolulu. Well, Annie was staying right here with me, but the day after my confrontation with Randy Entwistle at the hospital the "little something" arrived in the mail. Good thing I wasn't counting on it for immediate relief. The small box contained a pair of heirloom earrings that belonged to our ancestor, Mazie Wildethorne. I was particularly fond of them, mostly because Mother rarely wore them.

An old-fashioned mine-cut canary diamond sat in the center of each gold filigree star, with garnets set in each delicate point. Hanging from gold hooks, the earrings resembled red hibiscus from a distance. Although exquisitely crafted and loaded with sentiment, they were not terribly valuable. Mother had once sniffed that the jeweler had committed an unforgivable *faux pas* by mixing precious stones with semi-precious. In other words, the earrings weren't grand enough for her. Perhaps that was why she was willing to give them away. If Mother intended me to sell them to make ends meet, she'd misjudged my desperation. I'd never part with such a family treasure. Instead, I'd enjoy them for a while, then give them to Annie, who reminded me so much of Mazie. If the baby was a girl, Annie could pass them on.

Still piqued at my mother for this ostentatious but impractical gesture, I put the earrings on the next morning, along with white slacks and a red blouse. As I drove to my office, I admired the pretty effect in the rearview mirror. It pleased me to have this tangible connection to the madcap Mazie.

After greeting Peggy at the front desk, I went directly to the message boxes behind her. Thumbing through the usual assortment of promotional flyers from loan officers, escrow companies, and listing agents, I heard the front door open with a metallic creak.

A loud female voice demanded, "Where's that bitch, McDaniel?"

I froze in place, papers crushed in my hand, too stunned to turn my head. Peggy, never at a loss for words under any circumstances, stood up. "I beg your pardon?" she asked, in high dudgeon.

"McDaniel. Fucking Laura McDaniel. Where the hell is she? I need to talk to the bitch."

"Well, you'll do no such thing until you put a civil tongue into your mouth," Peggy replied.

"Look, bitch, I don't need any fucking lip from you."

As my blood began flowing again, I forced myself to turn around. There stood Moana, gray corkscrew hair quivering, knobby fists clenched on her hips, fire spitting from her narrowed eyes. A rush of nervous sweat broke over me. I stepped toward her, hoping she didn't have a weapon, then recoiled at her miasmic sandalwood aroma.

"I'm Laura McDaniel. What do you mean by bursting in like this?"

Moana limped past the barrier of Peggy's desk, pinning me with an evil glare. "Well, little Miss Real Estate. How many innocent people have you made homeless today? You must find that highly satisfying."

Gaining strength from her ridiculous accusation, I stood my ground and answered in what I hoped was a no-nonsense tone of voice. "I beg your pardon?"

"Oh, come off it, you back-stabbing bitch. You got two of my tenants so upset with those eviction notices, they packed up and left without paying this month's rent. Now what am I supposed to do?"

It registered in the back of my mind that two of our four eviction problems were solved. That gave me a shot of increased confidence. "Look, the house is sold. All the tenants have to leave, yourself included. The sooner you understand that, the better for everyone involved."

She rocked from foot to foot, as if winding up to spring at me. "Yeah, well, that isn't the way it is, shitface. I'll never leave that house. It belongs to me. You'll close that sale over my dead body!" Her last words exploded in the air like a rifle shot.

I put my hands on Peggy's desk to steady myself against the blast. "I'm afraid there is nothing you can do about it unless you produce that deed," I countered.

"Fuck the deed," she spat. "You just wait and see, Miss Prissy Realtor. I'm suing you and those hotsy-totsy clients of yours for major loss of income, in addition to everything else I have on them."

With that, she spun around and barged out the glass door, leaving behind a malevolent eddy of perfume. Until that moment, sandalwood had been one of my favorite scents. Half a second later she turned around, poked her head back in and shouted, "By the way, ask the fucking sheriff's deputy why he bought me groceries yesterday." She cackled with laughter and exited for good.

"Whew," Peggy exhaled when the door finally shut. "What was that all about?"

I gave her a tremulous hug, as much for my sake as hers. "Just another disgruntled tenant who doesn't like her home being sold out from under her. Thanks for running interference for me."

Sniffing indignantly, Peggy sat down again and started jiggling her computer mouse. "Sounds a little more disgruntled than most."

"Yeah, just my luck," I muttered, wondering what in God's name Moana had meant by her final remark. The deputy sheriff, who had delivered the eviction notices, had bought her groceries? More shaken than I cared to admit, I watched Moana's white pickup wheel out of the parking lot, then strode back to my cubicle, ignoring the curious stares of the other agents. I called the sheriff's office and asked for the process server for Haiku. Deputy Roman Corpuz came on the line. I'd had dealings with him before and knew him for a bumbling incompetent.

"Hey, Roman, Laura McDaniel at Blue Rock Realty."

"Eh, Laura. How you stay?"

I slipped into Pidgin. "Pretty good, brah. You?"

"Yeah, yeah, okay. What's up?"

"You wen' serve one eviction notice on Moana Entwistle, also known as Corrine Suzanne Urquhart, up Kauhoku Road, Haiku?"

"Uh, yeah. At least . . . I wen' try."

"When you wen' try?"

"Uh, las' Friday."

"An' wat?"

"She nevah wen' take 'um."

Enough of the Pidgin. I needed clarity. "She refused to accept it, you mean?"

"Yeah. Li' dat. Poor t'ing, you know. All limping and stuff. I feel sorry for her."

"Pardon me, Roman, you felt sorry for the poor thing, so you never served the notice?"

"Eh, she go t'row 'em back at me! But she know what stay inside the envelope."

"Yeah, but it doesn't count if you didn't leave it with her. Why didn't you post it on the door and be done with it?"

"Eh, no get all upset. You know da judge no going kick her out anyways. She all bust up. Her leg, you know. You saw how she limp?"

"I know nothing of the sort. She needs to get out. The house has been sold."

"She tell me *she* own the house, and she no selling."

"That's not true, Roman. She's a guest, not really even a tenant. We're just being nice by giving her official notice." That might or might not be true, but what did he know?

"No shit?" he said.

"Yeah, Roman, no shit." I rolled my eyes at the ceiling, realizing there was no point in grilling him further. "You didn't buy her groceries, by any chance?"

His silence confirmed it. *Men*, I thought, always suckers for a "poor me" story from a woman. I wondered what he expected to get in return. There was no point in prolonging the conversation.

I hung up and called again, this time asking to speak to Roman's boss. Sheriff Gonzales coughed a few times after hearing my tale, then allowed as how Roman might have handled things more professionally. Assuming he was also ignorant of the grocery-buying business, I shared that juicy morsel. Properly embarrassed, he assured me Deputy Corpuz's extracurricular activities would be investigated, and that he himself would deliver the notice that afternoon.

That nailed down, I went outside the office for a breath of hot, humid air. Leaning against the sun-baked lava façade, I closed my eyes against the afternoon glare. The warmth of the blue-gray, quarried stone for which Blue Rock Realty was named seeped through my blouse, melting away some of the chill Moana had left behind. I decided I'd better drive over to the Colemans and let them in on the latest developments.

"But, darling, they're exquisite." Diana exclaimed over my new earrings. "You mustn't give them to Annie. That girl will never appreciate them. If you want the baby to have them, you must give them to her directly when she's old enough to wear them. If it's a girl, of course."

I sat back on Diana's lanai swing, crossed my arms, and chose not to react to her dig about Annie. "Right, so I'll just enjoy them until then. Listen, I have news. Not good news."

Her smile turned to a frown. She gripped the back of a lounge chair and leaned toward me. Her scrunch-curled dark hair dipped forward to frame her aristocratic cheeks.

"Bad news? About the house?" She turned in a panic, pushing her hair behind her ears, and called down the hill over the lanai railing "Darling, you'd better come up and hear this."

We waited while Jerry trudged up from his gardening, skirting riotous banks of cup-of-gold underlaid with *mundo* grass. He wore dirt-smudged shorts and a T-shirt full of holes, complete with filthy old running shoes, untied and sockless.

"Hey, Laura. How goes the battle?" He flopped onto an aluminum lawn chair, the only one Diana let him sit on in his earthy condition. I caught a sour whiff of sweat, the odor of a man engaged in honest manual labor. In other circumstances, I might have enjoyed it.

"Get me some ice water, will you, kid?" Jerry said to the air over his shoulder. Diana obediently slid open the screen door and stepped into the house. Turning to me, he asked, "So, what's the latest?"

"Not real good, I'm afraid. Not impossible, but not good."

Diana set down a tray of ice-filled tumblers and three bottles of Maui Springs filtered water. We each uncapped a bottle and poured our drinks. The icy glass felt shivery cool in my warm hand. I ran it against the inside of my arm to get the full effect, then gave it to them straight. "Our close personal friend Moana trounced into my office an hour ago, called me every filthy name in the book, and said she's suing you for loss of income, among other things she deigned not to mention."

Jerry wiped the sweat off his forehead with the front of his shirt, leaving a red dirt swath above his eyebrows. "What the hell does that mean?"

I related the scene, conveying the drama without parroting her scummy words, emphasizing the good news that two of the four tenants had moved out already.

"Oh, darling, I'm so sorry you had to face all that," Diana said, looking sincerely shocked.

"Bitch," spat Larry. "Didn't I tell you how it is when two women—"

"Oh, Jerry, don't," said his wife. "Let's not sink to their level."

He brushed her off with a wave of his hand. "Well, she can't do that, sue us for loss of income and a bunch of other crap. Income to which she's not entitled in the first place."

"Anybody can sue anyone for anything, Jerry. It's a ghastly process, even if she has no chance of winning. I suspect Moana's just blowing smoke, but it's one more layer of unpleasantness we have to deal with. Frankly, I've about had it with this whole transaction."

"You're not going to desert us now?" Diana cried.

"Don't be ridiculous," Jerry said, refusing, happily, to take me seriously. "You want to close this sale as badly as we do. Has anyone seen Moana's so-called deed yet?"

"Not that I know of," I replied. "And that's still our best ray of hope. If Moana has a deed, surely she would have waved it in my face today.

I'm convinced she's bluffing, but we have to keep in mind the outside chance that she's not. Have you consulted with your attorney, by the way, Jerry?"

Jerry tipped his chair back, balancing on two legs with his feet on the coffee table. "Yeah, I called him this morning."

Diana gasped, "Jerry, you never told me that. What did he say?"

"Pretty much what Laura just said. The question of the deed is in Moana's hands. If we're willing to proceed, knowing she could produce it at any time and derail us, we can go ahead and try. Cross our fingers that she's bluffing. We also talked about Moana's rights as a tenant, and the rights of the jerks renting the rooms downstairs. Sounds like we got rid of two of them, eh, Laura? Good work. The other set, the ones who say Randy owes them for loss of door prizes and other crazy stuff, they've said what it will take to buy them off. Even though their claim is preposterous, surely the doctor will settle with them just to get them out. So we're left with Moana and Prakash. If we can get her out, I'm betting Prakash will pack up and leave, too. In the unlikely event he's cooking up illegal drugs, it would be too dangerous for him to stay around."

"We should be so lucky," I said.

"So it all boils down to Moana again," Jerry continued. "Even though she doesn't exactly fit the usual description of a tenant, my attorney says we've got to give her the full forty-five days from when she received her eviction notice, just to play it safe. When was that, Laura?"

My stomach did a somersault. "Ah . . . last week, but it seems Moana refused to accept it."

"What?" Diana and Jerry asked simultaneously.

"Apparently she gave the process server a big sob story, and the *lolo* believed her. He walked away with the notice in his pocket. Not only that, he felt so sorry for her, he brought her two big bags of groceries after he got off work."

"My God," exclaimed Jerry. "Is that the kind of law enforcement we have on this island?"

"I couldn't believe it, either. I called the sheriff and told him what a scammer Moana is. He was pretty embarrassed. Promised to deliver the notice personally this afternoon."

Diana cried, "But that gives her forty-five days from *today*. A month and a half for her to record her deed, and we sit here wondering all that time? I'll go crazy. We've done everything we're supposed to do. That isn't fair."

"You haven't heard the best part," I said, reaching out a hand to steady her. "I finally hit pay dirt with Randy Entwistle. Did a stakeout at the hospital surgery center until she showed up. She finally broke down. She's in deep *kim chee*. Moana's blackmailing her, big time. If Randy sells the house, Moana's threatening to expose her."

Jerry sat forward and snapped his fingers. "I knew it. Moana tells the hospital board Randy's gay, and out the door she goes." He nodded at his wife, lips pursed with satisfaction. "Didn't I tell you Moana had some cat-pussy on her? Go on, Laura. Give us the juicy details."

I gritted my teeth at Jerry's unshakable lesbophobia. "It doesn't work that way anymore, Jerry. Where have you been? You can be gay these days and still have a life. No, it's something else entirely. Seems Randy's been supplying Moana with narcotics." I explained about Moana's injuries and how Randy wrote illegal painkiller prescriptions for her for the past four years.

"Good Christ." Jerry lowered his head and stroked his eyebrows, mentally salivating over how to use this information to his advantage.

Diana jumped up out of her chair and raised her fist. "I don't care about their personal situation," she said. "It has nothing to do with us. Give her ten days to get all those people out. Otherwise *we're* canceling the sale. There are bad vibes everywhere in that house. I've had a funny feeling about it from the beginning."

Last I heard, Diana would have killed for that house. Now it had bad vibes?

Before I could frame a response, Jerry snapped at her. "Oh, for heavens sake, Diana. We won't get anywhere issuing crazy ultimatums. The doctor could end up in prison. No wonder she's behaving strangely."

Diana began to pout. "It would serve her right if Moana did rat on her and send her off to the slammer." She stood above her husband, looking down, hands on hips. "Jerry, I've changed my mind. I don't want that house. I wouldn't be able to sleep a wink in that bedroom, knowing that horrid woman slept there. Why, the doctor probably shoots Moana up herself, right there on the bed." She closed her eyes and shuddered.

Diana's lightning change of mind set my head spinning. It wasn't the first time I'd encountered such emotion-driven irrationality. The fate of a sale often hinges on moments like this: illogical, passionate, and, once dug in, irreversible. I hadn't figured, however, on Jerry being every bit as illogical, passionate, and unwilling to be bested in what was turning out to be, in his mind at least, a rollicking battle of wits. He nudged Diana aside and faced me.

"Look, Laura. We *are* buying that house. No ands, ifs, or buts about it." He leaned precariously back in his chair, glaring at his wife. "Diana, don't give me any nonsense about bad vibes. It's an incredible property. Best we've seen in a bloody year of looking. And we're paying ten-K below appraisal. It's the best deal in town." He smacked his lips in joyful contemplation.

"But I'd feel that woman's presence in every room," Diana exclaimed. "Moana's a blackmailer who does drugs! And we still don't know what's going on in the garage. Who knows what kind of people might come knocking on the door in the middle of the night? I don't want to live with that kind of negative energy. Laura, cancel the sale. We're not buying it."

Jerry crashed forward on the front legs of his chair and stood up. Abruptly he pushed his wife back down into her seat. "Shut up, my darling. I'm not letting a whacked-out aging hippie and her pussy-whipped doctor beat me out of that property. Laura, from now on, you communicate directly with me. You take instructions only from me. Understand? I'm taking over. No more cozy little afternoon tea parties for you two. I'm tired of women mucking about here. This is serious business."

Speechless, I called on every ounce of tolerance I possessed. This purchase was no longer a husbandly indulgence to keep Diana happy. Once the high appraisal had been revealed, he wanted the property even more than she did. He didn't care who he insulted or what it took. Before

I could reply, Jerry continued. "Maybe if you had worked directly with me in the first place, we wouldn't be in this mess."

I couldn't have been more taken aback if he had punched me. "Jerry, that's darn unfair. I have kept you in the loop every step of the way. And it hasn't always been easy."

Behind me, Diana burst into tears. Jerry threw up his hands and stalked away from us. Diana crumbled in her chair, sobbing into a pillow. Picking up my bag, I murmured a hasty goodbye. Neither of them responded.

When I reached the wrought-iron gate, I paused and looked back, expecting Jerry to come forth with an apology. Instead, he stood at the far corner of the lanai, his back to both of us, one foot braced on the wooden railing, leaning into the breeze as if scanning the horizon for war canoes. I half expected him to turn around and rattle an *ihe pakelo*, a wooden spear, at me as I hurriedly shut the gate.

At home, Annie thumbed through a *Rolling Stone* magazine, with, for once, the television off. In return for a pleasant, "Hi, Ma," she received the full brunt of my wrath. What luxury to have someone on whom to unload it.

"Why is it always my fault when something goes wrong?" I grumbled as I banged a can of tuna and a can opener onto the counter. "I didn't find the property in the first place. I didn't tell the seller she should go it alone without an agent. I didn't invent this harridan who fouls us up at every turn. Nor did I create the bad vibes Diana now says afflict the place. And I most certainly have not been doing business at cozy little female tea parties without including Jerry."

From across the kitchen counter, my daughter laughed. "Whoa, Ma. Cool out. You can't save the whole world."

Stung, I turned away, cranked open the tuna and squeezed out the juice. My nose wrinkled at the fishy smell. I dumped the tuna into a bowl, added mayonnaise, pickle relish and capers, and beat the hell out of it with a fork.

Maybe Annie was right. Maybe I did need to loosen up. I had learned that when the mechanics of closing a sale got hopelessly tied in a knot, the best strategy involved stepping back and removing myself from the arena. Both sides now had lawyers. Let them duke it out, with Jerry and Randy shouting instructions from opposite corners of the ring.

"What say we visit Grandma and Grandpa in Honolulu for the weekend?" I asked Annie. "We could both use a change of scene."

Annie brightened at the idea. "Yeah, Ma. I've been thinking a lot about Pua Olena. Let's go, but only for the weekend." She raised her fair eyebrows. "I couldn't stand Grandma's bossiness any longer than that."

"You and me both." I chuckled, my spirits lifting already.

Taking furtive pleasure at the thought of playing hooky, I called my parents, packed minimally, and booked a five-thirty flight. I left messages for my broker and the Colemans, letting them know I'd be on Oahu until Monday, telling them I'd check my answering machine daily in case anything came up. I also left a message for Randy Entwistle, asking if she had ordered the survey and termite inspection. I'd given her names and phone numbers a week ago, but so far I'd had no feedback. I purposely refrained from giving anyone the number at Pua Olena. It was my turn to be incommunicado. I struggled with a rush of guilt for about three seconds, then laughed out loud at the wonderfully liberating feeling.

As the plane accelerated down the runway, I closed my eyes, delighted to have a break from my high-intensity business. A relaxing weekend in my childhood home had the enticing appeal of a trip to Shangri La. Now that Jerry and his attorney were fully engaged, I felt confident that the sale would close, in spite of his insults and Moana's machinations. Regardless of the unhappy note on which I'd left them, I felt the Colemans and I had weathered a crisis that had cleared the air.

Now that I knew why Randy squirmed so miserably in Moana's iron grasp, I understood her fearful, erratic behavior. Despite my best efforts to remain detached, I felt a nagging sense of responsibility for the doctor creeping in. By pushing the sale to a close, I would precipitate events that might ruin her life. Maybe Diana and Jerry could ignore these consequences, but they were becoming more and more troublesome to me. Not as a Realtor, but as a human being.

Chapter 24

Everything is different at Pua Olena.

High in Nuuanu Valley, we drove through the imposing lava rock gateposts and down the ancient, root-buckled driveway lined with royal palms. All thoughts of another life slipped away. The encroaching jungle air closed in, heavy and rank with decay.

By contrast, the manicured estate lawn, wrested from the jungle by generations of brown arms hacking with machetes, glistened with succulent life. Pampered garden foliage—hibiscus, bird-of-paradise, bougainvillea, plumeria—surrounded the white, single-story plantation-style house, screaming in primary colors, unfazed by a late afternoon shower. Two clumps of *olena*, the exotic East Asian turmeric ginger for which the estate was named, flanked the far end of the driveway. Carried from India by one of my seafaring ancestors to flavor his curries, this robust plant had become one of the treasures of Mother's annual charity garden tour.

Calixto, Mother's young Filipino chauffeur, swung the car under the porte-cochère and opened our doors with great ceremony. The rambling old house reached out—enfolding, embracing, enchanting, seducing—its whispered creaks and tightly held secrets waiting to echo our every step. Mother stood in the shelter of the wide wooden porch, dressed in crisp white sharkskin slacks, a pale blue silk blouse, and gold leather sandals. Platinum hair waved perfectly in place; she looked ready to receive the garden club ladies for tea. Annie climbed the steps to her grandmother's eager embrace. Following, I received a kiss in the air near my ear.

"So you've come to your senses at last," Mother exclaimed, clapping her hands together. "I'm so glad you've brought Annie to stay. I have your old room all ready for her." She smiled at me with tissue-paper-thin sincerity. "And how long are *you* staying, dear?"

I had mentally rehearsed this scene all the way over on the airplane. Why was I able to engage in hair-raising negotiations with strangers over a real estate deal, yet utterly unable to stand up to my own mother? Although I hadn't anticipated a confrontation on the doorstep before we even took off our shoes, I knew I'd better settle things right here and now. When I spoke, my voice sounded shrill and overly emphatic.

"We're both staying until Monday, Mother. That's all."

She looked as if I'd announced we weren't having Christmas that year. "But I thought—"

I placed one deliberate, practiced word after another, like pieces into a jigsaw puzzle. "I already told you, Mother. Annie is having her baby on Maui. That's the way she wants it. That's the way I want it. We're just here for a little visit with you and Dad, a mini-vacation from the business hassles at home. But only until Monday."

A flush crept up my neck as I braced for her inevitable rebuttal. To my surprise, she didn't even try. She merely huffed in her imperious way, clearly meaning, "We'll see about that." Putting a cosseting arm around Annie, she led her into the house. "Come along, dear, let's see what we can do for you. Would you like some of Tami's pineapple and lime ice tea? She picked fresh limes this morning, especially for you. It must have been a dreadful trip from Maui."

Firmly in tow, Annie looked back at me as if to say, "Mom, are you sure this was a good idea?"

I shrugged and followed helplessly in their wake. What did she mean, a dreadful trip from Maui? It was a twenty-two minute flight. There was nothing the least bit dreadful or even uncomfortable about the journey. Mother's remark was simply another veiled dig at my unfavorable adult life choices.

The whispering drizzle through open windows drowned out anything further between Mother and Annie as they crossed the living room and disappeared down the *lauhala*-matted hallway. Stepping out of my shoes just outside the front door, I paused to inhale the scents of my youth: damp grass, rain-drenched flowers, mildew, and the musty lauhala.

The living room was lit to dispel the late afternoon gloom. Lamplight gleamed on exquisite museum-quality koa wood tables and chairs. During the recent restoration of Iolani Palace, Mother had donated several pieces whose provenance led back directly to Queen Liliuokalani at the time of the overthrow. A momentary feeling of suffocation came over me, as it always did when I came home. As I walked across the dark eucalyptus planking, I clutched my purse a little tighter, reminding myself I had a ticket back to Maui on Monday. I did not live here anymore.

I'd not had an unhappy childhood, but a lonely one with parents too busy for me, Father with his restaurant and Mother with her volunteer work. The servants tended me, entertained me, kept me busy, played and laughed with me as I tagged along after them. No other children lived nearby. Pua Olena will always be the home of my heart, but I'm eternally grateful to Frank, regardless of the way things ended, for rescuing me from this stultifying realm, and giving me a real home with children and carpools and neighbors. In spite of what I now realize was an extraordinary upbringing in a bygone era, my life began when I married him.

Tami had prepared a guestroom for me down the hall from my old bedroom. She had placed one of Mother's prize-winning orchids in a raku pot on the bedside table. Five white blossoms crowned the long, arching stem, like virgin moths fluttering in the lamplight. I quickly unpacked and joined Mother and Annie.

"I've given Annie your old room because of the adjoining bath," Mother said as she helped her granddaughter hang up her two muumuus and several T-shirts, holding them gingerly away from her body as if they might sully her spotless white slacks. "You don't mind using the bathroom down the hall, do you, Laura?"

As far as I was able to tell, Annie, even at eight months, never had to get up in the middle of the night to use the bathroom. While I, having had my bladder sat upon and kicked about during three full-term pregnancies, never missed a night.

Let it go, I thought. There will be more important battles to fight this weekend. I was kidding myself if I believed Mother would meekly let Annie return to Maui with me on Monday. This was the woman who had once chained herself to a historic tamarind tree across the street from my high school to prevent it being bulldozed to widen the road.

Nothing would do that first night home but dinner at Dad's restaurant, the Woodrose in Waikiki. He was "on" that night, as he'd been every night of my life but Sundays. When I called him to let him know we'd arrived safely, he insisted we all come down as soon as we'd freshened up and said hello to Tami.

I found her seated at the kitchen table, rolling butter balls for break- fast with scored wooden paddles. I stood at the door, wanting to run across the room and give her a big hug. But that wasn't done.

She looked up and grinned at me while smoothing a wisp of gray hair into her bun with a gnarled hand. I waited for her to speak first. "You home. Good. And Annie." It would be impolite to mention the baby.

"Yes. I wanted to come see you right away."

"You go to Father's restaurant tonight." It was not a question.

"Yes. He insisted."

"Tomorrow I make you noodles."

"Great! I love your noodles!" Even though she was Japanese, Tami made the best Chinese noodles in town, rich with wood ear mushrooms, cilantro, and sweet *char siu* pork. She beamed. Compliments on her cook- ing were all she would accept in the way of affection. Of all the adults in my world, I loved Dad and Tami best.

"You go now. Father waiting." With that, she picked up the bowl of iced butterballs, stowed them in the refrigerator, and untied her apron in preparation for going home.

***

The *kiawe* wood char-broiled aroma set my mouth to watering as we strolled in from Kalakaua Avenue, Waikiki's bustling main thoroughfare. An old-fashioned survivor of *la nouvelle cuisine*, the Woodrose epitomized a man's restaurant: huge portions, sizzling platters, cholesterol be damned. When tourists had enough of strange, exotic Island tastes, they found real American food at Dad's restaurant and loved it. He blithely ignored culinary trends, serving only the finest Midwestern beef and Idaho potatoes, loaded with butter, bacon, sour cream, and chives.

Thirty-some years ago he had daringly installed the first salad bar in the state, a great innovation at the time. Numerous dining trends later, it remained the only grand salad bar in Waikiki and still a huge favorite. Although Father clearly adored his wife, I understood from an early age that the restaurant served as his escape from Mother's haughty ways. Passé but popular, the Woodrose had long since become my Dad's *raison d'être*.

His face lit up when he saw us. Someone once described Jack Henderson as the last of the old-time Honolulu gentlemen. He certainly looked the part as he strode over to greet us, arms outstretched, white mustachioed smile beaming. He wore light tan slacks with a long-sleeved *tapa*-pattern aloha shirt, the geometric black, brown, and white fabric sewn inside-out in modern Island fashion to subdue the loud print. A priceless peacock feather band circled his ivory Panama hat, which he always wore on duty. Tucked into the turquoise feather band was a rosette of miniature brown wood roses.

"Isn't this just grand," he exclaimed, encircling me in a big bear hug. "You had us convinced we'd have to go to Maui to see this little girl again." Somehow, coming from him, his statement attached no blame. He engulfed Annie, rocked her back and forth. In his joyful embrace, she looked like a floss-headed doll. He released her and turned to his hostess, a tall, slender woman of mixed Island heritage. "Say hello to Kaulana, my love. She's been pestering me about you all afternoon."

My children and I adored Kaulana. Just a few years older than I, she'd been with Dad since I was in high school. Stately and graceful, she'd won the Miss Hawaii title and gone on to the Miss America contest, taking the honors, as Island girls often did, as Miss Congeniality. Dad hired her the day after her Miss Hawaii reign ended. She'd been a fixture at the restaurant ever since. Her black hair pulled tight in a low chignon, jade earrings dangling, she was even more stunning in the ripeness of maturity than when she'd won the crown.

Kaulana laughed and held out her arms to Annie. For the first time since our arrival, Annie responded with genuine delight.

Father called out to the dining room, "Hey, folks. Here's my little granddaughter. Everyone say hello." Mother, quite used to Father's exuberant nonsense, led me to a red velvet banquette while Dad, ever the genial host, escorted Annie around, introducing her to his patrons. Annie went gamely along with her grandfather's performance, but I could see she was embarrassed. Mother sat beside me, beaming at them as they progressed from table to table. How different things would have been with me in a maternity smock at her age, I thought. Perhaps a grandchild is not such a direct reflection of one's self.

Saturday we lounged around. Neither Annie nor I wished to move from our comfy *punee* on the shady rear lanai. Beyond the reaches of the rolling lawn, the jungle-clad ridges of the Koolau Mountains towered above us, creating a sense of safety and security I felt only at Pua Olena. *Ti* leaves and *lauae* ferns rustled against the lattice work that hid the post and pier foundation. Intermittent rain showers drifted by. Along with the moldy scent of the outdoor furniture, everything conspired to gently settle our energies. Our skin drank in the upland coolness, a welcome contrast to the Kihei heat.

I read. Annie dozed while listening to her portable tape player. Mother went off to a bridge tournament. When the subdued rock music began to distract me, I quietly got up and took my book to my room. No aggravation, no apologies. Annie rested happily in one space, I in another. But we were still together, breathing the same damp, refreshing air. What luxury. Truly at peace for the first time since Annie's return, I enjoyed the simple fact of her presence.

At four o'clock I mustered the strength to check my messages on Maui, using the phone in my father's den. I hated to lift the veil of serenity that had so gently drifted over me, but I had to keep tabs on the Coleman sale. The first voice on the tape, shot with indignation as only Pidgin English can be, ripped the veil off completely.

"Laura, dis is Leebrick Kinimaka, Kamaaina Surveying. Sorry for break up your vacation. You told me dat woman stay difficult, but you never tell me she stay crazy. I wen' up Haiku for do da survey, and she wen' follow me around, yelling and screaming that she own da place. She tell me she not selling. I try fo' do da job, but she follow me and pull up da stakes as soon as I put 'em in da ground. She wen' throw 'em down da gulch, *confunnit*. She say she goin' shoot me if I try complete the survey. I finally wen' call da police on my car phone. She tell the police *I* wen' threaten *her*, so they try fo' arrest *me*. Dis is heavy hazard duty. I cannot do nothing. You gotta call me and tell me what's goin' on. I no goin' back 'til she outta dere."

Irritation clamped down hard. Where was the blessed peace I felt just moments before? I took deep, cleansing breaths while the machine beeped to the next message.

"Laura, Darlene here, Bugs Rn't Us Pest Control. I sent Roger up to do the termite inspection in Haiku. The police were arresting the surveyor when he got there. That crazy woman yelled at Roger and threatened to have him arrested, too. You better call me. We don't appreciate being sent to a lunatic asylum."

I sank onto the chair behind my father's desk, waiting for my heartbeat to slow down. Damn that Moana. Every move we made, she checked us. On a positive note, it looked like Randy had made good on her resolution to carry on with the sale. She'd ordered the survey and pest inspection. A good sign. When buyers or sellers are upset, they frequently make promises in the heat of the moment and then do exactly the opposite—or nothing. A report from a tradesman often provides the only clue that they are indeed moving ahead with the sale. With someone as non-communicative as Randy, I felt like a hunter reading scat on the trail.

Neither Leebrick nor Roger was at his office that late on a Saturday afternoon. I left messages apologizing to both. I left one for Randy, too, telling her what had transpired and instructing her to reschedule the survey and termite inspection at a time when she could be there to keep Moana out of their hair.

I returned to my room, pulled a light blanket from the closet and stretched out on the bed. Eyes closed, I tried to put the tangled mess out of my mind. We were so close. All we had to do was complete the survey and termite inspection, obtain final loan approval, and we could close. Provided that Prakash didn't get the property confiscated first. And that Moana neglected to record her alleged deed. The solution seemed clear— move with lightning speed before either of those disasters could strike. Unless Moana experienced a miraculous change of heart and meekly moved out before her forty-five days expired, that was about as likely as awakening to a snowfall on Pua Olena's rolling lawn the next morning.

As my mind quieted, my inadvertent role as a catalyst for disaster in Randy's life loomed again. Randy's involvement with Moana, the illegal prescriptions, Moana's blackmail, Prakash hovering like a dark shadow in the background, were all woven into place before we ever met. When she put up the For Sale sign, Randy had embarked on a last, desperate attempt to reclaim her life. Diana, Jerry, and I had simply walked into the web. My duty to my clients was clear: Close the sale. Randy would have to take care of herself.

I must have dozed off, because the next time I opened my eyes deep shadows filled the room. The hall light cast a textured glow across the *lauhala* mat. Feeling groggy, I listened to the low hum of voices floating in. Assuming my mother had invited guests for dinner, I changed into a fresh muumuu: turquoise cotton, floor-length and long-sleeved, and joined them.

To my relief, it was just the family enjoying cocktails. Father rose to greet me. He'd taken the night off in our honor. Tami handed around a *pupu* platter of crackers topped with cream cheese and Mother's green pepper jelly. We dined by candlelight, served meticulously by Tami. Annie seemed withdrawn throughout the meal, but no more than usual. Father entertained us with hilarious stories of his mainland haole patrons. Mother brought us up to date on her ongoing city beautification crusade.

Later Dad and I played cribbage. Moths flitted against the window screens, attracted by the light inside. Bufos, common land toads, dotted the lawn, ever hopeful of a tasty morsel. How I'd hated those ugly, hopping things as a child. I'd rarely played outside after dark for fear of squishing one beneath my bare feet.

We all retired early. Nothing further had been said about our departure on Monday, but I remained determined that Annie and I would both be on that plane. I fell asleep wondering what the nearby rain forest would look like covered in snow.

"Mommy?"

I sat bolt upright, all senses fine-tuned in the dark. Annie's voice sounded as clear as if she stood at my bedside. Not a shout, not a cry. Just one word, spoken more in wonder than in fear. I knew my little girl was in trouble. I raced along the *lauhala* matting to her bedroom and found her sitting curled over her stomach on the edge of her bed.

"Mommy, I think it's happening," she gasped.

"What's happening, sweetheart?"

"I think the baby's coming."

Was it possible? She had a month to go. I put my hand on her stomach. "Are you having contractions?"

"I think so." Her voice quivered. "I woke up with the most horrible cramps. It's getting worse. I've never felt anything like this before. It comes on real hard like I can't control it, then it goes away." She grabbed my arm and stiffened as another pain hit. "Mommy, I don't know what to do." She threw back her head and moaned. After a few moments of panting, she crumpled forward. "Mommy, make it stop." She began to cry.

"Honey, there's only one way to make it stop. You're going to have a baby." Chills ran up my arms, covering me in chicken skin. My grandchild!

"I don't want to have a baby," she cried. "Make it go away!"

I tried to keep the panic out of my own voice. "Annie, listen to me. It's not going to go away. Not the labor nor the baby. You've got to buck up."

"I'm scared. I don't want to." She sobbed into my shoulder.

I held her for a moment, torn between comforting her and needing to take action. Finally I released her and switched on the bathroom light. Memories of my long ago miscarriage flooded over me, all that blood on this same white tile floor. It couldn't end that way with Annie. It just couldn't! She looked so small and desperate, sitting on the edge of the unmade bed, clad only in my awful frog-green T-shirt. The huge sleeves hung down below her elbows, making matchsticks of her forearms. I dampened a washcloth and sponged her sweat-beaded forehead.

"We've got to get you to the hospital," I said. "I'll call Calixto and have him bring the car around."

"No. Don't take me to the hospital yet." she wailed. "I want to stay here. It can't be time yet." Her sobs turned to hiccups. I wiped the tears from her cheeks, then sat on the bed beside her and put my arm around her narrow shoulders.

"Sweetheart, you're a month early. The baby may be in trouble. We can't take any chances."

She looked at me, pleading. "It can't be time. It just can't."

"We'll go straight to Kapiolani. Your baby will get the best possible care."

"I'm not ready to be a . . . a . . . mother," she moaned, rocking back and forth in my arms.

I hugged her tight. "It's not the worst fate in the world, sweetheart."

Her next words came out between sobs. They were almost unintelligible. "I'll never be able to be . . . as good a mother . . . as you are."

My breath caught in my throat. My heart expanded to a size it had never been before. I closed my eyes, nuzzled her hair, and inhaled deeply, borne away on long-ago scents of ribbons and sunbonnets and wispy tow-headed curls.

"Honey, it's the most wonderful thing you can imagine. Motherhood powers the world!"

"Yeah? What if I don't like it?"

I pulled away and looked at her. "Motherhood, or the baby?"

She stared back with the intense desperation of her nineteen years. "Both. Either."

I squeezed her shoulder. "Let Mother Nature do her thing, sweetheart. You haven't much choice now, anyway. They even let Queen Elizabeth and Princess Diana do this, you know." I brushed back her fair hair and tucked it behind her ears. She looked about ten years old. Her lips twitched. Not exactly a smile, but close enough.

Another contraction hit. Her body stiffened. She closed her eyes, grasped her stomach and groaned. They say you forget your labor pains as soon as they put your newborn baby in your arms. Hogwash. That's a blatant old-husband's tale, fostered on wives of previous generations to keep them reproducing without complaint. Seeing the pain and fear on my daughter's face brought it all back in living color, yet I would gladly have suffered it for Annie if I could.

"Let me get Calixto," I said. "I'll call the hospital, too, let them know we're coming. Will you be okay for a bit?" I didn't want to leave her, but she nodded as the pain receded. "I'll help you into some decent clothes when I get back. Good thing I bought you new underwear," I added with a twinkle.

Calixto, who lived in an apartment above the garage, had the car at the porte cochère in record time. Having heard the commotion, Mother swirled about the porch in a lavender silk negligee with a million questions and rafts of unwelcome advice.

"Are you sure she's really in labor? It doesn't do to get there too early. Those people just ignore you. The next thing you know, you're swimming in a pool of blood and nobody's around to clean you up. I'll come along and make sure she gets their full attention."

Annie stared at her grandmother, horrified. Whatever happened to Mother's glowing faith in the world's only adequate maternity hospital?

"Mother, for God's sake," I snapped. "Quit scaring her. It's so unnecessary. She's in heavy labor. It's time to go."

Just then Father stumbled onto the porch, bleary-eyed, bare-chested in his blue-and-white-striped pajama bottoms. He looked like a fuzzy, graying circus bear, half dressed for the next show. Annie reached out and latched onto his wrist. She gripped with both hands as a new contraction clamped down on her. He stood stock still, stricken with helplessness.

Calixto opened the car doors and paced the bottom step, his black eyes flashing with concern.

Suddenly Annie exclaimed, "Oh."

We all looked at her. A wet stain spread across the crotch of her shorts. Water trickled down her shins and ankles, cellophane ribbons gleaming yellow in the bug-repellent porch light. She let go of her grandfather and stepped back. The liquid dribbled into a glistening puddle on the porch floor.

"Grandma, I'm sorry! I can't stop it. It keeps coming down."

"Your water has broken," I replied. "A sure sign the baby's on its way."

Mother looked around. There were no servants about. "Don't worry, dear. I'll . . . I'll get you a towel. Don't move."

As soon as she disappeared into the house, I turned to my father, pleading, "Dad, please keep Mother here. I don't want her at the hospital. She'll make us all crazy. I promise I'll call you with every sign of progress. Can you do that for me?"

He cupped my chin in his hand and grinned. He wanted to help, but hadn't dared insert himself into this most female of feminine concerns. Now he had something important to do. "Of course, honey. I'll keep her right here. Never fear." I kissed him my thanks.

Mother reappeared, threw a towel on the puddle of water on the wooden porch floor and handed another to Annie. "Stuff it between your legs. That's a good girl. Here's one to sit on." She patted Annie on her back and guided her down the steps. "Now, don't worry. We'll be right behind you in your grandfather's car."

I looked at my dad in a panic. He winked. "She hasn't gotten away from me yet," he said. Mother shot him a look, but he ignored her. "You jump right in that car with Annie, Laura. Go on now, off you go." He shooed me down the steps.

Calixto tucked Annie into the back seat with her towels. I ran around to the other side and clambered in beside her. Cal slammed the car doors. We were off. I twisted around for one last glance out the rear window. Dad stood with his arm around Mother, the pair of them backlit by the golden porch light. With his free arm, he waved goodbye with his whole heart and soul.

CHAPTER 25

My mother engineered the whole thing. I just don't know how she did it. Annie gave birth at Kapiolani, just as Mother had planned. She had made Annie's reservation for a private room the very day she learned of Annie's pregnancy. A certain familiar bile roiled in my gut. As usual, I tamped it down.

That night remains a kaleidoscope of clashing lights, colors, and sounds in my mind's eye. Blinding headlights racing toward us as we careened in the dark around the narrow, vine-curtained curves of Old Pali Road, then the rush straight down Pali Highway and a manic swerve onto Lunalilo Freeway. No sooner did we bluster into the flowing three-lane traffic than Calixto veered up an off-ramp, ran a red light across Punahou Street, and squealed into the only empty spot at the hospital's emergency entrance. Beaming at our hair-raising approach, he helped Annie out of the car with great tenderness, walked her through the automatic doors, and assisted her into a waiting wheelchair.

Diverted to the admissions office, I filled out innumerable forms and questionnaires, pledging my own firstborn son as security for Annie's charges in lieu of her Ohana Care card, which she had carelessly left on Maui. At last the clerk gathered the sheaves, clipped them together, and set me free to track down my daughter.

Bright lights; gleaming floors; long hallways; uniformed staff striding along with important airs, gesturing, laughing, absorbed in their own theatrics; an elevator to the third floor, and finally a sign that read, OBSTETRICS.

I paused in the doorway of Annie's room, fighting back a sudden rush of tears. Clad in a white hospital gown, she was curled up under a coral cotton blanket, one shoulder exposed, her back to me. With her ash-blonde hair lying every which way across the pillow, she looked like an abandoned china doll that had been left behind when the little girl went off to nursery school. Once again I wished I could tap her on the shoulder and say, "My turn, sweetheart. I'll take it from here. You go on out to play."

While I fought to regain my composure, Annie heaved over onto her back and spotted me. Pale and scared, she pushed off the bedcovers and reached out a hand. "Mom," she pleaded in a soft, shaky voice.

My heart melted. "I'm here, baby."

She struggled to sit up. "I thought you'd gone home. I thought you'd left me here all alone." Her voice wobbled, her little chin quivered.

I smoothed the sheets across her legs and sat on the bed beside her. "Oh, honey, never. My fingers are numb from filling out a million forms. But I'm here now. I won't leave you."

She gripped my hand as a contraction seized her.

"Breathe, Annie. Take deep breaths. It helps." Oh, why had she so stubbornly refused to attend childbirth classes? Here I was, trying to coach a kid who didn't know the most elementary rules of the game, relying on a vaguely remembered playbook from almost twenty years ago.

Time passed. Nurses came and went, efficient, cheerful, and reassuring. I rubbed her back. I held her hand. I sponged her arms and forehead. Annie soldiered on bravely. She caught onto the deep breathing during contractions and worked at it with intense concentration.

Morning crept in, illuminating the green hills of Manoa Valley through the window. Meal carts rattled by, redolent of scrambled eggs and Portuguese sausage. Deep circles had developed beneath Annie's eyes. Her lips became parched and cracked. An aide gave her chipped ice to suck. Tired and discouraged, her breathing became ragged as she struggled to keep up with the contractions.

Sitting on a straight-backed chair beside the bed, I coached her through the hours. My back ached. My feet screamed for relief from my hurried choice of shoes. Annie began to pass out between pains. I eased off my shoes and walked around the room barefoot. The cool linoleum felt divine. For a moment, just for a moment, I decided to try the overstuffed chair by the window. The aide brought me a blanket and took my place at Annie's side.

The next thing I knew, lunch carts were rattling down the hallway, suffusing the wing with the pungent scent of teriyaki chicken. Suddenly I was famished. When the nurse returned to examine Annie's progress, I decided it was safe to duck out to the cafeteria. As I reached the door, Annie turned over on her side and vomited.

"Good," said the nurse. "The baby's moving down the birth canal." Before I could take another step, they threw open the closet doors and wheeled out an amazing array of equipment. "Time for delivery," the nurse stated. "She's fully dilated. Doctor's on his way. Are you staying, Mrs. McDaniel?"

Not for one moment had I entertained the possibility of witnessing the birth of my first grandchild. I'd simply never gotten that far in my vision of things.

"Annie? They say I can stay. Do you want me here?"

Panting like a racing horse, Annie's blue eyes widened with fear. "Mom, you gotta stay. I can't do it without you."

Feeling awkward and in the way, but propelled by an incredible sense of excitement, I gowned and masked under the aide's supervision, then stood at Annie's shoulder to prop her while she pushed. Before we knew it, an angry little bundle emerged, waving her arms and howling with indignation. Her fierce crying was Annie, all right. But that round face and those big dark eyes and hair—she looked like no child who had ever been born into our family.

My daughter and I cried and laughed and hugged each other like perfect fools. Reduced to our elemental beings, all animosity and antagonism dropped away. Annie had brought new life into the world, and I had assisted.

Without warning, the doctor turned toward me and held out the waxy, squalling infant. "Would you care to cut the cord, Mrs. McDaniel?" The nurse, nodding encouragement, held out a pair of blunt-tipped scissors.

Startled, I backed up and shook my head. Annie laughed. "Come on, Ma, you can do it. She's your granddaughter."

With shaking hands, I did as instructed: a nice, clean snip between the clamps. Beaming, the nurse reclaimed the baby, fussed over her for a few minutes, then returned her to me, fresh, open-eyed and swaddled in a pink blanket. She was exquisite. I held her first, even before her mother. It was a sweet, unforgettable moment to savor in drowsy dreams.

Calixto stood beside Mother's car in front of the hospital later that afternoon, waiting to take me home. When I arrived, I gave Mother and Dad a complete account of the baby's birth and answered their many questions. By the time I collapsed into bed, it was well into evening. I slept until noon the next day. By the time I awoke, they had been on the phone and spoken to Annie twice. Mother and daughter seemed to be doing fine, but my parents could barely contain themselves while I dressed, ate a quick bite, and joined them for their first visit with their great-granddaughter.

Annie appeared miraculously recovered. Her hair gleamed, and the purple circles under her eyes were almost gone. Flattening the bed sheet across her belly, she declared. "Look, I'm skinny again."

She insisted on getting up and walking to the nursery with us. Dad proudly offered her his arm as we progressed down the hall in regal splendor, his camera swinging importantly from a strap around his neck. A cheerful Filipino nurse met us at the entrance to the infant intensive care unit. She showed us how to scrub at a deep stainless steel sink and slip into cotton gowns from a nearby cabinet. She led us down a row of incubators, each one surrounded by tubes and wires that hung about them like anemic jungle vines, all attached to a confusion of keyboards, humming metal boxes, and blinking monitors. Each monitor flashed a continuous outpouring of indecipherable graphic data, translating the sacred essence of tiny living beings into impersonal blips and numerals.

The nurse stopped at the very last station. There she was, our little rosebud, lying on her side in her plastic Isolette, so tiny, so pink, so sweet. She fit right in with all the other dark-haired babies in the nursery.

"She's doing fine, Ms. McDaniel," the nurse assured Annie. "Dr. Leong is doing his rounds," she said. "He should be along any minute." The nurse reached into the Isolette and picked up the baby. She maneuvered the wires attached to that tiny chest and forehead with a practiced motion and offered her, wrapped tightly in a flannelette blanket, to Annie. "Would you like to hold her, Ms. McDaniel? Go ahead, sit in the rocking chair. Just be careful of the equipment."

Eyes open in surprise, Annie backed up and bumped smack into Dad. From behind, he took her by the elbow and guided her into the waiting chair. He held it steady while Annie eased onto the corduroy cushion, warily eyeing the baby in the nurse's arms. The rocker, an ordinary wooden one they might have picked up at K-Mart, lent a surprising air of hominess to the high-tech environment.

"Ouch," Annie exclaimed as she lowered her full weight onto the seat. Her exclamation broke the ice. We all laughed as she timidly reached out for her daughter.

"Here," said the nurse, at ease with nervous new mothers. "Let me show you how to hold her." Her manner was so warm, so sincere, that Annie visibly relaxed and nestled her baby to her chest. "You're bottle feeding, right?" The nurse asked casually, attaching no judgment to the decision.

Annie nodded vigorously. "No way I'm doing it the other way."

"In my day, only white trash breast-fed their babies," Mother contributed, backing Annie up in her own inimitable way. Dad rolled his eyes and hummed a little tune. Annie and I looked at each other and burst out laughing again. The nurse frowned, then turned away, opened a cupboard and took out a bottle of pre-mixed formula. She had sized Mother up for exactly what she was, a snob of the first degree.

"Now, dear . . ." Dad, ever the placater, lifted his camera and began snapping away.

Fighting a grin, the nurse pulled up a stool and sat down beside Annie. She twisted the cover off the nipple and handed the bottle to her.

"Just tease her lips a bit, that's it. She knows what it's for." The baby opened her precious mouth and began sucking with a vigor that belied her preemie size. Entranced, Mother, Father, and I watched quietly. Dad put his arm around my shoulders. As I leaned against him, a feeling of warmth and happiness flowed through me. Maybe, just maybe, this marked the beginning of Annie's acceptance of motherhood.

Dr. Leong, a short, stocky Chinese man with a military brush cut and rake-like mustache, introduced himself as a neonatal specialist. He reported finding no obvious signs of distress when he had examined the baby. Her Apgar scores were a bit low, but within the normal range. She seemed healthy, although he was watching for signs of in-utero substance abuse that sometimes didn't manifest right away. He gave Annie a run-down on the warning signs, telling her she'd have to be watchful after the baby was released. In his straightforward manner, he covered all the things I had been so worried about. For once, Annie appeared to listen. We all cheered when he finally said, "For the moment, we have to concentrate on fattening her up so she can go home. Judging by the speed with which she emptied that bottle, I'd say she's well on her way."

They released Annie alone the next morning, after a luxurious one-night stay. This incensed Mother.

"Why, in my day, they kept you in bed for two weeks," she declared. "On the tenth day, they let you dangle your legs over the side of the bed so you could get used to walking again."

"Mom, she'll be fine. And she'll have both of us, and Tami, to look after her."

"Humph. It's unnatural to leave the baby behind and go home alone."

"Annie's perfectly healthy," I pointed out. "Do you want to pay for her extra days at the hospital until the baby is ready to leave?"

The discussion ended then and there.

In spite of her apparent good beginning, the baby did not immediately thrive. Fussy and wakeful, she spat up her formula as soon as she drank it down. Her weight dropped to a little over four pounds. The doctor assured us that such a drop was normal after birth, but by the fourth day she hit a worrisome plateau. Her weight stabilized, but she wasn't gaining.

That afternoon, Annie and I went to visit the baby alone. Dad was at work, mother at a committee meeting. Annie had just settled into the rocker to give her a bottle when a social worker from the Department of Health came into the nursery with an important-looking clipboard, introduced herself as Mrs. Morales, and asked for the baby's name.

Annie fiddled with a corner of the baby's blanket. "She doesn't have a name yet," she said, without looking up.

Mrs. Morales' voice rose a notch. "But you gotta name her before she leaves the hospital so we can register the birth."

"I'm not ready for that," Annie replied.

Resting one hand on her hip, Mrs. Morales lowered her clipboard. A heavy Portuguese woman with gray hair and a lined, weary face, she had seen it all and wasn't interested in seeing any more. "You cannot take your baby home until she get one name," she declared in flat, assertive Pidgin.

Annie pushed her chin out defiantly. Despite everyone at home also asking, she had steadfastly refused to choose a name. Considering the baby's fragility, I'd begged Annie to give her a nice, solid name to hang onto. I had all kinds of grand ideas, clever combinations of ancestral and Hawaiian names, but I kept them to myself. If Annie named her, it would be part of the process of claiming her.

Stepping forward, I said to the social worker, "Let it go for now, please. My daughter will notify you when she's ready. We've lots of time. The baby won't be going home for a while."

Looking doubtful, the woman pursed her lips, scribbled a note on the clipboard, and departed with a stern promise to return the next day.

"Sweetheart, don't you have any ideas for a name?" I asked when we were alone again.

She shook her head stubbornly, pulled the bottle from the baby's mouth and held it up to see how many ounces were left. Furious, the baby flailed her arms and began to cry. Annie quickly stood up and handed her to me. She turned to the window and crossed her arms over her chest, shutting us both out. I picked up the bottle and held it to the baby's eager lips. As I swayed back and forth to settle her, it struck me just how tiny she was, how tenuous her hold on life. I ran my finger across her downy cheek, murmuring, "We need to fatten you up, don't we? Why, you're as light as a feather."

Annie spun around from the window. "That's it, Ma. You just named her. Feather."

I looked at her, startled. "Feather? What kind of name is that for a baby?"

"You said it. Now it's her name. Feather McDaniel."

"Oh, Annie. That's dreadful. It sounds like a hippie name. You might as well call her Sunflower Seed . . . or Rainbow . . . or . . . or Cabbage."

"Done deal, Ma. Her name is Feather. I kinda like it." She reached out and took the baby from me. She held the wrapped bundle up to her shoulder and spoke softly near the baby's ear, looking at me with narrowed eyes. "Feather. Your grandmother named you. Always remember that."

Her icy eyes dared me to get angry. My heart contracted. Was this her brutal way of telling me our closeness brought about by Feather's birth had ended?

CHAPTER 26

We settled into twice-daily drives to and from the hospital until one day when Annie refused to turn off the TV and leave Pua Olena at the appointed time for our morning visit.

"Ma, I'm tired of going twice a day. Why do we have to go so often? All we do is rock her and feed her. What's the point? Let the nurses do it. It's not like I'm breast-feeding." She shuddered at the very idea.

It took a moment, but I found my voice. "Sweetheart, you don't mean that. She needs you as much as possible. Babies don't thrive unless they're held a lot. They need touching as much as they need feeding. The nurses only have time for essentials."

Annie yawned. "Ma, it's a drag. I'll go this afternoon, but I'm not going this morning. I'm too tired." She turned back to her TV game show.

"Tired? From what?" I asked, incredulous.

She planted her elbows on the arms of the easy chair and pushed herself halfway up. "Well, duh, I just had a baby."

Anger rose up and threatened to choke me. "Sure, five days ago, and you haven't had to take care of her on your own for one second. I'd have a little sympathy if you were doing the middle-of-the-night feedings and up for all day at five a.m."

The chair creaked as she flounced back and looked away. "I don't care. I'm still tired. Go without me. I'll do my duty this afternoon." She picked up the TV remote control and started her defiant channel flipping.

I stared at her, immobilized with fury. To keep from slapping her, I turned around and hurried out to the front porch where the car was waiting.

When Feather was eight days old, she finally regained her birth weight. Annie's interest waxed and waned, but even she seemed pleased when the pediatrician announced that Feather's tests for prenatal substance abuse damage were all negative and that she would be released as soon as she hit five pounds.

Buoyed by that good news, I got home to find little yellow squares stuck to my bedroom door bearing messages from the Colemans and Randy Entwistle in Tami's neat printing. They must have gotten Mother's phone number from my broker.

While only a week ago those folks had been the driving forces in my life, I had to strain now to picture them. I'd monitored my answering machine daily, but not much had required my attention. The two attorneys were doing their jobs. Reluctantly, I went to Dad's den and picked up the phone.

"Darling," Diana breathed when I told her the news. "Congratulations on the baby! You must be thrilled. Do give me your mother's address so I can send her something frilly."

Before I could answer, Jerry picked up an extension. His voice was gruff and impatient. "Laura? Annie's had the baby? Everyone okay?"

"Fine so far, Jerry. Thanks for asking." I steeled myself for an unpleasant conversation.

"Glad to hear it. When are you coming home? There's no end of grief with those two madwomen."

My stomach flip-flopped. Nervously I began lining up the pencils on my father's desk in a neat row. "What now?"

"The doctor decided to enforce Moana's eviction notice by calling Maui Electric and cutting off the power to the house. She also had the phone and water disconnected. Thought she could force the issue. Miss Moana marched right downtown, declared she was Randa Entwistle, and demanded they turn them on again. Claimed she'd made a mistake. Of course they didn't know her from the washerwoman, so they complied just to get her out of there. Now she's threatening to sue Dr. Entwistle for harassment and constructive eviction. Apparently shutting off the utilities is a no-no."

I groaned.

"Meanwhile," Jerry continued, "the lock on our loan is about to expire. We have to pay another quarter point to extend it. That's serious cash, Laura. You better get home and kick some butt around here."

I scooped up the pencils with an irritated clack and dumped them point-down in a mug. *Here we go again.* First Jerry tells me to butt out; then when things get sticky, he wanted my butt on the line again. Typical. I made a snap decision. "Okay, Jerry. I'll be there tomorrow." I hated to admit it, but he was right. I would have to leave Annie and the baby in Honolulu and go home to tend my business. My pile of unpaid bills kept flashing before my eyes. "I'll ring you when I get in," I told him. "Would you call your attorney and tell him to expect a call from me? Authorize him to give me a complete update, nothing held back."

I returned Randy's call next, but of course I only got her machine. Whatever she had to tell me would have to wait.

It killed me to leave Honolulu. Annie didn't seem to care one way or another. Mother put on a good show, but the smug gleam in her eye betrayed her. Finally, she would have Annie and Feather all to herself.

After all my grumbling about close quarters and Annie's messy habits, my apartment seemed depressingly lifeless without her and the baby. I drew the drapes and slid open the glass doors to let in the warm air and sunshine. It felt marvelous after the chilly damp of Pua Olena.

I turned on the ceiling fan and threw my suitcase on the bed. I'd been dreading the idea of Annie, her baby, and me trying to manage in this small space. Now that I knew darling Feather, had witnessed her birth, had held her in my arms, and had fallen hopelessly in love with her, I couldn't wait to get her and Annie home and tuck them safely in with me. We would have to find a bigger place before she started to crawl, but we'd be cozy here in the meantime. The thought warmed me like a swig of *okolehao*.

I quickly unpacked, picked up a shirt and pair of shorts Annie had left on the bathroom floor, and began to focus on the details of the Colemans' closing.

First, I called their loan officer to verify what Jerry had told me yesterday. Buyers and sellers often get mixed up and panic over misinformation, but this time Jerry had gotten it right. Their lock was about to expire, and it would cost them almost $1500 to extend it. They'd simply have to bite the bullet.

The next item was a chat with the Colemans' attorney, Jeff Garagiola.

"Hey, Laura, how goes the battle?" If you only heard Jeff's deep, resonant voice, you would assume he had a bruiser of a body to match. In truth, he's a toothpick of a fellow, not much taller than me, with a sweet boyish face and a five o'clock shadow that gets ugly at noon. When he set his sights on the law, he discovered his voice was a serious asset in the courtroom. Drama lessons turned it into a lethal weapon. In trial, or just on the phone, folks sit up and take notice. The fact that he looks like someone's baby brother becomes a non-issue the minute he opens his mouth.

"One punch at a time, Jeff," I replied. "How's by you?"

"You keep sending me folks like the Colemans, I'm gonna retire and write a best seller."

I could envision his shaded face bent over the computer keyboard while his slender fingers picked away, proving once again that truth is stranger than fiction.

"I'll be happy to serve as a highly paid consultant," I joked. "But first, we have to close this deal. I've been out of town. What's the status?"

"According to the seller's attorney, Ji-Kwok Yuen, all the tenants but Moana have moved out. Dr. Entwistle settled with the folks who claimed they lost their door prizes at the employee picnic, and all that other crap. As you know, the other two up and left when the weirdness meter cranked up. But we've still got the housemate who refuses to move out, a threat of disputed ownership, and a surveyor and a termite inspector who got chased off the property. Oh, yeah, and the possibility of a drug lab in the garage. Other than that, everything's right on target."

I coughed. "So what are you doing about it?"

"The surveyor and the termite inspector went back yesterday. The sheriff was there himself to make sure they were allowed to do their jobs. Thanks for giving him a piece of your mind, by the way. Saved me the trouble."

"Easy," I replied.

He continued. "I did a background check on the woman. Seems she has an interesting litigious history." I could hear Jeff scratching his rough chin as he spoke.

Dread settled in around my ankles like a creeping black cat. "Why am I not surprised?"

"I've dug up two lawsuits, both pretty dramatic. You probably know about her boating accident. It made quite a splash." Jeff was notorious for making bad puns.

"And the other was a car accident," I added, in no mood to acknowledge his cleverness. "She got handsome settlements for both, I take it?"

"Yeah. But I wouldn't be surprised if that cash is running low, and she's looking around for another opportunity. Just in case renting rooms in someone else's house doesn't pan out."

"Well, hell. You think she picked me out as her next victim?" This wasn't how it was supposed to go.

"I don't know. But it's something to consider. You ought to get your own counsel, just in case."

My voice cracked with distress. "Jeff, that'll wipe me out."

"Better give it some thought, Laura. From what I can tell, she's a pro. If she decides to go after you, she'll get mean and ugly. There are attorneys in town, I'm sorry to say, who would salivate over this case. You being your mother's daughter and all."

My family history was no secret. What Moana didn't know, however, was how tight-fisted my mother was, and that I had no real assets of my own. But that wouldn't keep her from trying. I glanced around my peaceful apartment. The little straw carrying basket for Feather was packed with her layette. Annie and I had picked out each blanket, each nightgown, each little shirt with such loving care. All I wanted was Annie and Feather safely at home, and the rest of the world to leave us in peace.

"Just help me close the sale, Jeff. I beg you, let's shut the door on this one."

Chapter 27

I called Annie at Mother's and checked in with the nursery every day. Depending on how she felt, Annie would gush like a typical new mother with some cute tidbit about her daughter's behavior, or brush my phone call off as an imposition. My stomach tightened every time I waited for her to answer. I wanted so desperately to hear all the details, and for Annie to share them enthusiastically.

The calls to the nursery were easier. The nurses were always bright and encouraging, reporting day by day that Feather was slowly but steadily gaining weight.

Just over a week after my return to Maui, I called the nursery first, shortly before noon, only to be told Feather had been released that morning. Although we had expected it any day, it hurt beyond measure that Annie hadn't called to tell me herself. Surely she knew how relieved I'd be and would want to share the good news right away.

I quickly rang Pua Olena. Mother answered. "Mom? I just called the hospital. They said Feather's been released. Are she and Annie at home with you? Is everything okay?"

Mother's voice sang with delight. "Of course, dear, of course. Annie was just going to call you. We only got word this morning. One of the nurses phoned while we were having breakfast. We put down our napkins and left immediately. Isn't that wonderful?"

I swallowed my bruised feelings. If that was really how it happened, perhaps Annie hadn't had time to call me. Feather was safely out of the hospital and home with her mother—that's what really mattered.

"How is Annie doing with her, Mom?" Hopefully Mother hadn't whisked the baby out of Annie's arms and taken over. My daughter was going to need a lot of encouragement to become a confident mother.

"Why, they're sitting together in the living room in Dad's big chair, getting better acquainted. What an adorable picture! Tami's warming a bottle for her right now." While the enchantment in her voice reassured me, it deepened my sense of isolation.

"Mom, can I talk to Annie? I'd like to know when she's coming home."

Mother hesitated a heartbeat longer than necessary. With a sense of foreboding, I looked at the ceiling and tapped my foot. Her next words dripped with innocent surprise. "Why, they're staying here, dear. I thought you knew that."

I tightened the phone cord around my fist until it hurt. "Mother, that's absurd. You're not set up for a baby."

"I certainly have more room than you, dear." Said with such honeyed ingenuousness. "And Liberty House delivered a full set of nursery furniture yesterday."

I stifled a groan. "Would you let me talk to her, please?"

"I'll have her call you as soon as the baby's asleep. Tami just walked in with the bottle. Best we let them alone for the moment. Take care, dear." The phone went dead.

I dropped the receiver onto its cradle and whirled around to face the mountain. The morning clouds had lifted; the summit rose clear. At the top, the observatory sparked pinpoints of crystalline sunlight along the purple ridgeline. I took a deep breath and called Hawaiian Airlines. I arrived in Honolulu on the seven o'clock flight.

Hungry, tired, or bored, Feather screamed. No little "eh-eh-eh" windups, but open-mouthed, full-throttle screams. Or she screamed for no reason at all. Once in a while she condescended to doze in her bassinet, but not for long. The minute she realized she'd been left alone, she screwed up her face and wailed to be picked up. Occasionally, when satiated and snug in someone's arms, eyes wide open and curious, she was an angel. Entranced with her exotic, dark-eyed beauty, I held her and rocked her and thought of Annie.

Throughout her childhood, hardly a week went by that Annie didn't wake up in the middle of the night hysterical about something. Sometimes the shadows on the wall or a noise outside her window frightened her. Or she dreamed her brothers were strangling in tree-climbing vines in the jungle behind Pua Olena. More than a few times we found her cowering in the corner of her bed, terrorized by an imagined cockroach, grown to gigantic proportions and gnawing through the mattress to eat her.

We carried her down the hall to show her the boys tucked safely in bed, made the shadows disappear by turning on the lights, assured her the noise was just a branch rubbing against the house in the wind, or remind her the roaches were only small and very much afraid of her. But Annie held onto her fears like a treasured baby blanket, resisting comfort, unwilling to let them go. The doctor said she had an overactive imagination, that she would outgrow it. I don't think she ever did. She simply learned to keep her fears to herself while they continued to run her life. Was that another borderline manifestation of autism? Would Feather be subject to terrors, too, and Annie's other difficult behaviors? Would I be any better at dealing with her than I'd been with Annie?

I had planned to stay in Honolulu until midweek, so we'd be close to the hospital in case Feather took a bad turn. According to the doctor, she was progressing well with no signs of damage from Annie's prenatal lifestyle, but I wanted to be sure.

On Feather's first night home at Pua Olena, my eyes flew open the instant she begin to fuss in the wee hours. My bare feet hit the *lauhala* before I realized I didn't have to go to her. She wasn't my baby. Gripping the edge of the bed, heart pounding, I listened fearfully until I heard Annie pad down the hallway to the kitchen for a bottle. Perhaps I should have kept her company in her lonely vigil, but caution stayed me. I knew only too well the fragile state of the new mother-child bond. By the time Annie had the bottle ready, Feather was screaming. And I was remembering.

"Annie! Stop crying! Mommy loves you! Stop! Stop!" But she wouldn't stop. Her shrieks increased, high-pitched, piercing, relentless. Gripping her by her heaving ribs, my arm muscles cramped with tension, I thrust her out in front of me, eye to eye. Through clenched teeth, I shouted again, "Stop, damn you. Stop! I love you, Annie. Stop crying. Stop it now! Now!"

But she didn't stop. Night after night she screamed for hours, a high-pitched, nerve-grating scream. The more I tried to comfort her, the more she twisted and kicked away from me. She refused my every effort. And then one night when she kicked and twisted yet one more time in rage, I felt my arms go slack. I let her go. Purposely, deliberately. I just let her go, for the merest instant, heedless of the terrazzo floor at my feet. In that split second I didn't care if she hit ground or how badly she got hurt, just as long as she stopped that ear-shattering shrieking. I came to my senses in a heartbeat and swooped down to catch her before she hit the floor. She was as startled as I at the sudden movement. We stared at each other for a long, tense moment. And then her eyelids fluttered, and she fell asleep in my arms.

I had sat down with her in the rocker and cried and cried. How had I come so close to harming my child? My baby! I understood in that moment how even a devoted mother can be driven to desperation and pushed over the brink to actual physical harm. The only difference was that I had stopped myself at the very last. But the potential remained. For the rest of her childhood, I kept a steel band on my nerves, ever mindful of another time when I might not be able to hold myself back in the face of her incomprehensible behavior. It never happened again, thank God, but the memory haunted me. I never forgot.

Frank never knew. He never knew the desperation to which I was driven in the night with Annie. Like my father, he was rarely home in the evening. When he was home, he slept the deep sleep of exhaustion, out of earshot from the children's wing. It was all left to me. I tried. I truly tried. The boys had been easy. But not Annie. The doctor called it colic, but I was sure it was more than that. I should have demanded help. But I didn't know there was help to be had. When she finally slept through the night, the crying stopped, except for the nightmares.

I'd managed to bury the memories, out of sight, out of mind, until Feather's crying brought it all back again.

Shivering in the cool night air, I relived that desolate, exhausted, terrified feeling of being alone in the middle of the night with an infant. Nights Frank didn't come home. Nights an inconsolable child drove me to the brink. I slid back under my covers, glazed in cold sweat. Annie was all grown up with a baby of her own now. Surely that nightmare was long over. Surely the pattern would not repeat.

In a conscious effort to stop trembling, I paced my breathing to the rhythm of Annie and Feather in the koa rocker, the chair in which Tami had rocked me, the chair in which I'd rocked my boys and Annie when visiting my parents. The crying finally stopped. I listened while Annie patted Feather on the back, and she finally burped. The chair went quiet. Annie's footsteps whispered on the *lauhala* as she returned Feather to her bassinet. I held my breath until all was still. Relieved beyond measure, I finally nodded off. Everything would be fine in the morning.

Feather's first full day at home flew by in a flurry of baby care and photo opportunities. Toward late afternoon, I caught the girls relaxing in Dad's easy chair in the living room, Feather asleep and Annie gazing at her in a moment of unguarded affection. Beautiful as a Russian icon, I thought as I snapped the picture, Madonna and Child, framed by Annie's shimmering hair.

Attentive to her daughter, Annie nevertheless acquiesced when I offered to help. Mother had a full day of volunteer commitments, which left us a contented threesome. This time things would be different. The wisdom I had acquired over the years with Annie would temper Feather's demanding disposition. Raising her would be a joint undertaking, the two of us together.

That night I woke again with the baby's fussing. Again she didn't cooperate. I heard Annie click her tongue impatiently, urging her to take her bottle, but Feather just cried louder. Annie's footsteps whispered back and forth on the *lauhala* while she hummed a lullaby from her own youth. My stomach tightened at the haunting tune in my daughter's voice. Nothing seemed to work. I grasped the edge of my sheet, pulling it taut across my chest. I did not want to be with a baby in the middle of the night. But it was no use. I had to help my daughter. I threw off my covers and darted down the hall.

Annie's room was a shadowy mess—baby clothes and used diapers strewn on the floor, an earlier bottle overturned on the bedside table. Frustration curled the corners of her words.

"Ma, she doesn't want her bottle. What am I supposed to do? All she does is cry!"

"Is the bottle too hot?" I asked, hoping for an easy answer.

"No, it's not much over room temperature. She's never fussed about that before." Annie hopped up and down, jiggling the baby hard.

"Annie, be careful! You'll hurt her!" I grabbed the baby and backed away from Annie, holding Feather safely against my breast, my heart pounding against her cheek. Annie looked at me curiously, as if my reaction was way out of bounds. I asked the first distracting question that came to mind.

"Did you check for open diaper pins?"

"Pampers, Mom," she replied.

I took a deep breath. "Of course." Secure in my arms, Feather stopped crying and then yawned as if all that fuss had been a great big bore. I inhaled again and loosened my arms just a bit, repeating silently to myself that this was not Annie. I had only to look into her dark, foreign eyes to reassure myself. Everything would be okay. Feather had been reacting to her mother's inner turmoil. Oh, how I knew that routine. She'd calmed down the instant I picked her up. I felt a small flicker of confidence. Things *would* be different this time.

In the dim glow of the night light, relief softened Annie's face. She handed me the bottle. The baby immediately began sucking. Annie stood there like an abandoned waif, toes turned in, T-shirt hanging off one shoulder.

"Ma, what's wrong? Doesn't she like me?"

"Of course she likes you, silly. Who knows why babies act the way they do? You were just like this. Cried all the time. I never knew what would set you off."

She peered at me through her bangs. "Pretty awful, huh?"

I sat in the rocking chair with Feather and finally relaxed. "Honestly, it was tough. You were certainly different from your brothers. I thought I had babies all figured out, that number three would be a breeze. But you were completely different. Nothing that worked with the boys worked with you. I never did figure you out—not to this very day." I said it with a smile, not intending any offense.

For once, none was taken. Annie climbed onto her bed and leaned back against the wall, cross-legged, watching us. She was so child-like herself, the least likely portrait of a mother. I tightened the baby's blanket around her tiny body, a gesture that soothed me as much as it soothed Feather.

"Look how content she is now," I said. "All she needed was a different set of arms to hold her for a while. Nothing personal, honey. You lie down and go back to sleep. I'll finish her up." Flashing me a gamin grin, she sank down on the pillow. Soon she was breathing deeply.

While Feather put all her restless energy into making those four ounces of formula disappear, I watched her closely. Lush dark lashes curled on her cheeks; a swirl of black hair framed her doll-like face. As dreadful and unforgivable as the circumstances of her conception had been, those hateful feelings had nothing to do with this sweet baby girl. Had I been given a second chance to help raise a child so much like my daughter in temperament? Was Feather a gift sent to help me forgive myself? Had I learned enough from my mistakes with Annie that I could help turn the tide with her daughter? I didn't know.

Safely back between the shivery sheets in my own bed, I gave way again to the fear I had managed to stave off while helping Annie settled Feather. Those long nights with Frank at the hotel, and a child who would not sleep. Endless exhaustion, nerves beaten to the edge of combustion. By day I had managed to put one foot in front of the other and make it to bedtime for the boys. Then another long night began with Annie.

But that was a generation ago, another mother, another child. It was over. I forced my thoughts into a safer channel. I could handle this.

CHAPTER 28

At breakfast Annie announced, "We're going home today, Ma. This afternoon." In spite of my earlier plans to stay the week, I was ready to leave, too. It was no fun living in someone else's home with an infant.

Annie spent the morning throwing Feather's things into a suitcase. She waved me away when I offered to help. Mother, in high dudgeon at our sudden plans to depart, headed for her orchid house to check on her *honohono* starts, from whom, she announced on her way out the door, she received considerably more gratitude. Dad stayed in bed, conspicuously out of the fray. I felt like a piece of seaweed in a tidal pool, thrown this way and that by the crashing surf, never knowing the direction from which the next breaker would hit.

We had three o'clock reservations on Hawaiian Airlines, but Annie was chafing by noon, insisting we leave immediately after lunch, knowing we could stand by for an earlier flight. Mother took in this news too quietly. While Tami poured tea and offered her melt-in-the-mouth Russian teacakes for dessert, Father said his hearty goodbyes and left for the restaurant. The moment the gravel-crunch of his wheels faded down the driveway, Mother turned to me, her linen napkin uncharacteristically twisted into a rope.

"Laura, there's something I need to discuss with you before you leave. Annie, you'll make your flight, but don't count on anything earlier."

Her voice was so severe, so commanding that Annie acquiesced without a fuss. Leaving her to help Tami clear the table, I nervously followed

Mother down the hall, feeling once again like the rattled teenager who had scooped the boy's photo from the yearbook layout table and hidden it in her underwear drawer.

On she marched, ramrod straight, cinched tight at the waist of her crisply pressed slacks, her gold sandals marking a dire cadence on the *lauhala* mat. The fact that she wore footwear in the house lent extreme gravity to the situation. What on earth was she going to scold me about this time?

Without hesitating, she entered Dad's *sanctum sanctorum*, his holy of holies, and sat in the chair behind his desk. Was it something about his health, as I had feared almost thirty years earlier when she'd lambasted me about boys? I sat across from her, in deep trepidation, on the wood-and-leather chair where I'd had many happy visits with my father.

"Mom, what is it? You're scaring me."

"There's something you need to know." She forced her words through stiff, prim lips.

"About Dad? Is he ill?" My fingers tightened around the carved gar-goyle heads on the arms of the chair. I'd squashed peanut-butter sand-wiches into their mouths to feed them as a child, something else I'd been scolded for in this room. Dad had cancer, I knew it, with only two months to live.

"No, your father's just fine, blessed be the angels and the saints. This is something else. I've worried for months about how to tell you, when might be an appropriate time. Now that we have Feather, and your busi-ness is such a failure, I feel the time has come."

I took immediate exception. "What do you mean, my business is a failure? That's absolutely not true."

"Really? Then why did you call and ask for something to tide you over some weeks back?"

"Oh, for heaven's sake. That was just to help me stay afloat until my next closings. Annie's return threw my finances completely out of whack. You can understand that. The Schultzes just closed, and the Colemans are on the brink. Plus, I have two more in escrow. I'm doing just fine." Not exactly true, considering the state of things with the Colemans, but Mother didn't need to know that.

"Well, I'm glad to hear it. Because if you're counting on anything substantial from the estate after I'm gone, I'm afraid you'll be disappointed."

This was so far removed from any topic I had expected to confront that I could only stare at her. In spite of having worked with the orchids all morning, every platinum wave on her head stood teased precisely into place.

"Yes, I thought you'd be shocked. Well, it's true. I know you've always assumed you'll be an heiress some day, so it's time you knew the full situation."

My fingers loosened their death grip on the gargoyles. My hands dropped into my lap. Thank God Dad was okay. But how could Mother be sitting in this imposing historic house, on ten acres of prime Honolulu real estate, deeded to a trust in her name alone with funds to maintain it, telling her only child she would not inherit some day?

"What on earth are you talking about, Mother?"

"All this"—she made her familiar gesture of largesse—"all this is mortgaged to the hilt, and the trust fund is down to bare bones."

I could only gape. I wasn't exactly looking forward to her funeral, but I'd always assumed that someday my financial cares would cease to exist. My mind reeled at the idea that this might not be so.

She smoothed her hands over the green desk blotter. "It's true," she said, a little more relaxed now that her announcement was out in the open.

"But Uncle Harry would never allow that." Harry Broederbelt, my late grandfather's best friend, served as sole trustee of his estate. He'd been younger than Granddad by about fifteen years, which put him in his late seventies now.

"Your Uncle Harry is an idiot."

"How can you say that?" I adored Uncle Harry. A confirmed bachelor, he'd played hilarious games with me as a child and brought me outrageous gifts every time he visited, even though he was only a calabash relative. Just last week he'd sent Feather a pair of wildly expensive little dresses from Sak's Fifth Avenue with pastel satin shoes and bonnets to match.

"I'll say it again. Harry Broederbelt is an idiot. Equally as idiotic as my father for naming him sole trustee."

I frowned. "I don't get it."

"Your beloved Uncle Harry made a series of disastrous investments in recent years with the trust money. Then he tried to recoup by throwing good money after bad. It all went down the drain."

"I thought Uncle Harry was a financial wizard. Grandfather wouldn't have appointed him otherwise."

"Only Father believed Harry a financial wizard. He was dead wrong."

I couldn't take it in. "When did you learn all this?"

"Rather recently. But to no avail. There's nothing to be done."

"Sack him. Get rid of Uncle Harry if his management of the trust has been such a disaster."

"Easier said than done, my dear. I've had a battery of attorneys and CPAs look into it, which cost me a considerable chunk of the remaining funds. Your grandfather's will is air-tight. He wanted Uncle Harry to be in charge, and so it is. I've tried, so help me. There simply isn't anything I can do. In addition to providing for me, your grandfather wanted Harry to be taken care of, for some reason known only to himself. You know what kind of loyalty men create on the golf course—friendships deeper than blood, sometimes.

"Harry hasn't worked a lick outside managing the trust since Father died. He gets a healthy six-figure salary, which he clings to like *opihi* on the rocks at high tide. Simply can't pry him loose. My attorneys and CPAs ultimately arm-wrestled him into transferring the remaining money into a conservative mutual fund, with a promise to leave well enough alone. He now gets paid his outrageous salary for doing nothing. A modern-day remittance man. It was the best they could manage. I'm sorry, Laura."

For the first time in living memory, my mother apologized to me. My vision cleared as if an optometrist had flipped up a stronger lens. The doyenne of Honolulu charities looked shockingly beaten. Her mouth sagged at the edges; fine wrinkles crosshatched her cheeks under blotchy rouge. The skin beneath her chin had loosened into a wattle. Sometime when I wasn't looking, my mother had become an old woman. Oddly, that unsettled me more than her revelation about the trust. My first thought was to comfort her.

"Mother, obviously it's not your fault."

Bitterness laced her reply. "No, but I could have started paying attention a whole lot earlier. It just never occurred to me that it was necessary."

"What does Father say about all this?"

For the briefest moment, the wattle on her neck quivered, then she stuck out her chin and pulled herself up to her full imperial height behind Father's desk. The transformation was startling. "Your Father knows nothing about it. Nothing. And you will say nothing to him. Promise me, Laura."

"But why?" I cried. "Why would you keep this from him?"

"He has never had anything to do with my trust. Your grandfather set it up that way, to protect me. He always said that if a husband got his hands on his wife's money, he would 'take advantage.' His will stipulated that any man I married be kept at arm's length. Quite an advanced notion, actually, for his generation."

"But look what Uncle Harry did! He was looking out for himself, it seems, not you. Have you not discussed this with Dad? Surely he can help!"

Her chin jutted out a little further. "We've never discussed my trust."

Shades of a bygone era. How could a couple be so devoted to each other, and yet have such a huge area of non-communication? "So you've carried the burden all alone, Mom? You haven't even let him give you moral support while the attorneys and the CPAs investigated?"

"Oh, Laura, the truth would kill him. He loves our lifestyle, it means everything to him."

"But if it's crumbling beneath him, he needs to know!"

"Never. I'll beg, borrow, and steal before I ever tell him. In fact, I already have."

"But he still has the restaurant. That's what really means everything to him."

Mother began to fidget. Picking up Dad's white jade letter opener, she ran its point across the blotter, making a pattern of shallow grooves on the soft green surface.

"Mother? What else do you need to tell me?"

She looked up at me with weary eyes. "Jack's beloved Woodrose has been a drain on the estate from year one. Father set it up for him, you know. Huge investment. By the time Father died, the restaurant was mired in debt. The first payment out of the trust fund after I inherited was to put it in the black again. And the trust has been supporting it ever since."

"But it's one of the most popular restaurants in Waikiki. Continuously written up in travel magazines! How can he be running a deficit?"

"The Woodrose has never turned a profit—not once. Jack feeds his patrons, revels in being a glad-hand host, and I provide the means."

"How is it possible? It's always bursting at the seams!"

"As your dad boasts, 'top quality, reasonable prices.' In the account books, that amounts to monthly pools of red ink."

"But, Mother, why? Why did you allow it to go on?"

She slapped the jade opener against her open hand. "Because it pleased me to do so."

"But that's enabling. Didn't you think it might be better to force him into fiscal responsibility?"

She answered from the other side of an abyss. "There are things about our life before you were born you will never know. Suffice to say, I owe your father everything."

I knew my mother well. Her tone of voice and the severity of her expression told me no further questions would be brooked on that subject. I took a deep breath, distressed that there were more secrets, but relieved at the same time. Whatever else existed between my parents, I certainly did not want to be privy to it. I was already on overload.

"Oh, God, Mother. So what will happen?"

"I've put a reverse mortgage on the property. It works like a checking account. As I write checks, the amount of the mortgage increases. When I die, you'll need to sell the property and pay off the debt. Any remaining equity will, of course, be yours. But you won't inherit the property—unless you come up with some other means of retiring the mortgage."

"Sell it now! It's ridiculous to live like this if it's so far beyond your means. You mustn't hang onto it for me. I never imagined living here again."

She pouted like a child. "I couldn't do that to your Father. It would destroy him."

"Mother, be honest. It would destroy *you* if you had to sell Pua Olena and descend from the high-and-mighty valley into the lowland world of ordinary mortals."

She raised her chin again until the skin on her neck stretched taut, obliterating the wattle. "You're right. It would. It's all I know. I don't wish to embrace a new lifestyle at my age."

"Good Lord." Life outside the strictures and mores of Pua Olena was fascinating, but I knew she wouldn't listen. She had no desire to be liberated from the life her ancestors had handed down to her.

She sighed. "That's how it is with old money, Laura. The heirs of the heirs let it sift through their fingers until it's all gone. The process began way before I was born. The amount I inherited was greatly exaggerated, and it has continued to dissipate. We've been living on capital for years now. There will be something for you, I've made sure of that, but you won't be an heiress. Perhaps its just as well. Men won't take advantage."

"Oh, for heaven's sake, Mother. That's the least of my worries."

"Very well, then. Perhaps you'd better get going. Annie's probably pacing on the other side of the door. I'm so very sorry, my dear."

Standing with the help of the gargoyle armrests, I looked down at the elderly woman who was my mother, so diminished by Dad's oversized office furniture and the enormity of her confession. With the white jade opener she traced the outline of her doodle on Dad's blotter, refusing to meet my gaze.

All I ever wanted from my mother was a occasional kind word, some recognition for my achievements, and once in a while the feel of her arms around me. Eyes stinging, I walked behind the desk, placed my hands on her shoulders, leaned over and rested my cheek against her lacquered platinum hair. Her shoulders stiffened and began to tremble. Slowly she shook her head against mine, but made no move to turn into my embrace. Greatly saddened, I left her to her dignity. Two apologies in one day were all I was going to get.

CHAPTER 29

Settling the three of us into my small apartment that Saturday became a juggling act, to put it mildly. My kitchen cabinets quickly filled with baby bottles, cans of formula and distilled water. To make room, I packed my china and crystal and stowed them in my storage locker downstairs. We wouldn't be entertaining much, anyway.

Feather's layette occupied every available flat surface, including the tops of the washing machine and dryer in the bathroom. I bought a dresser for her the next day and set it at the foot of my bed. Upon it I placed several framed photos of Feather, including the one I'd taken of Annie holding her in Dad's easy chair. Annie's countenance showed placid affection as she gazed at her daughter. A rare shot, and certainly my favorite.

Space in which to move around diminished exponentially. Infants nowadays require an extraordinary amount of equipment, most of which had not yet been invented when my children were born. Gone was any pretense of neat and tidy. Feather and her gear reigned supreme, her two handmaidens ever at her beck and call.

Annie tried her best. Reasonably attentive, she beat me as often as not to the baby when she cried. Which was frequently. But I could see my daughter's interest was tentative.

I stayed home with them for a few days as planned, encouraging Annie to get out for a breather now and then. Looking back, that wasn't such a hot idea. If I hadn't suggested it, however, she would have gone out without any prompting.

Feather liked to snack. She'd sip just enough formula to take the edge off her appetite, then lose interest. She'd be hungry again in an hour. As a result, Annie and I yo-yoed up and down all day and night. When I couldn't take it anymore, I suggested that we force her onto a schedule before the feeding-on-demand did us in.

Annie looked at me as if I'd suggested we starve her to death and be done with it. "Ma, she's not even a month old. Already you're trying to run her life."

"Annie, be fair. That's not what I meant at all. It would take three or four days to get her organized, if we cooperate. All we have to do is watch the clock and distract her, walk her around when she cries too early, and gradually lengthen her times between feedings. She'll drink more and stay satisfied longer. I don't know about you, but this nibbling business is driving me batty. It's so unnecessary."

"No, Ma."

I persisted. "How many times were we up last night? I fed her twice and I heard you get up a couple of times. I don't know about you, kiddo, but I'm tired and ready to crash."

Annie stood firm. "Ma, I am not raising Feather by dumb, old-fashioned rules. They didn't work for me, and I'm not laying them on my daughter. I might as well have stayed at Grandma's."

We'd just have to play it out, day by day, and see how long we could stand it. I resolved to step back, be less helpful, especially in the middle of the night. Perhaps Annie would change her tune if she had to do most of it by herself. I'd focus on the cooking and cleaning, and oh, yes, earning us a living. To wit: The Colemans were still pending. I called Jerry at work the day we returned to let him know I was home.

"Hey, Laura. Welcome back. Baby okay? Annie?" The heartiness of his greeting encouraged me. When you're not quite sure how things stand, a transaction's temperature is often discernible by the tone of a client's voice.

"Yes, they're fine. Thanks for asking. Camped out in my apartment as we speak. Huge mess, but my granddaughter's a little doll."

"Good, good. Glad to hear it."

"I understand you've moved ahead with extending your loan lock?"

"Yeah, we had to take a dump, but what can you do? We're all set to close—at least on our end."

"So, are your funds for the down payment ready to transfer to escrow?"

"Yup. Sold off a bunch of stocks yesterday. Lucked out on that. The ones I earmarked to sell actually went up while we were waiting and took a dive the very next day. Can you believe it?" He chuckled. I could picture him slapping his thigh in delight. "Escrow called and said the papers are ready for signatures. All signals are go. We can't wait to move in. What's next?" His exuberance was catching.

"Well, I need to check on what progress Randy's attorney has made on Moana's eviction. I'll call Ji-Kwok Yuen and see what gives. So far, still no sign of her alleged deed. She's got to be bluffing. We're ready to close the day we get her out. We're so close!" I could smell the ink on my commission check.

"Great. Let me know what he says. Have you heard from the other crazy bitch?"

"Dr. Entwistle, I presume?"

"You know damn well who I mean. The nutcake female doc. Jesus, what a pair, those two dykes." He paused. When I didn't respond, he demanded, "Well?"

As hard as I tried to maintain it, my façade cracked. "Damn it, Jerry, they're not dykes. And, no, I haven't seen or talked to Dr. Entwistle lately." They were certainly nutcakes, both of them, but his unbending assumption that two women living together automatically had a physical relationship just plain aggravated me.

He snorted. "Don't you think you'd better get on the stick and find out when she's going to sign her papers? Doesn't do us any good if only Diana and I sign. Don't let us down now, gal, after all we've been through."

"Come on, Jerry. Give me a break. I've left message after message for her. She hasn't returned my calls. And don't call me 'gal.' I'm as old as you are."

"What's new, huh? Keep the pressure on, gal. We're almost there. Gotta go. Keep me posted."

That man was beyond irksome. Sometimes I wondered how Diana put up with him. But then, she was the ultimate kept wife, as I had been, once a upon a time.

To calm myself, I folded a load of Feather's laundry before calling Ji-Kwok. If I couldn't contact Randy, her attorney would be my best source of information. Ji-Kwok and I went way back to high school, where we had been biology lab partners. Our frog dissection had been a disaster. Ji-Kwok got sick and ruined our specimen. We'd had many a laugh over the memory when we were thrown together in real estate deals over the years.

"I suppose you're calling about Dr. Entwistle?" he asked immediately.

"Indeed."

Ji-Kwok was surprisingly forthcoming, considering he represented the other side. "I gotta tell you, Laura, this woman, Corrine Suzanne Urquhart, or 'Moana' as she fancies herself, is pure *pilau*. She has Dr. Entwistle in a stranglehold. I understand the doctor has told you about the blackmail. I'm doing what I can to protect her, but she has instructed me to proceed with the sale of the home regardless of the outcome. She wants this over and done with, and says she's willing to accept the consequences."

"That will be a huge relief to my clients, Ji. I hope it won't go too badly for Randy. I feel somewhat responsible."

"Well, get over it. You are a very small cog on a huge, nasty wheel. It would eventually have come to a head whether or not she put the house up for sale. Like I said, I'm doing what I can to protect her. Deputy Corpuz lost his job, by the way, after going back up and buying Moana those groceries. What an idiot."

"'S why hard, yeah?" I replied.

"Yeah. He deserved it. When the surveyor and the termite inspector went out again, along with the sheriff, Moana watched very conspicuously from an upstairs window. Gave 'em big stink eye, according to the sheriff, but she didn't interfere. So far no sign of the woman vacating, however. Her white truck was still there last night. I drove up myself to check. She'll likely play out the entire forty-five days. Assuming she'll leave even then."

"Are you in touch with Randy?" I asked hopefully, as if she had any power to get Moana out.

"Surely you jest. Leaving messages and waiting for her to return calls doesn't exactly constitute being in touch. Last time I spoke with her was five days ago. How does she expect me to represent her if she won't talk to me?"

"Tell me about it. Does she know the papers are ready at escrow for her to sign?"

"Maybe. I've left her the message. She can go ahead and sign even if the Urquhart woman is still in residence. Then as soon as she moves out, if she moves out, we do a final inspection, notify escrow, and the deal's done."

"Do you honestly think Moana will leave?" I asked.

"I heard via the grapevine she's been all over town, shopping for a lawyer who would take her case as an aggrieved tenant. She doesn't have a leg to stand on, not even a gimpy one. So far, she hasn't found anyone desperate enough. Nobody will take a case like this on a contingency. There's no real grounds for damages."

I exhaled my relief. "That's good to hear. So maybe if she can't find any legal help, she'll just go away?"

"You wish. People like her rarely just go away. But we'll keep pressing until she sees the error of her ways. I've got one more ace up my sleeve."

"Which is?"

"Can't tell. That would be cheating."

"Pull it off, I'll take you and your wife out to the best dinner in town."

When we'd been home for a week, it was time for Feather's first checkup with a Maui pediatrician. I booked Annie to see Lily Fujikawa the same morning for a postnatal exam. The only available appointments were overlapping, so I took the baby to her appointment, leaving Annie down the hall in Lily's waiting room.

Feather had gained weight during the week. The doctor pronounced her the picture of perfect health. Beaming as any proud grandmother would, I carried her through the sunny lobby of the medical center and found a chair in Lily's reception area. Annie was still in the inner sanctum.

Making Feather comfortable on my lap, I realized the tall, solidly built fellow seated next to me was turning the pages of a magazine far too quickly to be reading them. At a glance, he looked familiar. Fair-skinned and dark-haired, his Hawaiian ancestry showed only in his expressive brown eyes and generous, bow-curved mouth. I turned toward him with a smile. He frowned at me for a moment, then grinned widely in recognition.

"Laura! How you? Long time!" He leaned over and kissed my cheek.

"I'm great," I replied. "Meet my little granddaughter, Feather." I proudly pulled back the pink blanket so he could see her sweet face. Feather obliged with a blink and a yawn.

I'd met Kamuela Smith and his wife Ginger at an open house a few years ago. After several months of showing them properties, we found a perfect starter in a neighborhood full of young families. Ginger had been expecting their first child. After a series of earlier first trimester losses, she was aglow with excitement, confident she would carry this one full term. Then, with loan approval only days away, Kamuela called and tearfully asked if the seller would let them out of the deal. Ginger had miscarried at five months. Devastated, they couldn't bear the thought of moving into the home where all their dreams were vested. I hadn't seen them since.

"She's beautiful," Kamuela said, running a wistful finger over Feather's dark curls. "How old?"

"Just turned four weeks. She was premature, had to stay in the hospital in Honolulu for a while after her birth, but now she's doing fine." I opened the blanket completely so she could kick and wave her arms.

He leaned over and touched her cheek again, his yearning palpable.

"And Ginger?" I asked. "I assume you're at the ob-gyn for her, not for yourself?" I expected a chuckle, but he only shook his head. "What's the matter?" I asked.

He bit his lower lip. "It's been so hard for her. Trying to have a baby, I mean. Nobody should have to try this hard."

I hesitated. "Is she . . .?"

He shrugged. Lines of concern deepened around his mouth while he gathered himself to continue. "Yeah, she's *hapai* again. Seven months this time." His voice choked. He rubbed his hands over his lips to stop them from quivering. I cupped my hands protectively over Feather's knees as a wave of his sadness washed over me.

Kamuela leaned toward me and continued earnestly. "I get upset because it's so hard for her, Laura. Sure, I'd like children, too, but for me it's not a life mission. For Ginger, it's all she thinks about. It kills me to see her so disappointed every time. We never imagined it would be so much *pilikia*." He looked at me in despair.

"What happened this time? You said she was seven months along?"

"Yeah, everything was just fine. We were sure this was it. Seven months! We never got that far before. Even if she delivered early, the baby would probably live. We were all set. In fact, we were thinking about giving you a call to start looking at houses again."

I smiled at the happy prospect. Just then, the door to the examination suite opened. We both looked up. It was neither Ginger nor Annie. I turned back to Kamuela, waiting for him to continue. He sprawled in the chair, legs extended, and looked at the ceiling, his hands laced behind his head. "A couple days ago, when we were lying in bed, Ginger mentioned she hadn't felt the baby kick the last few days. I told her he was probably worn out riding along on all the work she'd been doing in our apartment, getting the nursery ready and all. She laughed, but last night she mentioned it again. I told her to call Dr. Fujikawa, see if she could put her mind to rest. And so we're here." He straightened up and looked at his watch. "She's been in there an awfully long time. If a baby dies in the womb, does it just stay there? Wouldn't a woman go into labor right away?"

I shook my head. "I don't know. Look, let's not be negative. You don't see the doctor the minute you go in. Lily has five or six exam rooms. You usually sit around and wait, freezing to death in a little paper robe until it's your turn. Surely that's what's taking so long."

"I hope to God you're right. I don't think Ginger can handle another disappointment." He was silent for a moment, then he looked at me as if he'd just remembered something. "Your daughter . . . may I ask? When we were looking at houses, she had just run away. I remember how hard it was for you to carry on, being so heartbroken and all. Did she come home? Is this her baby?" He gestured toward Feather with his chin.

I happily reassured him. "Annie came home in August. Pregnant to the max." I jiggled Feather on my knees. She waved her arms wildly. "This little doll is the result. Annie's inside seeing Lily. Probably one of the reasons it's taking so long for Ginger."

He looked momentarily interested, but his own worries dragged him quickly back to the here and now. "I'm glad you're here, Laura. It helps, having a friend to sit with me while I wait. I hope you don't mind."

"Of course not. If it helps, I'm glad to be here."

The inner door opened. Ginger walked out, Lily holding her by an elbow. By the look on Ginger's pale face and her red, swollen eyes, the news was not good. Kamuela lurched from his seat and rushed to her. He stopped short of throwing his arms around her, giving her one last chance to say it wasn't true. "Honey?" he asked, his voice laced with concern, not wanting to believe what he already knew.

"Uh, uh," she sobbed, shaking her head. Tears welled in her sad blue eyes and spilled down her freckled cheeks. Her sun-streaked hair hung straight down over her shoulders. She looked so young, so fragile, like a flawed porcelain cup that would shatter at the first splash of hot tea. He closed the gap between them and gathered her bulging figure into his arms. Together they rocked in silence, broken only by her sobs.

Lily looked on for a few moments, her Oriental face inscrutable, then laid a hand on Kamuela's shoulder. "She needs to be admitted. There's no big rush, but the sooner the better. We can do a Caesarean, but I hate to if it isn't necessary."

Ginger looked up at her husband, a plea for understanding in her eyes. "I want . . . I want to give birth naturally . . . even if the baby's dead. I want it to have a real birth." Tears coursed down her cheeks, but she ignored them.

"Honey, that sounds so depressing. Do you really want to go through all that pain?"

"Yes, I do! I love this baby!" She wrapped her arms around her lifeless stomach. "I want it to be born properly and then . . . and then.... buried in a real grave . . . with a real headstone in a cemetery near the ocean. It's the only thing I'll ever be able to do for our baby!"

Fighting tears myself, I caught sight of Annie standing motionless in the doorway behind Ginger and Kamuela. Lily ushered the couple back inside, presumably to make further arrangements. Looking shaken, Annie stepped aside to let them pass.

CHAPTER 30

The image of Ginger and Kamuela Smith's heartbroken embrace at Lily's office haunted me for days. I wondered how the birth had gone for Ginger, and imagined them placing a white *pikake* lei on a small gravesite by the sea.

Annie announced one night, as she often did, that she was going out to meet her friends after supper. Having no plans of my own, I could think of no reason to keep her from having a little fun. Memories of my nights alone with her had faded as I gained confidence with Feather. I was content to stay home, just the two of us.

When Feather awoke at a little after 3:00 AM, Annie hadn't returned. Somehow I wasn't surprised.

I fed Feather and tucked her in with me. For once she went right back to sleep. With a protective arm around her, I lay awake listening to her soft breathing, inhaling her milk-sweet breath. I don't know how I knew Annie wouldn't be home that night, but I did.

I remained surprisingly calm, as if something within me had disconnected. I believe I finally understood that Annie would live her life exactly as she pleased. Although she found Feather enchanting at times, being a mother wouldn't change anything. She knew I would take care of her daughter. If I balked, she'd go down her particular path anyway, leaving us to make the best of it. All the love and care I had so desperately and hopelessly tried to impart to Annie, I saw myself now refocusing on little

Feather. When I finally dozed off, I slept with the knowledge that certain pieces of my life had shuffled about and realigned, not in a way I anticipated or wanted, but in a way that gave me some measure of peace. Whether Annie might return the next day or next week, I drifted off knowing that for all practical purposes, Feather and I were alone.

Several busy days of property showings loomed ahead. Since one of us had always been available to care for Feather, I hadn't given a thought to babysitters. I had no idea where to find one, and no time to try.

Off we trooped, my trunk stuffed with real estate files and baby gear. We showed my finds to prospective buyers, chased after listings, and viewed new MLS entries with other agents on Broker's Caravan. I handled the routine details of my two transactions in escrow—the small house in Waiehu and the Le Boeufs' condo —which would close within the month.

Not quite believing it, I accompanied the Colemans to sign their closing papers. There was still no word from Randy. We could only rest content that we'd taken care of the final business on our end, and that Randy and Ji-Kwok Yoon would find a way to get Moana out and close the sale. Or not.

The Colemans remained optimistic. With Feather as my first priority, my anxiety regarding their closing simmered down to mere curiosity as to how things would turn out. Wrestling Feather in and out of her bulky car seat, often with the help of an understanding client, stopping on the roadside to feed her before she worked herself into a frenzy, coping with middle of the night feedings and early morning wakeups had me in such a frazzle I couldn't even begin to worry about what might be happening with Dr. E. and Moana.

Annie stayed away for five long days. When she finally moseyed back to the apartment one morning, insolent, defiant, and smelling like a swamp wrestler, I was not happy to see her. I had reorganized my life without her, albeit with great difficulty. Incapable of welcoming her home, I picked up the baby, the diaper bag and my briefcase, and brushed past her without a word.

When I got home that night, hot, tired, and hungry, Annie sat poised like a cougar on a cliff, every muscle tightened to spring. She ripped right into me. "What's the big idea, Ma, walking out on me like that? You've been gone all day. I never even got to see Feather." She had at least showered and put on clean shorts and a T-shirt. *Eau de* festering swamp had been replaced by the gingery scent of *awapuhi* shampoo.

I dumped the diaper bag in the middle of my bed, but held onto Feather. "As if you care, Annie."

She raced over, plucked Feather from my arms and cradled her defensively. Her blue eyes blazed. "I *do* care."

"About her and who else? Me? You leave me with an infant for five days without so much as asking if I mind? Do you have any idea how difficult it is to do my work with a baby in tow, traipsing around with her all day in this awful heat?"

"Jeez, get a sitter!" As if it were as simple as buying shaved ice at Suda Store.

"*Me* get a sitter? Whose baby is she? What about you? She's your responsibility. Besides, she's not even six weeks old. I don't know anyone I would trust to take care of her."

"Well, I'm back." She jabbed her chin at me. "You can leave her with me tomorrow and have a nice day. If she needs a sitter, I'll find one." The sarcasm in her voice was as thick as seven-day-old *poi.*

"I don't think so. For all I know you'll prop her bottle on a pillow and run out to play with your disreputable friends. Or dump her on some filthy tramp sitting on the sidewalk. I don't trust you, Annie. Especially if you're back into drugs. Which I assume you are." I pinned her with my most severe gaze, silently begging for a denial. I couldn't put a finger on it, but something about her cocky expression when she walked in the door that morning had aroused my suspicions. She looked away, as good as confirming my accusation.

"I see."

"Well, she's *my* daughter," Annie declared. "I get to say who takes her and who doesn't."

I turned away and pawed through the diaper bag, pulling out a plastic sack of soiled diapers and three empty bottles. I marched them to the kitchen. "Don't you dare pull that high and mighty stuff on me, young lady. You'll take her for as long as she amuses you. When it starts to feel like work, you'll leave her with the most convenient person, suitable or not, and get back to your fun. I'm not going to let you do that."

"Oh, yeah? Well, there's nothing you can do about it. She's mine. If I want to take her out to visit my friends, you can't stop me."

I bit my lower lip to keep myself from issuing an ultimatum. If I threatened to throw her out, she would march right off with Feather to spite me. By law, she had that right. If I wanted to make sure Feather was properly cared for, I saw no alternative but to keep my daughter close at hand.

"What about your agreement with Dad to get some counseling now that the baby is born?"

"No way. I changed my mind."

"Annie, you promised."

"I don't care. I won't do it, and you can't make me." She tightened her arms around Feather and turned her back on me. That was true. One had to enter the process with a degree of willingness. Maybe she'd come 'round in a few weeks, when we were more settled in our *ménage a trois*.

The evening ended in a shaky truce, with Annie making a dramatic fuss over Feather while I watched with a wary eye.

Annie came and went. While I adjusted my comings and goings around her, anxiety over her lifestyle festered in my gut. I felt as if I were witnessing my child's self-destruction day by day. She never used in my presence, but I recognized the signs. Listless and argumentative by turn, manic when least expected, she lavished attention on Feather one moment, then couldn't be bothered to so much as wipe her nose the next. Her behavior kept me in a ferment of anger and guilt—anger because of the burdens she imposed upon me, and guilt because I resented it so. As much as I worried about Annie while she was out, life became more manageable when she wasn't home stirring things up.

Like her mother, Feather continued to be an uneasy child. She demanded constant attention and never settled into a predictable routine. Of course, there wasn't much hope of that with my own erratic schedule. What could I expect when I interrupted her nap to rush to an appointment, or held off her feeding until I finished a showing? Lulled by the rhythm of the road, she catnapped in the car, then stayed awake all hours of the night, leaving me ragged and on edge with no time to myself.

By the greatest of luck, I found a middle-aged woman in my building, Nancy Godfrey, who lived on a disability pension resulting from a back injury she had suffered while working as a nurse at Kula Sanitarium. Her references were impeccable, her medical background reassuring. While she couldn't take Feather full time, she was more than willing to earn a little extra money when Annie wasn't home and I really needed to hustle.

At six weeks, Feather was thriving. She outgrew her infant-sized clothes, and her dark curls began to look like real hair. With her round, olive-gray eyes and generous mouth, she was an exquisite baby. When she'd been with Nancy all day, we often enjoyed an evening of peace and tranquility. We ate dinner with Larry King and fell asleep to reruns of "Cheers." I lived from one day to the next, praying for the physical stamina to care for her, do my work, and make it to bedtime, hoping she'd only wake up once during the night for a quick feeding. It was rarely that simple, however.

About that time, I suggested to Annie that she finish her GED so she could find a job. If she'd contribute to the rent, we could move to a larger place right away. Once she had that under her belt, I'd take the next step and insist on the counseling. In response, she stayed away three days. By then I was so angry, I was ready to kick her ass out for good.

"Why don't you?" Barbara asked one afternoon when we met up by chance and ducked into the picket-fenced sidewalk café for a quick latte.

"Because she'd take Feather with her out of spite. I couldn't bear that. She refuses to work. Even if she got a job, God knows how she'd care for the baby. I have to keep close tabs on her in order to protect Feather."

"Are you enjoying this?" Barbara asked, biting into a sugar-dusted lemon bar.

"Are you crazy? Taking care of an infant is the last thing I want to do. But she's my granddaughter. I'm stuck."

"So if Annie's the problem, why don't you go to court and get custody? Then you can kick her out."

The idea had never occurred to me. I munched on a brownie while I tried to take it in. The rich, chewy chocolate had its usual edifying effect.

"A day-by-day commitment is one thing, Barb, but assuming full legal responsibility until Feather's eighteen? That would be a path of no return."

Barbara licked a white smear of sugar off her upper lip. "You'd probably have to show she's an unfit mother."

"Well, she is, but how would I prove it? Right now her only sin is neglect. She knows Feather is safe and cared for. She's never done anything to actually harm her. Part of me still holds out for Annie to shape up and do her duty. I'm very reluctant to rock the boat as long as there's any hope in that direction. And what if I proceed and fail? Annie would never forgive me. She'd likely take off for good. I'd lose them both."

"You've got a point," Barbara said, flicking crumbs off her plate for the birds.

We both looked at Feather, dozing in her carrier on the floor beside us, adorably exotic in a ruffled pink sun suit and frilly white bonnet. One hand curled against her cheek while her mouth made little sucking motions in her dream. The sweet picture tugged at my heart. How could I possibly risk Annie running off with her?

"Well, lots to think about," Barbara said. "You can't go on with a drug-using daughter bouncing in and out of your life, and an infant to care for without any real authority. Something's got to give."

"You're probably right," I replied. "But what?"

A tourist dressed in rubber slippers, baggy shorts and a DIVERS DO IT UNDER WATER muscle shirt set his steaming coffee mug on the table next to ours, then walked the few steps to a newspaper vending machine. He clanked in some coins and pulled out the last copy of the day's *Maui News*.

"Hey, that reminds me," said Barbara. "I think Grant's big story broke today. He left all smug this morning, still refusing to tell me anything. 'Wait 'til you see it in print,' was all he'd say. Bastard."

We both glanced over at the tourist's newspaper. He had pulled out the sports section and left the front section folded on the table, headlines up, facing us. We couldn't have missed it if we tried:

FORMER MAUI TEACHER DENIES INVOLVEMENT
IN CHILD PORNOGRAPHY RING

Realization crashed down on me like a truckload of wet sand. Jumping up, I whipped the front section off the startled tourist's table. The fellow yelped, "Hey, what's up wid you two broads?"

Barbara hissed at him, "Never mind, stupid." Several nearby patrons stared at us. One I recognized as an ad salesperson for the *Maui News*.

I'd never seen the man in the photo, so I didn't recognize him, but the name in the caption fit: CHARLES "CHAZ" CAMPBELL. The photo, which must have been taken from the high school yearbook, looked disgustingly clean-cut and attractive.

"Oh, my God. It's him. It's Annie's teacher!"

"But why was Grant asking me about Prakash? What's he got to do with Campbell?"

My eyes flew down the printed column. I gasped, then read aloud, "'Campbell, known to the hippie population on the North Shore as Prakash' . . ."

Barb jabbed at the photo over my shoulder. "Wait a minute—don't tell me Moana's Prakash is the same guy who ran off with Annie?"

"Dear God. According to this, he must be. How many Prakashes can there be on a small island?" My hands shook so much, I couldn't read the rest of the story. Barbara snatched the paper from me and spread it out on our table.

"Hold on. Let me get more details." She quickly scanned the column beside the photo, then looked up, her eyes alight with excitement. "Damn. It wasn't drugs at all. Prakash has a sex-tour business in Thailand, and he's been bringing kid porn videos back in his luggage and duplicating them here. That's what all the equipment was in Randy Entwistle's garage. He was apparently trying to save on postage, the dolt, by mailing them to his U.S. customers from the little old Haiku post office. Charles Campbell—Prakash. A high school social studies teacher until he went full time with the sex-tour biz. What a sleazebag."

I picked up the paper and slung it back onto the bewildered tourist's table. "I've got to get home. Annie'll freak if she sees this."

She grabbed my arm. "Wait a minute. The story's still unfolding. She might have some valuable information for Grant. I'm coming with you."

I rounded on her. "Absolutely not. This is not about Grant getting a scoop. This is my daughter! Don't you dare tell him Annie's involved. Promise me. The last thing she needs is to have her name plastered all over the paper. I'll figure out how to handle this. Just let me out of here."

I hoisted the baby's carrier and sprinted for my car.

My own *Maui News* lay on my doormat, as calmly and coolly as if the lead story were nothing more than another Gilbert and Sullivan scrape between the mayor and the county council. I scooped it up, fumbled for my keys and burst through the door. Thank God Annie was home, sober and alert, standing at the kitchen stove heating a pan of soup. The chicken noodle smell nauseated me.

"Here, take the baby," I said as I kicked the door shut.

"Whoa, Ma. What's happening?"

"Just take her."

I shooed them out of the kitchen and forced myself to calm down. I snapped the rubber band off the newspaper, smoothed out the pages on the counter and read the entire story. Former Maui high school social studies teacher Charles "Chaz" Campbell, known to the North Shore crowd as Prakash, had been arrested at the Haiku post office trying to mail child pornography videotapes. Between Grant's sleuthing and the rural route carrier's growing uneasiness about the myriad small boxes he regularly picked up from Randy Entwistle's garage, the cops set up a sting. When the carrier deliberately failed to stop by, Prakash took the boxes to the post office himself. The cops were there to greet him. He was being held at Maui Community Correctional Center pending arraignment. Bail was denied, as he was considered a flight risk. The front page, above-the-fold coverage ran under Grant Kneubel's prominent byline.

"Well, I'll be damned," I said, struggling to grasp the big picture. The adrenaline that had propelled me home to protect Annie slowly seeped out of my system. I held onto the edge of the counter to steady myself.

I couldn't believe it. Chaz was Prakash—making copies of those filthy videos right there in Randy's garage. Stringing beads, indeed. At least I'd been a little closer to the truth with my drug suspicions. Good thing I never saw him at the property. If I'd known who he was, I'd have killed him.

"Killed who?" Annie asked from the living room, where she was changing Feather's diaper. I must have muttered my last thought aloud.

I walked to the sofa and sat beside her. "We can relax, honey. That horrid man is behind bars. And the Colemans' house won't be confiscated for illegal drug activity on the property."

"What do you mean? What horrid man?"

I put a hand on her knee. "Chaz Campbell. Also known as Prakash. He's been arrested. As far as I'm concerned, they can give him the death penalty."

Annie plunked Feather back into her carrier and stood up. "Chaz? He's in jail? Here?"

"See for yourself." I pointed toward the kitchen.

Following, I watched her scan the article on the counter. It didn't take her long to get the drift. She looked at me with stricken eyes. Was she frightened *of* him, I wondered, or *for* him? If she had one iota of affection left for that man, I would cheerfully wring her neck. Before I could question her, however, the phone rang. I reached for it and said a rather brusque hello.

"Laura, this is Grant Kneubel with the *Maui News*. I understand your daughter has some information on the Chaz Campbell story."

"Grant, we have no comment." Damn that Barbara. How could she?

"May I speak with Annie, please?"

"Absolutely not. She has nothing to do with this."

"That's not what I heard."

"Grant, I know you have a job to do, but please leave us alone."

"It's not that easy, Laura. Once the police get onto this, they'll issue a subpoena and she'll have to talk. I was just hoping to get a jump on them."

"Well, you just go jump in a lake. And tell Barbara I'll never forgive her for this."

"Wait, it wasn't—"

I slammed down the phone.

Annie had blanched the color of raw almonds. "Ma, what am I going to do?"

"The man's been caught, honey. He's in jail, and likely to stay there. After everything he's done to you, aren't you glad?"

"You don't understand! He'll find a way to get out. He'll come after me and kill me!"

"But that's impossible. He can't get out."

"What if they let him out? All he needs is a clever lawyer. You know how they screw with the law. It's all in how much you pay them. And Chaz has lots of money."

"We have to have confidence in the law, Annie."

"You can say that, after your experience with that goofy deputy sheriff? The reporter knows I have information, Ma. He'll tell the police, and they'll make me testify. I can't let that happen. Chaz'll get me, I know he will."

"Annie, you're being illogical. He's in jail."

"Ma, people walk all the time. He's clever, sneaky, *evil*. He'll find a way to get out and come after me."

She was clearly terrified. I did my best to calm her down, but her fear of Chaz was real. I only knew the barest outline of her life with him. Still, I had faith in the system, bleeding-heart deputies notwithstanding.

"Honey, the best thing you can do is to cooperate with the investigation so they can put him behind bars forever."

She turned on me, horrified. "Are you whacked, Ma? He'll get me. I know it. I'm not having anything to do with it."

Before we could say any more, the phone rang again. This time it was the police. They wanted to question Annie and were on their way over.

"See, Ma, it's happening already. That friggin' reporter friend of yours told them. I can't do it. I won't."

"Sweetheart, I don't see that you have any choice. Isn't this why you brought the tape home? It's vital evidence. If you don't cooperate, they may not manage to convict him. Then what?"

"At least he won't blame me for going against him. He's a maniac, Ma. Have you ever seen anyone strangled right in front of your eyes?" She skittered out onto the lanai, sliding the screen door shut with a crash. I couldn't begin to imagine what was going on in her tortured mind.

"Annie, come back inside. You're making me nervous at that railing."

"Crap, Ma. You think I'm stupid? Suicide's only for drama queens."

I shuddered, but didn't say anything more. Two plain clothes detectives arrived within minutes. Seated on our dining chairs, the dark-haired local woman took notes while the *haole* fellow with a clipped blond mustache asked questions. Annie answered minimally, truthfully as far as I could tell, but volunteered nothing. The officer seemed intent on establishing that she had known Chaz in Thailand and had been aware of his sex-tour business. He didn't bear down too hard, possibly to ensure her cooperation at a later date. At no time did he suggest Annie had been anything more than an innocent bystander. If there had been the slightest intimation that he thought otherwise, I'd have stopped everything and insisted an attorney be present. Concluding the short interview, he advised her she was a material witness, and that she must make herself available for further questioning and possible testimony at Chaz's trial.

Annie stared down at her white-knuckled fists knotted between her knees, but remained silent.

"This is a serious business, Ms. McDaniel. I hope you understand that. Campbell is the lowest kind of criminal, a child pornographer. They don't come much lower than that. With your help we can nail him. We'll make it as easy for you as possible. But you mustn't leave the island. We need to be able to reach you. Do you understand?"

Stone-faced, Annie nodded.

The detective turned to me. "And you, Mrs. McDaniel. I understand you have that property where Campbell duplicated and packed his tapes under contract for sale."

It never occurred to me they'd want to question me. I felt ambushed. "Uh, yes, that's correct."

"Did you have any idea what was going on in the garage?"

"I suspected something. The owner of the property thought they were stringing bead necklaces to sell."

He snorted. "Come on, Mrs. McDaniel."

"Well, she hoped so anyway."

"And you?"

"It did occur to me that it might be drugs."

"And you never thought to call the police?"

"I immediately thought to call the police. The owner, Dr. Entwistle, had a fit. We both figured if we closed the sale quickly, he'd pack up and leave. Like turning over a rock and all the cockroaches skittering away."

"No thought for your own danger?"

"Officer, you just don't think this kind of thing happens in real life. Everyone—buyers, seller, and myself—just wanted to get the sale closed."

He sucked his blond moustache with his lower lip, no doubt trying to decide how I could possibly be that naive. "And no idea this guy Prakash was the man involved with your daughter?"

"Never! How could I possibly have known? Nothing Annie told us about Chaz Campbell connected to Prakash. If I'd even suspected, I'd have had you folks out there so fast—"

I could see him thinking, *They never learn . . .* He shook his head and stood up and gave me his card. "Thank you, ma'am. Call me if you or your daughter thinks of anything that might help. You stay on-island, too."

As soon as the door was shut, Annie started in. "You see, Ma? There's no escape. The police are after me, the newspaper's after me, and Chaz will be after me. I'm road kill."

"Annie, it's not like that."

"You don't know anything, Ma. You don't know anything at all."

Nothing I said would calm her down. She paced the floor, bit her fingernails, stubbed her toes into the carpet, as agitated as I'd ever seen her. "I've got to get out of here," she finally declared.

"Where are you going?"

"Out. Where nobody can get me." In a swirl of flaxen hair, she snagged her fanny pack and was gone. Once again, I stood facing a slammed door.

Annie's fear was real. I could feel it in the eddy of foreboding she left behind. But it also seemed irrational, way beyond normal bounds. Chaz was in jail, bail denied. He couldn't possibly harm her. I remained convinced that the very best thing she could do was tell the police everything so Chaz would end his days in a federal prison on the mainland.

Sitting with Feather, feeding her a bottle, and trying to subdue my own fears, it came to me. A mind muddled with drugs often became paranoid, creating imaginary fears or exaggerating real ones. Annie was no longer rational. And once her involvement in the story became public, heaven only knew how much further that would push her.

I called Grant back at the newspaper.

"Hey, Laura. Annie ready to talk yet?"

"No, Grant. She's terrified. You've got to leave her out of it, I beg you, as a personal favor."

"Sorry, Laura. You know I can't do that. Her involvement with Campbell is hot news right now."

"Grant, she's so emotionally fragile. She's terrified Campbell will somehow get out of jail and come after her if she gives the police any information about him."

"Sorry, Laura. My job is to get the news. Nothing personal."

"Where have I heard that before?"

"Look, I can give you this much. Tomorrow's story on Campbell doesn't name Annie. I haven't got enough facts yet. You could help me get it straight."

"Don't be preposterous."

"I figured. Well, her name won't appear until day after tomorrow. I'll have the depth I need by then. You've got a forty-eight-hour breather. That's the best I can do . . . and don't think I'm doing it to be nice."

CHAPTER 31

Jerry called to crow, of course, the minute he read the story. "Some news, eh, Laura? The scum's in jail and there's no need to worry our house will be confiscated. Unless . . . there's no federal law that allows confiscation in the case of child pornography, is there?"

Weariness weighed down my voice. "No, Jerry. We're safe on that score."

"Hey, what's the matter? This is great news. Now all we have to do is get Moana out and we're home. Literally."

"Sorry, Jerry. There's more to it than that. Day after tomorrow the *Maui News* will break the rest of the story. Prakash, a.k.a. Chaz Campbell, is the one who took Annie when she ran away three years ago. He took her to Thailand and forced her to work in his business."

"You mean his sex—"

"Yeah."

For once Jerry was speechless. Finally he recovered. "Jesus, Laura. You never said a word. I mean, we knew she'd run away and come home pregnant, that you were worried about drugs, but . . ."

"I only found out in bits and pieces, Jerry, and fairly recently. I just couldn't talk about it. It was too awful. My focus was on helping Annie get her life back together. You understand."

"Well, of course. Hey, sorry. We had no idea you were going through all that. Is she okay?"

"The news was a shock. She's very frightened of Campbell, even though he's in jail. She left in a panic this afternoon and isn't home yet. I'm at my wits' end."

"Do you want us to come over? Keep you company? Help you look for her?"

"That's lovely of you to offer, but no, Feather and I will be fine. We really can't do anything but wait."

"If you're sure . . ."

"I'm sure, Jerry. *Mahalo*. I really am happy it's turning out well for you and Diana."

"Don't forget, you'll get paid!"

"Yeah." There was that.

Annie pulled an all-nighter. My apartment was still empty when Feather and I returned the following afternoon. I was beyond frantic, but didn't know what to do. In her confused state of mind, she could be up to anything. I called Frank several times in Maine, wanting to update him on Campbell, hoping for moral support, but his machine picked up every time. Giving him the benefit of the doubt, I concluded he was out of town. I left a message, saying Chaz Campbell was in jail so I didn't think we'd need the services of his international criminal attorney buddy after all.

My good friend and confidant Barbara was off limits, due to her relationship with Grant at the newspaper. I felt totally betrayed, certain she'd gone right home and told him about Annie and Chaz. I hesitated to call anyone else, not wanting to spread the story myself. My parents were undoubtedly following events in the *Honolulu Advertiser* without realizing their granddaughter had a part in it. As promised, Grant hadn't mentioned her name today, but he would tomorrow, and the other papers in the state would pick it up. I wondered if I were becoming as paranoid as Annie. If she wasn't home by morning, I'd have to call the police.

As I rocked Feather that evening, still in a dither, my personal attorney, Sally Mitchell, rang. Immediately my mood lightened. Why hadn't I thought of calling her? She could advise me and help me protect Annie.

Sally knew Annie and loved her. Her daughter Nani had been Annie's best friend in grade school. Sally had handled my divorce, prepared my will, and advised me on various non-real estate matters over the years. Annie's involvement with Chaz was probably out of her realm, but she could tell me if Annie needed counsel, and if so, recommend the right person. But Sally's familiar voice sounded strained. I held back and waited to hear why she was calling.

"I've got a legal matter to discuss with you, Laura. I wonder if you could come by my office tomorrow afternoon, say one o'clock?"

The muscles between my shoulder blades tightened. "Sounds serious. Is somebody suing me?"

She chuckled, a mechanical sound with no warmth. Not like Sally, who was always the soul of good cheer. "No, no, nothing like that. But I do need to see you."

"Gee, can't you tell me what it's about?" Panic slithered up my shins. "It's not Annie, is it?"

"I think it's better if we wait until tomorrow afternoon. I have a deposition in the morning, which I can't reschedule. One o'clock?"

I found it difficult to keep the alarm out of my voice. "Are you sure this isn't about Annie?"

She maintained her professional distance. "Sorry. Sometimes I have to pull the curtain and be official. This is one of those times."

My imagination rushed to the worst-case scenario—Chaz breaking out of jail and tracking her down. "Annie's been killed. Tell me. Tell me now."

"No, Laura, please. It's nothing like that."

"Well, what else can it be? Somebody suing me over a real estate deal? Moana Entwistle?" In my panic, I called her by the doctor's last name.

"Who?" She sounded genuinely puzzled.

"Corrine Suzanne Urquhart? Moana Entwistle?"

"No," she replied. "I've never heard of anyone by those names."

"Then who?" I demanded.

"Look, this has nothing to do with real estate, or being sued, or Moana . . . Corrine . . . whoever. Please trust me on that. And Annie is fine."

"But if you know she's fine, then—"

"Trust me, Laura. I'll see you tomorrow, okay?"

Rosen, Yoshinaga, and Mitchell, Attorneys at Law, occupied a two-story wood-frame house with a wide front porch and double-hung windows. It stood in a section of old Wailuku town that had once been residential, but had recently been rezoned for small business. Restored old-fashioned homes now served as offices for lawyers, chiropractors, acupuncturists, holistic counselors, massage therapists, and Chinese herbalists. By the time I arrived at one o'clock the next day, I could have used them all.

The receptionist ushered me into Sally's upstairs office. She was the only attorney I knew who didn't consider it part of her professional duty to keep people waiting. She held rigorously to her appointment schedule, which her clients appreciated. Not knowing what the afternoon would bring, I had left Feather with Nancy.

Standing to greet me, Sally smiled but didn't come around her desk for a hug as she normally did. Shorter than I by a few inches, she had a buxom figure and graying hair that always needed a brush and a trim. Slightly overweight, rather plain, her crinkly blue eyes were clear, intelligent and sincere. One usually had the impression that just seeing you had made her day. Now, however, she stood behind an uncharacteristic shield of reserve. Nothing in her manner invited our usual friendly repartée.

My misgivings grew as she shuffled papers on her desk, looking for something that obviously wasn't there, then punched a button on her phone and leaned toward the speaker.

"Hold my calls, please, Maryanne." Another stalling tactic. What lawyer's receptionist wasn't trained to hold calls while her boss was in conference?

I sat forward on the edge of my chair. "Sally, what in heaven's name is going on?"

She looked at me with those clear blue eyes lined with concern. Picking up a pen, she flicked it nervously against her palm. "In all my years of family law practice, Laura, I've never been in a position like this. I'm very uncomfortable with my role. I want you to know that."

A shard of dry ice dropped into my stomach and began to burn. "For God's sake, Sally. What in the world are you trying to tell me? It must be Annie. What's happened to my daughter?"

She dropped the pen, put both hands palm down on her desk and looked straight at me. "Annie's gone to the mainland. She left yesterday."

My body recoiled against the back of the chair as if it hit the bottom of a bungee jump. I searched Sally's face for a denial, willing those radiating lines of concern to turn to laughter, her next words to tell me she was kidding. The moment stretched forever. Finally, she picked up the pen and tapped her palm again.

"Annie came to me the day before yesterday, very distraught. I've always been fond of her, you know that. So I let her talk. She insisted that our conversation be kept confidential. She gave me a buck, like they do in the movies, as a retainer."

Apprehension gnawed. "Go on."

"She'd have walked right out if I hadn't given her complete assurance. She made me repeat over and over again that I wouldn't contact you or tell you anything until she gave me permission. Which she now has."

My speech came back in a rush. "It's Chaz Campbell, isn't it? He's gotten out of jail—"

"What?"

"You know she's a material witness in the Chaz Campbell investigation?"

"Oh, my God! The fellow they arrested for mailing child porn? She never said a word about that. She told me some local boy from high school was chasing her, that she needed to get away so he would leave her alone."

"That's a cover-up. She's running from Chaz Campbell. Her part in the story will break today. In fact, it's probably in the stands in the *Maui News* street edition right now. If she's run away, she's going to be in trouble with the law. She's a material witness. But where did she go on the mainland? For how long? How did she get the money for a ticket? How does she plan to live?" Questions tumbled through my brain almost quicker than I could ask them.

"She didn't tell me where she was going. She didn't want me to know. She certainly was afraid. She wasn't faking that. Oh, God. Now I get it."

"Yes. She's terrified of Campbell! He was her social studies teacher. He seduced her and took her to Thailand. That's where she's been these past three years. She's afraid if she testifies against him, he'll kill her. The police have already questioned her."

Sally lowered her voice. "And I helped her leave. I didn't give her any money, but I agreed to keep quiet until she was gone. Laura, I'm so sorry."

I pulled my fingers though my hair. "It's not your fault, Sally. Annie's a master manipulator. She would have found another way if you didn't cooperate. She's been on drugs, probably dealing, too. I suppose that's where she got the money to buy a plane ticket. She cleaned up during her pregnancy but went right back to it afterward. I think the drugs have affected her mind, made her paranoid. She was afraid of the police and even the newspaper reporter. She wasn't thinking straight at all. I begged her to cooperate with the investigation, to help put Campbell away for good, but she wouldn't hear of it."

"I don't know what to say. I had no idea." She paused for a moment, then walked back to her desk, opened the top drawer and removed a video cassette. "Does this have anything to do with it? DreamSeed Tours? She asked me to give it to you, to tell you she erased everything so it couldn't be used. She said you'd understand."

I didn't make any effort to take the disgusting thing, nor did I have the strength to give Sally more than the most cursory explanation. The images may have been erased from the tape, but not from my mind. "It's the one piece of evidence that would have tied Annie to the case, filmed when she was in Thailand. I guess that's her final way of saying she refuses to be involved. Throw the filthy thing away."

Sally shrugged her shoulders, then dumped it in the wastebasket.

I stood and paced to the open window, arms across my chest. The window looked down on a tranquil Japanese rock garden shaded by strawberry guava trees trimmed to perfect symmetry. Such cultivated perfection offended me. I turned around to face Sally. "What about the baby? She can't just walk out on us."

"Laura, I did everything I could to stop her. I cancelled the rest of my appointments and took her home with me. She spent the night at my house. We talked endlessly. But she refused to let me call you."

Hurt turned to anger. "But you're only an attorney. Did you suggest counseling, by a qualified psychologist or psychiatrist? Perhaps she'd have listened if the suggestion came from you."

"Oh, yes. I had someone standing by, ready to talk the moment Annie agreed. I know my limits, believe me. When I mentioned counseling she got hysterical. She ran out of the house, and I had to chase her down the road in the rain. Lucky we didn't get pneumonia . . . or run over. She's a handful, that daughter of yours."

"Tell me about it. But what about the baby? Am I supposed to raise her alone? I'm not sure I want to go through Brownies, and school conferences, and proms again. It's a whole different scene out there now. Sex. Drugs. I'm worried enough about Annie. Do I have to go through it all over again with Feather? I love her, damn it, but I'm tired. D'you know how hard I've struggled to make a life without Frank? Getting my boys through college and coping with Annie's disappearance? Finally, I'vd begun to think I'm on an even keel, with a semblance of a normal life. When am I going to be allowed to stop paying the price for not understanding Annie, for not being the mother she needed me to be—" I stopped abruptly, realizing I sounded like an idiot dumping all my baggage on Sally. Annie was gone. She hadn't taken Feather with her. The baby was safe with Nancy. Thank God for that. I looked at Sally blankly. She leaned back in her chair, aware, apparently, that my tantrum was over.

"Annie was thinking clearly in one respect," she said. "She asked me to draw up consent papers for you to adopt Feather. She signed them

before she left. All you have to do is execute them, and you'll have full
custody, pending court approval, of course. I don't expect any problem
there." Her face remained expressionless, waiting for my reaction.

"Oh, Jesus," I moaned, fighting back a rush of tears. "I'd willingly
help Annie raise Feather, but to do it alone . . . I didn't sign up for that."

"Well, there is another possibility."

"What do you mean?" At this point I felt totally numb.

"Adoption by someone else."

"What?" I turned to face her, my mind dodging the impact of her
words.

"You don't have to take this on, raising Feather alone, I mean. Adoption outside the family is an alternative."

My voice rose several levels. "You mean give my precious granddaughter away to strangers?"

She held up a hand. "Laura, you don't have to make a decision today,
or next week, or even next month. Take some time to let this all soak in.
When you've had a chance to think about it, you'll know what to do. Annie
prepared for either eventuality. She signed a separate set of adoption papers
that are non-specific as to the adoptive parents. She granted you power of
attorney to act on her behalf, if that's the route you choose."

Trapped by conflicting emotions, I floundered once again on a rising
tide of hysteria. "So what am I supposed to do, go out and canvas the
streets looking for someone who'll take her?"

Sally put a steadying hand on my arm. "Laura, you've had enough
for today. You need to be with Feather and absorb the shock. I'll work
through this with you, as I promised Annie I would. Is there anyone I can
call to stay with you this afternoon?"

I shook my head. She was right. I needed to go home. I wasn't sure
whether to thank Sally or not. Right then I didn't feel very grateful. After
all, she had conspired with my daughter to bring about this desperate
state of affairs. But, if not Sally, who? Annie could have run off and left
me with all the responsibility and none of the legal rights. Then she could
drop back into our lives any time she pleased and spirit her daughter

away, leaving me no way to stop her. At least if I had custody, Annie could never threaten to take Feather again. And I'd have full say as to how she was raised.

Sally said, "I know you're angry right now, Laura. That's natural. It'll all work out, if we both just keep in mind what's best for Feather." Shades of Kathleen, always reminding me to think of what's best for my clients. Nodding, I reached out for a hug.

When I got home, Nancy handed me the baby. I buried my face against her, inhaling her powdery baby smell. She began to squirm and fuss, but I didn't care. She was here, safe and well. I sat down on Nancy's couch with Feather on my knees and told her that Annie was gone.

"That girl," Nancy exclaimed. "There's no telling about young 'uns these days. You'll forgive my saying this, but I've seen Annie hanging around South Kihei Road in the evenings lately. She runs with a rough bunch, y'know? Dreadlocks, tattoos, bellybutton rings. I worried about her, but didn't want to say anything. Nobody appreciates a busybody, y'know?"

I nodded. "Annie's been lost to us for a long time, Nancy. I'm struggling to accept that. But how am I going to raise Feather alone? I'm forty-six. I'll be sixty-four when she graduates from high school. Sixty-eight when she graduates from college. It's hard enough being a single mother in your twenties and thirties, but in my fifties and sixties?"

"You're a lot wiser now. That'll help."

"Wise enough to know my limits."

"Look, as that attorney gal said, you don't have to decide now. Go home and get a good night's sleep. Things always look better in the morning. Give Annie some credit for taking care of business and giving you choices. She could have dumped it all in your lap with no legal rights. Then you'd be stuck whether you liked it or not."

"Sometimes having choices is what makes life so difficult," I mused.

Annie's yearbook photo and family history were lying in wait for me on the welcome mat at my front door, face up above the fold. Grant Kneubel had ferreted out an amazing amount of background tying Annie as a victim to the Campbell case, most of it accurate. As a result, my answering machine was full to overflowing, the messages no doubt from both sympathizers and curiosity seekers. I simply couldn't deal with it. With an evil glare, I did something I've been dying to do for years. I hit the erase button and sent the unheard messages flying to perdition, the highlight of a rotten day.

By way of penance for that dastardly deed, I called my parents immediately. They'd have read about Annie in the *Honolulu Advertiser*. Surely half the erased messages were from them. Mother was terribly distressed and of course wanted to fly right over. Once again, I begged her not to. "It would just add to the confusion, Mom. Annie has made her choice—she's gone; she's left us. This time I have to focus on Feather. She needs all my love and attention."

"But I can help you, dear."

"Mom, please, I have to face this alone. I promise I'll keep you posted. As soon as I have a handle on things, Feather and I will come over for a visit. Soon, I promise. I really appreciate your concern. Truly, I do."

She had no choice but to acquiesce, however reluctantly.

Feather had no sympathy for me at all. She fussed all evening, no matter what I did for her. I could only quiet her by walking her in a circle from the coffee table, through the kitchen, back through the living area, past the bed, into the bathroom, back past the bed, and around the coffee table again. On and on, endlessly into the night. She'd drift off, her sweaty little body slack against my shoulder. I'd carefully put her down, and just when I was beginning to relax in my own bed, she'd start to scream again. Up once more, endless walking, put her down, more screaming . . . as if she knew her mother had deserted her. I didn't have the heart to let her cry it out, even though her mother's behavior certainly was something to cry about.

Well after midnight Feather finally gave up, but not for long. She awoke again at 1:30 PM and didn't settle until 3:15 PM, leaving me in a state resembling a soapy dish rag. Morning dawned with birds chirping and Feather howling again. When she hadn't settled down again by 8:00 AM, I called Nancy and begged for some time off. Nancy came right over and got her, bless her heart. I fell back into bed.

As I rolled over to get more comfortable, I glanced at the framed photos of Annie and Feather on the dresser at the foot of my bed. My favorite shot of mother and daughter in Dad's easy chair at Pua Olena was missing. How long had it been gone? I had no idea. I'd been so pre-occupied lately, someone could have moved my refrigerator out, and I may not have noticed. Who else but Annie could have taken it?

That small gesture meant a million times more to me than the legal steps she had taken to secure Feather's future. It meant she cared enough to want a little bit of her daughter with her wherever she was. Giving in to freshets of weeping, I finally dozed off to visions of Annie in some for-lorn mainland bus station, cold and hungry, huddled on the cement floor in a corner with her photo of Feather tucked in her arms. I vowed to make a copy for myself from the negative, taking comfort in the thought that we would both be looking at the same image from time to time.

The twirping phone jolted me awake just before noon. It took a moment to realize I could let it ring without fear of disturbing Feather. Lying back, I let the answering machine click on. For a moment I half listened to the female voice.

"Laura, this is Lily Fujikawa. I was hoping to speak to Annie. Could you have her give me a call at her earliest convenience?"

I pushed over and grabbed the receiver.

"Lily? It's Laura. Hold on a sec. Let me turn this beast off." Push-ing up on an elbow, I reached across the bedside table to punch off the recorder.

"There." My voice was groggy. "Hi, Lily. Is anything wrong with Annie, health-wise I mean?"

"No, no, I had something else entirely I wanted to discuss with her. Will she be home this afternoon, do you think?"

I took a deep breath. Here we go. Time to face up to it. Lily must have been the only person on the island who hadn't been following the Chaz Campbell story in the newspaper. Too busy delivering babies, no doubt. "As a matter of fact, Annie's gone. She flew to the mainland day before yesterday."

"Oh, dear. Indefinitely?" Lily was well aware of Annie's flight-not-fight tendency.

"As far as I know. She didn't communicate with me directly. Did sort of a 'Dear Mom' thing via Sally Mitchell."

"Oh, Laura, I'm so sorry. You've really had your hands full with her."

"True. How did I manage so well with the boys?"

"Annie's just different, my friend. Some kids are born with their own agenda. Nothing and nobody can deflect them from it. You did your best for her, there's no question about that. Who's to say she isn't happy with her choices? Not everybody wants to lead a plain vanilla life."

"Thanks, Lily. I know you mean well." I hoped I didn't sound ungrateful. She was trying to help.

Lily graciously let it pass. "Will she stay in touch this time, do you think? At least let you know how the baby's doing?"

"Oh, well, she left Feather with me."

"What?" That one word came back like a shot.

"Yup, lock, stock, and diaper bag. I'm faced with single motherhood again at forty-six." Contrary to Nancy's cheery prediction, it did not sound better in the morning.

"Dear God. Is that okay?"

"I've hardly had a chance to comprehend it. Just found out yesterday. Annie had Sally prepare adoption consent papers."

"For . . . ?"

"Me, and as an option, a separate set for a third party adoption, should I choose that route. It's my decision . . . power of attorney, and all that."

Lily sucked in her breath. She tred very cautiously with her next statement. "As it happens, Laura, that's why I called. A third party adoption, I mean." She stopped to let me absorb her words.

I struggled to sit up on the wrinkled bed clothes. "What? Are you in on this, too, Lily? Has Annie set up all my friends in a plot against me?"

In the space of Lily's hesitation, sweat broke out along my ribs.

"Well, now that you're telling me this," she said, "I think I may have been a party to it, inadvertently, that is."

"What are you talking about?" I kicked my feet free of the twisted top sheet.

"Remember that day when Annie was here for her checkup, and one of my patients was so upset about her failed pregnancy?"

"Yes. The Smiths. I know them. They're former clients." I could see Lily's next words coming around the bend like a runaway truck on the Kailua side of Pali Highway.

"I had just examined Ginger Smith and given her the bad news. I left her with the nurse for a few minutes while I tended Annie. We could hear Ginger crying through the wall. I was terribly concerned about her. I didn't think she could go through any more disappointments. I planned to bring up adoption to her after I finished with Annie, so it was on my mind. I happened to mention to Annie that for some people, adoption would be a gift from heaven. I believe those were my exact words. I didn't mean to suggest it to her, it just slipped out as a solution for the Smiths. I swear I wasn't thinking about Feather."

My hands moistened against the receiver. "What did Annie say?"

"Nothing. I finished her exam, told her she was doing fine. We both walked out into the scene you witnessed in the waiting room. I haven't seen or talked to Annie since."

"Obviously she took your words to heart. Oh, Lily, how could you?"

"That wasn't my intention, I swear. But . . . the Smiths would be wonderful adoptive parents, Laura, if you'd consider it."

I fell back against the pillows. Lily's heart was in the right place, but I was still so raw from being dumped on—yes, that's how it felt —that I could barely answer her civilly.

"I'm going to raise Feather myself, Lily. The Smiths will just have to look elsewhere."

CHAPTER 32

In spite of my brave statement to Lily, over the next few days indecision weighed me down. Why didn't I enthusiastically accept the challenge of raising Feather, while blessing dear Annie for giving me this once-in-a-lifetime opportunity? The fact that I hesitated, questioned, stepped into the traces most unwillingly showed me dark places in myself I trembled to see. I bitterly resented Annie for holding the mirror to my innermost feelings of selfishness.

I put my best face on it, however, and did what had to be done. *Duty*, I could hear my mother exhorting. *Just do your duty. If you don't like it, too bad. You've made your bed, now sleep in it.* Only I hadn't made the bed—nor slept in it. Annie had.

Feather and I had good moments and bad, with tolerable stretches in between. I kept telling myself we would adjust, we would get used to it. Things would get better—if only she would sleep through the night.

As for work, the fun part of real estate evaporated. With Feather claiming all my personal time, I no longer had the luxury of socializing with my clients or fellow agents. I rushed from appointment to appointment, showing to showing, sometimes with Feather, sometimes alone. It looked as if a few listings or sales might pan out while the wait with the Colemans continued. I lived one day at a time, praying each morning we would make it through the day. And the night. When would Feather relent and let me catch up on my sleep—and allow me finally to let go of my fear of being alone with her in the night?

***

Three days after Annie left, at 3:30 PM Hawaiian time, six hours later on the East Coast, it was still a decent hour to call Frank. He would blame me again for everything, but he needed to know Annie had left. After all, he was an interested party in Feather's fate. Grandparents rights had become a big thing in recent years. I didn't want any complications on that score.

When he answered, the rumble of a ballgame in the background muffled his voice. Frank hated to be disturbed when he was tuned into football. His anger erupted immediately.

"Goddamn it, Laura. Why didn't you stop her? We've probably lost her for good." Shards flew through the receiver like ice crystals swirling atop Mauna Kea. "How could you let this happen again?"

"Frank, if you take that attitude with me, I'll hang up and tell you nothing more."

"Jesus, Laura—"

"I mean it, Frank. Do you want to hear the whole story, or shall I stop right now?" Had I, not so long ago, nestled lovingly in his arms, cried out with passion?

He bellowed, "For Christ's—"

"Frank!"

"All right. Go on." The football noise went dead. He must have zapped it with the remote.

I told him about Chaz Campbell, Annie's fear and her running away. "Annie left the baby with me, Frank. She signed adoption consent papers. To me, or to a third party, giving me full authority to make the final decision. All done secretly, but legally, behind my back." I explained that Annie had gone to Sally Mitchell as a client, holding her to full confidentiality. "Sally told me she tried every way she knew to stop her, but . . . I don't know. We have to face it, Frank. She's been running all her life. There's so much about Annie we'll never understand."

His breath exploded. "Fuck."

Familiar prickles of old aggravations buzzed in my ears. "Frank, please. This is difficult enough without that language."

"You really know how to irritate me, Laura."

I let that little gem of insanity pass. "That's the situation. She's gone. I don't know about you, but I don't think I can go through the business of hiring a detective to look for her again. And now there's Feather. She shouldn't have to pay for her mother's mistakes."

I paused, waiting for Frank to comment. He remained silent. I took that to mean he agreed with me about not hiring a detective again. As tough as that might be, I truly felt, for everyone's sakes, that we had to let Annie go. I could see him run his free hand over his hair and twist the curl of his ponytail around his finger. Heart pounding, I forged on. "Frank, I need to be certain that whatever decision I make about the baby, you won't interfere."

"Why in God's name would I do that?"

"I don't know, Frank. I'm a little shaky right now regarding other people's behavior in general. I don't want the added element of having to deal with your resistance in whatever I decide."

Frank clucked his tongue. "You've become a very hard woman, Laura. I'm not sure you *should* keep the baby."

I spoke through gritted teeth. "Damn it, Frank, just promise me you'll stay on the sidelines. Annie set it up for me to make the decision. You were not included. That's what she wanted. Unless . . ." I hesitated to play my trump card, but saw no alternative, "unless you and Holly want to take Feather?" I'd die rather than let them have her, but I had to get it out so I could cross it off the list of worrisome possibilities. Or begin right now to worry like hell.

His voice became wildly agitated. "Oh, no, oh, no. Don't even suggest it, Laura. You have no idea how difficult it is with Georgie. He consumes every waking minute of Holly's time. She's beyond obsessive. No, don't even imagine we could do that. You do what you like. If you need money, maybe I can help a little. I promise, I won't interfere. I promise."

I could see him gesticulating wildly, thrashing the air, tearing the band from his hair, letting it fall loose in wild mahogany waves. In the background a woman's voice murmured. Holly must have just walked in the room. I relaxed and enjoyed the vision—him upset, her not knowing why.

"So no matter what, if I keep her or find her a good adoptive home, you'll stay out of it?"

"Yes, yes, I promise!" He paused. "Hey, you're not really thinking of giving her up?"

"No, not at all."

"Well, that's good. That would be pretty cold-hearted."

"Stop. I just needed to know how you felt about it, either way."

"It's up to you, Laura, totally up to you."

"Thank you." Time to change the subject. "How's Georgie?"

"Ah, well, no signs of progress that I can see." Holly must have left the room again. His voice was shrouded in defeat. "It's just a damned shame. I'm ready to accept the finality of it, arrange for a full-time helper so Holly can have a life. She refuses to see it that way. She'll soldier on until she draws her last breath."

"Well, I give her credit. But . . . that doesn't exactly make for a good marriage, I don't suppose." Strangely, I found no satisfaction in saying it.

"No, it doesn't." The sadness in his voice sounded all too real.

"I'm sorry, Frank." What else could I say? His dreams of conquering the New York hotel world with the vivacious Holly on his arm had ended in a bitter pyre of cranberry-flavored ashes. I took no satisfaction in it at all.

It wasn't quite four o'clock. Normally, I'd be wrapping up paperwork at the office, or perhaps finishing showing property to prospective buyers, silently and hopefully evaluating their every comment for buying signs.

When I lived alone, I often took a quick sunset dip in the ocean to get the cobwebs out of my head, or swam laps at the pool. Both were delicious ways to work off stress at the end of the business day. Then I'd shower, return the last of the day's phone calls, rattle around in the kitchen for a bit, and sit down to a simple dinner. Toward ten o'clock, I'd go to bed with a good novel and be asleep before I knew it. Peaceful, quiet, well-deserved serenity in a world where buyers and sellers often jostled to get the better of each other while trapping me in their schemes.

I looked at Feather, asleep in her basket. With all of my real estate activities and worries about Annie, I'd had so little time to relax with her. Annie had either been with us, or likely to burst in at any moment with her disruptive energy. Now it was just Feather and me. We could make it together. The wisdom I had acquired while raising Annie and her brothers would make all the difference. If I really concentrated on Feather, truly devoted myself to her, I could turn the tide and give her what I had failed to give Annie. As for the sleepless nights, we only had to survive them one at a time. Surely we could manage that.

A horn honked in the parking lot below the lanai. Feather started and screwed up her face to cry. I picked her up quickly, nestled her to my breast, and patted her on the back.

"Ssh, sweetheart, it's only a car. No need to cry over that. Come on now, calm down. It's okay. I'm here. Ssh, ssh."

She gulped down several frantic breaths, then gradually relaxed. Just like her mother, she overreacted to outside stimuli. Things her brothers took in stride often set Annie howling. A long, tedious evening loomed over us. Exercise might help, but swimming was out of the question. I'd picked up a lightweight baby carrier that strapped on for walking. We'd give it a try at the beach.

My feet sank deliciously into foam-drenched sand, refreshing my entire body as I walked. Misty air redolent of salt and seaweed cleared my head. Trade winds whipped my hair and caressed my cheeks. Worries flew away like seabirds, off to find less fortunate isles on which to settle. The whisper and wash of gold-capped waves slowly soothed away all remaining cares, leaving behind only immediate sensual pleasure. Strapped across my chest, Feather lay snug, awake but quiet, sharing her warmth with me.

As we walked, the sun sank slowly behind a layer of low-lying clouds. As the gilded disk emerged beneath them to kiss the horizon, the underside of the clouds took on a molten glow. Intense turquoise blended to lavender where sun and water met. I stopped and watched, spellbound, as the gleaming sphere shimmered, flattened, and sank out of sight. No matter how many times I had stood in the shore break and marveled at the sun's last act, it was always glorious and entrancing. My own personal drama retreated into manageable perspective. We headed for home, renewed and invigorated.

Feather fussed and sputtered all evening. If I held her, walked her, rocked her, she condescended to a wary silence. If I put her down for a second, she objected long and loud. Even the act of leaning forward, preliminary to setting her down, was enough to trigger her wrath. For a while I feared she was in pain, but it mysteriously disappeared at the lift of human arms. In spite of Annie's clear imprint on her personality, and her frequent impatience with me, this one difference lifted the shadow of autism. Feather loved to be held.

Somehow during the evening I managed to gather our dirty laundry and throw it in the washer. When I could stand Feather's fussing no more, I powdered Feather's bottom, fastened on a dry diaper, and tucked her into her little rush basket. I carried the basket into the bathroom and laid it on the agitating washing machine. I closed the door and left her to cry it out. Miraculously, she quieted down immediately. The noise and rhythm of the washer must have done the trick. Maybe I had stumbled onto something.

My broker Kathleen called the next morning as I was bathing Feather. The baby truly enjoyed her daily splash in the plastic tub on the bathroom vanity. Not wanting to cut short her delight, I let the machine pick up the call. When I heard Kathleen's voice, however, I swooped Feather up in a towel and dashed for it.

"Hey, Kathleen, I'm here. Just keeping a low profile. Let me turn this thing off." I clicked off the echoing recorder. "There. We can talk without that awful squawk in the background."

"What the heck's going on?" Kathleen asked. "I've left messages, but you never called back."

"Sorry, Kathleen, it's been unbelievable. It's all I can do to put one foot in front of the other."

"You're okay?"

"Yeah, not to worry. We're managing."

"That's good. Look, I know you're in a bind, but I have to ask what this all means in terms of business. Are you going to be able to carry on? Do you want to turn your business over to someone else for a while? Take time off to get into being a mother again?"

Her suggestion sent a panicky shiver across my shoulders. "No. Perish the thought. I *have* to work. I've got bills up the kazoo."

Distracted by the fear of not earning a living, I forgot to watch where I was going and snagged my toe in the handle of Feather's diaper bag. Tipped off balance, I careened into the coffee table. The sharp edge clipped my shins with the force of a machete. I dropped the phone, tossed Feather over the low table onto the couch, and caught myself just short of falling.

"Ouch!" I cried, hopping from one foot to the other, frenzied by the pain in my legs. One glance told me Feather was momentarily safe on the couch, but not liking it at all. If I didn't get to her fast, we'd be in for another wailing spree. I scrabbled for the phone and spoke through clenched teeth as I danced around the coffee table.

"Sorry, Kathleen. Small bump in the road. Hang on a sec." I picked up the baby with my free hand and nestled her against my shoulder. That reassured her for the moment. "As for work, we just have to get into a rhythm here, you know? I've been taking Feather with me when I'm on the road. That's no problem. She's too young for a full-time sitter. I'd be on pins and needles all day, worrying about her . . . and the sitter."

Kathleen laughed. "Well, as long as you can keep your clients happy. By the way, you're still working on that Haiku closing, yeah?"

"Yeah, I think we have all but one wrinkle ironed out. Our fear of a drug lab in the garage went away when it turned out Prakash was Chaz Campbell, and the equipment involved his sick videotapes."

Kathleen replied, "Wasn't that the most bizarre turn of events? My eyes almost fell out of my head when I read about it."

"Dr. E.'s attorney has taken over getting the last so-called tenant out. She has about ten more days on her eviction notice."

"Excellent. You'll be glad to get that one out of your hair. Listen, I have a great lead for you, if you're up to it." She filled me in on the details: a retired couple from Seattle, the Maguires, who wanted a high-end condo in Wailea.

"You're singing my song, girl," I declared. "I'll get right on it. Thanks for the lead."

Whirling into motion, I sponged the blood off my legs, smeared the cuts with antibiotic ointment, and plastered them with Band-Aids. The pain died down to a dull ache. Fortunately, the cuts were not as desperate as all that blood would have indicated.

I gave Feather a bottle, then sat down by the phone, catching the Maguires as they returned from a snorkeling expedition to Molokini Island. We made an appointment to meet late that afternoon. Fueled by a sizzling charge of excitement, I checked the MLS to update my knowledge of inventory and recent sales in the resort.

To the rhythm of soft rock, I tore about the apartment, straightening up; Feather cooperated to the extent of lying quietly on a blanket on the floor, eyeing me warily to make sure I didn't throw her halfway across the room again. Having only the Maguires to concentrate on for the moment, I could devote myself to them and still be attentive to her. Whether the Colemans closed or not, business was looking up. Maybe I could stop worrying about finances for a while.

CHAPTER 33

I showed the Maguires several spectacular Wailea Resort properties that met their requirements. They had touring activities planned for the next few days, so they asked for time to think it over. There was nothing I could do but bite my fingernails while they enjoyed themselves. I was helpless, too, with Diana and Jerry Coleman while we waited out Moana's last days in the house. My immediate financial future was entirely out of my hands. I'd been there before. You hoped for the best and prepared for the worst.

I devoted the next two days entirely to Feather, walking her on the beach, rocking her while watching movies on TV, cruising the mall with the stroller, giving her long, tender massages with baby lotion after her bath. I made a conscious effort to tune into her rhythms, to observe closely what made her happy, what upset her. It became clear that she needed a constant, predictable, stable daily life with one reliable person in charge. She simply didn't do well with constant interruptions, frequent car trips, broken naps, ringing phones, ever-changing scenes, and shuttling at odd hours between myself and Nancy. In just two days of sensitivity to her needs, she became surprisingly manageable. We even got through both nights with quick feedings, after which she went right back to sleep. My washing machine proved a godsend, although the condominium association wouldn't be pleased with the increased water bill.

With a pricey new sale in sight, my own energy miraculously rebounded. Life regained its flavor. I began to feel confident that I could provide the serene atmosphere Feather needed, while earning our living at the same time.

When I didn't hear from the Maguires by early the third afternoon, I became concerned. Frissons of anxiety raced across the back of my neck while I listened to their phone ring. And ring and ring. I tried repeatedly throughout the day, but there was never any answer. By late afternoon I was pacing the floor, fit to be tied. Feather picked up on my nervousness, and began to fret. She refused to settle for a nap, and by 4:00 PM we were both in a frazzle. I rang them one more time. A strange voice answered.

"No, this is not Pat Maguire," he said. "My name is Ventitucci. Whoever was here yesterday checked out. That's how we got the unit a week early. Incredible luck."

"My God, what happened?" I exclaimed.

"How would I know, lady? I don't know Maguire from that coconut tree out there."

I managed to thank him, then called the rental office at the Breakers. The agent there had once worked for Frank.

"Oh, hi, Laura. Yes, the Maguires. They checked out yesterday, a week early. Something about their son, arrested for stealing a car back home. Big flap, lots of tears, out of here within a couple of hours. Luckily we re-rented the unit. That's all I know."

I hung up, concerned about my new friends, not to mention a very dead deal. My clients had lost their focus, and rightly so. Rescuing their child was more important than buying a condo. I moved about the apartment, struggling to accept this turn of events. Slowly I became aware of feelings I'd experienced many times before: the unexpected calm that replaces the roller-coaster anxiety of an iffy deal once all is irretrievably lost. There is a certain backhanded relief when you know you can quit trying. You may not like the conclusion, but it's over. You don't have to fight any more. Just as I didn't have to fight any more about Annie.

I picked Feather up and swayed back and forth, soothing us both, heartsick over what this tragedy would mean to the parents of the boy in trouble. I could relate—heartache, legal expenses, beating yourself up for being a bad parent—I didn't want to go there. I forced my thoughts onto a more practical track. Financially, Feather and I would just have to manage. I'd been running on hope. It hurt like hell to see that juicy commission evaporate. Five figures and change would have bought me a lot of time at home with her. The business was fraught with disappointments, big ones, little ones, and everything in between. You take it, but it's never easy.

Frankly, it also hurt that the Maguires hadn't called me before they left, but that wasn't unheard of either. Visitors did it all the time—wildly enthusiastic about buying, then disappearing without a word. To give the folks credit, their minds had been otherwise engaged. They probably flew off without giving the condo another thought. Or maybe each thought the other had called me.

Without knowing it, however, they had given me the gift of uninterrupted time with Feather. In those two days I'd gotten a clear glimpse of what she needed—a calm, predictable life—demonstrated plainly today as my own escalating tension had riled her up again.

I walked her back and forth from the kitchen to the sliding glass doors, humming softly. The rainbow shower trees beyond the lanai railing shimmered pink and gold in the late afternoon heat. Finally her little eyelids fluttered one last time, and she gave up the ghost. I sat down in the rocker and held her, enjoying the downy softness of her hair against my cheek, her trusting heart beating against mine.

First thing the next morning, Ji-Kwok Yuen called to say that Moana had up and moved out of Randy Entwistle's house the previous day. Just like that.

I was stunned. "What happened? She's still got time!"

"The ace up my sleeve, which will forever remain a secret. The neighbors saw her hauling stuff away all day. I went up in the evening. The house is empty."

"Did you go inside?"

"No, I just looked in the windows with a flashlight. It's vacant and deserted."

"Well, never underestimate the power of a clever attorney. It's too good to be true."

"Yeah, well, don't knock it. You owe me a big expensive dinner."

Not quite believing it, I requested a final walkthrough of the property at 5:00 o'clock the next afternoon. Ji-Kwok promised the house would be thoroughly cleaned. The signed documents would be flown to Honolulu, he said, and the sale would record day after tomorrow.

I picked Feather up and waltzed her crazily around the apartment, segueing into a full-on war dance, whoops and all. When I finally slowed down and held her up in front of me to make sure she understood what a big day this was, her olive-gray eyes widened with fright, her little chin quivered, and her perfect baby mouth scrunched down at the edges, ready to bawl.

"Go ahead, love, holler," I exclaimed. "We've been waiting for this since before you were born." Seeing how truly frightened she was, I immediately stopped my silly antics. But, damn, I'd sweated that sale. It felt fantastic to let out some steam.

I called Diana and Jerry. They had just heard the news from their own attorney and were ecstatic. We met at the property the next day as planned. Aside from a few minor details that the Colemans were happy to overlook, everything appeared to be in order. For the first time we looked about leisurely without Randy's nervous presence spooking us, or a gray-haired fury in a red broomstick skirt screeching at us to get out. The house was cleansed not only of dust and furniture, but of the dissonant presence of the mismatched duo. All the downstairs bedrooms were open and empty. For the first time we entered the garage where Chaz Campbell had copied and packed his unspeakable sex tapes. The locks and window cardboard had been removed, along with any trace of equipment. Nothing remained but empty gloom. I exited as quickly as possible, shivering at what the man had done to Annie. The Colemans were too excited to notice.

As we walked from room to magnificent room in the house, Diana babbled on about furnishings, paint, wallpaper, and landscaping. The house came alive for me as it never had before. Her unwavering vision had kept the purchase firmly on track, aided of course by Jerry's furor at the threat of being outwitted by women. We laughingly recalled their tag team tactics—when Jerry lost the faith, Diana regained it; when Diana wanted to bail because of bad vibes, Jerry kept going because it was a superb investment. In spite of their differing motives, the strategy had worked. Caught up in their excitement, I found myself believing, for the first time, they could truly be happy here. As we locked the front door and strolled down the steps, I glanced around one last time to make sure the malevolent Moana wasn't lurking behind a bird-of-paradise bush.

We made a date to meet the next day for a celebration lunch, after which I would accompany them to the property for the last time to make a small ceremony of handing over the keys along with a Welcome Home basket of edible goodies. Although this is by no means necessary, it's always a good opportunity to heal any wounds still open, to allow the clients to forgive me for any perceived screw-ups, and for them to express their sincere thanks for a job well done. Ending on a happy note allows us all to remember our last professional interaction as a pleasant one, in spite of any nastiness that might have occurred along the way.

I tossed and turned in bed that night, getting up twice with Feather. Every time I closed my eyes again, dastardly visions of Moana in that horrid red skirt and tie-dyed T-shirt blocking the property recordation appeared. Would I turn on the TV news in the morning to see her engulfed in flames on the steps of the Bureau of Conveyances in Honolulu? Would a time bomb explode in the lobby, set by Moana to go off at precisely 7:55 AM as the state employees streamed in to work? Drenched in sweat, I struggled to wakefulness at dawn, realizing the shrieking and wailing came from Feather.

We were dressed and waiting when the phone rang at 8:05 AM. I grabbed it.

"Laura, this is Nadine at Valley Isle Title. Your sale in Haiku recorded."

Relief shot through me. "Thank God. You don't know how I've waited for this day. It's done. I'm free!"

Nadine continued in a oddly flat voice. "Don't you want to pick up the commission check this morning?"

"Well, no, just send it over by messenger, like you always do. I've waited this long; I can wait a few hours longer." I giggled, listening for Nadine to giggle with me.

She didn't. "Don't you want to come over and pick it up right away?" she repeated.

That was strange. I'd never picked up a commission check after a closing. The escrow company delivered it, Kathleen deposited it in her trust account at the end of the day, and the agent got paid the following day. At least, that's how it's done at Blue Rock Realty.

"Well, I really wasn't planning to go anywhere this morning, Nadine. The buyers are meeting me for lunch, and we're all going up to the house afterward. I was going to take my granddaughter to the beach before I leave her with the sitter for the rest of the day." I warmed at the thought of Feather's squeals as her little toes dipped into the shoreline foam.

Nadine's voice dropped like a lead sinker. She articulated each word with surreal clarity. "Laura, don't you want to come and pick up the commission check now." It was not a question. No word was emphasized more than another. But the word "now" crashed in my ears like the dumpster in my condo parking lot hitting the ground after being emptied.

"Now," I repeated, suddenly catching her sense of urgency, though not understanding it. "Give me fifteen minutes. I'll be there."

She hung up without another word.

The check was waiting for me in an envelope at Valley Isle Title's front desk. The receptionist handed it to me with a cheery smile, obviously not a party to Nadine's strange insistence. I asked if Nadine were available, thinking to defuse the mystery, but she was doing a closing. Feeling the punch seep out of my triumph at having earned it, I delivered the check to my broker.

"I don't quite get it," I said to Kathleen. "But something tells me we should deposit this right away."

Kathleen waved her hand across the pile of papers and files on her desk. "Are you kidding? I'm tied up here until late this evening. I'll deposit it on my way home, like I always do. Milton Green just called with another asinine snarl he's gotten himself into. I'm expecting him any minute. Who knows how long that'll take. He's gone beyond even his limits of legal creativity this time. I fully expect we'll both end up in jail."

Milton was our resident sales genius cum sleaze bucket. He sells like a pit bull crunched onto the jugular. He never lets go until they buy or die. I knew Kathleen would be tied up with him all afternoon.

Echoes of Nadine's odd persistence played back in my mind. "Kathleen, just make out a deposit slip, endorse the check and let me take it to the bank. I'll go right now. I don't know what's going on, but if you'd overheard my conversation with Nadine, you wouldn't argue. This transaction has been jinxed from day one."

In the moment she hesitated, Milton blustered in the front door. "God almighty," Kathleen said, reaching for a pen. "Here we go. Okay, I'll trust your gut. Bring me back a turkey sandwich. Dealing with Milton always leaves me craving."

I met a jubilant Diana and Jerry for lunch at a little café in Kahului near Jerry's office. We sat outside under canvas umbrellas, while business traffic rolled by on the other side of a pink hibiscus hedge. Diana couldn't begin to contain her excitement. Jerry ordered for her, but she paid no attention to her salmon in dill sauce when it arrived.

I subscribe to the same sensible school as my broker. After surviving a tense situation, I eat. I have no memory of my own lunch that day, but I do recall polishing off Diana's salmon after cleaning my own plate. As we were leaving the restaurant, the hostess stopped me at her stand and held out the phone. My guard shot up immediately. It was Kathleen.

"Are you sitting down?" she asked.

"Not at the moment. What's up?"

"Your gut was right. Nadine at Valley Isle Title just sent me a copy of a fax she received this morning. It's a letter from the IRS, demanding all of Dr. Entwistle's proceeds from the sale, minus only the mortgage payoff.

Apparently she's megabucks behind in her income taxes. The IRS called Nadine first thing this morning regarding Dr. Entwistle. It was only an inquiry, but Nadine knew what was coming. That's why she leaned on you to pick up the check *wikiwiki*. I just wanted to make sure you'd deposited it."

"Good heavens, yes." As the dill sauce clotted around the salmon in my stomach, I fished in my purse for the deposit slip. "Don't tell me we have to give it back?"

"No, I just checked with our attorney. The commission funds were dispersed prior to escrow's receipt of the demand letter. The phone call doesn't count. The fact that you deposited the check just adds good measure. As for everyone else involved in the sale—the surveyor, the termite inspector, and the rest of them—they're out of luck. And of course Randy Entwistle won't get a dime."

There went Randy's mother's retirement home, I thought. "God bless Nadine,"I whispered aloud.

"Yeah," Kathleen continued. "That would have been a heck of a note to go through the entire mess only to find out we weren't getting paid. I hope Nadine doesn't get into trouble."

"Me, too. It had to be Moana. She did the doctor's books."

Kathleen snorted. "She's probably been skimming for years, using the money to set that Prakash up in his sex-tour business instead of paying the doctor's taxes. Then she alerted the IRS to the sale, the spiteful bitch." I could see Kathleen's perfectly tucked eyebrows arching. "Pretty brutal."

My knees wobbled as we left the restaurant. On the drive to Haiku, I explained to the Colemans what happened. We were all awestruck at the scope of Moana's vengeance. Finally the conversation tapered off, each of us sunk in our own thoughts, grateful that woman was out of our lives.

Recent rain had left the asphalt slick on the narrow country road. The overhanging vegetation glistened. The speeding tires sloshed over the rough pavement, sending earthen scents into the muggy air as Jerry negotiated the red-dirt-banked curves. Alone in the back seat, I curled up against the door. What a close call. I don't know if I could have carried on in the business if my commission had been grabbed by the IRS, especially on the heels of my disappointment in Wailea. I said a fervent prayer of thanks to the saints who preserve us, and wondered how Randy would take the news. Happily, it wasn't mine to deliver.

My clients got their house, and nobody had died. I had a big, fat check waiting for me. I could pay off debts and think of the future. Lulled by the swaying car and the moist, warm air, I dozed off.

Suddenly Diana gasped, "Oh, that little shit!"

"What?" I asked, straightening up, trying to get my bearings.

With a sharp turn that threw me back against the door, the car lurched into the driveway of the Colemans' new home and skidded to a halt at the top of the hill, sending mud flying in every direction. The open driveway in itself was remarkable, as we had been stopped by the locked gate on previous visits. This time, there was no gate. Nor gateposts. Someone had pulled them right out of the ground, leaving nothing but two yawning holes in the dirt. White scrape marks lined the pavement behind us.

"That bloody bitch pulled the gate right off and took the posts with her," Diana gasped. "How dare she?"

Jerry was ominously silent. There was no question in any of our minds that Moana was the culprit. "Looks like that's not all she took out," he growled.

He eased the car slowly down the driveway into a wasteland of dead trees and shrubs. The entire yard had been uprooted, one plant at a time. Those too big to manhandle had been decapitated at the knee with a chainsaw. Bird-of-paradise, tree ferns, gardenia, heliconia, monstera littered the lawn like corpses on a battlefield. Adding insult to injury, the vandal had driven a heavy vehicle back and forth across the spongy yard, spinning the tires and carving deep, muddy ruts in the grass.

"How could she?" Diana cried. "Those poor plants. What a depraved monster!"

Jerry was fuming, but not ready to explode yet. Mentally, he was way ahead of us. He sped us around to the back of the house and jerked to a stop on the terrace.

"Don't waste your tears on the yard, ladies. You don't think she quit there, do you?" He stomped up to the kitchen door and turned to me with his hand out. "Laura, give me the goddamn key."

There went my little ceremony. Jerry barged into the kitchen, stopped dead, and cursed. "Goddamn it all to hell. She's raided the fucking place."

Sure enough. Nothing but shadowed indentations marked the slots for the range, the refrigerator, the dishwasher, and the microwave.

"The bitch would have taken the brick fireplace if she could've figured a way to do it," Jerry muttered.

We followed the trail of destruction down the hall to the front entryway, where the antique chandelier near the foot of the sweeping koa staircase had been reduced to a dangling collection of frayed wires.

Right then the stench hit us. We gasped at the huge pile of manure dumped in the center of the living room carpet, then tracked star-wise in every direction. At the end of each smeary trail, our girl had wiped her boots on the soft Berber carpet and gone back for more.

Gagging and choking, we doubled back and raced upstairs. The doors to the master suite were locked. When Jerry hurled his weight against them, they gave with a loud crack. He stumbled in, with me and Diana right behind. We halted a few steps inside, all senses alert in the eerie quiet. The room smelled oddly of sandalwood and candle wax. How dare that bitch leave her scummy scent behind.

At first glance, it looked as if there had been an overnight frost, with glittering ice piled on the sills and floor beneath the open windows. Impossible, of course. Then we realized all the windows in the master suite had been smashed. Glass littered the carpet.

Diana screeched, "That damn bitch! If I ever get my hands on her—"

Jerry pushed past her and leaned out the window. "Well, at least the gulch and the ocean are still there. She left them alone."

Then I saw Jerry's eyes flick toward the half-closed bathroom door. He sniffed a couple of times. Once again, he was way ahead of us. Ashen-faced, he strode over to Diana, who stood in the middle of the room weeping, put his hands firmly on her shoulders and walked her toward the landing, whispering in her ear as he guided her out of the room. He looked back at me once, stricken, as if to say, *Sorry, you're on your own. I can only protect my wife.* Puzzled, I walked toward the bathroom to see what he feared. As I pushed open the door, a whiff of gasoline fumes stopped me, but only for an instant. Jerry's voice from the hallway cut through me like a garrote.

"Don't. Go. In. There."

But I was already through the door. Somehow I knew before I looked. There was only one more thing Moana could have done to complete the ruination of the house for the Colemans.

CHAPTER 34

Red . . . red . . . everywhere . . . where no red should be.
Red blood, red skirt, red water.
Red candles lined up on white enamel bathtub.
Red spatters on white tile backsplash.
Innocent sandalwood flames
sputtered out in puddles of hardened red wax,
framing a scene of obscene horror.
Ripped flesh, chainsaw splattered.
White face half-submerged, gray hair
swirled in red . . . red . . . RED.
Searing Haiku red burned in consciousness,
Moana's final legacy, haunting red dreams forever.

One glimpse propelled me, gasping and screaming, backward into Jerry's arms. My mind registered, but did not compute, that the only other note of color in the ghastly red-and-white scene was a quarter-folded sheet of lined yellow paper on the white marble floor.

I shivered uncontrollably in the windowless, air-conditioned interrogation room at the Wailuku Police station, squirming on the unforgiving wooden chair. They read me my rights, told me I could call an attorney. I said I had nothing to hide. The questioning proceeded endlessly. What had my relationship been to the deceased? Why had I wanted her out of the house? Ah, you're a Realtor. You folks will do anything to close a sale, yeah? What steps had I taken to effect her eviction? What were the names of the sheriff's deputies who had delivered the eviction notice? What did I know about the doctor's relationship with the deceased? And what about the handwritten deed on yellow paper found beside the tub?

What could I say? Moana had apparently had the deed all along. Why had she not used it to stop the sale? I couldn't begin to comprehend the reasoning of her twisted mind. I told the cops what I surmised—that the deed was more effective as a threat than a *fait accompli* in controlling Dr. Entwistle. But the truth had died with Moana. We would never know for sure.

I had not seen Diana or Jerry since we were escorted into town in separate squad cars, but I prayed our identical stories would convince them we were not responsible for Moana's death. They finally let me go close to midnight.

As I put out a shaky hand to push through the lobby door into the night, Randy Entwistle materialized on the other side of the dark glass, a police officer at her elbow. Startled, I stepped back to let them enter. Eyes crazed, hair awry, she stopped dead when she saw me. Her clothes were wrinkled, her bare feet encrusted with sand. They must have found her camped in her van at the beach. My heart tripped, shattering every coherent thought my mind struggled to form. What could I possibly say? What words were appropriate? Had *she* done it? Surely she didn't think *I* had? However deteriorated their relationship, Moana's brutal death had obviously hit her hard.

His hand still gripping her arm, the policeman turned to say something to a colleague. Randy halted squarely in front of me. Like a cane-grabber opening and shutting its maw, her lips pursed and retreated several times over her barnacle teeth. She snaked her head at me and blurted, "She was everything to me. Everything. And then you . . . you . . . you *sold* the house and ruined it." She exhaled the last words in a snarling whine, as if it were incomprehensible that I could have done such a thing.

I steadied myself against the wall, shaking my head. "But, Randy, you hated her. You wanted your house sold so you could get her out of your life . . . didn't you?"

"I didn't hate her! I loved her! I've never loved anyone the way I loved Moana."

"But I thought . . . I was only—"

"My life is ruined, thanks to you. She'd have taken me back! Prakash is in jail now, out of the picture. She'd have taken me back, I know it. We'd have left the Islands, found a nice little place, maybe in Bali . . ."

Twisting away from the distracted officer, she sprang at me, teeth hideously bared, saliva foaming in the corners of her mouth. I stumbled sideways, hitting the sharp edge of a redwood planter. Pain shot through my knee. I hopped crazily away from her on one leg. The officer quickly restrained her and hustled her down the hallway. She twisted around one more time and shouted over his shoulder. "She needed me. I told you to call it off, but you pushed and you pushed. You just wouldn't let go. I hope you're damned well satisfied."

That was the last time I ever saw or spoke to Dr. Randa Entwistle.

How I got home, I didn't remember. The scene with Randy threw me into an emotional blackout. My car was in the condo parking lot the next morning, but I had no recollection of driving home.

Memory began again as I frantically, sobbingly stripped off my clothes in the bathroom, ridding my body of impediments to cleanliness. I leaned over to turn on the bathtub tap, and . . . red . . . red . . . *red* . . . The bathtub . . . the chainsaw . . . *the red* . . . Oh, God. Moana.

Somehow I got myself into bed, shivering in the warm Kihei night, chilled bone-deep by the frigid police station air. The horrific visions wouldn't stop. Moana, hacked to death in a mad butchery, aswirl in red, red water. And Randy shouting at me that she loved her.

I lay in bed trembling, utterly unable to comprehend the back-twist of Randy's revelation. Was everything she'd told me throughout our long and tedious dealings a lie? Was her real motive in selling the house to boomerang Moana back into her arms? In spite of the vicious black-mail threats that could have ruined her medical career? Whatever her true motive, Randy's plot had backfired hideously, with me an unwit-ting accomplice.

My mind turned in on itself, harrying me as to how I could have allowed myself to be the catalyst in such a tragic denouement. I had indeed pushed and pushed Randy to get Moana out and close the sale. But that's what I thought she wanted. Sure, she had tried to rescind after Moana discovered the sale, but then she vehemently revoked it three days later, telling me to proceed, which the Colemans would have forced her to do in any case.

But if I were to be completely honest, soul-deep, alone-in-the-middle-of-the-night honest, I had skillfully employed Randy's wavering as a sales technique to get Diana and Jerry to dig in deeper whenever their resolve appeared to falter. Throughout the transaction I was the supreme driving force. Doing my job, yes, but at what cost to another human being? I certainly had no love for Moana, but my God, I didn't want her dead.

I rolled over, trying to find a comfortable position in which my knee didn't hurt. But there was no comfort that night. Where along the way had I turned into a cold, grasping selling machine, capable of being ma-nipulated by two sick and desperate women, intent on closing the sale in spite of every sign that begged me to leave Randy and Moana to work out their craziness in some other way? What right did I have to hound Moana, alone, through Randy, through attorneys, and the sheriff, to the point of self-destruction?

I was sure it was suicide. There were no signs of struggle, no bloody footprints leading away from the bathtub. Besides, no murderer would have set the scene so carefully with sandalwood-scented candles. Not a single one was disturbed. Deep in my bones, I knew Moana had done this to herself. Her lover Prakash was in jail, and she had lost control of Randy. In one outrageous gesture, she ended her own struggle and ruined things for everyone else.

My mind refused to shut off. The phone rang.

"Laura? Are you home? It's almost three a.m."

"Oh, Lord. Nancy! Is Feather all right? Tell me she's all right." My ribs contracted on my wildly thumping heart.

"Well, she's pretty hungry. I've run out of formula. When did you get home? Why didn't you stop by and pick her up?"

"I don't know. I forgot. It's been an awful night. I'll be right there." I grabbed my key and raced to her apartment in my T-shirt and underpants, mindless of who might be prowling the hallway in the wee hours.

Guilt added to guilt, I fed Feather and tucked her into bed with me for the rest of the night. She fell asleep easily for a change, but I didn't dare shut my eyes. How could I have walked right past Nancy's door and not thought to pick Feather up? Traumatized, yes, but that was no excuse. I'd forgotten her. What a terrifying thought.

The sweaty sheet pressed down upon me with the weight of a wet canvas tarp. I bicycled it off in a frantic flurry and sat straight up in bed, biting my lip to keep from screaming into the ever-listening night. The sudden movement jostled Feather awake beside me. I picked her up and hugged her, pressing my face against hers, but she refused to settle. *Oh, Annie. Why did you leave me to face it all over again?*

It was only 5:00 AM, but we were up for the day. The morning newspaper spared no detail:

WOMAN FOUND DEAD IN BATHTUB, MAULED BY CHAINSAW

The rattling that filled the room was the newspaper in my hands, shaking so badly I dropped it without reading further. I needed no black-and-white description of that red-and-white scene of mechanical self-immolation.

I was still staring into the distance beyond the mountain with Feather fussing on my lap when Barbara banged on the door, and kept banging until I let her in. Without a word, she took the baby and walked her until she settled down. She laid Feather in her basket on the washing machine, turned it on as she had seen me do, closed the door, and sat down with my telephone on her lap, a firm hand on the receiver.

"You're resting, the baby's asleep. If anyone calls, you'll call back later," she ordered. "I did not tell Grant about Annie's involvement with Chaz. It was that ridiculous ad salesperson, remember? She was seated a few tables away from us at the café the day we saw the newspaper head-lines. She's always wanted to be a reporter. Figured that was her big chance, so she went straight to Grant with what she saw. So get over it."

"Oh, Barb, I'm so sorry."

"Never mind. Just talk. What happened with Randy and Moana?"

Nothing I said surprised her. She'd seen it all, and more, at the LAPD. Her calm acceptance helped me regain some emotional footing. She assured me that if my movements were as traceable as I remembered, I would be cleared immediately. But I wasn't worried about being charged with Moana's death. On the contrary, I'd led the assault that resulted in her suicidal desperation. And was duped into doing it by Randy Entwistle.

"Look, Laura, Moana was a psycho. I lived across the street, remember? Dr. Entwistle wasn't far behind. People attract who they are, you know."

"Psycho or not, I had no business pushing so hard. I played right into Randy's hand."

"Weren't the Colemans pushing *you*? Seems to me I heard you say you should get them out of it more than once. They wanted that house badly. If you'd turned them loose, they'd have gone after it on their own."

"That's probably true, but—"

"You'll make yourself sick if you insist on taking responsibility for this. Moana was wacko. Everyone who knew her will tell you that. Suicide is not the normal response of a tenant who receives an eviction notice. All the other tenants left quietly, didn't they? Sure, they grumbled a bit, but they've all relocated and moved on with their lives. You cannot, must not, feel responsible for the act of a madwoman. As for Randy, sure she lied, sure she used you. But even she had no idea things would go that far. She must not have realized, or allowed herself to admit, the extent of Moana's derangement. She expected them to patch things up once Moana realized she really meant to sell the house, for heaven's sake. Randy was delusional, but that's not your fault, either."

I so wanted to believe those deep brown eyes that looked at me with utter sincerity. Logically, I knew she was right. But I had bushels of unused Catholic guilt roiling in my catechized soul, rising up and clobbering me from every direction. And beneath it all now was my unthinkable neglect of Feather.

"The guilt runs pretty deep, Barb. You weren't raised by a Catholic mother."

"Oh, so now we're going to blame it on your Mom? That's handy."

"My mother. Oh, God." I glanced at the clock on the bookshelf across the room: 8:40 AM. Unless Diamond Head had erupted and engulfed Honolulu in glowing lava overnight, my mother had just padded across the living room at Pua Olena and picked up the morning newspaper on the front porch. Tensing, I stared at the phone on Barbara's lap. I swear I felt the 11-digit long distance signal from Nuuanu Valley crackle through the wire.

Right on target, the phone rang on Barbara's lap. I reached for it, but Barbara turned her back to me, answering it herself.

"Oh, hello, Mrs. Henderson. Yes, yes, Laura's here. She's just fine, but she's resting right now . . . I know, grim. I'm sorry you had to read about it in the newspaper . . . Yes, the police questioned her. She was there when the body was discovered, but there's no indication they believe she had anything to do with it. Not at all. In fact, it appears to have been a suicide . . . Yes, ghastly. Not exactly what a Realtor expects to encounter in her daily business . . . A teacher? Don't you think she'd find that rather boring?"

I shook my head at Barbara and rolled my eyes. When would my mother let it go?

"Oh, I'm her friend, Barbara Jaworski. I was a cop once myself. Perhaps she's spoken of me?" Barb flashed me a wink and a grin.

"No, no relation to the Honolulu Jaworskys. I believe they spell it with a 'y.' Yes, yes, Polish as well, but no relation." By now, she was rolling her eyes, too, at my mother's nonsense. I felt the first vague intimation that my sense of humor might be alive and well in a distant galaxy far, far away.

"No, Mrs. Henderson, she really can't come to the phone. As I said, she's resting. As you might imagine, she's had a pretty rough night . . . Indeed, very tragic all the way around. But Laura's okay. She just needs to rest. I'm here to help with Feather so she can do just that . . . No, no, Mrs. Henderson, I think it's better if you don't come over." Barbara raised questioning eyebrows at me. I shook my head frantically. The last thing I needed was for my mother to descend upon us, all misguided solicitation and overbearing bossiness. "No, no, truly, Mrs. Henderson, everything's under control. Laura's just fine, the baby's fine. Listen, no crying." Barbara held the phone away and pointed it toward the closed bathroom door. When she returned it to her ear, she opened her mouth to speak, but apparently Mother beat her to it. She listened, frowned, then answered. "No, not the San Francisco Jaworskys, either, I'm afraid. No, I didn't know they'd given such a large donation to the Honolulu Academy of Arts. Perhaps I should change my spelling to 'y' and see if they'd like to adopt me."

God help us, the minute she got my mother off the phone, we collapsed into fits of laughter. Oh, dear, how good it felt. We shrieked and pounded our chair arms and our thighs. We bent over double with our hair falling over our faces and then swooped upright, sending it flying backward with wild abandon. Happily, Feather slept through the torrent behind the bathroom door. Finally, stomach muscles aching from the unaccustomed exercise, I collapsed lengthwise on the couch, the laughter trickling down to my bare feet doing butterfly kicks against the cushions. Barbara half slid off her chair, tangling her long legs on the floor, and giggled into her T-shirt. Granted, there was an edge of hysteria to it on my part, but I didn't care. It felt good. I wondered if I might, given a great deal of time, survive Randy's treachery and Moana's suicide after all. And banish once and for all the memories of my bad times with Annie.

Barbara stayed on, fending off dozens of well-meaning phone calls, including several more from my mother. Conspicuously absent were the

Colemans, probably, understandably, wanting nothing to do with me for a while. Diana had once declared the property had bad vibes. Jerry had scoffed. Well, now the bad vibes were real. Diana had been spared the sight, but certainly not the knowledge. How could they possibly think of living there now? So much damage, inside and out. I couldn't guess what they intended to do, but the property was legally theirs. Surely they'd seek damages from Randy, and I would be dragged into it. Then they'd put it back on the market, a stigmatized property impossible to sell except to someone titillated by its gruesome history.

While Barbara took Feather out for a walk after lunch, I turned off the phone and slept. When I awoke, sluggish and dull, she offered to stay through the evening. I thanked her for her solicitude but sent her on her way. I'd have to begin coping on my own.

The police spent the next few days tracing our movements, seeking an unaccounted hour amongst us the morning of Moana's death. They were out of luck. Jerry had been at his office since 4:00 AM, verified by his fellow stockbrokers and his phone records to New York. Then he drove the few blocks to meet us for lunch. Diana had had an early massage, facial, manicure, and pedicure in celebration of the closing. She'd had only just enough time to meet Jerry and me at the restaurant at noon. I, of course, was seen at the title company, Blue Rock Realty, and the bank. After returning to the office with Kathleen's sandwich, I left to meet the Colemans, arriving the expected number of minutes later. The restaurant staff and guests verified that we departed at about 2:00 o'clock. According to the coroner, Moana had been dead since mid-morning. As for Randy, she had been in surgery since 6:00 AM, with two cases back-to-back. She had not left the hospital until well after sundown.

Within the week, the coroner ruled Moana's death a suicide, officially clearing us all as suspects. The press had a field day speculating on the mechanics of killing oneself with a chainsaw, but Grant dredged up several precedents on the mainland and crowed in purple prose as to how it could be done. No other victim had shown such aplomb, however, as carefully staging the scene with sandalwood-scented candles and wearing her best red broomstick skirt.

Moana had laid low, according to Grant's reporting, while the Colemans and I did the final walkthrough the day before. She returned to the property that evening, working through the night and early morning to commit her final mayhem. When finished decimating the house and yard, she set the scene in the bathroom and lit the candles. She started the motor, got in the tub, lay down in the water, reached for the buzzing saw, and let it drop on her neck. By some unlikely miracle of physics and duct tape, it actually worked as planned.

I was relieved to be cleared of suspicion, but knowing the facts did not make life any easier. The red nightmares continued. Things went from bad to worse with Feather, as well. Once again, I vowed to throw myself into her care at the expense of everything else. I'd leave her with Nancy when necessary, but for the most part I promised to give her my full attention. I'd do the minimum required to close the small house in Waiehu and the Le Boeuf's condo, but otherwise felt quite justified in slacking off for both our sakes.

In fact, I had serious doubts about returning to the business at all. It seemed to be just one heartbreak after another, punctuated by the occasional thrill of a sale. By the time they closed, however, sales were rung dry of any feeling of triumph or even satisfaction. People lied and used me for their own ends, or walked away without so much as a word of farewell. Commissions went to pay debts with nothing left over to keep me going until the next closing. Admittedly, all sales weren't as rough as the Colemans', but I wondered how I could bear to carry on, sensitized now more than ever to anticipate the worst.

Then again, how else could I possibly earn a living on this rock? It always came back to that. Entry-level hotel work, waitressing, selling activities, driving a tour bus, clerking at a rental car agency? How much time would any of those give me for Feather, never mind the low wages that couldn't possibly support us? Perhaps I could run for public office. What a nauseating idea. The public exposure would be a hundred times more intense than real estate, especially now with my unwanted notoriety. At least my known poison, no matter what toll it took, always got me excited for the next big sale, just a phone call away. Love it or hate it, it's truly addictive.

Good soldier that she was, Barbara came over every day. Only then did Feather settled down. The minute Barbara picked her up, she smacked her little fist against her mouth, found her thumb, and uttered not a peep the entire time Barbara held her. When Barbara handed her back to me, awake or asleep, she opened her mouth and bawled. My only hope for a few hours of peace during the day was to have Barbara feed her, rock her, and put her in her basket on the washing machine without any interference from me.

When I threw up my hands one day in defeat, Barbara frowned. "I don't get it, either. Maybe it's because I'm neutral, not involved. She must be picking up on something when you hold her. That's all I can think of."

I remembered Feather's second night home at Pua Olena. She cried relentlessly in Annie's arms, yet settled down when I took her. What was so wonderful about me that night?

"If that's the case, she should be picking up that I love her," I exclaimed.

"Love her, but don't necessarily want to care for her."

"Barbara, don't say that."

"Can you honestly tell me you're enjoying this?" She waved her hands at the wadded-up diapers, the overflowing laundry basket, and the clotted bottles from Feather's last two feedings tipped over on the coffee table.

"No, I'm not. I went through this with Annie. It wasn't normal three-month colic, either. More like three years. It was horrible, but I was much younger then, way more energetic. And I had a husband. And maid service from the hotel. And I didn't have to work."

Barbara raised an eyebrow. "Sounds like you were a bit of a spoiled brat."

"Maybe." I lowered my gaze and smoothed the hem of my shorts.

"Never mind growing up at Pua Olena," Barbara added, staring at me until I had to look back. "All those servants . . ."

"Oh, stop. I've come a long way since then. If I'd been asked . . . if I'd been consulted, or if it had been an act of God . . . Annie killed in a car accident, God forbid, that would be one thing. But to have a baby dumped on me by an irresponsible kid . . ."

"That really rubs, doesn't it? You're still angry with Annie."

"Yes, damn right I am. Can you blame me? She panicked when she learned Chaz was here and in jail. She felt he'd blame it on her, that he'd somehow get out and kill her. She was back on drugs, I'm sure of it, and fully paranoid. It all happened so fast, she'd left before I knew anything. Signed the baby over to me legally. All I have to do is accept, and I have a new daughter to raise."

Barbara's eyes widened. "So?"

"I . . . really . . . don't . . . want . . . to . . . do it." For the first time, I said it aloud. I tensed, waiting for lightning to strike me dead. The sky above Haleakala remained clear with no hint of hurling thunderbolts. Birds twittered cheerfully in the rainbow shower trees off the balcony. Coconut fronds rustled reassuringly outside the bedroom window. Mother Nature had prevailed again. The propagation of the species had continued through Annie. Beyond that, Mother Nature didn't care a jot.

"And Feather's so much like her mother. I don't want to go through Annie all over again. What kind of a teenager is Feather going to be, with me in my sixties? I failed with Annie, and I'm sure to fail with Feather. I already have. She goes ballistic every time I pick her up. You want the truth? I think she hates me. No, I don't want to raise her. I've had exactly two good days with her since Annie left. Not that I haven't tried. I've tried in every way I know how. I just don't know what else to do."

Barbara looked at me steadily, her dark velvet eyes never wavering. "You can get help. Counseling, maybe medication. It would be very different this time. But if you're not up for it . . ."

"Don't go there. I couldn't give away my flesh and blood, Barbara. I love Feather. Believe me, I do. I was in the delivery room when she was born. That's awesome! I cut the cord." My lips quivered, my throat closed. I had to force several deep breaths before I could continue. "We forged a bond right there on the spot. She's part of me. So how can I not want to raise her?" I blinked hard, a useless effort against welling tears.

Barbara replied simply, "Because you've been there, done that, with your own three children."

"Yes." I gulped through the tears. "I had a husband who supported me and was a partner in raising them until they were in their teens. Now I'm single. I'm forty-six. I have a wildly unreliable income. You know that scene. And staggering debts, thanks mostly to Annie."

"What about your mother? Surely she'd help financially?"

"Forget that. I just found out my mother has run through most of her trust fund and mortgaged her home to the hilt. Then she tells me Dad's restaurant hasn't turned a profit since the day he opened it. She's been bailing it out all along. I'm still in shock over that. There's nothing but quicksand everywhere I look. For the first time, I feel truly alone. And this." I gestured across the room. "This condo isn't the least bit suitable for a small child. I don't even have a bedroom door I can shut when she cries."

Barbara lowered her eyes and studied her tea, as if the loose jasmine leaves would reveal an answer. When she looked up, I caught a glimpse of humor in her expression. In my self-pitying distress, I could see she was fighting to feel sorry for me. "If you decided not to keep her, what's the worst thing that could happen?"

I blew my nose into a tissue. "Somewhere in her right mind, Annie signed a second set of papers for adoption by a third party, giving me power of attorney to make the decision."

Barbara thought this over for a moment. "Would the baby go into foster care until they found suitable parents?"

That possibility had never occurred to me. With a jolt, I imagined my precious Feather lying in a fouled crib, her tiny wrists tied to the bars, alone in a dark, fetid room, neglected for days while strangers collected payment for keeping her and spent the money on booze and gambling. Surely I'd read about that somewhere.

I clutched the baby to my breast. "Don't even think it. I'd never allow that to happen. Are you crazy?" My skewed vision of the foster care system was frighteningly vivid. The image gave me shivers.

She looked at me curiously. "It's not that bad, you know. I dealt with lots of foster kids on the mainland. Sure, there are some abusive foster homes, just as there are abusive natural homes, but there are also many good and loving ones. You've seen too much TV, Laura."

I kissed the top of Feather's head, caressing her silky black hair with my lips. I closed my eyes for a moment, inhaling the scent of baby shampoo. "Well, maybe. But I would never put her in foster care. Forget that right now." I willed my stirred-up emotions to simmer down.

"Okay, strike that one. Just checking." She shifted her frame on the sofa, switching her tucked legs to the other side.

I looked over the lanai railing to the mountain. Its lavender peak rose serenely above the afternoon clouds, oblivious to human turmoil below. "How would I ever live it down?"

"You mean, what would the neighbors think? It's none of their darn business."

"But everyone knows I've got her."

Barb tucked in her chin. "So you'd keep her, just because some folks might disapprove?"

"Like my parents."

"That'd be a tough one. I won't deny it."

"Thanks a lot."

"But your mother and father are not the ones stuck with raising her." Her terminology stung, all the more because it was exactly what I was thinking.

"I'll bet my mother would make the grand gesture of offering to raise her herself. Another of her benevolent projects. That would make me feel even worse."

The fact that we were discussing giving Feather up, to my parents or anyone, distressed me terribly. I got up and lifted her from Barbara's arms. Sound asleep, with a crusty drop of milk on her chin, her cheeks were flushed in the hot afternoon air. I sat down with her on the couch, wanting nothing more than to hold her, to feel her warmth against my breast, to reassure myself that I truly wanted us to be together. I smiled down at her and smoothed her rumpled T-shirt over her belly, savoring the sweet moment. The instant I relaxed against the cushions, her eyes flew open. She took one look at me, and we both burst into tears.

"I can't do this," I wailed as I thrust her back at Barbara. "I cannot cope with a baby who cries every time she looks at me."

Barbara walked Feather up and down, jiggling her against her shoulder. In fewer than three round trips from kitchen to the glass doors, Feather was once again the picture of perfect contentment.

Chapter 35

Diana called toward the end of the week. A zing of anxiety shot through me when I heard her unmistakable British lilt. I should have been the one who called first, but Diana brushed off my apology.

"Listen, darling, what a horrible experience for all of us. That dreadful woman, killing herself with a chainsaw in our bathtub. Honestly. Not to mention the awful mess she made of our house and garden. Jerry and I are still breathless over it."

"Our" bath tub? "Our" house and garden? What did she mean? They owned the property, yes, but this sounded like emotional attachment. I started to ask, "Surely you're not—?"

"There's been enough moping around, darling. The police are satisfied it was suicide. No more questioning, thank God. Wasn't that bloody awful, by the way? I think the only thing they didn't ask me about was my menstrual cycle. Anyway, you must come up for lunch tomorrow. Everything's still a mess, but the police have released the property. We ripped the yellow crime scene tape off this morning, had great fun wadding it all up. I've got a cleaning crew here now. The carpet's pulled out—God, that awful manure—the floor's been resealed and new broadloom's on order. Do come up, darling, won't you?"

"You're not serious? You're at the house?" Not in my wildest dreams did I imagine them simply cleaning up and moving in.

"Well, yes, after everything we went though to get this place, did you think we were going to let the bitch win in the end?" Diana sounded mortally offended at the very notion. "Our attorney's been in touch with Dr. Entwistle's. She's agreed to compensate us for all the damages. It's the least she can do."

"What about the bad vibes?" I asked weakly. Would I ever understand people?

"Why, they're jolly gone. All down the drain with Moana's mess. I had to pay extra, by the way, for the cleaning crew to tackle all that blood and gore everywhere. They freaked dreadfully when they saw it. But, darling, we're thrilled with the place. There are all kinds of wonderful aspects we couldn't possibly have known about before moving in. You should hear the birds first thing in the morning. A celestial symphony. And the rain . . . lovely showers that cool everything off at night. A world away from Kihei."

"You mean you've actually slept there?" I could barely ask the question.

"Yes, yes. As soon as they got rid of the mess and the carpet, we brought up our camping gear. We're spread out on plywood, but our new furniture's on the barge, arriving from Honolulu next week, along with the carpeting. Painters are booked for day after tomorrow, inside and out. We chose a marvelous pale green for the exterior that will make those jade roof tiles positively glow. By the time I'm finished there'll be no trace of Dr. Randa Entwistle or that . . . that Corrine 'Moana' Urquhart."

I struggled for something, anything, to say in reply, but failed utterly.

"Come on, darling. We thought you'd be pleased. I could be reaming you up one side and down the other for getting us into such a jumble, but we really love the place. I'm so excited I can hardly bear it, just dying to get it all done up. And the yard. I'm almost grateful to that woman. You know I was going to rip most of it out anyway. Now I don't have to squabble with Jerry over my plans for an English country garden. Really, Laura, it all worked out for the best. Do say you'll come for lunch."

Lunch? How could she extend such an ordinary invitation? But I couldn't possibly say no. For everyone's sake, I needed to support Diana and Jerry in their decision to make the best of things and keep us out of a lawsuit. Perhaps there was some value, too, in desensitizing myself by exposure. If I experienced the property again in broad daylight, with all the gore cleaned up, perhaps my nightmares would cease.

"I'll have to bring Feather," I said, trying for a last minute reprieve in spite of my brave thoughts. "Her sitter wrenched her back yesterday, and has to lie flat for a week."

"No problem," Diana exclaimed. "I'm dying to see her. I do admire you so, taking her on like this. I certainly wouldn't have the patience."

The deeper I drove into Haiku late the next morning, easing my car along the twisting, vine-draped road, the more nervous I became. Moana's suicide may have been mopped up, but my memories had not faded a jot. I didn't believe a word of my earlier thoughts on desensitization. You might as well tell a rape victim to go out and get raped again to help her get over it.

The gate and gateposts had already been replaced. Beyond the garage, I spotted the uprooted and decapitated plants in a gnarly pile. It wouldn't have surprised me if Diana and Jerry were planning a huge celebratory bonfire.

Diana greeted me in cut-off jeans and a sculpted white T-shirt, her dark hair tucked under a blue silk bandana. Even in the midst of a moving orgy, she looked impossibly glamorous.

"Darling, come right in." She pecked my cheek and stooped to admire Feather in her baby carrier. "Oh, the little mite. What a precious pet!" Bubbling with enthusiasm, Diana led us on a tour of the first floor. Our footsteps echoed on the bare plywood. The rooms appeared cavernous without the furniture and carpeting. The pig manure stench had been overpowered by Pine-Sol.

"Everything that could possibly remind us of those two harridans is out the door or down the drain," Diana declared with a dismissive wave of her hand. "Two weeks from Sunday we're having a blessing. You must come. I've asked the Reverend Samuel Kinimaka to do the most potent ceremony possible—hula dancers, chanters, kava bowl, the works—to make sure there's nothing left of their bad karma. Look, here's where I'll put . . ."

She went on to describe her furniture arrangements in great gushing detail. Surprisingly, Feather watched from my arms with mild interest, quietly chewing on her hand, as if she understood and approved every word Diana said. I did my best to respond, but couldn't get past feelings of dread, thinking of what I'd have to face upstairs. They couldn't possibly have gotten all that blood off the white tile backsplash. When Diana led us toward the koa wood staircase and started up, I began to tremble. I stopped on the bottom step.

"I can't, Diana. Not today. I just can't go up there."

She looked a bit offended, then stepped back down to my level. "Come on, darling. It'll be good for you. You have to face things, you know, to get over them." She took Feather from me and laid her in her carrier at the bottom of the stairs. Feather uttered not a peep.

With Diana's arm around me we ascended the stairs, pausing on the landing. The double doors to the master suite were wide open. Diana led me through. The room was bare, except for two sleeping bags on the floor and an open suitcase with clothing spilling out. The only reminders of the past were the crushed silk drapes framing the windows and the window frames empty of glass.

Diana turned me toward the bathroom. I shook my head, terrified to go any farther.

"Come on, darling. Let's get it over with. You've got to face it." She tightened her grip on my shoulders and led me forward.

I stood at the bathroom door peering in, shocked at the pristine whiteness of the tub and the tile. Diana was right. Not a trace of the foul deed remained, yet my mind saw it clearly, every gory detail.

"There, darling, that wasn't so bad," she prattled, leading me back downstairs. "The frightful visions will fade, they always do in time. We're going to gut this room, replace the tub, the tile, the vanity, everything. Nothing will be left to remind us."

Happily smug, she led me to the kitchen where she quickly peeled and sliced a mango and put the finishing touches on our chicken salads. We took our plates outside and sat at a table on the shady terrace. Still disturbed by the blank whiteness upstairs, I could barely look at the salad, croissants, and mangoes in champagne.

"Jerry and I are ever so grateful to you for everything you did to complete the sale, oh yes. When we first found the property, we were quite prepared to go it alone, remember?"

I nodded, recalling how furious I'd been at their initial plan to proceed without me.

"But, remember, right up front I said there was something queer about the doctor. Truly, we could not have done it on our own. You were the key to securing this marvelous home for us. We both appreciate it. You got paid. Those two ghastly women deserved what they got." She picked up her bowl of champagne-drenched mangoes and a silver spoon. "Come on, have a taste. I picked the mangoes myself in the gulch this morning. Snitched a bottle of Jerry's best champagne to pour over them, just for us."

A gold filling on the side of Diana's mouth gleamed as she opened her mouth for a bite of bubbly goodness, utterly pleased with her own cleverness.

CHAPTER 36

My lunch with Diana unnerved me in ways I couldn't possibly have antici-pated. Every trace of Moana's demise had been erased with lightning speed, as if it hadn't happened at all. But nothing could erase the searing vision in my consciousness. Nor could I reconcile Diana's punchy joy at finally be-coming chatelaine of the manor. She had downright salivated at the endless hours of renovating and decorating pleasure that stretched gloriously ahead of her. In the light of Moana's hideous end, her attitude struck me as unbe-lievably callous.

As I drove home through the lowland cane fields, Feather asleep in her car seat, the warm, humid air became more and more oppressive. The water had been shut off to the ripened fields, allowing the crop to dry prior to burning. Bent khaki leaves rattled forlornly on curved, juice-laden stalks. I felt hollow, empty, as if, like the cane leaves, I was sucked dry and awaiting my doom.

Ever sensitive to my moods, Feather was restless and needy the rest of the day. I fought for enough breathing room to indulge in a cleaning jag, scrubbing the bathroom and kitchen that afternoon, promising the dusting and vacuuming in the morning.

That night I had my worst nightmare yet about Moana. Instead of a chainsaw, she grasped the knife with which Diana had sliced the mangoes for our lunch. Nor was Moana in the bathtub, but curled in the dark space that once held the refrigerator she had maliciously hauled away the morning of her death. Staring at her, thinking she looked like an overgrown wasp grub wriggling in its mud nest, I slowly became aware that I couldn't move my feet. They were stuck to the slate floor tiles. Looking down in horror, I saw her blood oozing between my toes.

Laughing hysterically, Moana sliced at her neck, her chest, her stomach, her legs, daintily almost, as if she were dabbing on perfume. Above her diabolical grin, her wild gray eyes never wavered from mine, accusing me of all that was disastrous in her life. Bonded now to the floor by her coagulating blood under my feet, I screamed back at her, "No, no, it isn't my fault," louder and louder to drown out her shrieked accusations. She slashed at me like a fencer with the dripping blade, swishing it back and forth just out of reach, then swiped it across her neck to open another gaping wound. Frantic, I stretched forward to wrest the knife away, to rescue her from her self-destruction. One of my feet suddenly ripped loose from the blood-stuck floor, pitching me forward into the carnage. Unable to stop myself, I screamed until I woke myself up, pushing madly against my pillows to escape the bloody gore. Moana's shrieks segued into Feather's high, piercing wails. Reality rushed back into my veins.

I staggered from my bed and picked the baby up from her basket on the washer. She looked at me as I must have looked at Moana, wild with horror and fear. She twisted in my arms, screaming and wailing as I tried to calm her. She would have none of it. Waves of nausea washed over me as flashes of the nightmare repeated. Pacing up and down the carpet, frantically jiggling the crying baby against my shoulder, I lost track of what was real and what was not. All I could see was Moana's ghoulish face, laughing and cursing, as I fell into her slashed and bleeding body. Feather's cries pummeled the night, pushing me beyond hysteria.

I made one more frantic loop, around the living room, back past the bed, into the bathroom, and turned. My toe caught where the bathroom tile ended and the carpet began. As I stumbled, I felt the baby loosen in my arms. For the merest instant, I let my arms go slack. Then with a moan I jerked back upright, pulling Feather in, safe and secure. I hadn't done it deliberately—had I? I clasped her so tight neither of us could breathe for a moment. I bowed my head over hers, my cheek against her hair.

The movement in the mirror above the dresser caught my eye. We were framed in the ambient light, Feather and I, in a stark standoff. As I loosened my hold, her wails redoubled. Her body went rigid with exertion. But I had the power. I saw it in my face in the mirror—grim, haggard, lined with desperation. Yes, I had the power in this dusky tableau—the power to make everything right.

The strength leached from my arms. Trembling, I lowered Feather to the bed. Releasing my hold, I stepped back and saw her as she truly was, an innocent victim of birth to an unwilling mother. And deserving of more than a fear-driven grandmother could give her. Slowly, carefully, as if she were the most delicate hand-blown glass ornament, I, barely able to breathe, moved her to the safety of her basket.

It was done. I called Sally Mitchell, who called Lily Fujikawa first thing in the morning, catching Lily as she left the hospital after an emergency Caesarian section. Barbara drove us to Sally's office at 9:00 AM. Although she transferred Feather's car seat from my car to hers, I couldn't bear to strap Feather into it. Caution, the law, and good sense be damned, I held her in my arms, wet-eyed all the way. When Barbara stopped the car in Sally's parking lot, she turned to me and asked, "Are you sure?"

"Yes," I lied. I blew my nose, wiped my cheeks and carried the baby upstairs. Barbara followed with the diaper bag and her rush basket, both packed with as much formula, clothing, and diapers as we could cram in.

Before she would agree to facilitate the adoption, Sally questioned me relentlessly. Barbara waited with Feather in the reception area on the other side of the closed office door.

"You've just been through a horror with that Moana person's suicide," Sally began. "You mustn't make a hasty decision."

"It's not that so much, Sally. I'm afraid I could harm her. I don't trust myself. I've never told this to another living soul, but there were times with

Annie . . . I came so close to hurting her, Sally. She was a baby! We didn't understand child abuse back then, but I came so close one night. She could have died! I was too ashamed and confused to ask for help. If you'd seen me with Feather last night, you'd understand. God gave me strength one more time to pull back. But I'm terrified to take any more chances. She deserves a happy life with truly devoted parents. A different emotional environment will make all the difference. I absolutely know she'll thrive with Ginger and Kamuela. She'll fit right in. She even looks *hapa*."

Sally stared at me, stern as an old schoolmarm. "She's your flesh and blood. Your only grandchild. Your only link with Annie. Shouldn't you give yourself more time? You've just been through a major trauma. Sometimes that sets us off, but as you say, you stopped yourself. You've broken the cycle. Surely things will be different now, especially with some good counseling."

I threaded a tissue over and under my fingers in my lap. "I was the wrong mother for Annie, and I'm the wrong mother for Feather. If I give myself more time, Sally, I'll lose my will to let her go. I have to do it now, while I'm still horrified by what could happen. I truly believe this is best for Feather. She'll have two young parents who'll be devoted to her. That's the only thing that matters. Do you hear me? If I kept her, I'd be doing it out of a white-knuckled sense of duty. I'd be continually on edge, wondering when I might be driven to the brink again. And whether I'd be able to stop myself the next time. I'm a wreck just thinking about it."

Sally looked at me sternly. "Laura, you'll cause all kinds of havoc if, a week or three months or even a year from now, you decide you want her back. So many people will be hurt."

"Right now I feel like I'm in the darkest pit of hell," I said. "There's no light at the surface, except for the merest pinprick, if I hold my breath and squint my eyes really hard. That pinprick is Feather's future with the Smiths. They'll be marvelous parents to her. They've got enough willingness and love for a dozen children. They're economically stable. They'll adore her as they adore each other. I can't give Feather anything like that. You don't know how close I came to harming her, the same way I almost hurt Annie all those years ago. I'd be on pins and needles every moment I was alone with her. I can't trust myself. As much as it tears me apart, I know it's the right thing. The most difficult and, more importantly, the most loving thing."

She slowly shook her head.

"Sally, can you deny it's best, when you look at it entirely from Feather's point of view? Without any other consideration? It's an act of love. Annie knew that. That's why she signed that second set of adoption papers. She knew I wasn't the best mother for Feather, too."

"What about your parents? Your sons? Will they understand?"

"Does it matter?" I asked. "For the sake of the child, I have to do this!"

She looked at me for the longest moment. Then, without another word, she pushed a button on the side of her desk. Her assistant entered with her notary book and seal, then sat down in the chair next to mine. Although she must have witnessed countless tragic scenes in Sally's inner office, her face paled at the enormity of the decision she was asked to acknowledge. We were like three reluctant soldiers, ordered to execute a deserter from our own brigade in cold blood. Only this was no execution. It was my ultimate gift of love to Annie's daughter.

Sally informed me there would be a legal process to follow, and that nothing would be final until the court gave the adoption its blessing. I nodded, certain there would be no reason for the court to object.

"They'll want to have her examined by a pediatrician, too. They'll need full disclosure of Annie's history with drugs. And your suspicion of Annie's autism, borderline though it may be."

I clutched the front of my shirt. "You don't think . . .?" After all I'd been through to make this decision, it never occurred to me that the Smiths would say no.

"Relax. From what I know of the Smiths, they'd welcome a child from the leper colony at Kalaupapa. They're that kind of loving. They can take custody right away, since that's your intention, but we will have to go through the formalities. We'll take it one step at a time."

Sally opened her file drawer and slowly pulled out the adoption papers. Annie's childish signature, half cursive, half print, jumped off the page at me. *Oh, Annie, I hope I'm doing the right thing.*

As I signed on the remaining blank line, my hand shook so hard I barely recognized my own signature.

I said goodbye to Feather in Sally's outer office. Even now, I cannot revisit the sorrow that wracked me in those final moments. Suffice it to say, I almost caved in and changed my mind. But the ghostly memory of my tortured face in the mirror, a face I'd barely credited as my own even then, and knowing myself fully capable of losing control . . . No, I had to let her go. There was a higher love to be honored.

I didn't break down until we were in the parking lot, just Barbara and me. I watched her unhitch the baby's seat from the back seat of her car and run it up the stairs to Sally's office. I sank into the front seat and gave in to deep, soul-wrenching weeping.

Barb drove me home and stayed with me. There was very little to say. I felt as if my soul had been ripped from my body, leaving me with nothing but an all-consuming emptiness. There seemed nothing left inside, as there was nothing left of Feather, save the rocking chair and a load of her clothes we forgot in the dryer. And the photo of her and Annie that I'd had copied and replaced on the dresser at the foot of my bed.

I slept. Barbara read. When I awoke in the afternoon, I found she had packed the clothes from the dryer and taken them to her car. I was profoundly grateful to be spared that task. I sent her home, reluctant to face my apartment alone, but knowing it had to be done.

That was all I could do: sit there and face it. I tried to imagine the Smiths' joy when they received Lily's phone call, painted a picture in my mind of them walking down the steps from Sally's office with their baby girl in their arms. Did it help? Not really. But it was the one positive thing I could focus on. It was true and right. No matter how bereft I felt, I knew I had done the right thing. That certainty, I prayed, would see me through.

I slept the sleep of the dead that night—no dreams, no terrors, nothing but deep, enveloping blackness.

Early the next morning the doorbell rang. I smothered the annoying racket with my pillow, trying to ignore it. I didn't think I could get out of bed and walk as far as the door. Nor did I wish to see anyone. I wanted only to lie there and slip back into the serene, unfeeling darkness. The bell rang again and again, with great persistence, interspersed with relentless knocking. Shrouded in a body that no longer felt like my own, I forced myself to get up, if only to shut off the wretched noise.

Lily stood on the doormat, peering cautiously from behind a huge bouquet of tropical flowers.

"Laura, thank God. You had me worried when you didn't answer the door." She thrust the flowers toward me. "These are from the Smiths. I offered to bring them myself so I could make sure you're okay. May I come in?"

I began to shake. Lily moved fast. Before I knew it, she was out of her sandals and in my kitchen, topping the vase with water. She wiped the vase dry, placed the flowers on the kitchen counter and led me by the elbow into the living room. There she stood, barefooted, pigeon-toed, her sleeveless denim mini-shift barely covering her slender brown thighs. She looked as uncertain as an orphan waif just off a transport from Japan. No one would ever have guessed she was head of obstetrics at a bustling county hospital. Her glance flew from me to my unmade bed and back again.

"Well, I see you at least tried to sleep. Did you manage?"

"To be honest, I hit the sheets and then it was morning." I paused for her to tell me I was a bad person, not only for giving Feather up, but for sleeping so soundly afterward.

Instead, she beamed. "Good. Your soul must be finding peace. You've done a truly magnificent thing, Laura. Ginger and Kamuela are deliriously grateful. And someday Feather will be, too." She gestured toward the flowers through the kitchen pass-through. "Ginger worried that you might think the flowers are in bad taste. I hope not. It's only a tiny gesture to express their thanks . . . thanks that are entirely inadequate."

I sat down on the couch and motioned her to the rocker. At once, memories of myself and Feather in that chair threatened my self-control. I knew I'd never be able to sit in it again.

Lily leaned forward, her elbows on her knees. Her straight black hair, gleaming in the morning light, fell diagonally across her cheeks. "I know you're suffering," she said. "But I thought if I could tell you how overjoyed the Smiths are, it might help. If you don't want to hear about it, I'll leave. And I'll take the flowers with me."

Suddenly, I couldn't bear to be alone. "No, Lily. Please stay. This is all so crazy. I absolutely know I did the right thing, but it's a real struggle to accept it emotionally. Tell me, shine some light on it for me, help me to feel in my heart what I already know in my mind."

Her black eyes snapping, her ebony hair swinging just below her ears, she described the scene as the three of them arrived at Sally's office half an hour after Barbara and I left. "They were ecstatic," she said. "Ginger immediately picked Feather up, nestled her to her breast. You would have thought you were looking at the Madonna and Child."

My eyes flew to the copied photo of Annie in Dad's chair looking just so with Feather. I tried to smile, but only succeeded in bringing fresh tears to my eyes.

"Oh, I'm so sorry," Lily said. "Really, this is too much for you. I shouldn't have come."

I clamped down on my heaving chest. "No. Any adoption is going to have a happy side and a sad side. I happen to be on the sad side, doubly sad as it's all wrapped up with Annie. But I know, as time goes by, I'll see it only from the Smith's side. You're helping me just by being here, believe me. Please go on."

She relaxed into the rocker and continued to describe their unquestioning signing of the papers, their chatter about how they would do up her nursery, and how excited they were to tell their parents they'd suddenly become grandparents. "They're flying to Honolulu tomorrow to surprise his folks," Lily said. "Then I understand they're going to Philadelphia as soon as possible. Ginger wants to take her home."

"To Philadelphia?" My mind took a flying leap. *They're moving to the mainland.* It was one thing for them to be living with Feather on Maui, where I might occasionally glimpse her in the mall or the grocery store, but Philadelphia? That was half an ocean and a continent away.

Lily saw my agitation, and again apologized. "I just seem to make one mistake after another, Laura. I'm sorry. I wanted to help, but everything I say upsets you."

"No. Please. Oh, Lily. It's not your fault. It's just such uncharted territory . . . a minefield of emotions. If you said it was a beautiful day, I'd probably cry. Let them take her to Philadelphia. I'll have to get used to it. I can't put any geographical conditions on the adoption. It's too late, and it's not fair. I really do appreciate knowing they're so happy, though. If I hang onto that, perhaps it'll be enough. I can't tell you how much I appreciate your coming over. Truly, Lily. And the flowers are beautiful. Please tell them. It was a lovely gesture."

I went to the kitchen and carried the flowers into the living room. The arrangement of red antheriums, pink shell ginger, and yellow pincushion protea, interspersed with dark green ferns, was as stunning as it was thoughtful. I set them in the center of the dining table and turned to Lily. "Please tell Ginger and Kamuela that I hand-picked them to love Feather, and that I know they'll be wonderful parents for her. I'd never have considered adoption to anyone else. Will you do that?"

"Of course. That will complete their happiness."

"Thank you." I bit my lip and reached deep inside myself to put forth the question I hardly dared ask. "Do you think . . . I might be able to see her one more time before they leave for the mainland?"

Lily shrugged as if she wanted to promise me but wisely refrained. "We didn't discuss anything about you seeing her. Things happened so quickly. As I recall, there was nothing about visitation in the adoption agreement. But . . . I'll see what I can do."

For the moment, that would have to suffice. Lily glanced at her watch and sighed. "Time to run. Babies have no respect for my personal life."

We stood, and she gave me a hug. Over her shoulder I saw the rocking chair, still moving from the lift of her body. "Lily, would you take that chair with you? Call the Smiths and see if they'd like it? I can't bear to have it here."

She nodded. Silently, we carried it to her car.

How do you pick up a life that no longer matters? To keep my body moving, I plowed into more cleaning—closets, drawers, cupboards, under the bed, even my storage locker got thoroughly sorted and purged. What an accumulation of nonsense that had once been important. Everything that reminded me of Feather and Annie went out the door, except for the photos. Framed and unframed, I packed them in a box, hoping someday I would be able to look at them again. At the last minute I kept one out—the shot of Annie and Feather in Father's chair, the one Annie had taken with her.

Once everything was in order, it stayed that way. I wandered aimlessly through the neat, tidy emptiness, aching for a wet diaper on the coffee table, a sink full of sour bottles waiting to be scrubbed. I picked up a magazine and tossed it aside. Making a snap decision, I pulled on my bathing suit, grabbed a towel and walked down the road to the beach. No bottle, no diapers, no extra clothes, no baby carrier, no synchronizing timing with a nap schedule. I just walked out the door. I sat on the beach for as long as I felt like it, letting the warm sun toast my skin. Again when I felt like it, I ran into the surf and dove into a cresting wave.

The cool water sluiced down my back, my legs, my feet. Dolphin-like, I emerged on the other side and paddled around until I'd had enough. Refreshed, every pore zinging, I walked back across the hot sand, picked up my towel, threw it over my shoulder and walked home. As simple as that. Nothing to carry but my apartment key; no baby paraphernalia to slow me down, I noticed. It was the first minute step toward reclaiming my life. And being okay about it.

My business, of course, was in ruins. The Coleman commission had flown out the window like a gust of trade wind. But, for the first time in a long while, my finances were current, and Annie's detective was probably doing cartwheels with how much I'd been able to send him. My credit cards were paid off, as well as parts of Annie and Feather's medical bills not paid for by Ohana Care, despite their promises to take care of everything, but I had been so consumed with the girls that I had not done any prospecting and had no deals in the works. It was back to square one. That night I sat down and outlined my plan of attack. Cold calls, strolling the mall with my name badge on, calling friends, acquaintances, fellow committee workers, enemies—everyone was a possibility. Prospecting was not my favorite activity. But make enough calls, talk to enough people in the grocery-check out line, at meetings or at the dentist, and sooner or later, a live one comes along.

Within a few days I had sniffed out several who might get me past "just current and finally get that useless detective out of my life for good. I began to feel alive again, revitalized, challenged, interested in what would happen next. I was on the treadmill again, and, damn, it felt good.

Thoughts of Feather filtered in constantly. Reminders were everywhere. Whenever I felt myself slipping, I pictured her happy with the Smiths, and the Smiths' delight in having her. Giving myself permission to enjoy simple pleasures and professional triumphs might come later, if I could just get through the first difficult weeks.

I made a quick trip to Honolulu to tell my parents that I had given Feather up for adoption. I faced them with trepidation. They were visibly upset about Annie running away again, but they quickly came to realize that there was nothing we could do but love her from a distance. When I got to the part about Feather, I bravely said the words. They sat quietly, side by side on the couch in the living room, while I explained about the Smiths and my sincere belief that she would be much better off with them.

They didn't move, except to turn their heads to look at one another. Then my father reached over and took my mother's hand. It was a gesture of infinite tenderness, one that excluded me once again from their world. Finally my mother spoke.

"As I said the last time you visited, dear, there are things you don't know about your father and me. Things you may never know."

Dad spoke up. "Perhaps it's time, my love, to tell her."

Confused, I looked from one to the other. "Dad? Mom? What is it?"

Mother stood up and began to wring her hands. "I can't, Jack . . . Really, I can't."

"Let me tell her, Margaret. Spare yourself." Dad turned to me. "When I met your mother, Laura, she was *hapai* . . . with another man's child. He was charming, handsome in his army uniform . . . and part Hawaiian. Totally unsuitable. These things happened in wartime, you know. Honolulu swarmed with soldiers and sailors, mad with gaiety in the face of the daily casualties overseas. All the rules were suspended."

I turned to my mother, expecting to see her eyes downcast in shame. Instead, she met my gaze frankly, unapologetic for her youthful sin. I felt we were having our first personal, intimate conversation ever, even though Dad did the talking.

"We met at a canteen. I fell madly in love with Margaret." He stopped, choking for a moment as he relived those dizzy first moments of infatuation. "Once she understood my feelings, she began to avoid me. After much dogged persistence, she finally told me why. She didn't think I'd want her if I knew about the baby. Of course, she was wrong. We got engaged, and I went off to war. By the time I returned she'd had the baby. Your grandparents insisted she give it up. An informal adoption, *hanai*, to the boy's family. The child was a girl."

Speechless, I could only stare. *I had a half-sister somewhere.*

Dad lifted Mother's hand and kissed it. Mother finally spoke. "So you see, dear, history repeats itself. You may have wondered why we weren't upset at Annie's condition when she came home. We knew better than to judge."

How ironic, I thought: my mother, the opinionated judge of everyone else. "You never made any attempt to find her as time went by?" I asked. "Or she you?"

Mother replied, "It wasn't done, my dear. We're from different worlds."

And that was the end of the conversation. They thanked me for coming, walked me to the car, kissed me goodbye.

Each day it became more and more important that I see Feather before the Smiths took her to Philadelphia. When I didn't hear from Lily, I ached to call her. I refrained, however, believing the best thing I could do for the Smiths and Feather was to stay silently in the background until they were ready.

Toward the end of the week, I got home one night, dead on arrival. I'd spent the day showing condominiums in Lahaina to a tourist couple from Ohio, then wrote up an offer for them to sign first thing in the morning. When the phone rang, I set my Lean Cuisine aside, forced my lips into a smile, and answered as cheerfully as possible. *Please God, don't let it be my buyers, reneging after all that work.*

It was Lily. "Laura, how are you?"

My heart sped up a bit. "Tired. But okay. And you?"

"One delivery today, and another mother in labor as we speak. Now, listen. I'm sorry I haven't called you. I thought I'd better give the Smiths a little time before I told them about your request to see Feather. Good thing I did. When I finally called this afternoon, Ginger freaked out when she recognized my voice. She begged me to tell her I wasn't calling to tell them you'd changed your mind. It took me five minutes to reassure her. She went almost hysterical with relief. After all her losses, she still can't believe she actually has a baby. But listen, Laura. They're leaving for Philadelphia tomorrow evening. They're on a seven-thirty American flight."

"Oh, my God," I said, steadying myself against the back of a chair. "They're really taking her away?"

"Apparently they were able to get last-minute seats, so they went for it. But Laura, I just couldn't ask her to let you see the baby. You do understand? She was so upset."

My heart contracted. "But all I want . . ."

"I know. I just couldn't do it. But then I got to thinking, what if you just show up at the airport, like you were meeting someone else? It wouldn't be much of a visit, but at least you'd be able to see her. They couldn't very well object in such a public place."

"But that's not . . . I want to spend some time with her."

"I know. I just don't know what else we can do, Laura. I feel certain that I if I asked, they'd say no. Then you'd be stuck. As grateful as Ginger and Kamuela are, Ginger's a basket-case over that baby. I shouldn't be telling you any of this, but after all you've been through, I think you deserve to see her. Especially as they're going so far away."

"So I just show up and act surprised?"

"That's the best idea I can come up with."

The November days were noticeably shorter. The sun was low behind the West Maui Mountains, igniting the fish-scale clouds to a brilliant salmon against the turquoise sky. It would be dark by the time I reached the airport. Memories of my dash to pick up Annie flooded in as I sped past the *wiliwili* on Mokulele Highway. How frightened I'd been that she'd disappear again before I could reach her. Now I fretted that Lily had gotten the time or the date wrong, and I would miss the Smiths altogether. Once again that half-hour race across the island's central plain seemed endless. Could I really stand by and let them to take her all the way to Philadelphia?

On the departure board at the top of the escalator I found American's 7:30 PM flight and raced down the concourse toward the gate. By the time I got there, I was doubled over with a stitch in my side. How would the Smiths believe I happened to bump into them if I collapsed at their feet?

I halted, deliberately slowing my breathing, willing my body to get a grip on itself. Then I spotted them, not thirty feet away, sitting with their backs toward me. Although Feather was not visible, my eyes began to sting, knowing she was only steps away. I forced myself to walk back and forth a few times in the waiting area behind them, until I felt I could act normally. Then I walked around their bank of seats and let my gaze fall on them.

Every synapse in my brain snapped, yet I found I couldn't utter a word at the sight of my granddaughter nestled contentedly in Kamuela's lap. In the ten days since I had left her at Sally's, she'd changed remarkably. Chubbier, prettier, dark hair a little curlier, black eyes more alert. I stood there gaping. Ginger saw me first. Her face went pale beneath her freckles. She immediately reached for the baby, gathering her into her protective arms. I tensed for Feather to cry at the abrupt movement, but she only looked around over Ginger's shoulder.

My hand went up in a peaceful gesture. Lily was right. Ginger was very insecure about the baby. "No, no. It's not what you think. I . . . I . . ." I couldn't speak the lie, that I was just passing by. "I came to say goodbye. That's all. Just to say goodbye."

Smiling, Kamuela stood, his arms open for a big local-style hug. "Of course, Laura."

We embraced, then he took Feather from Ginger and offered her to me. Ginger was so surprised, she didn't object. I took that sweet little one in my arms and blended her soft body into mine. Oh, that fresh baby smell. She squirmed a bit, but otherwise didn't fuss. I held her out in front of me to look into her round, ripe-olive eyes. Did she recognize me? She raised her hand and stuffed her thumb into her mouth, looking back placidly. Miraculously, she didn't scream.

Ginger took a step toward us, her arms open to reclaim the baby. Kamuela stepped behind her, wrapped his arms around her, put his cheek against hers, and whispered, "It's okay, honey. It's okay."

I looked at them over Feather's head. "It really is okay, Ginger. I just wanted to say aloha. I had no idea you were going so far away. I just couldn't let you go without saying goodbye."

Ginger looked around at her husband, her eyes asking if he believed me. He kissed her forehead and said, "Come on, honey. It's okay. We have to trust Laura. Remember, she hand-picked us to love her granddaughter."

I smiled. Lily had followed my instructions to the letter. "Did you get the rocking chair?"

Ginger looked a little braver. "Yes, I love it. Thank you."

"I have something else for Feather," I said, shifting her onto one arm and reaching into my pocket. "Here," I said, pulling out a small blue velvet box. "These were her great-great-great-great grandmother Mazie's. I saved them for Annie. I know she'd want Feather to have them."

Ginger looked at Kamuela, again asking if they could trust me. He laughed. "Come on, sweetheart. It's a gift for our little girl."

He reached out, took the box, and held it out to Ginger. She lifted the lid. There, on the white lace handkerchief I had carried at my wedding, lay the garnet and canary mine-cut diamond earrings Mother had sent me.

"Oh, my," exclaimed Ginger. "They're lovely."

"A family heirloom," I explained. "Perhaps someday you'll tell Feather where they came from. If you decide she should know about her birth family, that is." I held my breath at the mere suggestion.

"Oh," said Ginger, wiping away a tear. "Actually, we do think it's best to tell her about her adoption. Years from now, of course."

I hugged Feather closer. "I'm so glad. I have something else for you." I held out my favorite photograph of Annie and Feather. "Annie took this same photo with her. It's her only tangible reminder of Feather. Perhaps it will help you tell Feather her story when the time comes." For a moment I couldn't continue. Ginger and Kamuela stood quietly looking at the photo while I collected myself. "I don't know where Annie will be when that time comes, but you'll always know where to find me. Philadelphia's only a long-distance phone call away."

The couple exchanged a puzzled glance.

"We'll only be there a week, you know," Kamuela said. "After that, it's just a local call."

"But I thought you were leaving forever," I exclaimed.

"Who told you that?" he asked.

"Well, I mean, but . . ." I didn't want to betray Lily.

"We're just going for a quick visit so Ginger's parents can meet their new granddaughter. We'll be back before Thanksgiving. Feather is going to be raised right here on Maui."

My knees trembled with relief. My words to Lily, "Let them take her to Philadelphia," had been pure bravado. I desperately wanted Feather to stay right here, where I knew exactly where she'd go to school, where she'd play, and where she'd one day seek me out. I held that far-away vision in my heart.

The ramp attendant announced the boarding of the Smiths' flight. Ginger relaxed enough to let me continue holding Feather while they gathered their carry-ons. I walked with them to the gate, where other couples with babies and several passengers in wheelchairs were queuing to pre-board.

"Thank you for everything," I said. I kissed Feather and handed her back to her mother. "Thank you for the rest of Feather's life, and for this special moment."

"Will you be okay, Laura?" Kamuela asked.

"Yes. Much better now." I smiled at them both.

Ginger smiled back, then looked at her husband. "Do you think . . .?" she asked cautiously.

"You mean . . .?" he replied. A flash of communication passed between them. Ginger turned to me. Her color was back. With the baby safely in her arms again, she stood a little easier. "Yes, Feather's baptism. Laura, will you come? We planned it for the week before Christmas. At the old Makena Church, with a brunch afterward at our place."

Kamuela put his hand on her shoulder, giving her strength to complete her generous gesture. "We'd really love to have you there. Please say you'll come."

My heart tipped over with gladness. I enfolded all three of them in my embrace. "Of course," I said. "Just try to keep me away."

PUBLISHING, INC.

Quick Order Form For
Paying the Price

Fax orders: 719-527-0843. Send this form.

Telephone orders: Call 719-495-3755.

Mail orders: Dialogue Publishing, Inc.
16990 Cherry Crossing Drive
Colorado Springs, CO 80921, USA
Please enclose this form.

Order online at http://www.dialoguepublishing.com

Number of copies: __ at $15.95 = _____

Name:
Address:
City: State: Zip:

Telephone:
E-mail address:

Sales tax: Please add 4.9% for books shipped to Colorado addresses.

Shipping:
U.S.: $5.00 for first book, $2.00 for each additional book
International: $9.00 for first book, $5.00 for each additional book

Total enclosed: _____

Payment:
   Visa   MasterCard   Discover   American Express
Card number:
Name on card: Exp. Date:

Discussion questions for readers groups may be obtained at no charge at
http://www.payingthepricebook.com
Visit the author at www.hawaiirealbooks.com